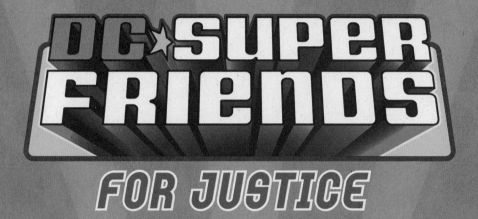

DC SUPER FRIENDS

FOR JUSTICE

WE ♥ U SUPERMAN
TRUTH & JUSTICE!
WE BELIEVE IN YOU!

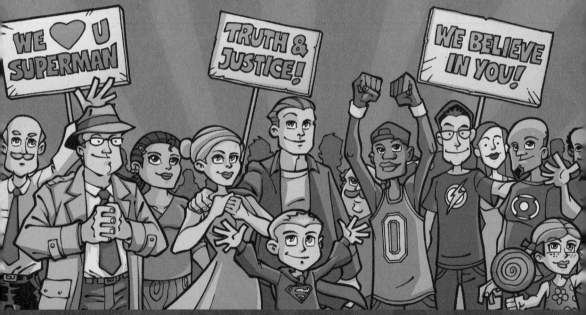

SHOLLY FISCH WRITER
J. BONE ORIGINAL SERIES COVERS

ROB CLARK JR. / RANDY GENTILE / TRAVIS LANHAM LETTERERS
HEROIC AGE COLORS

DAN DIDIO SENIOR VP-EXECUTIVE EDITOR

RACHEL GLUCKSTERN EDITOR-ORIGINAL SERIES

BOB JOY EDITOR-COLLECTED EDITION

ROBBIN BROSTERMAN SENIOR ART DIRECTOR

PAUL LEVITZ PRESIDENT & PUBLISHER

GEORG BREWER VP-DESIGN & DC DIRECT CREATIVE

RICHARD BRUNING SENIOR VP-CREATIVE DIRECTOR

PATRICK CALDON EXECUTIVE VP-FINANCE & OPERATIONS

CHRIS CARAMALIS VP-FINANCE

JOHN CUNNINGHAM VP-MARKETING

TERRI CUNNINGHAM VP-MANAGING EDITOR

AMY GENKINS SENIOR VP-BUSINESS & LEGAL AFFAIRS

ALISON GILL VP-MANUFACTURING

DAVID HYDE VP-PUBLICITY

HANK KANALZ VP-GENERAL MANAGER, WILDSTORM

JIM LEE EDITORIAL DIRECTOR-WILDSTORM

GREGORY NOVECK SENIOR VP-CREATIVE AFFAIRS

SUE POHJA VP-BOOK TRADE SALES

STEVE ROTTERDAM SENIOR VP-SALES & MARKETING

CHERYL RUBIN SENIOR VP-BRAND MANAGEMENT

ALYSSE SOLL VP-ADVERTISING & CUSTOM PUBLISHING

JEFF TROJAN VP-BUSINESS DEVELOPMENT, DC DIRECT

BOB WAYNE VP-SALES

SUPER FRIENDS: FOR JUSTICE

Published by DC Comics. Cover and compilation Copyright © 2009 DC Comics.
All Rights Reserved.

Originally published in single magazine form in SUPER FRIENDS 1-7. Copyright © 2008 DC Comics. All Rights Reserved. All characters, their distinctive likenesses
and related elements featured in this publication are trademarks of DC Comics. The stories, characters and incidents featured in this publication are entirely fictional.
DC Comics does not read or accept unsolicited submissions of ideas, stories or artwork.

DC Comics, 1700 Broadway, New York, NY 10019
A Warner Bros. Entertainment Company
Printed in Canada. Second Printing.
ISBN: 978-1-4012-2156-0

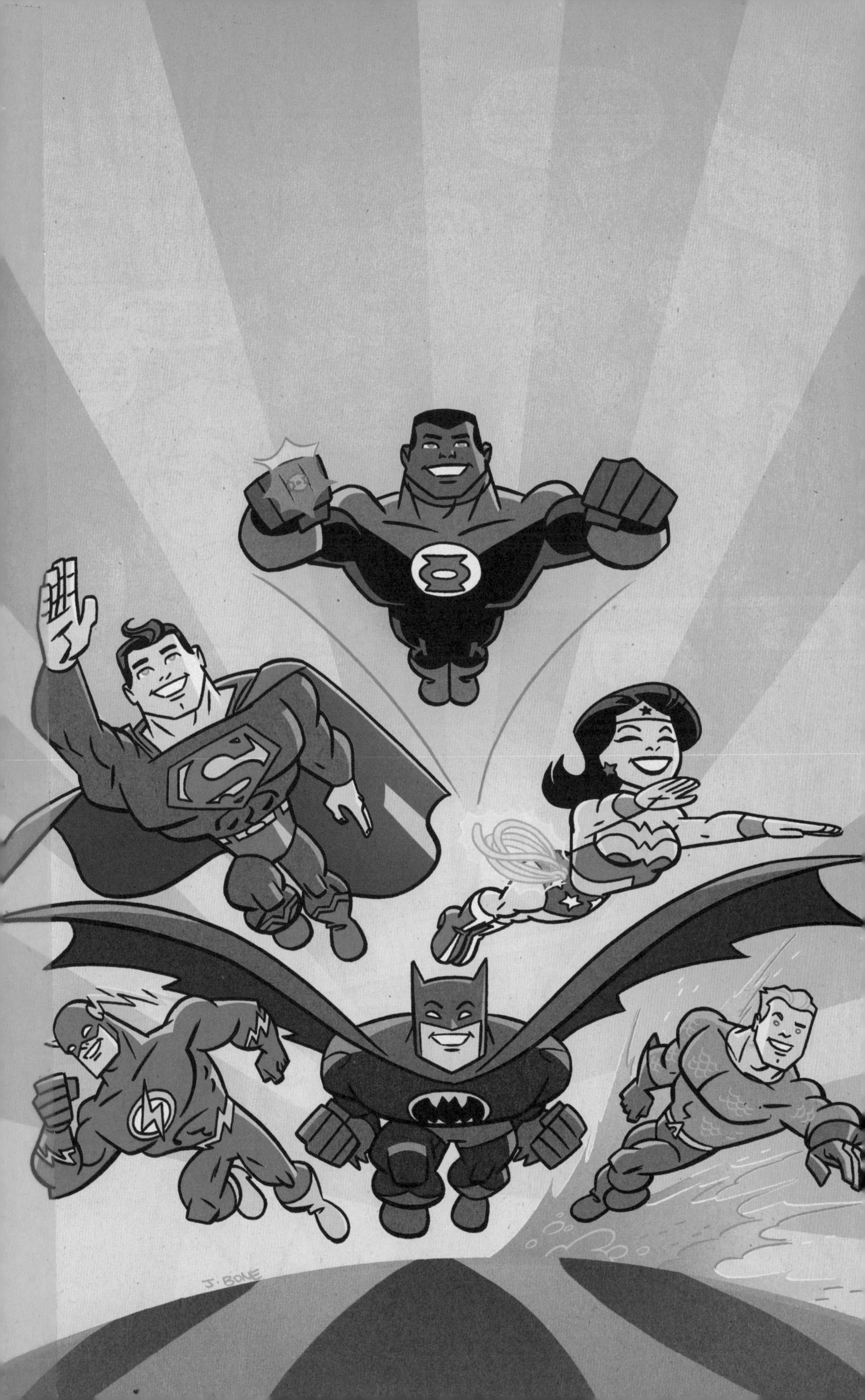
J. BONE

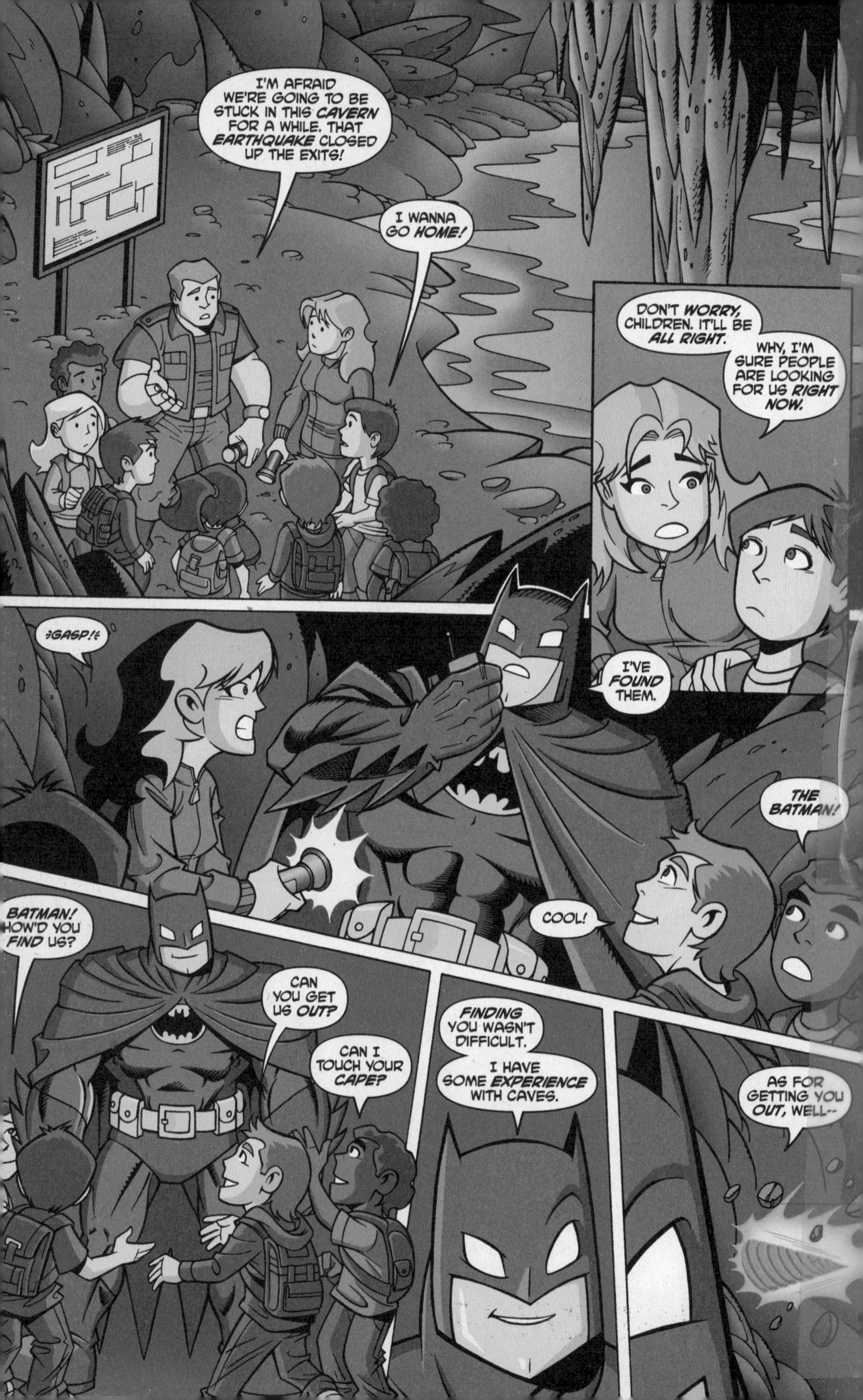
I'M AFRAID WE'RE GOING TO BE STUCK IN THIS CAVERN FOR A WHILE. THAT EARTHQUAKE CLOSED UP THE EXITS!
I WANNA GO HOME!
DON'T WORRY, CHILDREN. IT'LL BE ALL RIGHT.
WHY, I'M SURE PEOPLE ARE LOOKING FOR US RIGHT NOW.
GASP!
I'VE FOUND THEM.
THE BATMAN!
COOL!
BATMAN! HOW'D YOU FIND US?
CAN YOU GET US OUT?
CAN I TOUCH YOUR CAPE?
FINDING YOU WASN'T DIFFICULT.
I HAVE SOME EXPERIENCE WITH CAVES.
AS FOR GETTING YOU OUT, WELL--

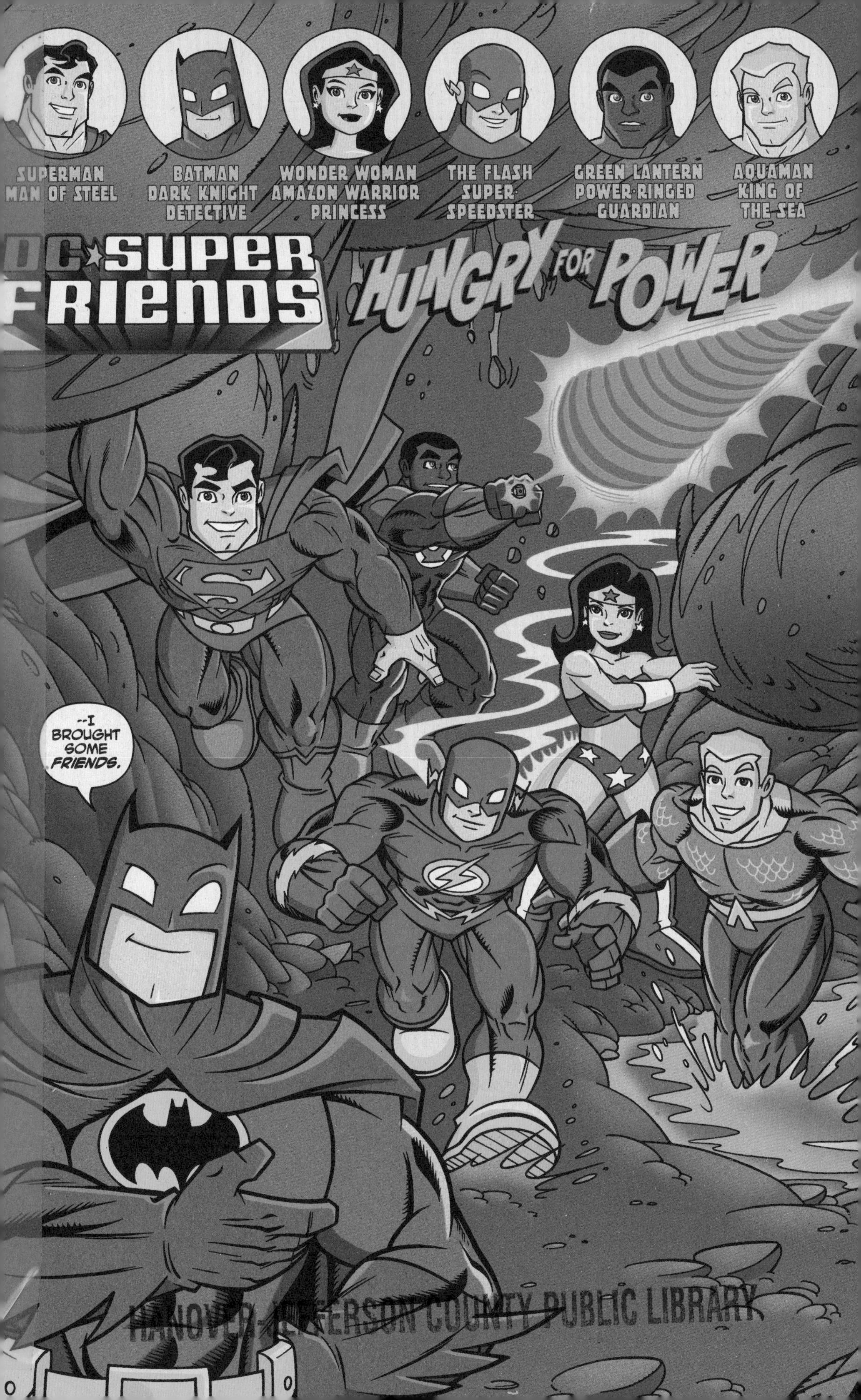
SUPERMAN MAN OF STEEL
BATMAN DARK KNIGHT DETECTIVE
WONDER WOMAN AMAZON WARRIOR PRINCESS
THE FLASH SUPER-SPEEDSTER
GREEN LANTERN POWER-RINGED GUARDIAN
AQUAMAN KING OF THE SEA
DC SUPER FRIENDS
HUNGRY FOR POWER
--I BROUGHT SOME FRIENDS.

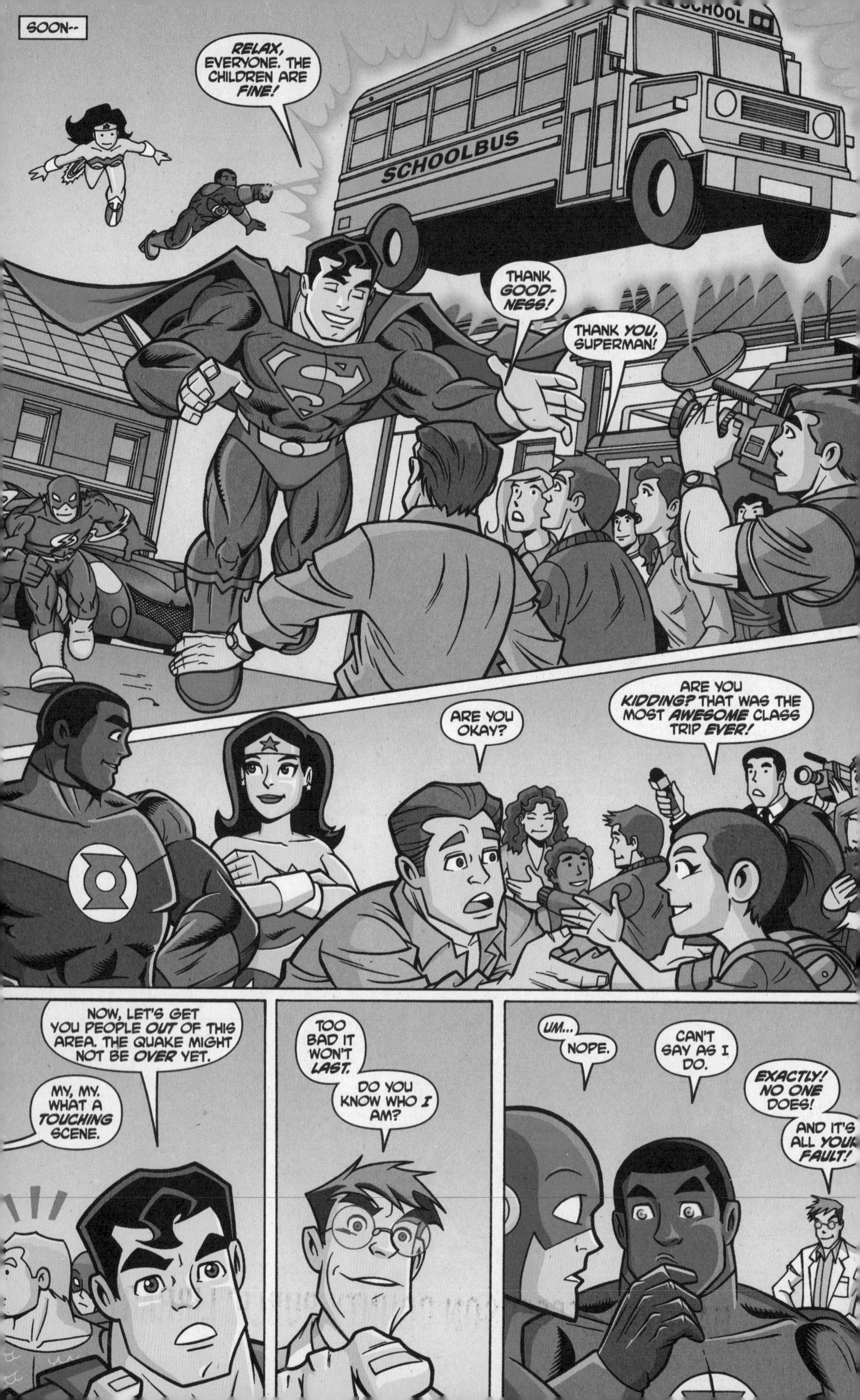
SOON--
RELAX, EVERYONE. THE CHILDREN ARE FINE!
SCHOOL
SCHOOLBUS
THANK GOOD-NESS!
THANK YOU, SUPERMAN!
ARE YOU OKAY?
ARE YOU KIDDING? THAT WAS THE MOST AWESOME CLASS TRIP EVER!
NOW, LET'S GET YOU PEOPLE OUT OF THIS AREA. THE QUAKE MIGHT NOT BE OVER YET.
MY, MY. WHAT A TOUCHING SCENE.
TOO BAD IT WON'T LAST.
DO YOU KNOW WHO I AM?
UM...
NOPE.
CAN'T SAY AS I DO.
EXACTLY! NO ONE DOES!
AND IT'S ALL YOUR FAULT!

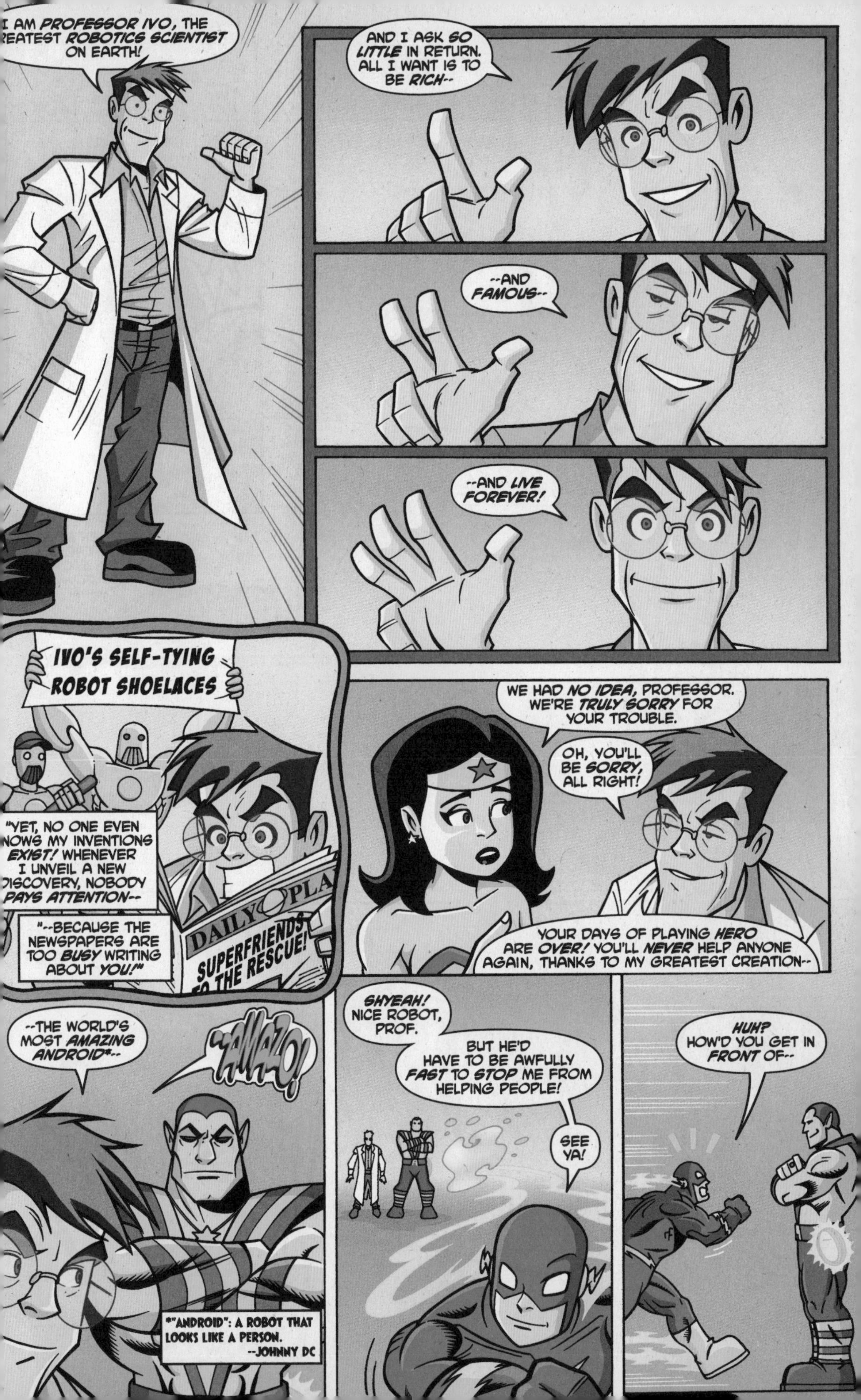

I AM PROFESSOR IVO, THE GREATEST ROBOTICS SCIENTIST ON EARTH!
AND I ASK SO LITTLE IN RETURN. ALL I WANT IS TO BE RICH--
--AND FAMOUS--
--AND LIVE FOREVER!
IVO'S SELF-TYING ROBOT SHOELACES
"YET, NO ONE EVEN KNOWS MY INVENTIONS EXIST! WHENEVER I UNVEIL A NEW DISCOVERY, NOBODY PAYS ATTENTION--
"--BECAUSE THE NEWSPAPERS ARE TOO BUSY WRITING ABOUT YOU!"
DAILY PLA
SUPERFRIENDS TO THE RESCUE!
WE HAD NO IDEA, PROFESSOR. WE'RE TRULY SORRY FOR YOUR TROUBLE.
OH, YOU'LL BE SORRY, ALL RIGHT!
YOUR DAYS OF PLAYING HERO ARE OVER! YOU'LL NEVER HELP ANYONE AGAIN, THANKS TO MY GREATEST CREATION--
--THE WORLD'S MOST AMAZING ANDROID*--
AMAZO!
*"ANDROID": A ROBOT THAT LOOKS LIKE A PERSON. --JOHNNY DC
SHYEAH! NICE ROBOT, PROF.
BUT HE'D HAVE TO BE AWFULLY FAST TO STOP ME FROM HELPING PEOPLE!
SEE YA!
HUH? HOW'D YOU GET IN FRONT OF--

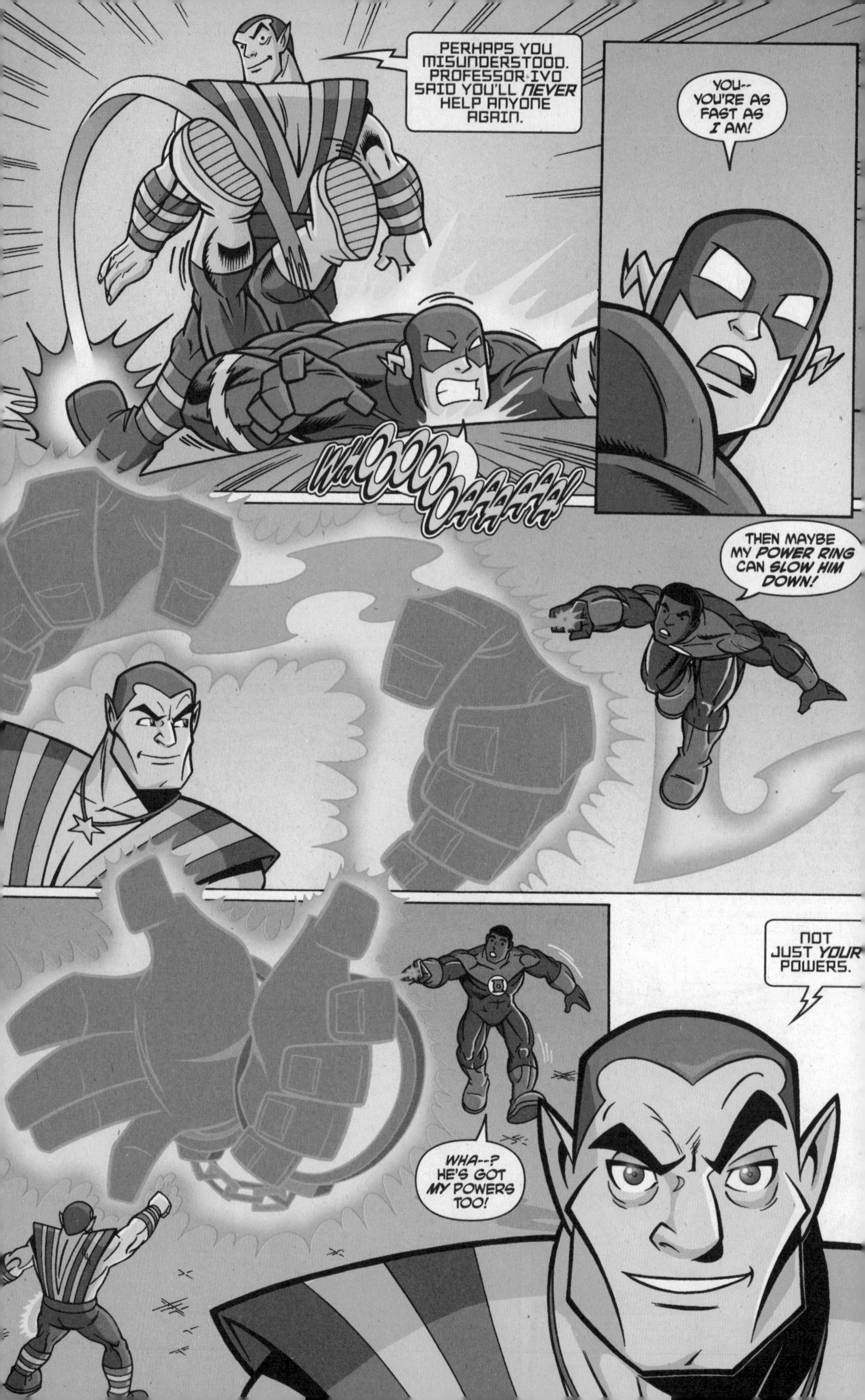
PERHAPS YOU MISUNDERSTOOD. PROFESSOR IVO SAID YOU'LL *NEVER* HELP ANYONE AGAIN.
YOU-- YOU'RE AS FAST AS *I AM!*
WHOOOOOOAAAAAA!
THEN MAYBE MY *POWER RING* CAN *SLOW HIM DOWN!*
WHA--? HE'S GOT *MY* POWERS TOO!
NOT JUST *YOUR* POWERS.

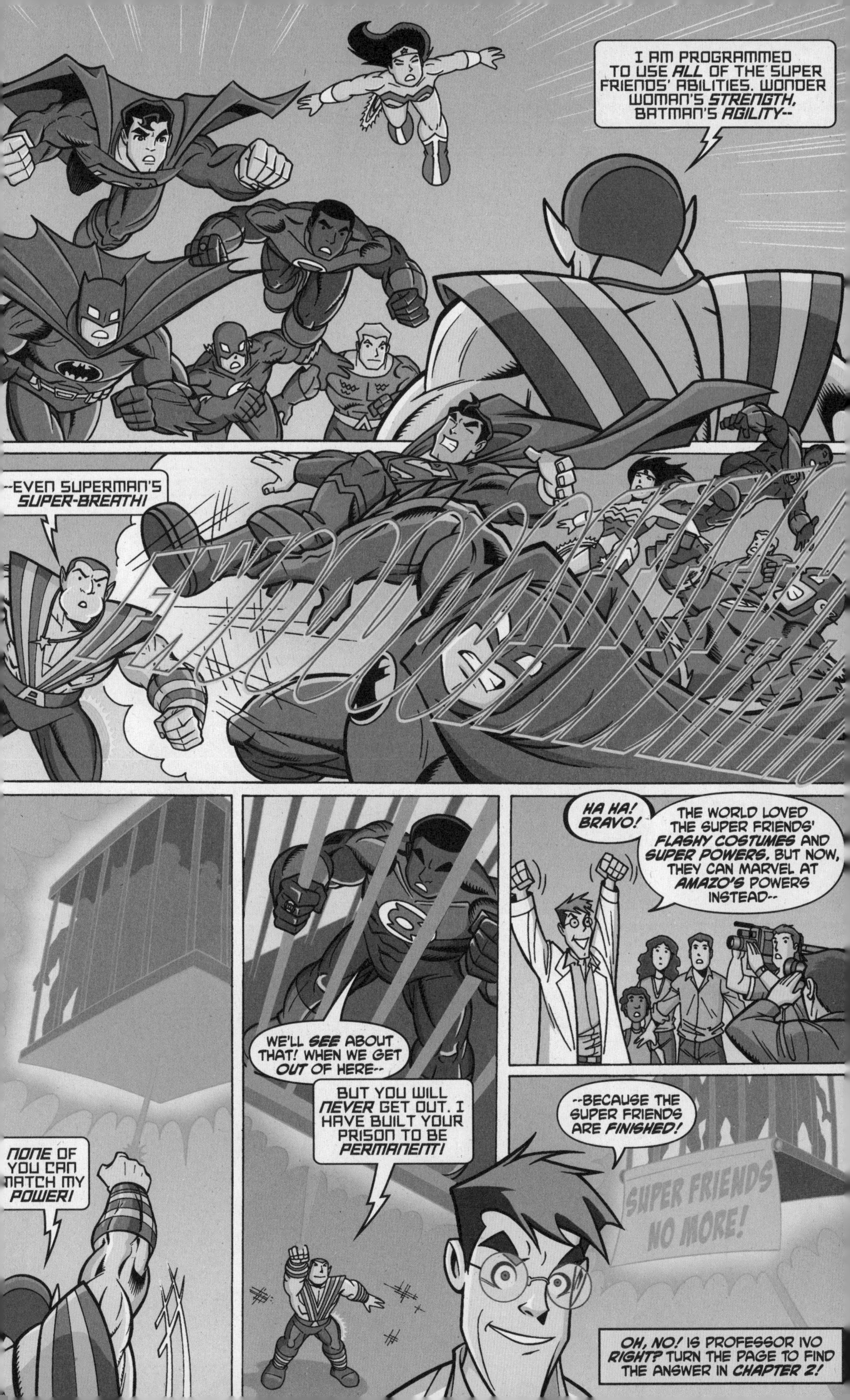
I AM PROGRAMMED TO USE ALL OF THE SUPER FRIENDS' ABILITIES. WONDER WOMAN'S STRENGTH, BATMAN'S AGILITY--
--EVEN SUPERMAN'S SUPER-BREATH!
NONE OF YOU CAN MATCH MY POWER!
WE'LL SEE ABOUT THAT! WHEN WE GET OUT OF HERE--
BUT YOU WILL NEVER GET OUT. I HAVE BUILT YOUR PRISON TO BE PERMANENT!
HA HA! BRAVO!
THE WORLD LOVED THE SUPER FRIENDS' FLASHY COSTUMES AND SUPER POWERS. BUT NOW, THEY CAN MARVEL AT AMAZO'S POWERS INSTEAD--
--BECAUSE THE SUPER FRIENDS ARE FINISHED!
SUPER FRIENDS NO MORE!
OH, NO! IS PROFESSOR IVO RIGHT? TURN THE PAGE TO FIND THE ANSWER IN CHAPTER 2!

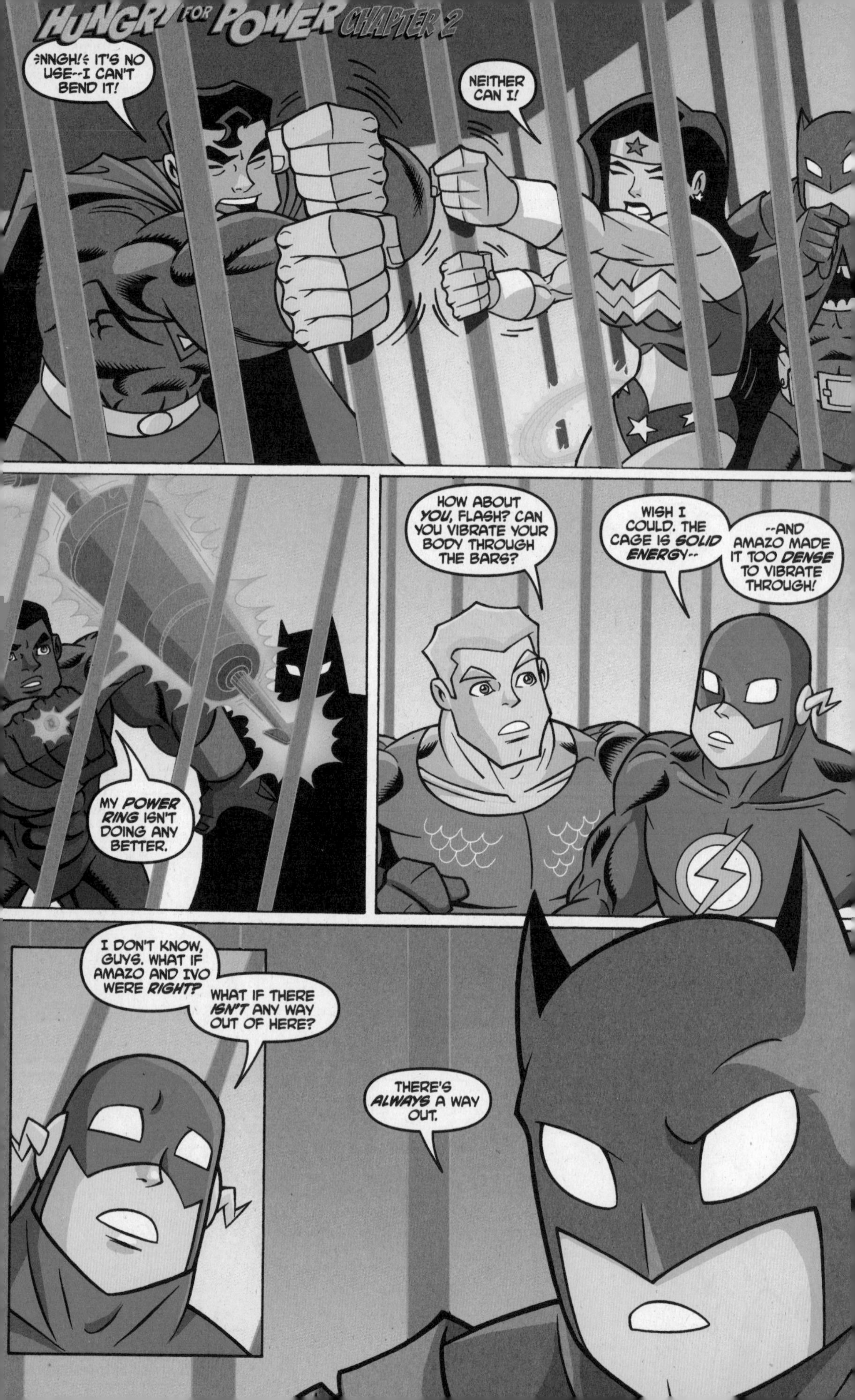

HUNGRY FOR POWER CHAPTER 2
=NNGH!= IT'S NO USE--I CAN'T BEND IT!
NEITHER CAN I!
MY POWER RING ISN'T DOING ANY BETTER.
HOW ABOUT YOU, FLASH? CAN YOU VIBRATE YOUR BODY THROUGH THE BARS?
WISH I COULD. THE CAGE IS SOLID ENERGY--
--AND AMAZO MADE IT TOO DENSE TO VIBRATE THROUGH!
I DON'T KNOW, GUYS. WHAT IF AMAZO AND IVO WERE RIGHT?
WHAT IF THERE ISN'T ANY WAY OUT OF HERE?
THERE'S ALWAYS A WAY OUT.

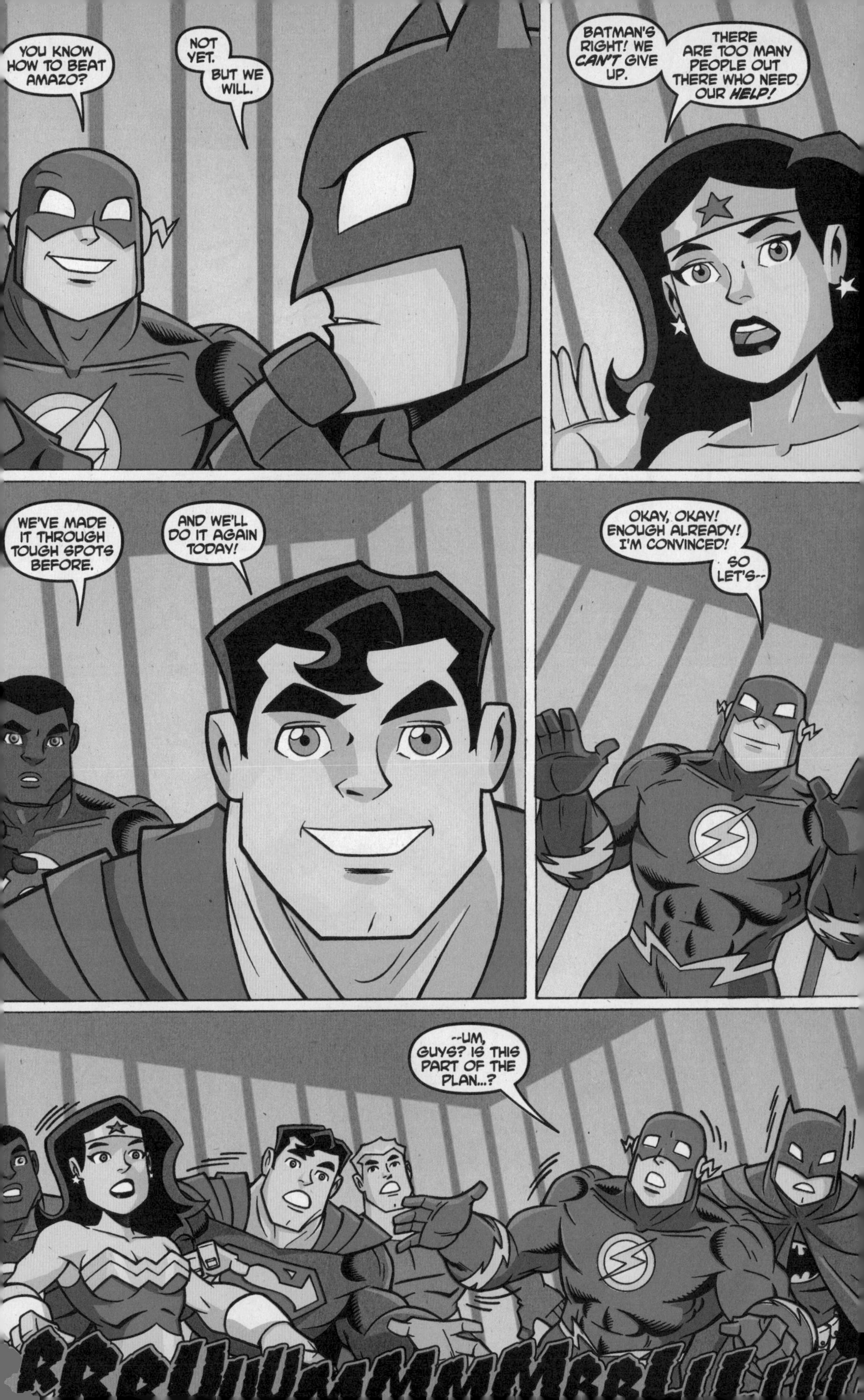
YOU KNOW HOW TO BEAT AMAZO?
NOT YET.
BUT WE WILL.
BATMAN'S RIGHT! WE CAN'T GIVE UP.
THERE ARE TOO MANY PEOPLE OUT THERE WHO NEED OUR HELP!
WE'VE MADE IT THROUGH TOUGH SPOTS BEFORE.
AND WE'LL DO IT AGAIN TODAY!
OKAY, OKAY! ENOUGH ALREADY! I'M CONVINCED!
SO LET'S--
--UM, GUYS? IS THIS PART OF THE PLAN...?

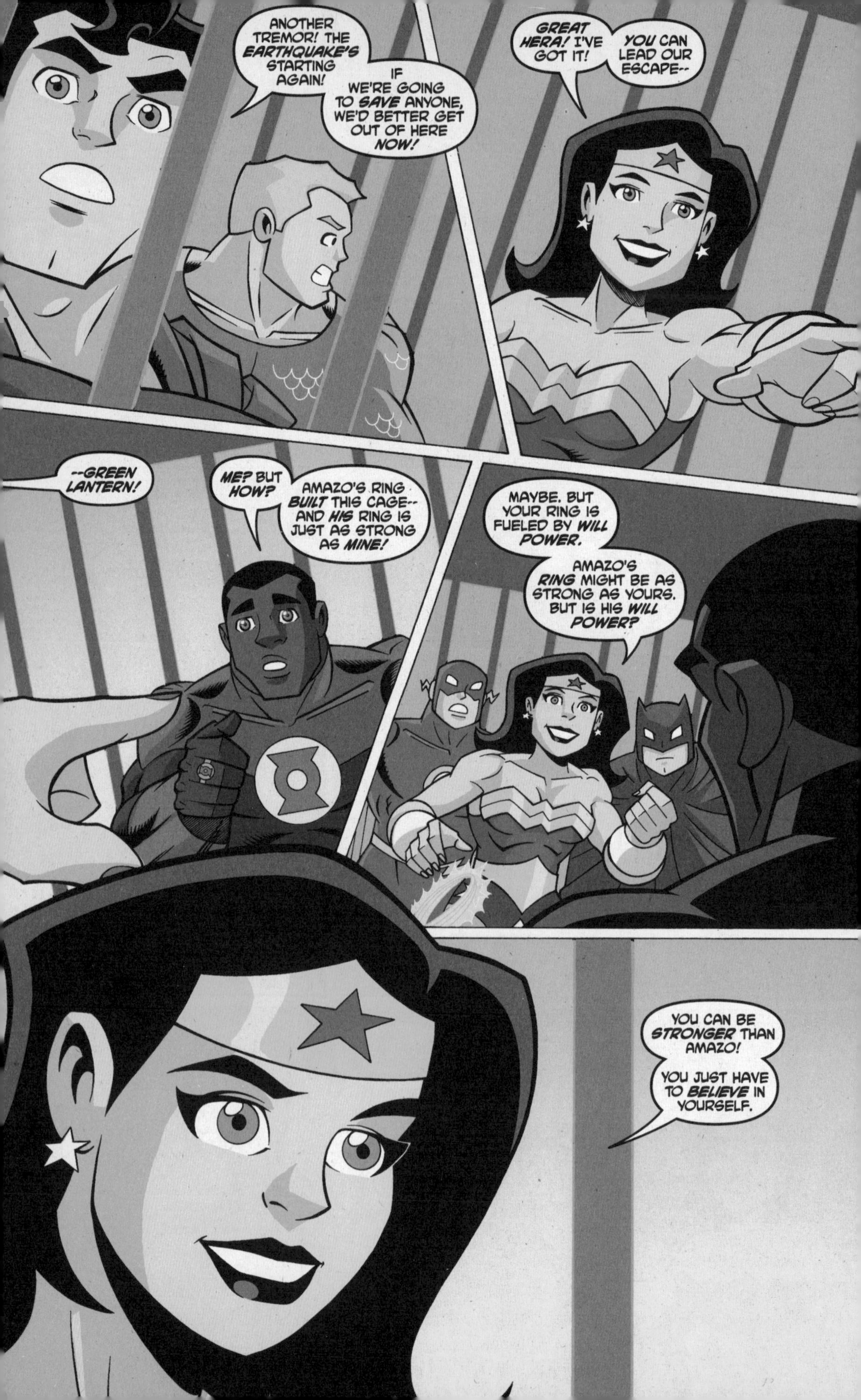
ANOTHER TREMOR! THE EARTHQUAKE'S STARTING AGAIN!
IF WE'RE GOING TO SAVE ANYONE, WE'D BETTER GET OUT OF HERE NOW!
GREAT HERA! I'VE GOT IT!
YOU CAN LEAD OUR ESCAPE--
--GREEN LANTERN!
ME? BUT HOW?
AMAZO'S RING BUILT THIS CAGE-- AND HIS RING IS JUST AS STRONG AS MINE!
MAYBE. BUT YOUR RING IS FUELED BY WILL POWER.
AMAZO'S RING MIGHT BE AS STRONG AS YOURS. BUT IS HIS WILL POWER?
YOU CAN BE STRONGER THAN AMAZO!
YOU JUST HAVE TO BELIEVE IN YOURSELF.

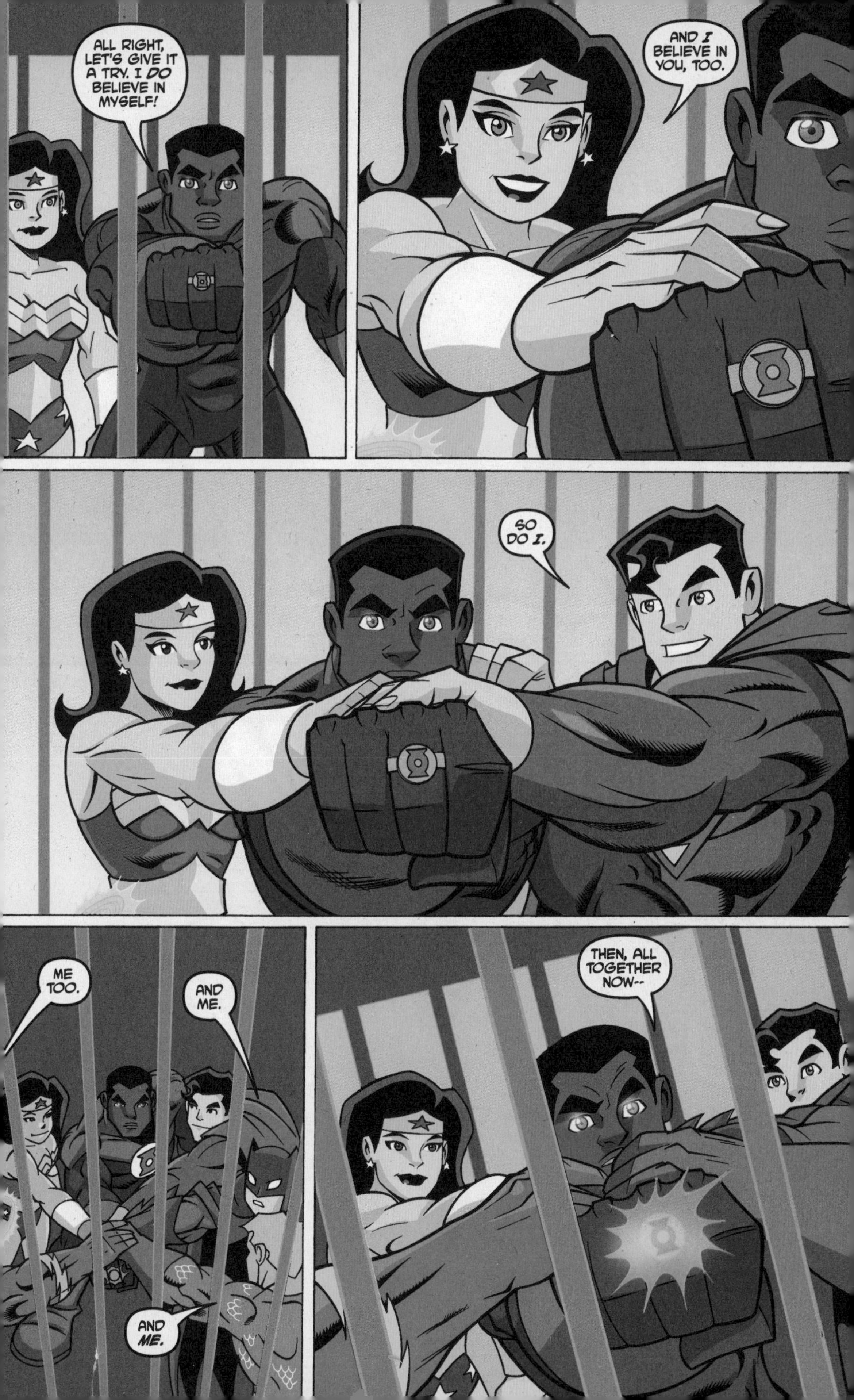
ALL RIGHT, LET'S GIVE IT A TRY. I DO BELIEVE IN MYSELF!
AND I BELIEVE IN YOU, TOO.
SO DO I.
ME TOO.
AND ME.
AND ME.
THEN, ALL TOGETHER NOW--

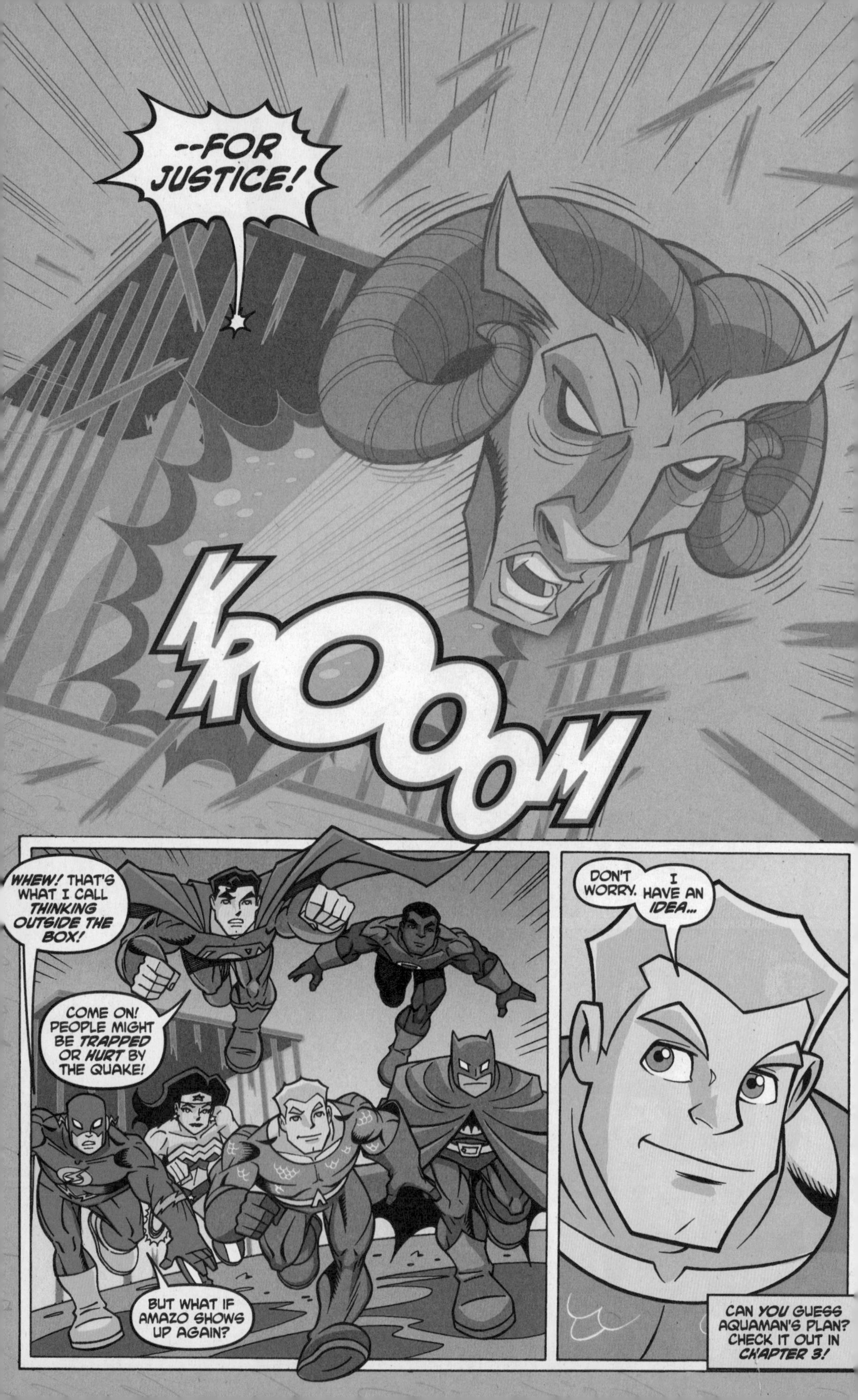
--FOR JUSTICE!
KROOOOM
WHEW! THAT'S WHAT I CALL THINKING OUTSIDE THE BOX!
COME ON! PEOPLE MIGHT BE TRAPPED OR HURT BY THE QUAKE!
BUT WHAT IF AMAZO SHOWS UP AGAIN?
DON'T WORRY.
I HAVE AN IDEA...
CAN YOU GUESS AQUAMAN'S PLAN? CHECK IT OUT IN CHAPTER 3!

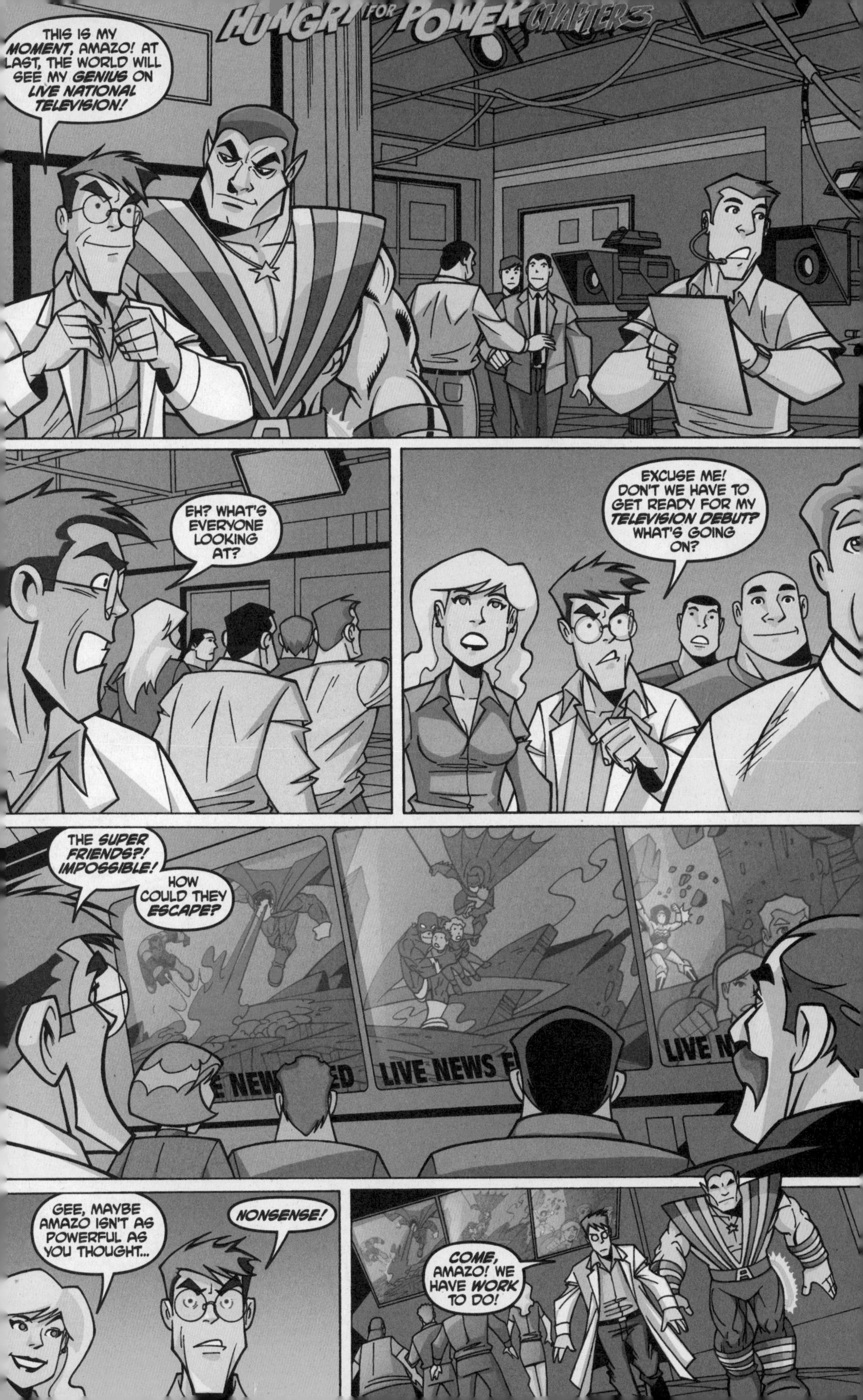

HUNGRY FOR POWER CHAPTER 3
THIS IS MY MOMENT, AMAZO! AT LAST, THE WORLD WILL SEE MY GENIUS ON LIVE NATIONAL TELEVISION!
EH? WHAT'S EVERYONE LOOKING AT?
EXCUSE ME! DON'T WE HAVE TO GET READY FOR MY TELEVISION DEBUT? WHAT'S GOING ON?
THE SUPER FRIENDS?! IMPOSSIBLE!
HOW COULD THEY ESCAPE?
LIVE NEWS
LIVE NEWS
LIVE N
GEE, MAYBE AMAZO ISN'T AS POWERFUL AS YOU THOUGHT...
NONSENSE!
COME, AMAZO! WE HAVE WORK TO DO!

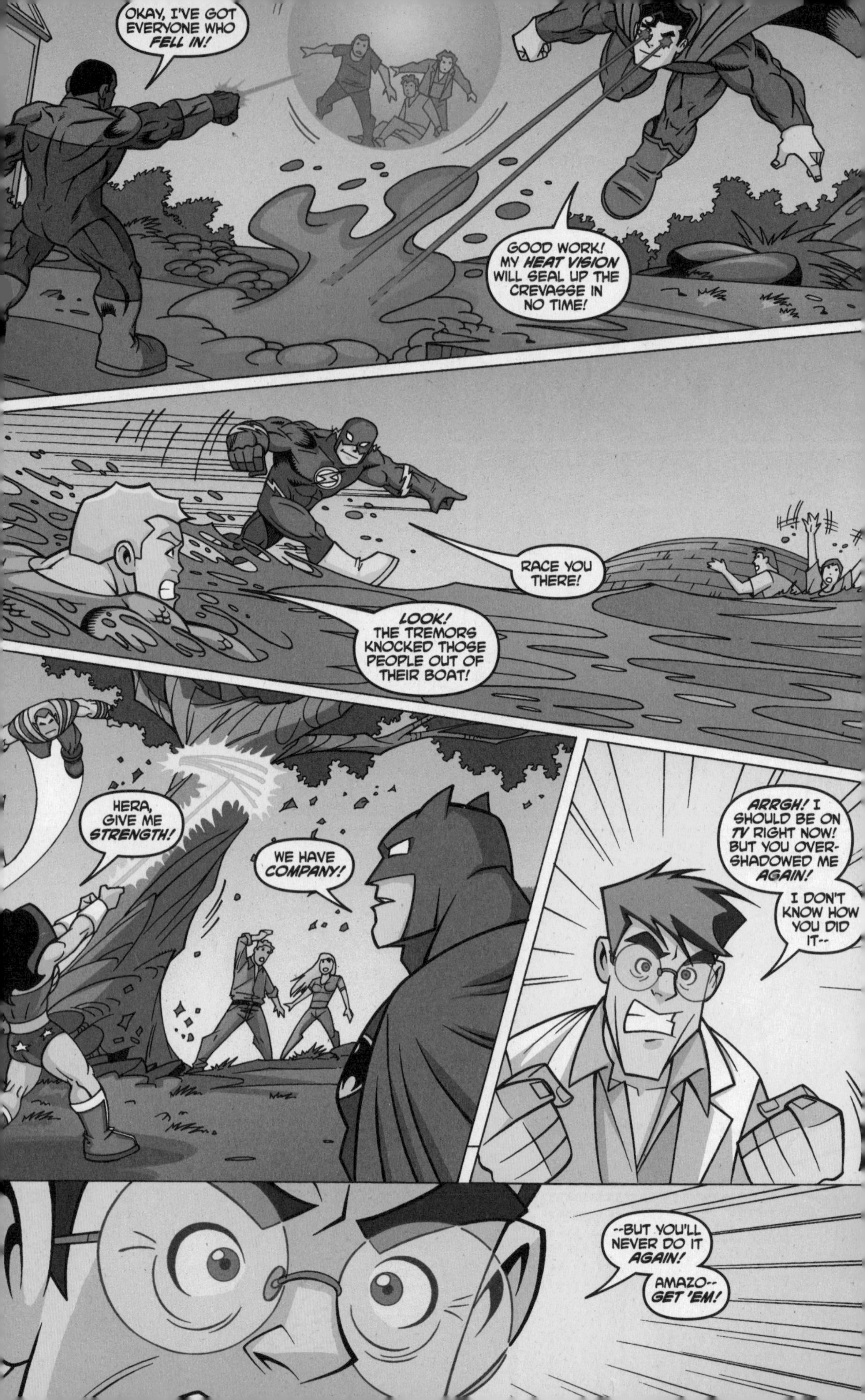
OKAY, I'VE GOT EVERYONE WHO FELL IN!
GOOD WORK! MY HEAT VISION WILL SEAL UP THE CREVASSE IN NO TIME!
RACE YOU THERE!
LOOK! THE TREMORS KNOCKED THOSE PEOPLE OUT OF THEIR BOAT!
HERA, GIVE ME STRENGTH!
WE HAVE COMPANY!
ARRGH! I SHOULD BE ON TV RIGHT NOW! BUT YOU OVER-SHADOWED ME AGAIN!
I DON'T KNOW HOW YOU DID IT--
--BUT YOU'LL NEVER DO IT AGAIN!
AMAZO-- GET 'EM!

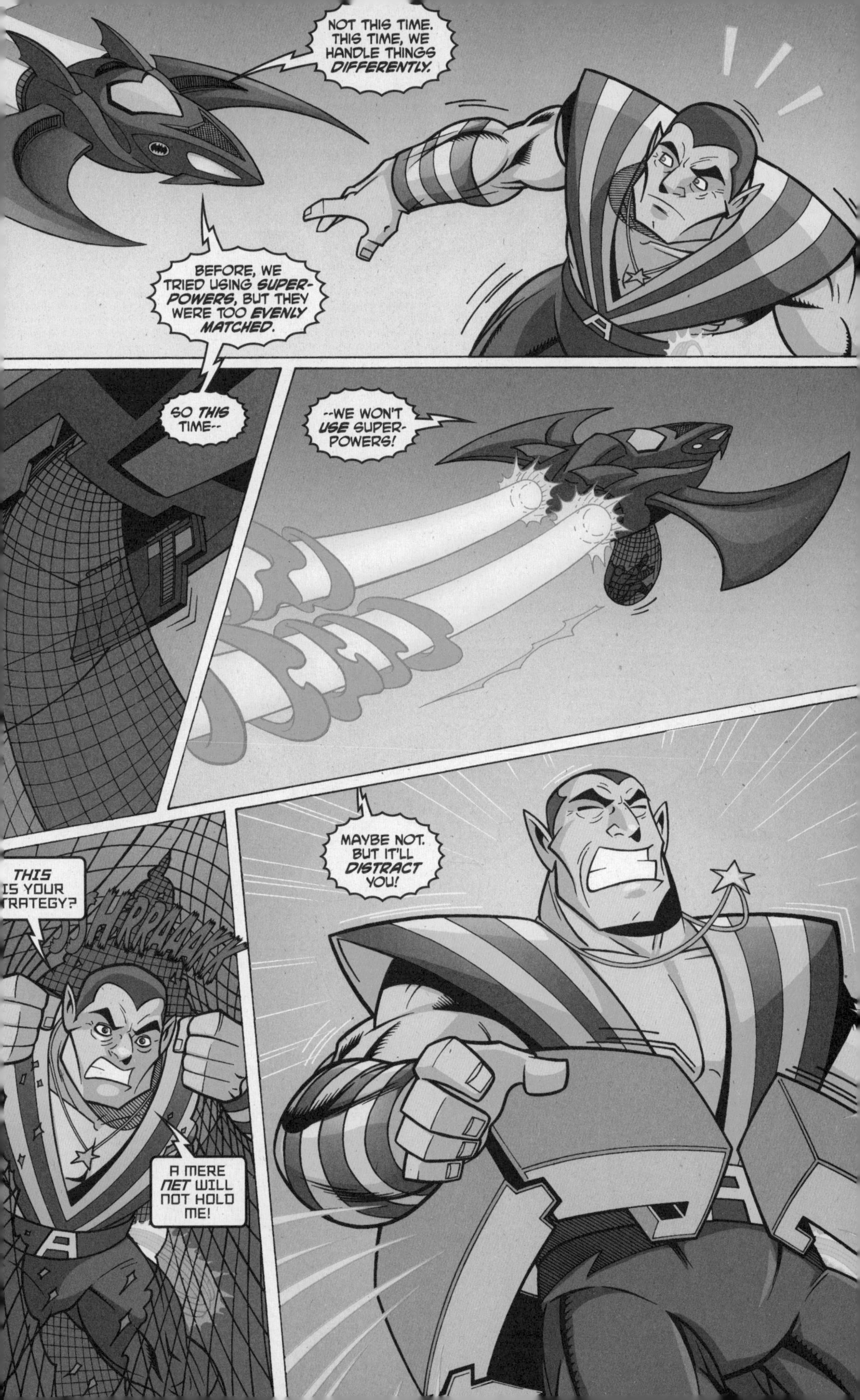
NOT THIS TIME. THIS TIME, WE HANDLE THINGS DIFFERENTLY.
BEFORE, WE TRIED USING SUPER-POWERS, BUT THEY WERE TOO EVENLY MATCHED.
SO THIS TIME--
--WE WON'T USE SUPER-POWERS!
THIS IS YOUR TRATEGY?
A MERE NET WILL NOT HOLD ME!
MAYBE NOT. BUT IT'LL DISTRACT YOU!

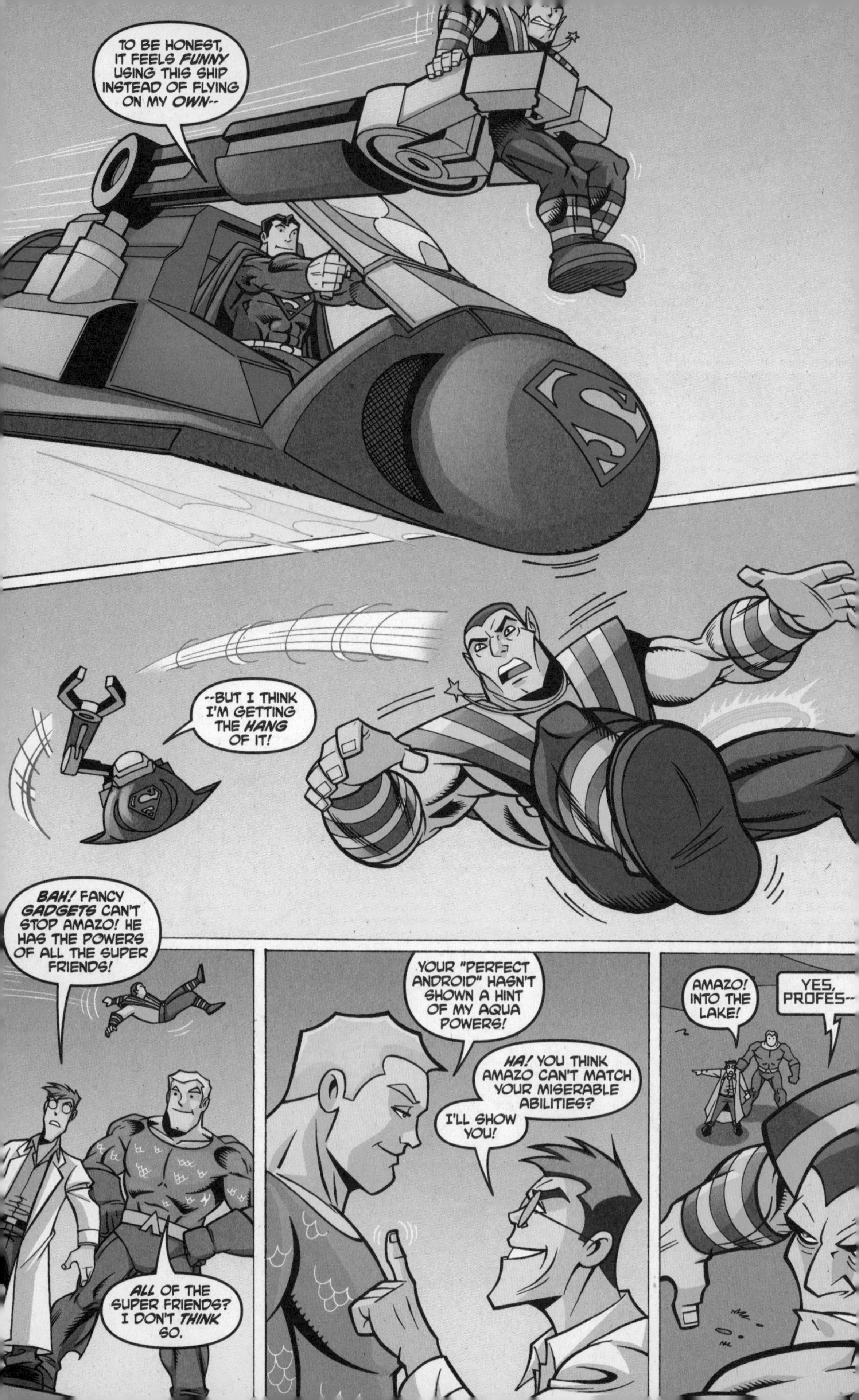
TO BE HONEST, IT FEELS FUNNY USING THIS SHIP INSTEAD OF FLYING ON MY OWN--
--BUT I THINK I'M GETTING THE HANG OF IT!
BAH! FANCY GADGETS CAN'T STOP AMAZO! HE HAS THE POWERS OF ALL THE SUPER FRIENDS!
ALL OF THE SUPER FRIENDS? I DON'T THINK SO.
YOUR "PERFECT ANDROID" HASN'T SHOWN A HINT OF MY AQUA POWERS!
HA! YOU THINK AMAZO CAN'T MATCH YOUR MISERABLE ABILITIES?
I'LL SHOW YOU!
AMAZO! INTO THE LAKE!
YES, PROFES--

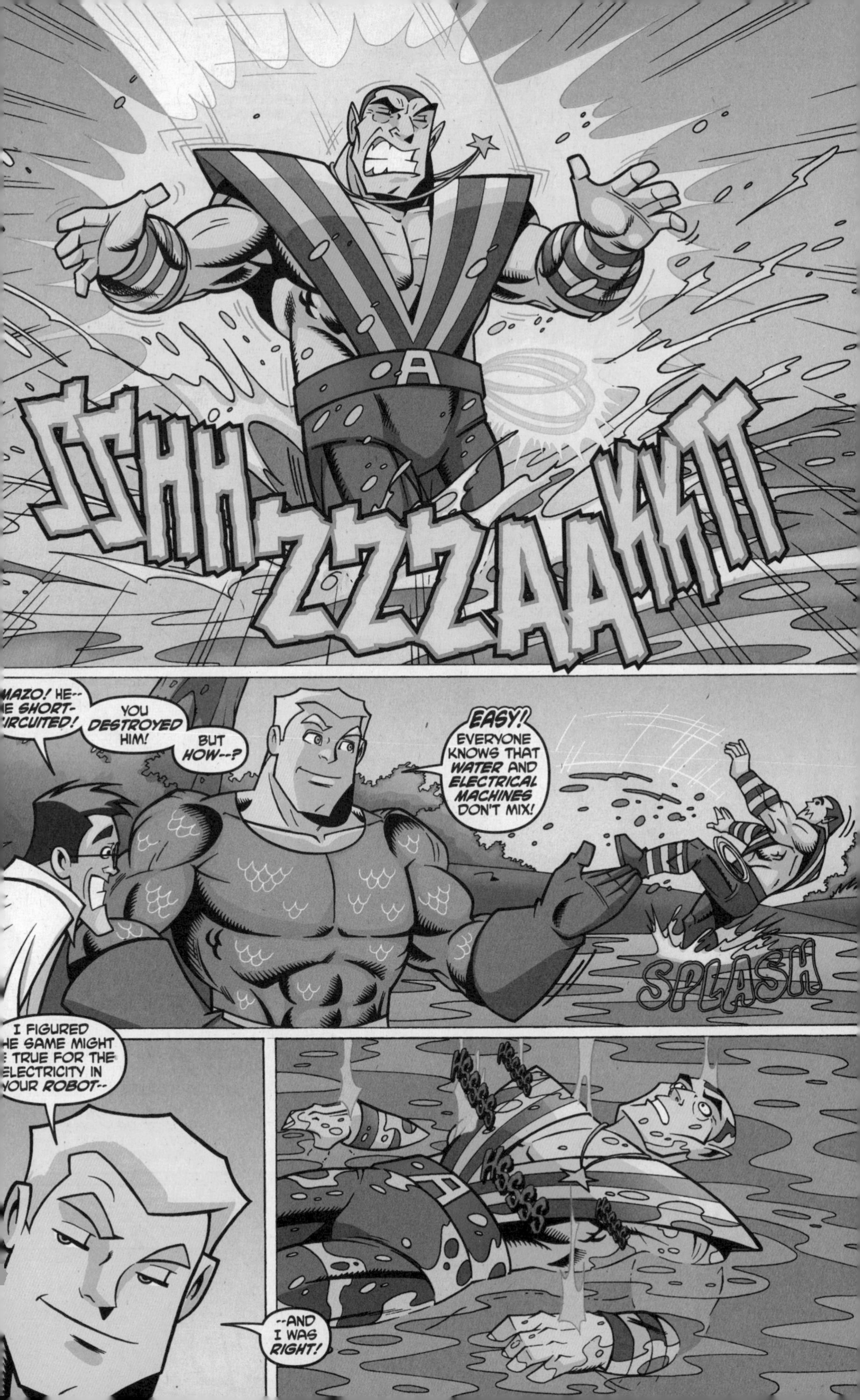
SSHH-ZZZZAAKKTT
MAZO! HE--
HE SHORT-CIRCUITED!
YOU DESTROYED HIM!
BUT HOW--?
EASY! EVERYONE KNOWS THAT WATER AND ELECTRICAL MACHINES DON'T MIX!
SPLASH
I FIGURED THE SAME MIGHT BE TRUE FOR THE ELECTRICITY IN YOUR ROBOT--
HSSSS
--AND I WAS RIGHT!

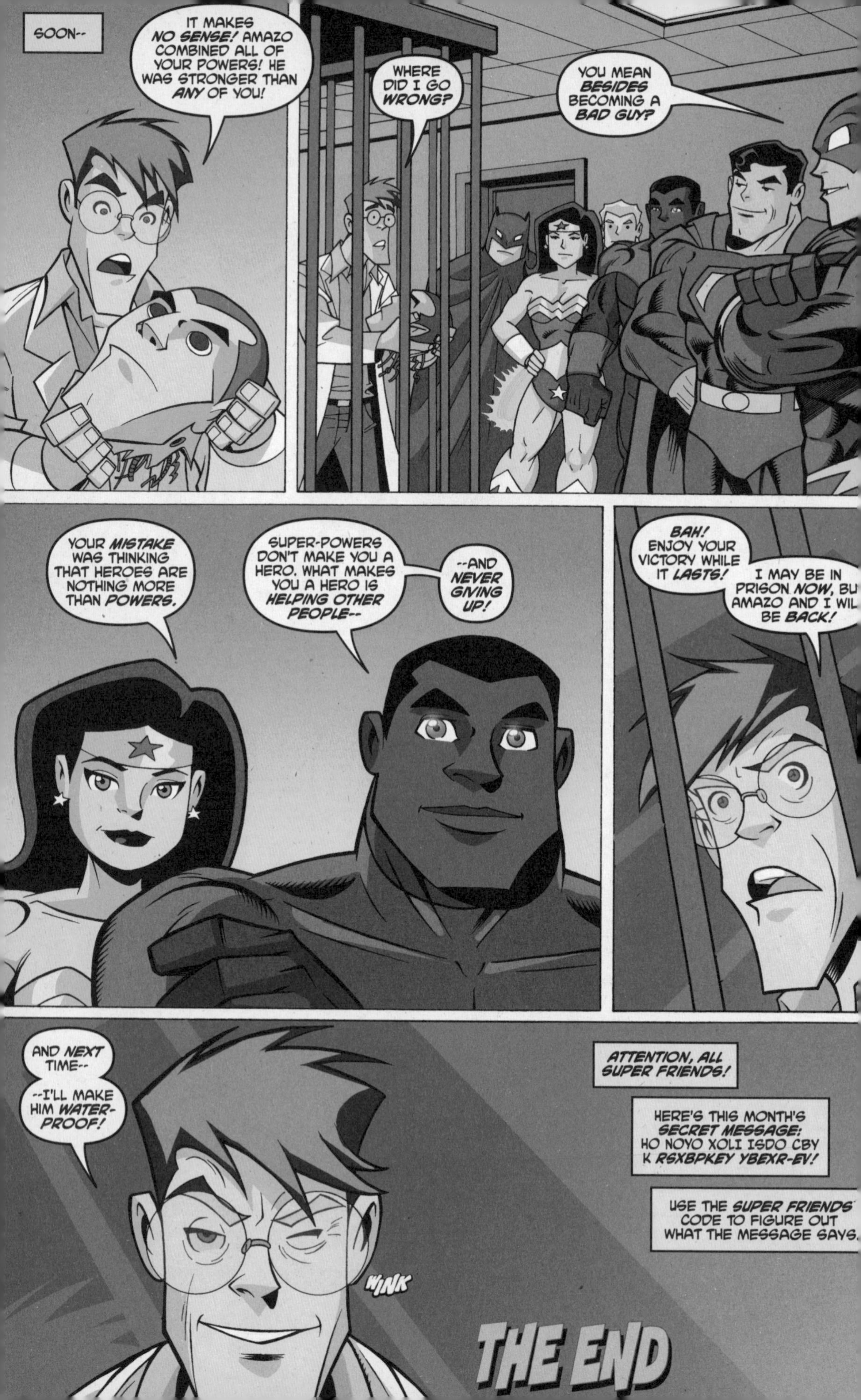
SOON--
IT MAKES NO SENSE! AMAZO COMBINED ALL OF YOUR POWERS! HE WAS STRONGER THAN ANY OF YOU!
WHERE DID I GO WRONG?
YOU MEAN BESIDES BECOMING A BAD GUY?
YOUR MISTAKE WAS THINKING THAT HEROES ARE NOTHING MORE THAN POWERS.
SUPER-POWERS DON'T MAKE YOU A HERO. WHAT MAKES YOU A HERO IS HELPING OTHER PEOPLE--
--AND NEVER GIVING UP!
BAH! ENJOY YOUR VICTORY WHILE IT LASTS!
I MAY BE IN PRISON NOW, BU AMAZO AND I WIL BE BACK!
AND NEXT TIME--
--I'LL MAKE HIM WATER-PROOF!
ATTENTION, ALL SUPER FRIENDS!
HERE'S THIS MONTH'S SECRET MESSAGE: HO NOYO XOLI ISDO CBY K RSXBPKEY YBEXR-EV!
USE THE SUPER FRIENDS CODE TO FIGURE OUT WHAT THE MESSAGE SAYS.
WINK
THE END

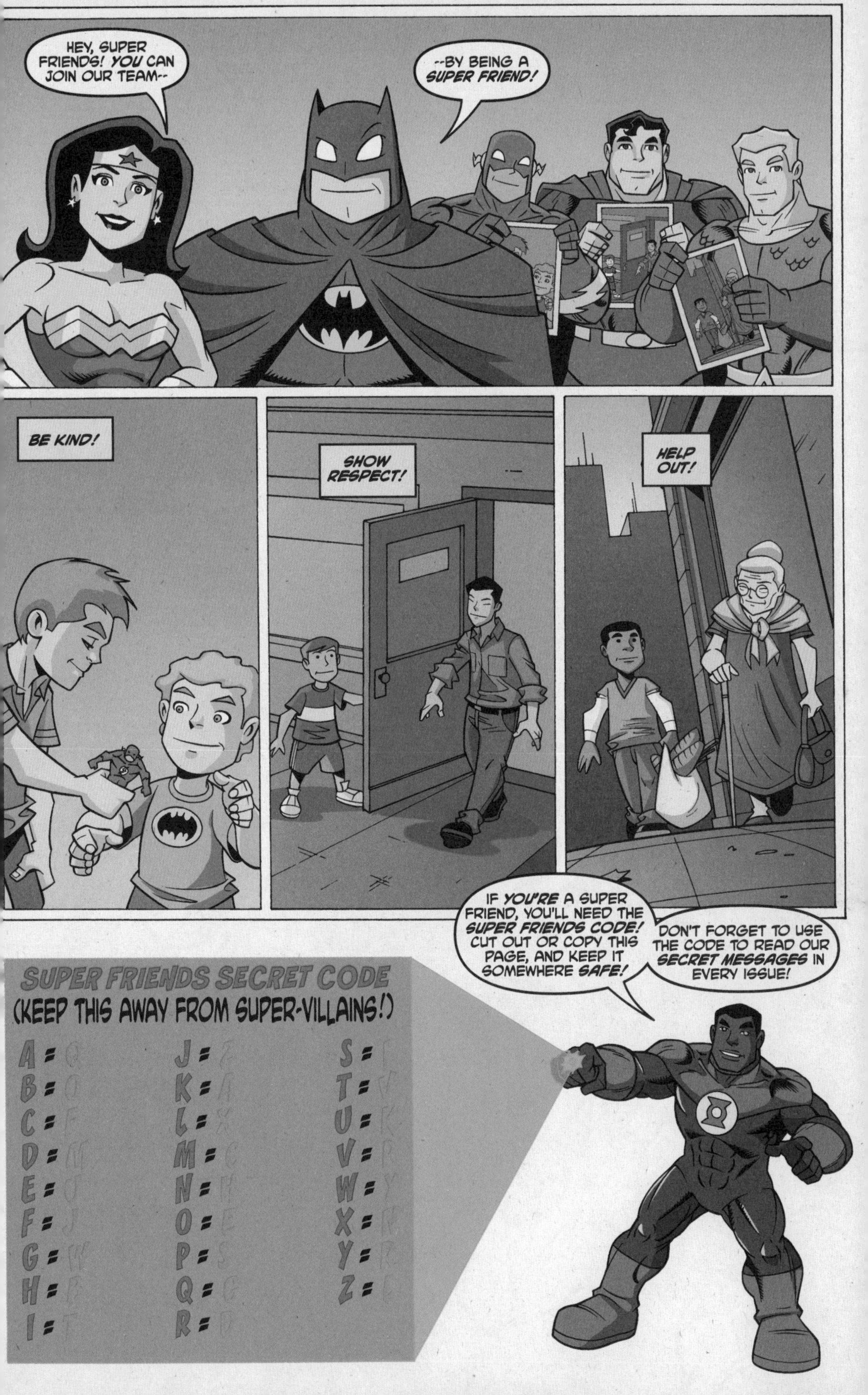

HEY, SUPER FRIENDS! YOU CAN JOIN OUR TEAM--
--BY BEING A SUPER FRIEND!
BE KIND!
SHOW RESPECT!
HELP OUT!
IF YOU'RE A SUPER FRIEND, YOU'LL NEED THE SUPER FRIENDS CODE! CUT OUT OR COPY THIS PAGE, AND KEEP IT SOMEWHERE SAFE!
DON'T FORGET TO USE THE CODE TO READ OUR SECRET MESSAGES IN EVERY ISSUE!
SUPER FRIENDS SECRET CODE
(KEEP THIS AWAY FROM SUPER-VILLAINS!)
A =
B =
C =
D =
E =
F =
G =
H =
I =
J =
K =
L =
M =
N =
O =
P =
Q =
R =
S =
T =
U =
V =
W =
X =
Y =
Z =

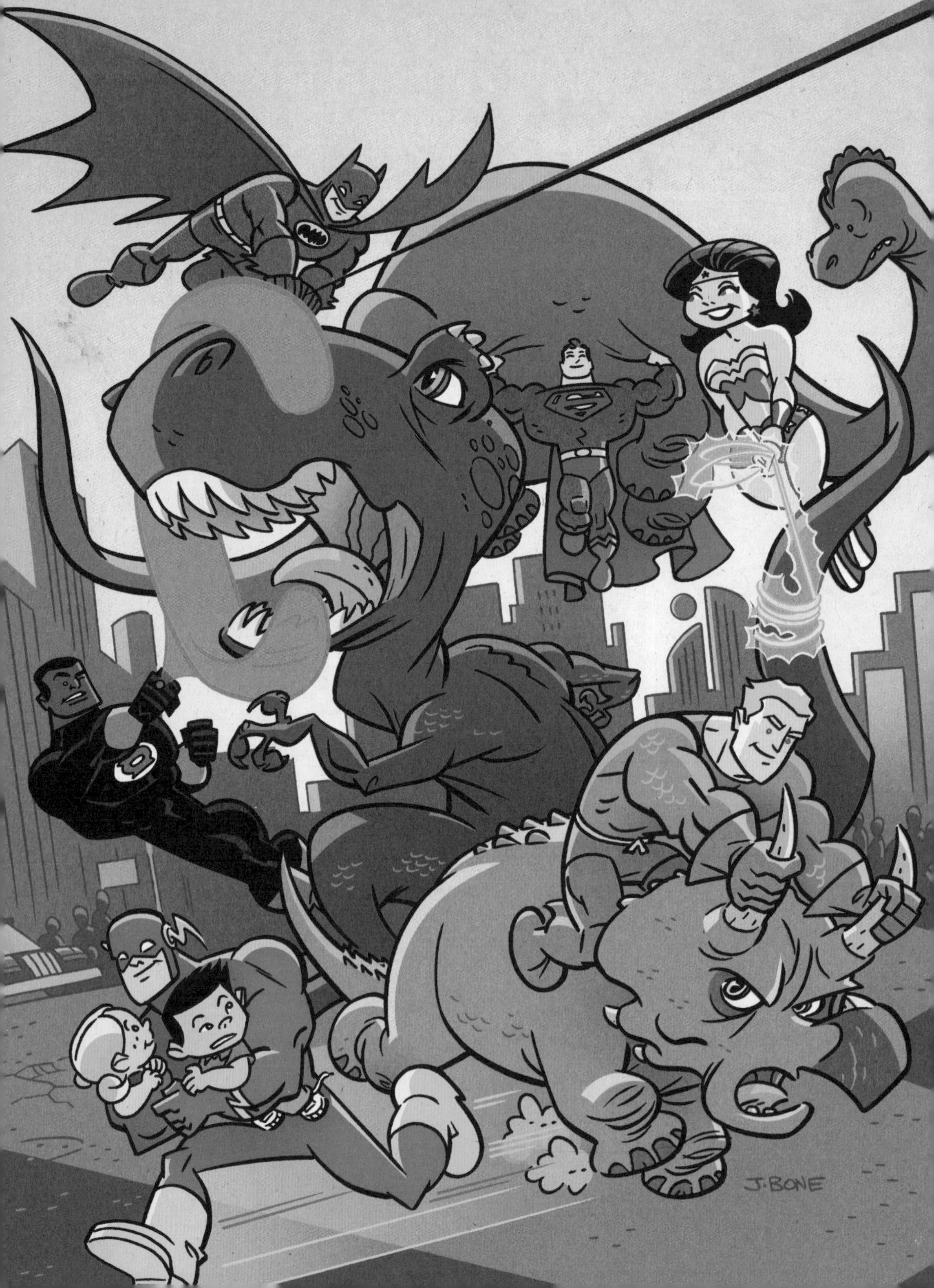
J.BONE

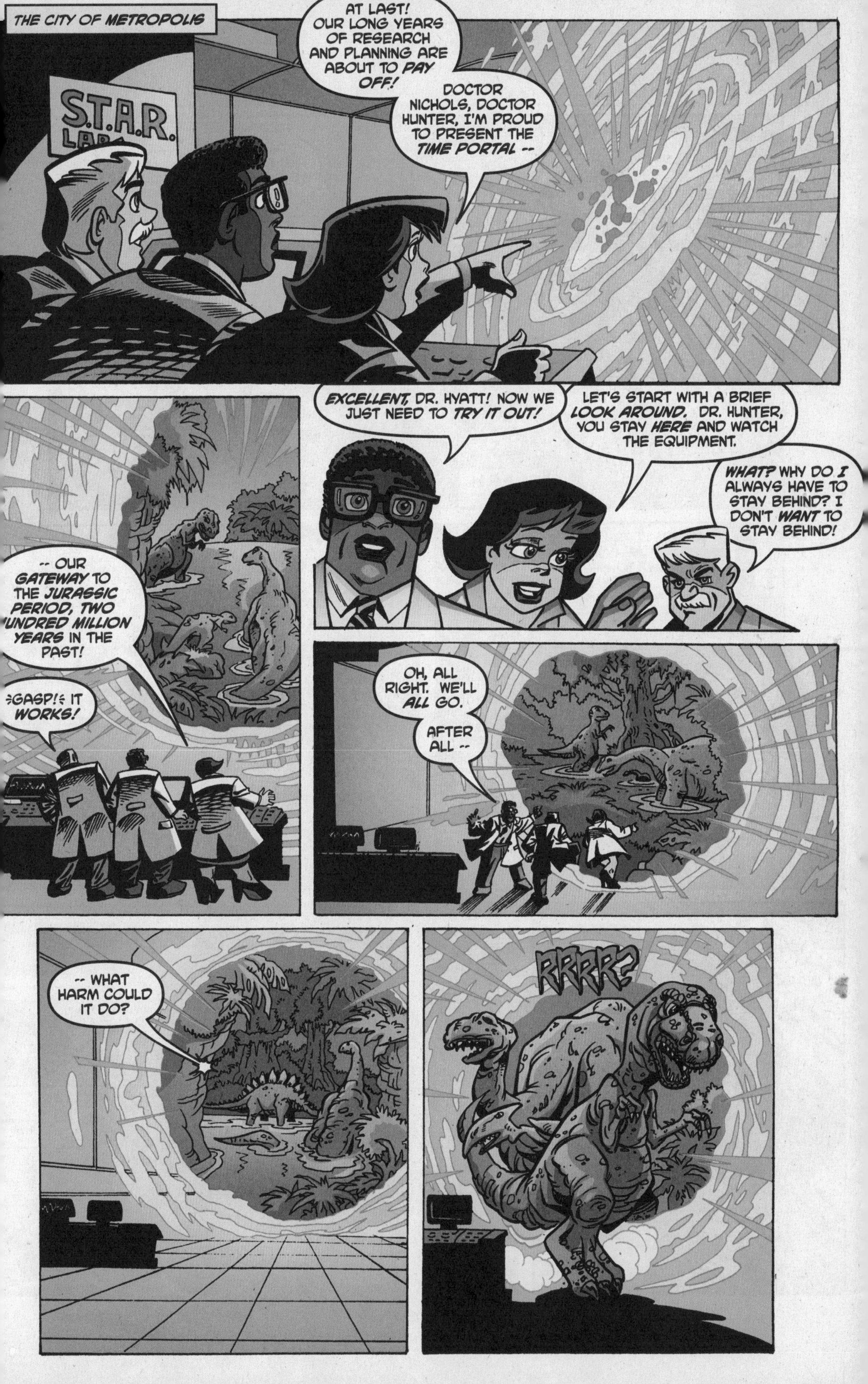
THE CITY OF METROPOLIS
AT LAST! OUR LONG YEARS OF RESEARCH AND PLANNING ARE ABOUT TO PAY OFF!
DOCTOR NICHOLS, DOCTOR HUNTER, I'M PROUD TO PRESENT THE TIME PORTAL --
S.T.A.R.
-- OUR GATEWAY TO THE JURASSIC PERIOD, TWO HUNDRED MILLION YEARS IN THE PAST!
GASP! IT WORKS!
EXCELLENT, DR. HYATT! NOW WE JUST NEED TO TRY IT OUT!
LET'S START WITH A BRIEF LOOK AROUND. DR. HUNTER, YOU STAY HERE AND WATCH THE EQUIPMENT.
WHAT? WHY DO I ALWAYS HAVE TO STAY BEHIND? I DON'T WANT TO STAY BEHIND!
OH, ALL RIGHT. WE'LL ALL GO.
AFTER ALL --
-- WHAT HARM COULD IT DO?
RRRR?

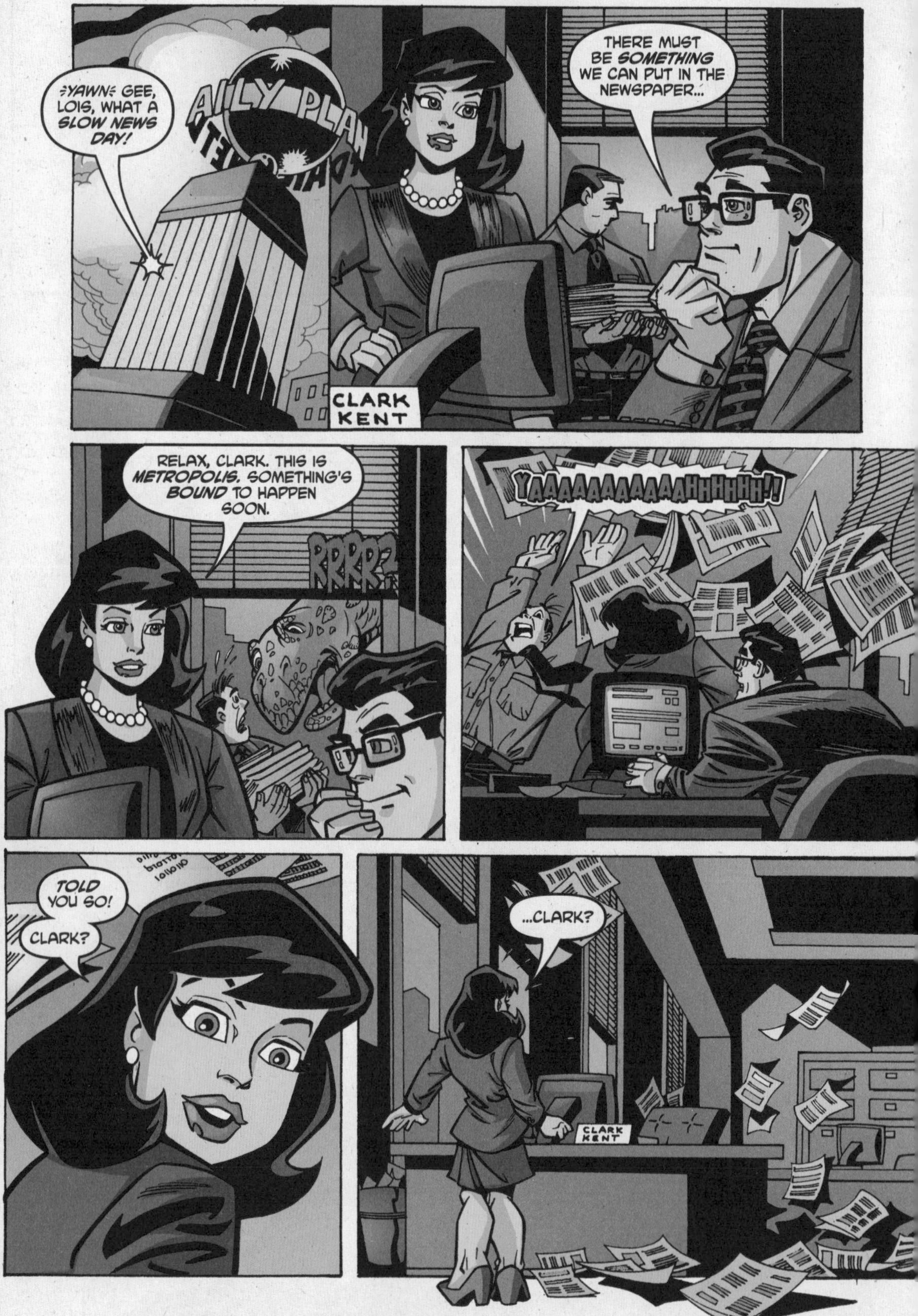

≈YAWN≈ GEE, LOIS, WHAT A SLOW NEWS DAY!
THERE MUST BE SOMETHING WE CAN PUT IN THE NEWSPAPER...
CLARK KENT
RELAX, CLARK. THIS IS METROPOLIS. SOMETHING'S BOUND TO HAPPEN SOON.
RRRR?
YAAAAAAAAAAAHHHHHH!!
TOLD YOU SO!
CLARK?
...CLARK?
CLARK KENT

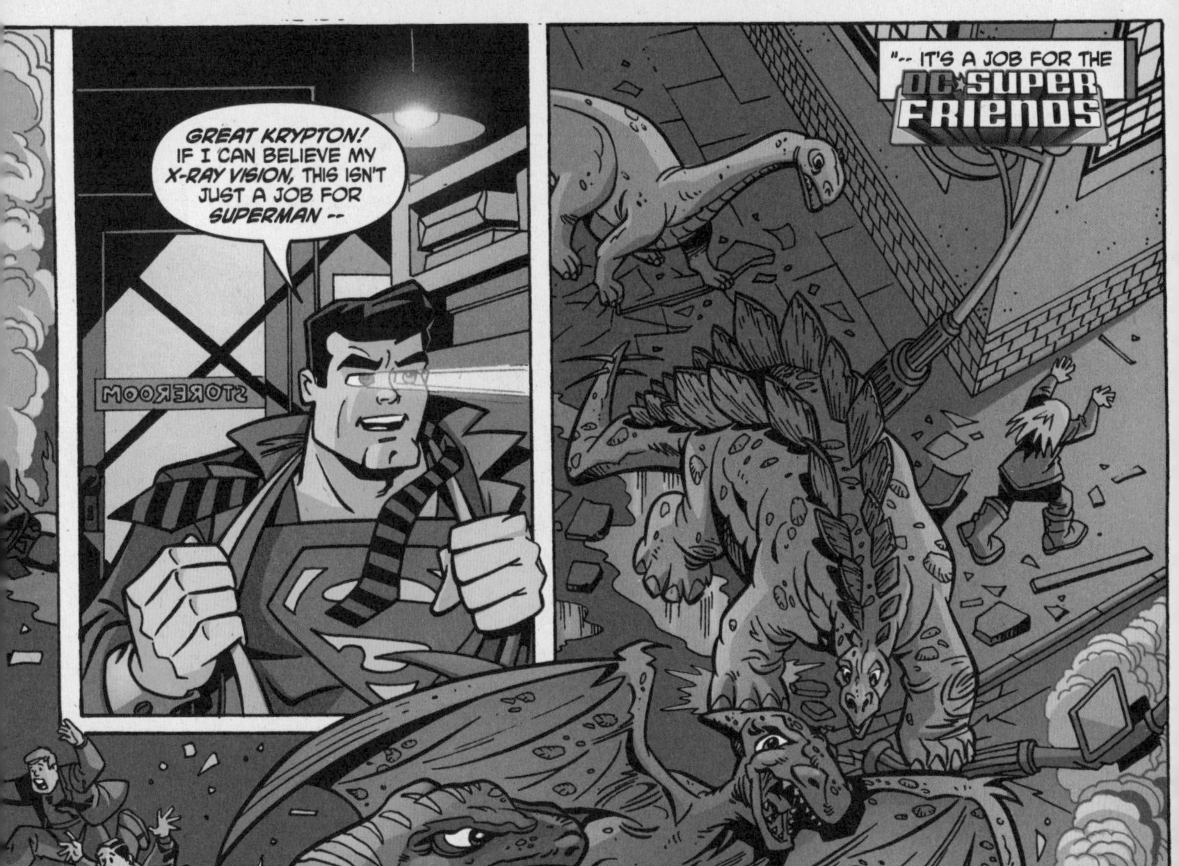
GREAT KRYPTON! IF I CAN BELIEVE MY X-RAY VISION, THIS ISN'T JUST A JOB FOR SUPERMAN --
STOREROOM
"-- IT'S A JOB FOR THE DC SUPER FRIENDS
DINOSAUR ROUND-UP

ROLL CALL!

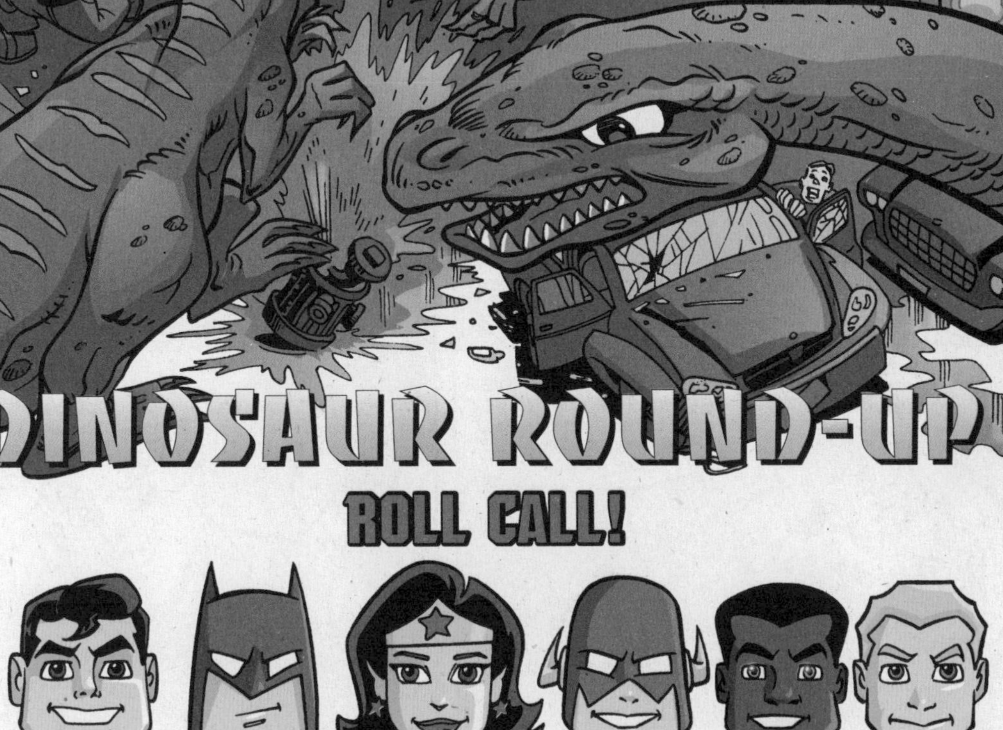
SUPERMAN
MAN OF STEEL
THE BATMAN
DARK KNIGHT DETECTIVE
WONDER WOMAN
AMAZON WARRIOR PRINCESS
THE FLASH
FASTEST MAN ALIVE
GREEN LANTERN
POWER-RINGED GUARDIAN
AQUAMAN
KING OF THE SEA

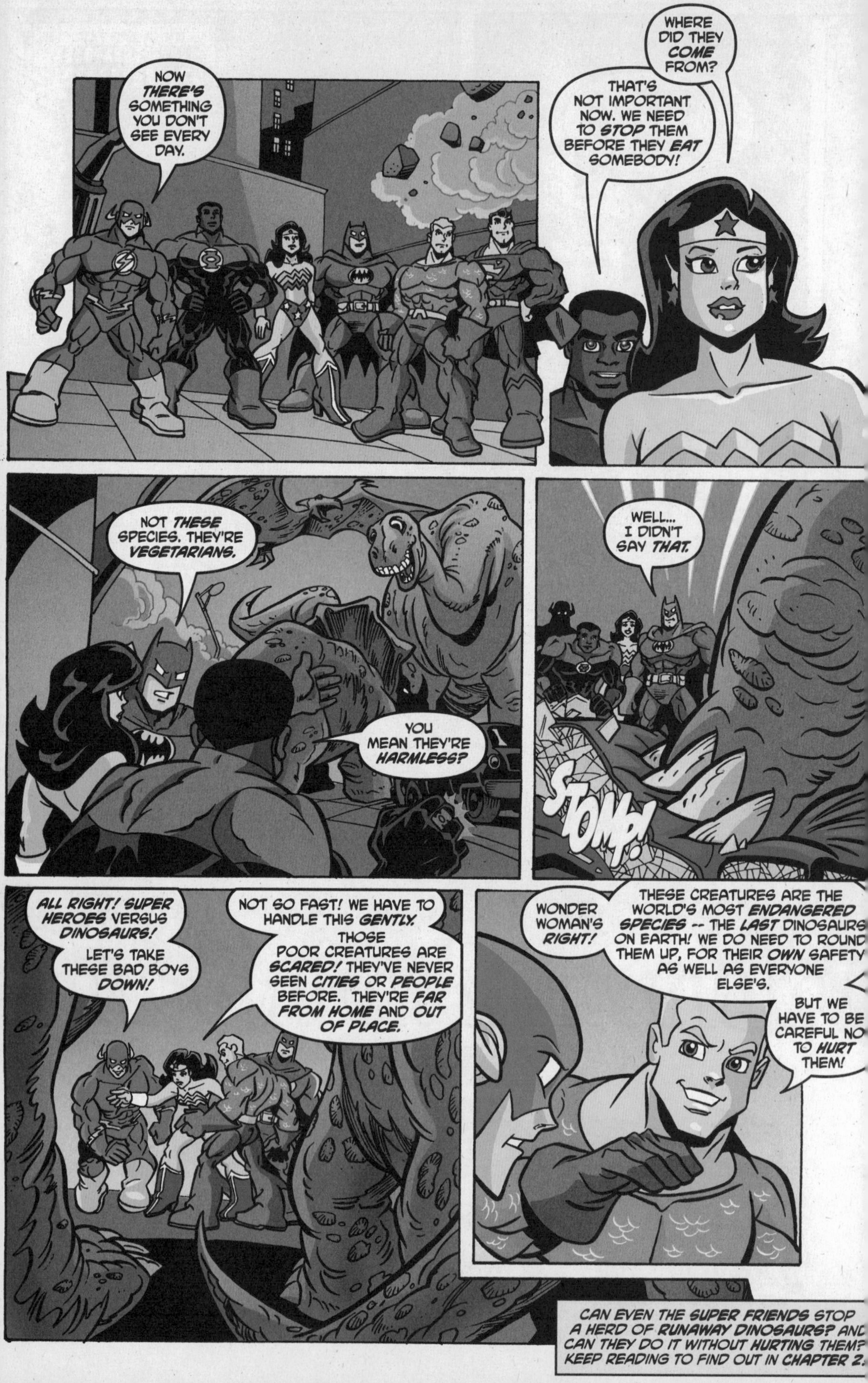

NOW THERE'S SOMETHING YOU DON'T SEE EVERY DAY.
WHERE DID THEY COME FROM?
THAT'S NOT IMPORTANT NOW. WE NEED TO STOP THEM BEFORE THEY EAT SOMEBODY!
NOT THESE SPECIES. THEY'RE VEGETARIANS.
YOU MEAN THEY'RE HARMLESS?
WELL... I DIDN'T SAY THAT.
STOMP!
ALL RIGHT! SUPER HEROES VERSUS DINOSAURS!
LET'S TAKE THESE BAD BOYS DOWN!
NOT SO FAST! WE HAVE TO HANDLE THIS GENTLY.
THOSE POOR CREATURES ARE SCARED! THEY'VE NEVER SEEN CITIES OR PEOPLE BEFORE. THEY'RE FAR FROM HOME AND OUT OF PLACE.
WONDER WOMAN'S RIGHT!
THESE CREATURES ARE THE WORLD'S MOST ENDANGERED SPECIES -- THE LAST DINOSAURS ON EARTH! WE DO NEED TO ROUND THEM UP, FOR THEIR OWN SAFETY AS WELL AS EVERYONE ELSE'S.
BUT WE HAVE TO BE CAREFUL NOT TO HURT THEM!
CAN EVEN THE SUPER FRIENDS STOP A HERD OF RUNAWAY DINOSAURS? AND CAN THEY DO IT WITHOUT HURTING THEM? KEEP READING TO FIND OUT IN CHAPTER 2.

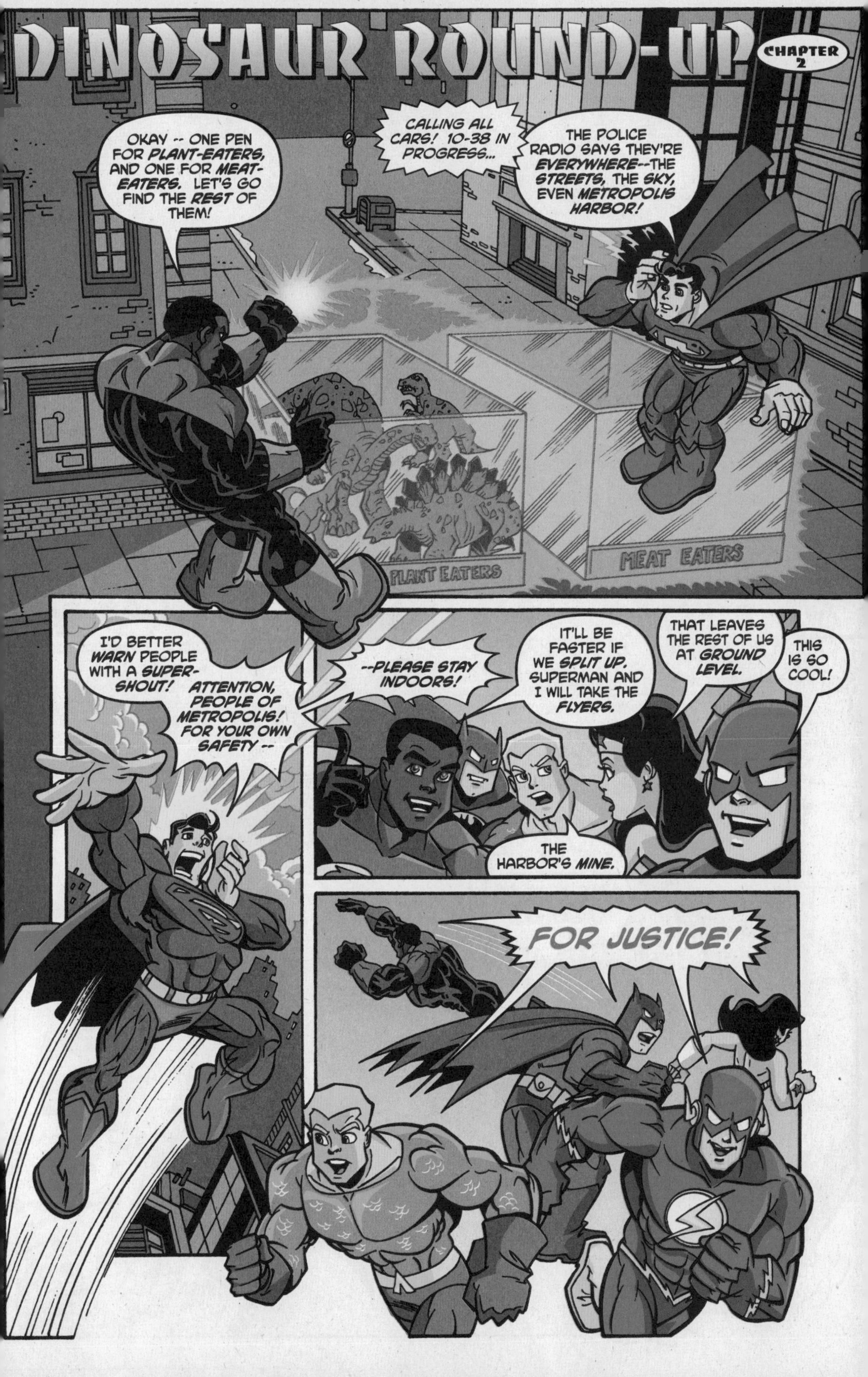

DINOSAUR ROUND-UP
CHAPTER 2
OKAY -- ONE PEN FOR PLANT-EATERS, AND ONE FOR MEAT-EATERS. LET'S GO FIND THE REST OF THEM!
CALLING ALL CARS! 10-38 IN PROGRESS...
THE POLICE RADIO SAYS THEY'RE EVERYWHERE--THE STREETS, THE SKY, EVEN METROPOLIS HARBOR!
PLANT EATERS
MEAT EATERS
I'D BETTER WARN PEOPLE WITH A SUPER-SHOUT!
ATTENTION, PEOPLE OF METROPOLIS! FOR YOUR OWN SAFETY --
--PLEASE STAY INDOORS!
IT'LL BE FASTER IF WE SPLIT UP. SUPERMAN AND I WILL TAKE THE FLYERS.
THAT LEAVES THE REST OF US AT GROUND LEVEL.
THIS IS SO COOL!
THE HARBOR'S MINE.
FOR JUSTICE!

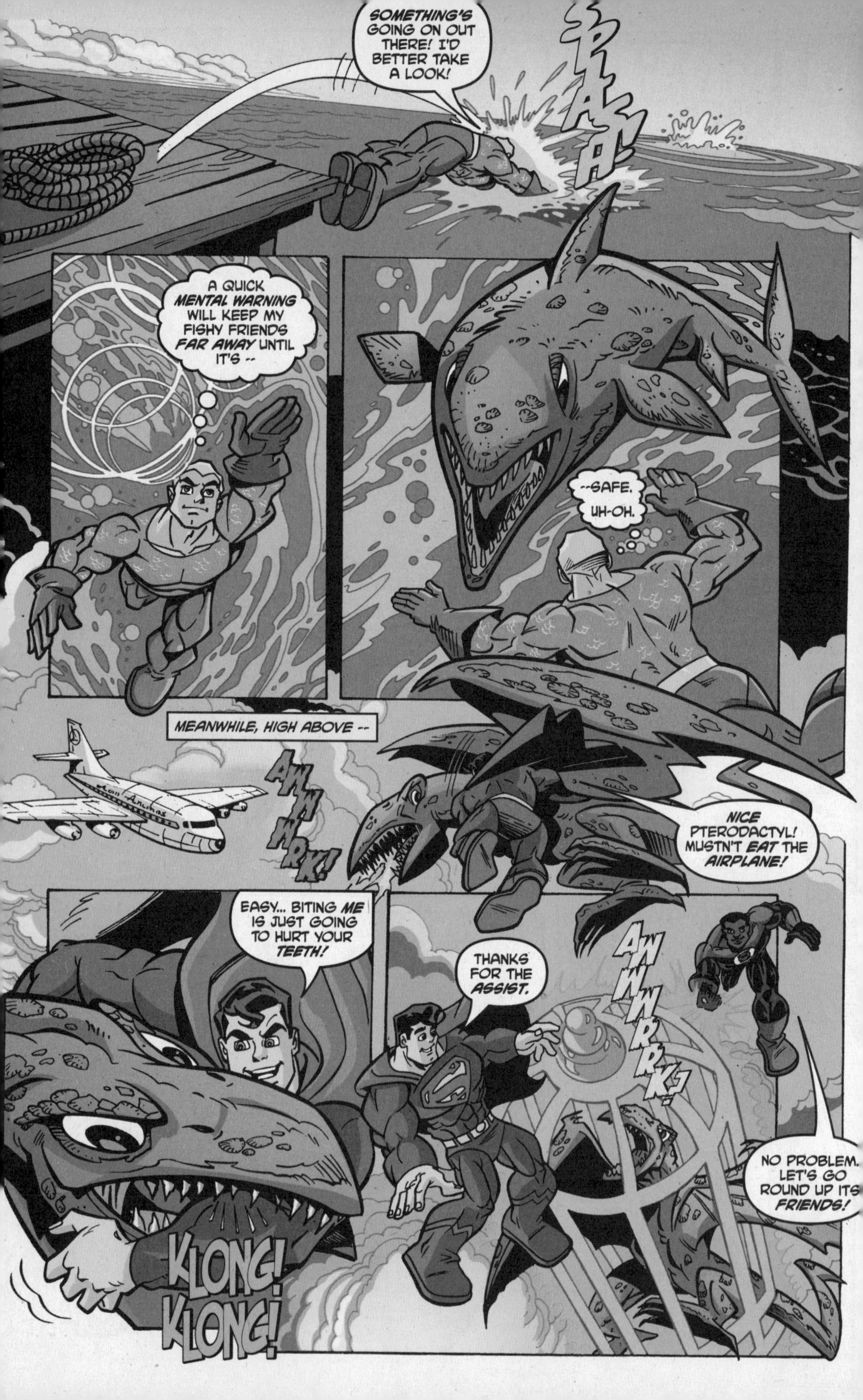

SOMETHING'S GOING ON OUT THERE! I'D BETTER TAKE A LOOK!
A QUICK MENTAL WARNING WILL KEEP MY FISHY FRIENDS FAR AWAY UNTIL IT'S --
--SAFE. UH-OH.
MEANWHILE, HIGH ABOVE --
AWWWRK!
NICE PTERODACTYL! MUSTN'T EAT THE AIRPLANE!
EASY... BITING ME IS JUST GOING TO HURT YOUR TEETH!
KLONG! KLONG!
THANKS FOR THE ASSIST.
AWWWRRK!?
NO PROBLEM. LET'S GO ROUND UP ITS FRIENDS!

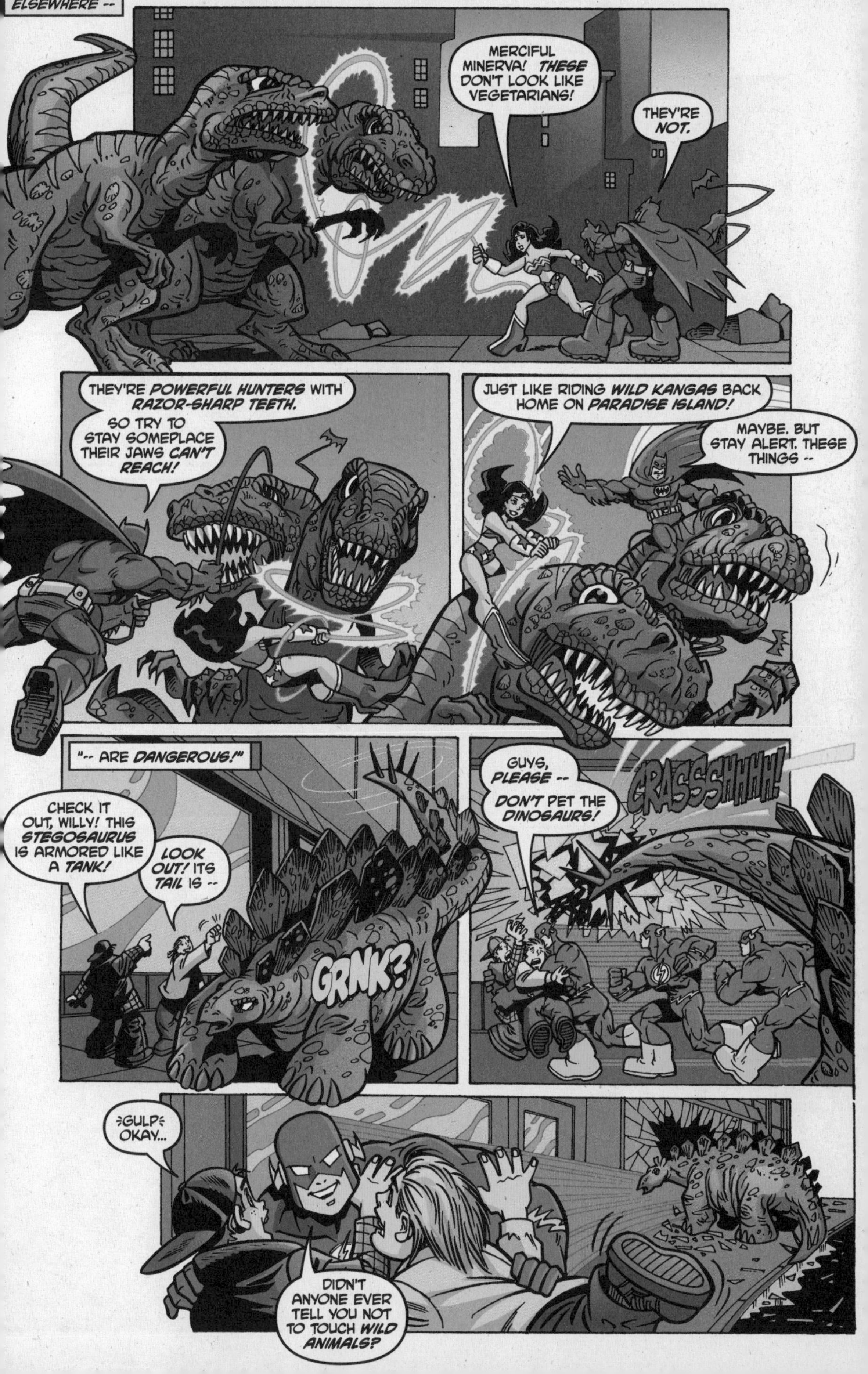
ELSEWHERE --
MERCIFUL MINERVA! THESE DON'T LOOK LIKE VEGETARIANS!
THEY'RE NOT.
THEY'RE POWERFUL HUNTERS WITH RAZOR-SHARP TEETH.
SO TRY TO STAY SOMEPLACE THEIR JAWS CAN'T REACH!
JUST LIKE RIDING WILD KANGAS BACK HOME ON PARADISE ISLAND!
MAYBE. BUT STAY ALERT. THESE THINGS --
"-- ARE DANGEROUS!"
CHECK IT OUT, WILLY! THIS STEGOSAURUS IS ARMORED LIKE A TANK!
LOOK OUT! ITS TAIL IS --
GRNK?
GUYS, PLEASE -- DON'T PET THE DINOSAURS!
CRASSSHHHH!
GULP OKAY...
DIDN'T ANYONE EVER TELL YOU NOT TO TOUCH WILD ANIMALS?

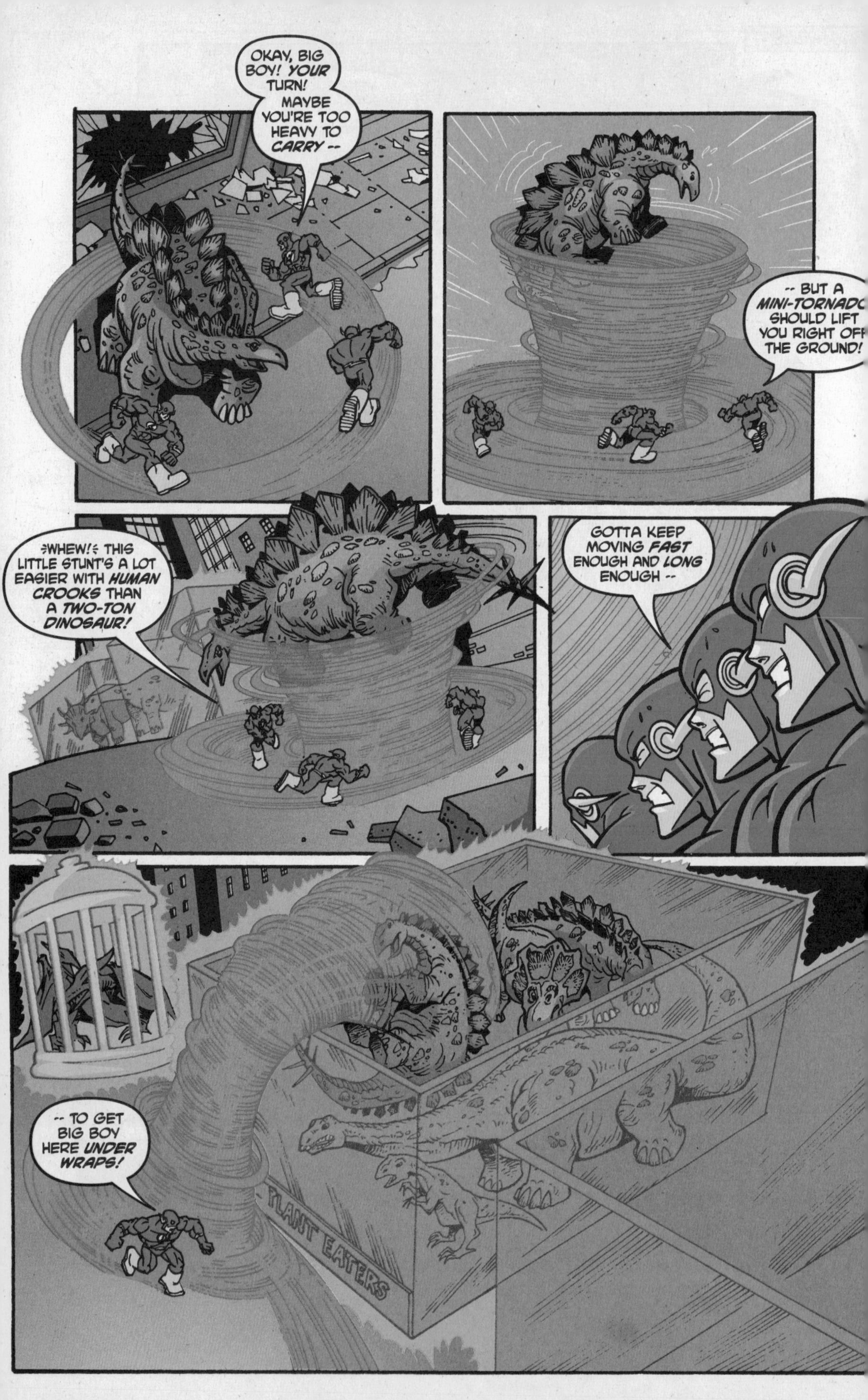

OKAY, BIG BOY! YOUR TURN!
MAYBE YOU'RE TOO HEAVY TO CARRY --
-- BUT A MINI-TORNADO SHOULD LIFT YOU RIGHT OFF THE GROUND!
WHEW! THIS LITTLE STUNT'S A LOT EASIER WITH HUMAN CROOKS THAN A TWO-TON DINOSAUR!
GOTTA KEEP MOVING FAST ENOUGH AND LONG ENOUGH --
-- TO GET BIG BOY HERE UNDER WRAPS!
PLANT EATERS

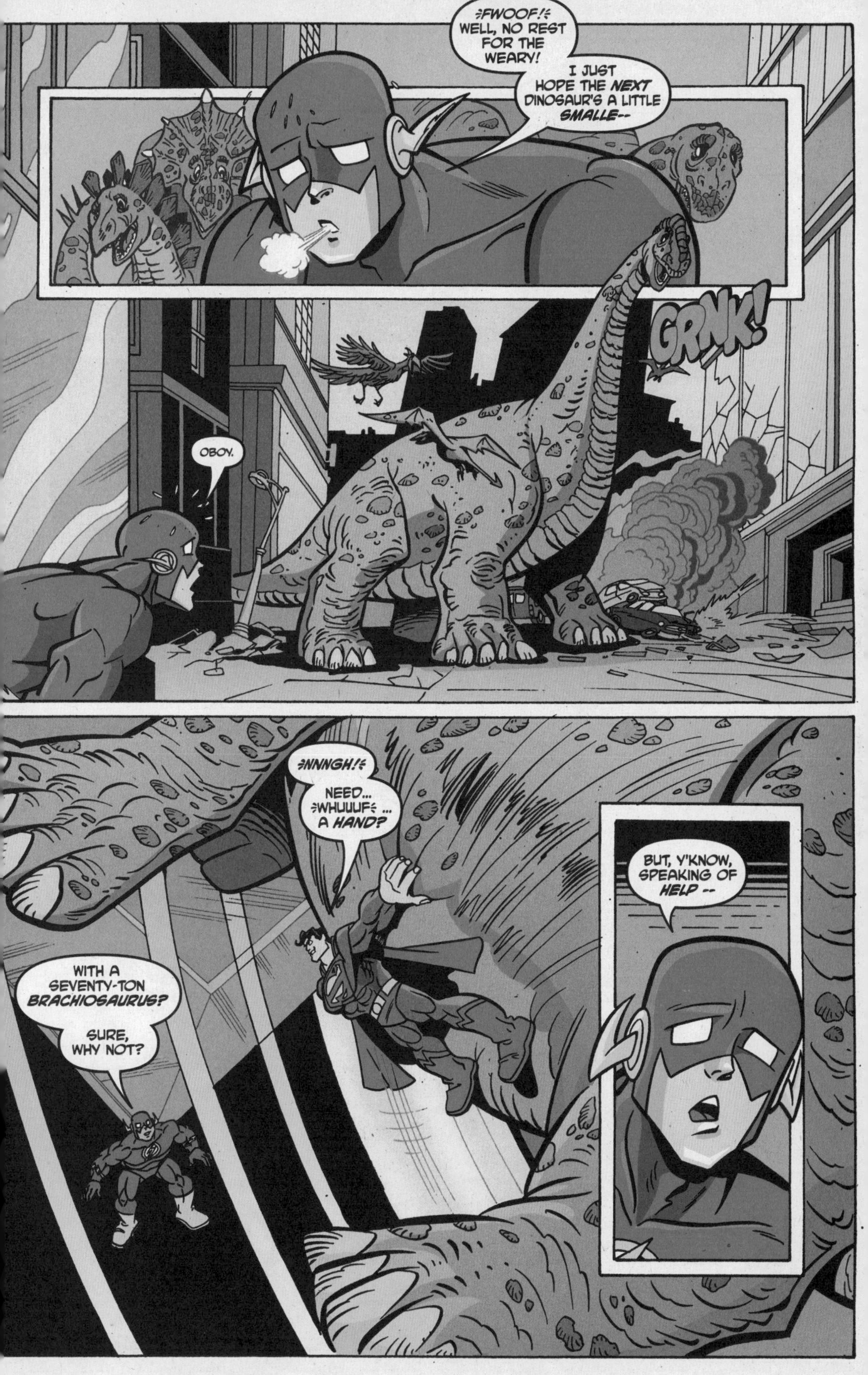

≠FWOOF!≠ WELL, NO REST FOR THE WEARY!
I JUST HOPE THE NEXT DINOSAUR'S A LITTLE SMALLE--
GRNK!
OBOY.
≠NNNGH!≠
NEED... ≠WHUUUF≠ ... A HAND?
WITH A SEVENTY-TON BRACHIOSAURUS?
SURE, WHY NOT?
BUT, Y'KNOW, SPEAKING OF HELP --

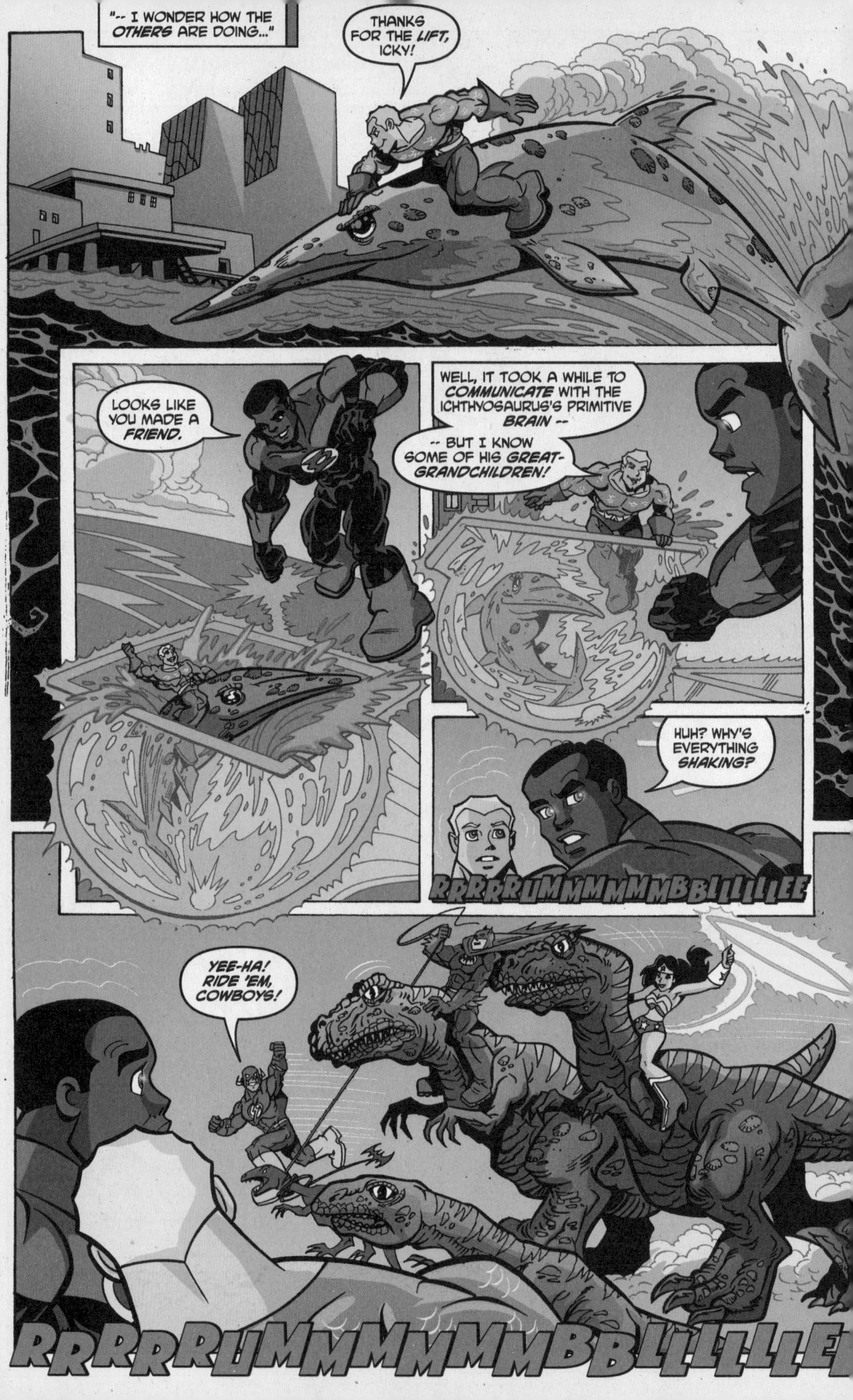
"-- I WONDER HOW THE OTHERS ARE DOING..."
THANKS FOR THE LIFT, ICKY!
LOOKS LIKE YOU MADE A FRIEND.
WELL, IT TOOK A WHILE TO COMMUNICATE WITH THE ICHTHYOSAURUS'S PRIMITIVE BRAIN --
-- BUT I KNOW SOME OF HIS GREAT-GRANDCHILDREN!
HUH? WHY'S EVERYTHING SHAKING?
RRRRRUMMMMMMMBBLLLLLEE
YEE-HA! RIDE 'EM, COWBOYS!
RRRRRUMMMMMMMBBLLLLLE

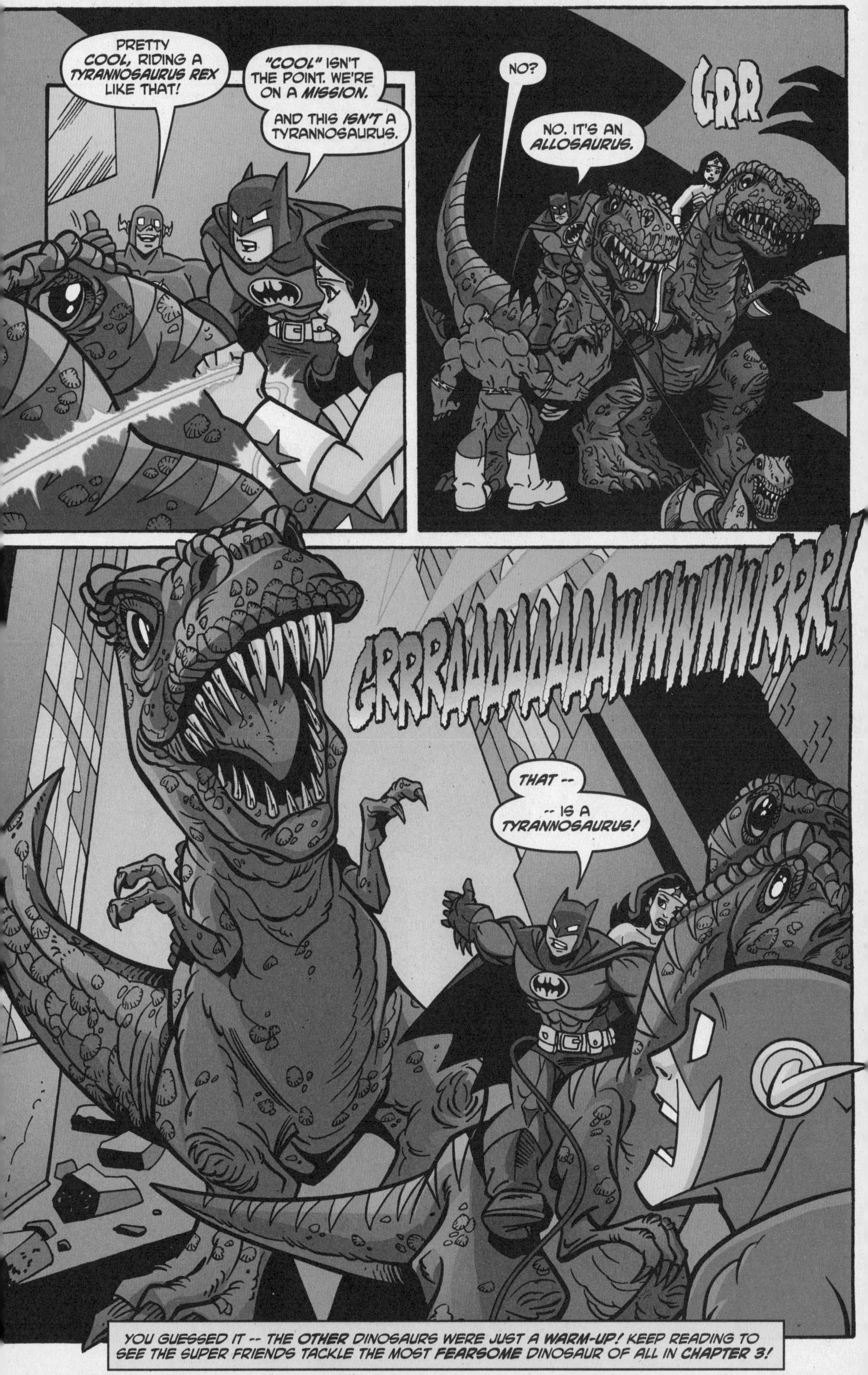
PRETTY COOL, RIDING A TYRANNOSAURUS REX LIKE THAT!
"COOL" ISN'T THE POINT. WE'RE ON A MISSION.
AND THIS ISN'T A TYRANNOSAURUS.
NO?
NO. IT'S AN ALLOSAURUS.
GRR
CRRRAAAAAAAAWWWWWRRR!
THAT --
-- IS A TYRANNOSAURUS!
YOU GUESSED IT -- THE OTHER DINOSAURS WERE JUST A WARM-UP! KEEP READING TO SEE THE SUPER FRIENDS TACKLE THE MOST FEARSOME DINOSAUR OF ALL IN CHAPTER 3!

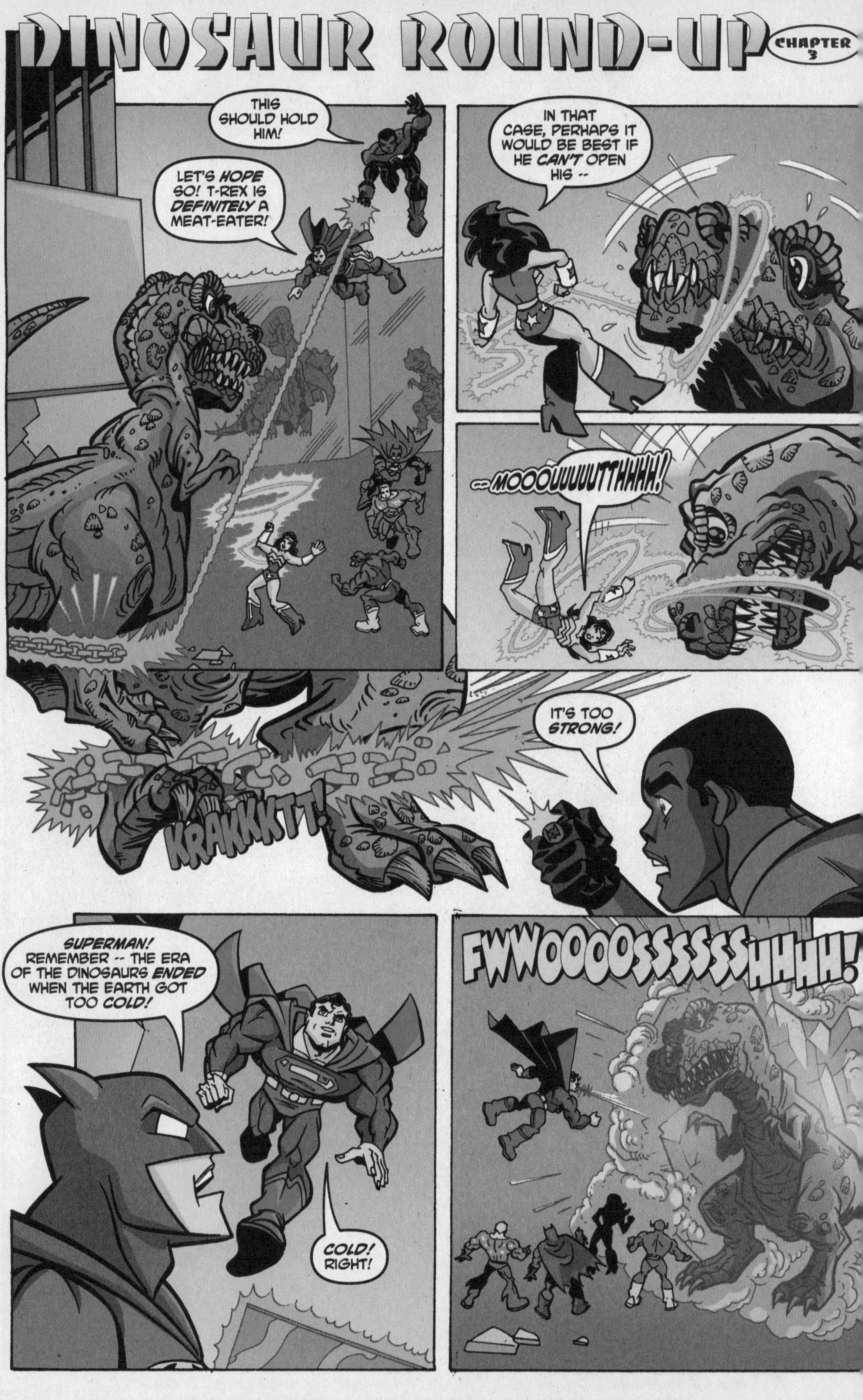
DINOSAUR ROUND-UP
CHAPTER 3
THIS SHOULD HOLD HIM!
LET'S HOPE SO! T-REX IS DEFINITELY A MEAT-EATER!
IN THAT CASE, PERHAPS IT WOULD BE BEST IF HE CAN'T OPEN HIS --
--MOOOUUUUUTTHHHH!
IT'S TOO STRONG!
KRAKKKTT!
SUPERMAN! REMEMBER -- THE ERA OF THE DINOSAURS ENDED WHEN THE EARTH GOT TOO COLD!
COLD! RIGHT!
FWWOOOOOSSSSSHHHH!

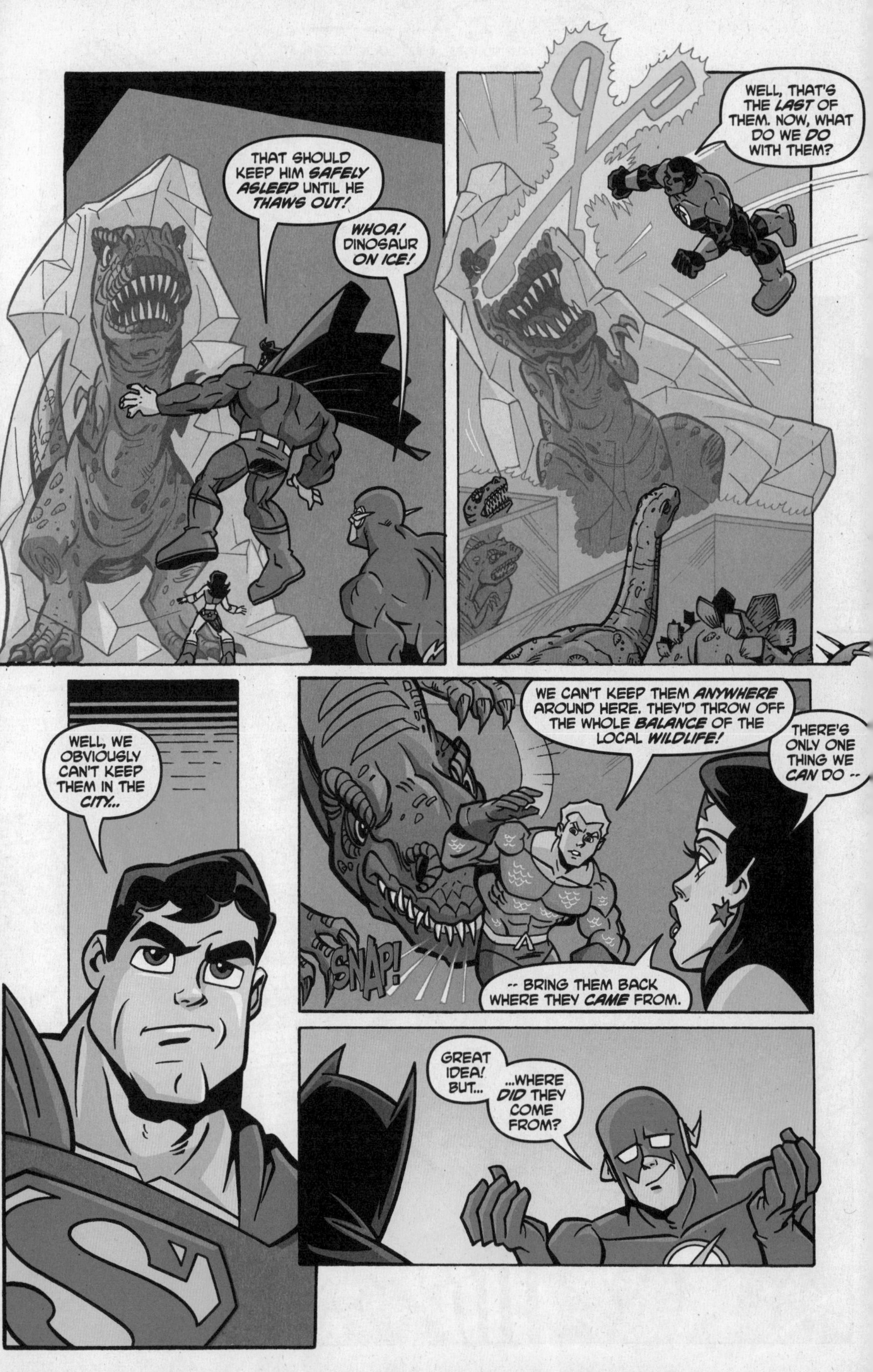
THAT SHOULD KEEP HIM SAFELY ASLEEP UNTIL HE THAWS OUT!
WHOA! DINOSAUR ON ICE!
WELL, THAT'S THE LAST OF THEM. NOW, WHAT DO WE DO WITH THEM?
WELL, WE OBVIOUSLY CAN'T KEEP THEM IN THE CITY...
WE CAN'T KEEP THEM ANYWHERE AROUND HERE. THEY'D THROW OFF THE WHOLE BALANCE OF THE LOCAL WILDLIFE!
THERE'S ONLY ONE THING WE CAN DO --
SNAP!
-- BRING THEM BACK WHERE THEY CAME FROM.
GREAT IDEA! BUT...
...WHERE DID THEY COME FROM?

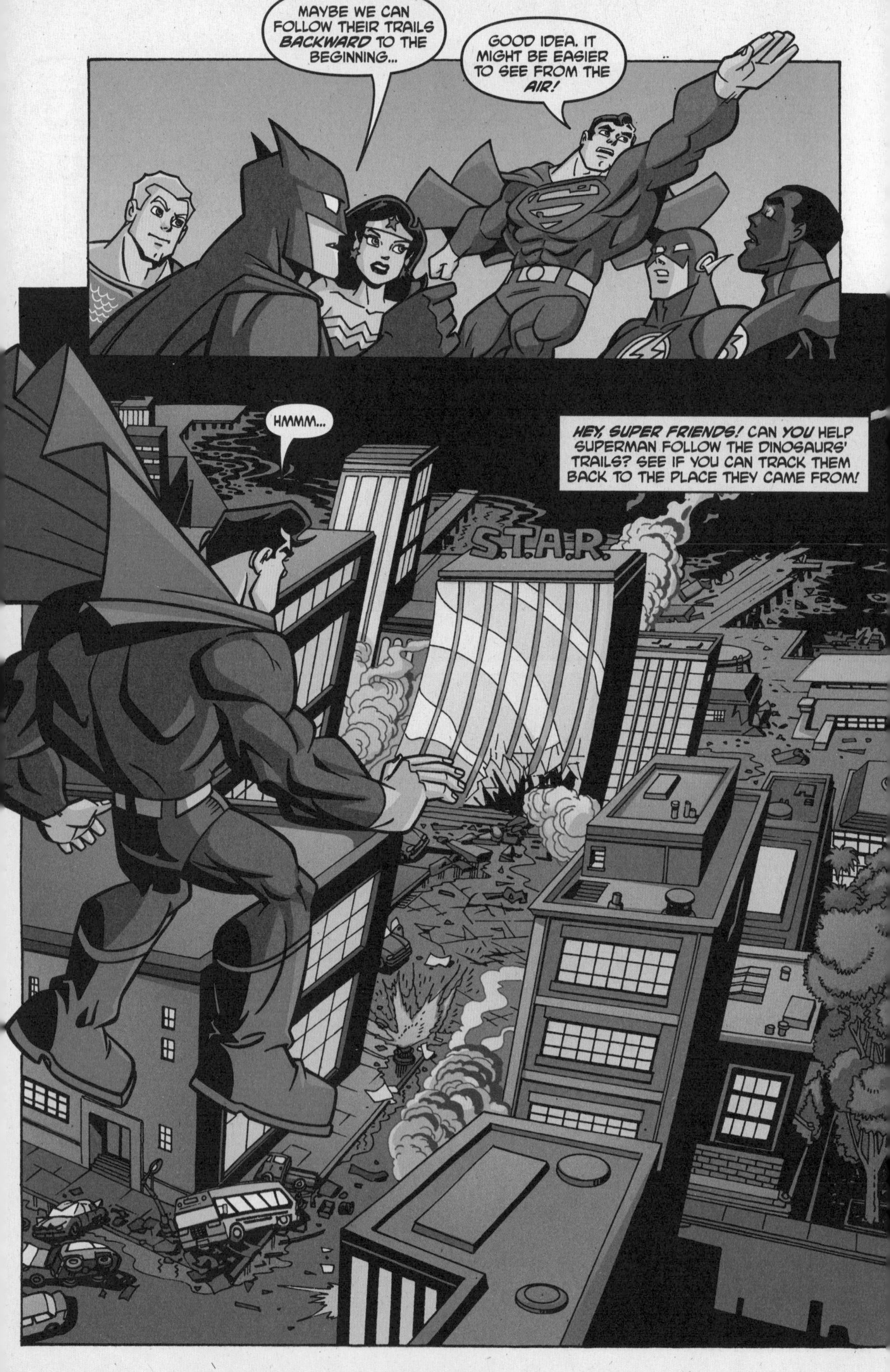
MAYBE WE CAN FOLLOW THEIR TRAILS BACKWARD TO THE BEGINNING...
GOOD IDEA. IT MIGHT BE EASIER TO SEE FROM THE AIR!
HMMM...
HEY, SUPER FRIENDS! CAN YOU HELP SUPERMAN FOLLOW THE DINOSAURS' TRAILS? SEE IF YOU CAN TRACK THEM BACK TO THE PLACE THEY CAME FROM!
S.T.A.R.

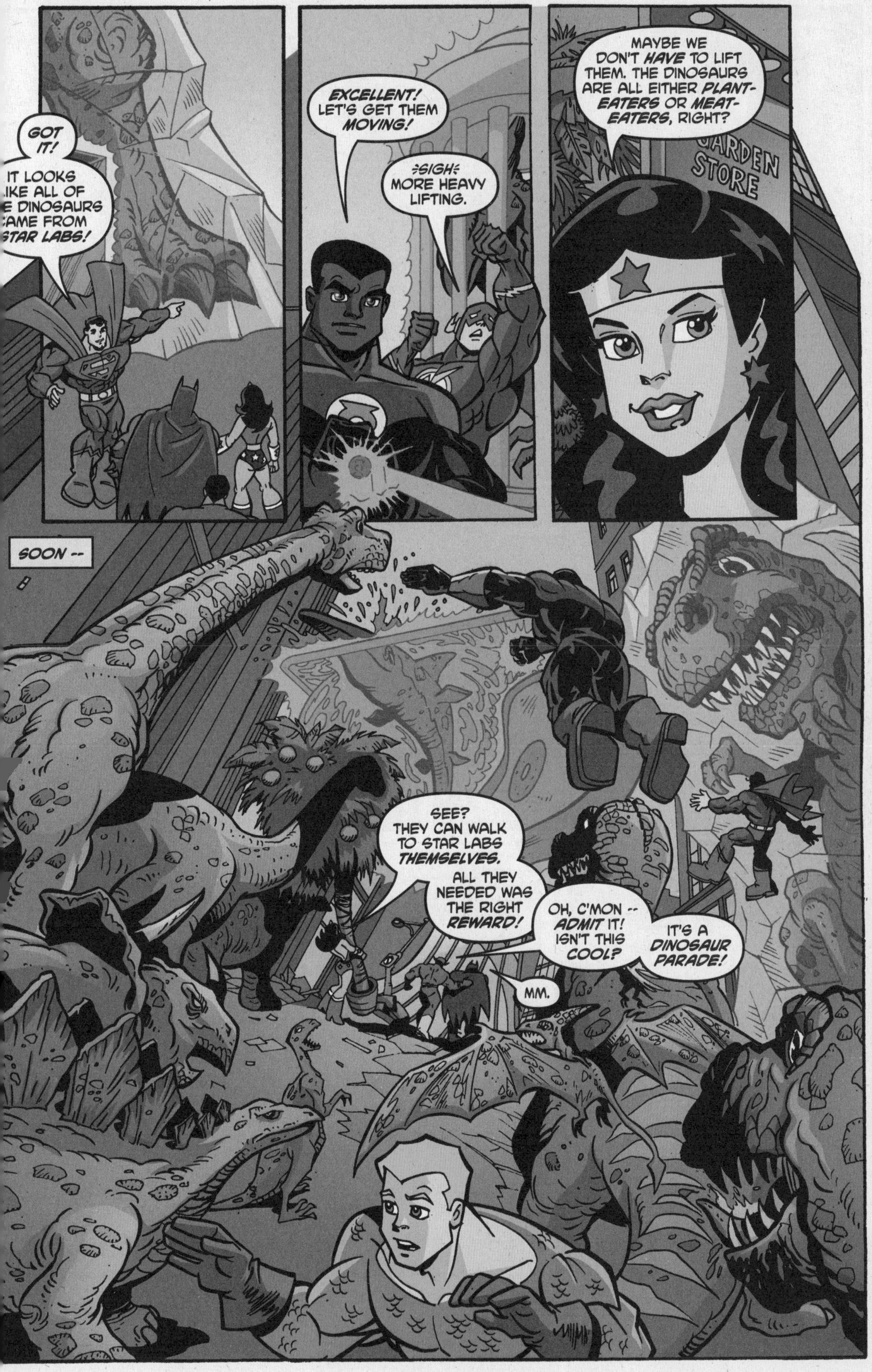
GOT IT!
IT LOOKS IKE ALL OF E DINOSAURS CAME FROM STAR LABS!
EXCELLENT! LET'S GET THEM MOVING!
SIGH MORE HEAVY LIFTING.
MAYBE WE DON'T HAVE TO LIFT THEM. THE DINOSAURS ARE ALL EITHER PLANT-EATERS OR MEAT-EATERS, RIGHT?
GARDEN STORE
SOON --
SEE? THEY CAN WALK TO STAR LABS THEMSELVES.
ALL THEY NEEDED WAS THE RIGHT REWARD!
OH, C'MON -- ADMIT IT! ISN'T THIS COOL?
IT'S A DINOSAUR PARADE!
MM.

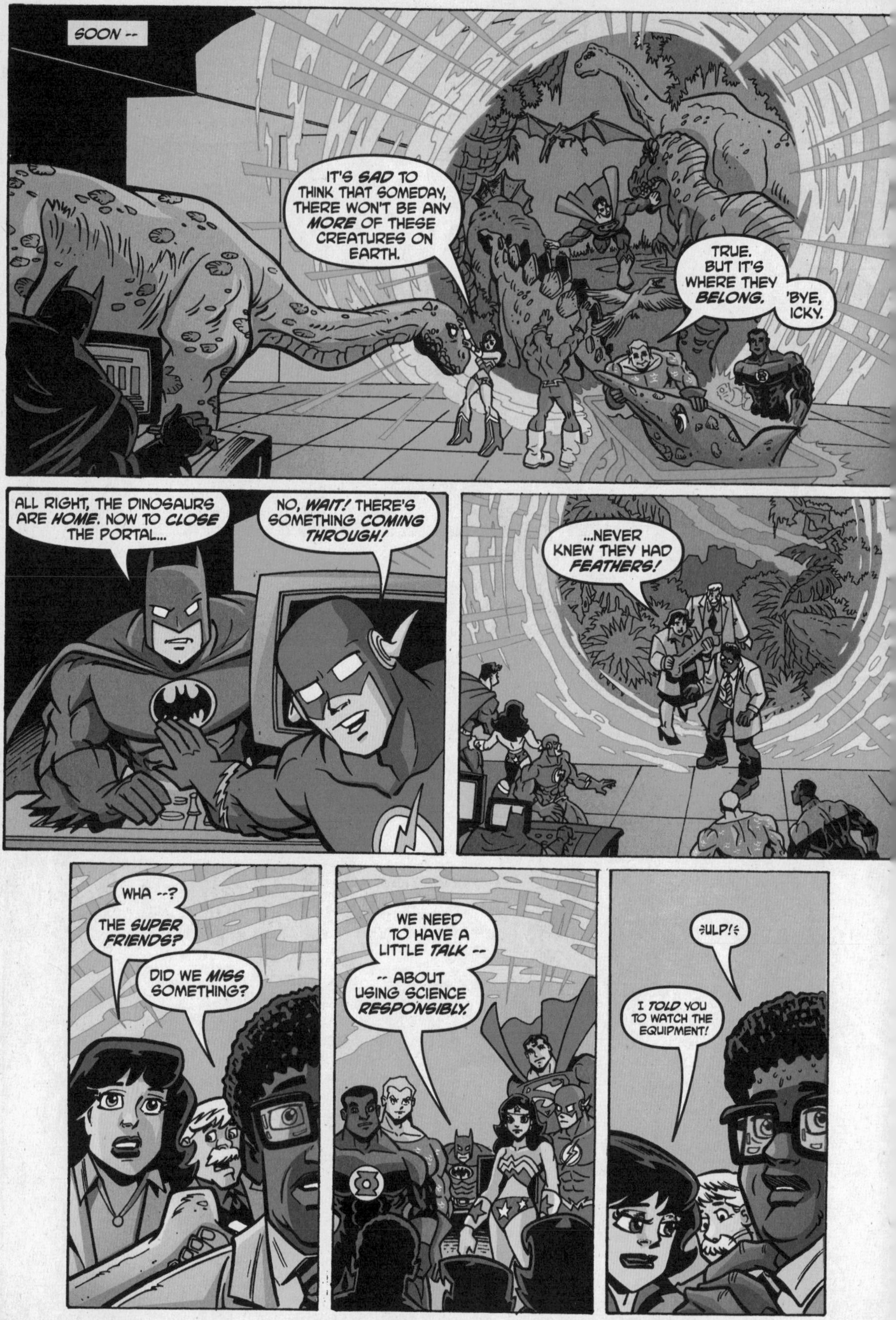
SOON --
IT'S SAD TO THINK THAT SOMEDAY, THERE WON'T BE ANY MORE OF THESE CREATURES ON EARTH.
TRUE. BUT IT'S WHERE THEY BELONG.
'BYE, ICKY.
ALL RIGHT, THE DINOSAURS ARE HOME. NOW TO CLOSE THE PORTAL...
NO, WAIT! THERE'S SOMETHING COMING THROUGH!
...NEVER KNEW THEY HAD FEATHERS!
WHA --?
THE SUPER FRIENDS?
DID WE MISS SOMETHING?
WE NEED TO HAVE A LITTLE TALK --
-- ABOUT USING SCIENCE RESPONSIBLY.
ULP!
I TOLD YOU TO WATCH THE EQUIPMENT!

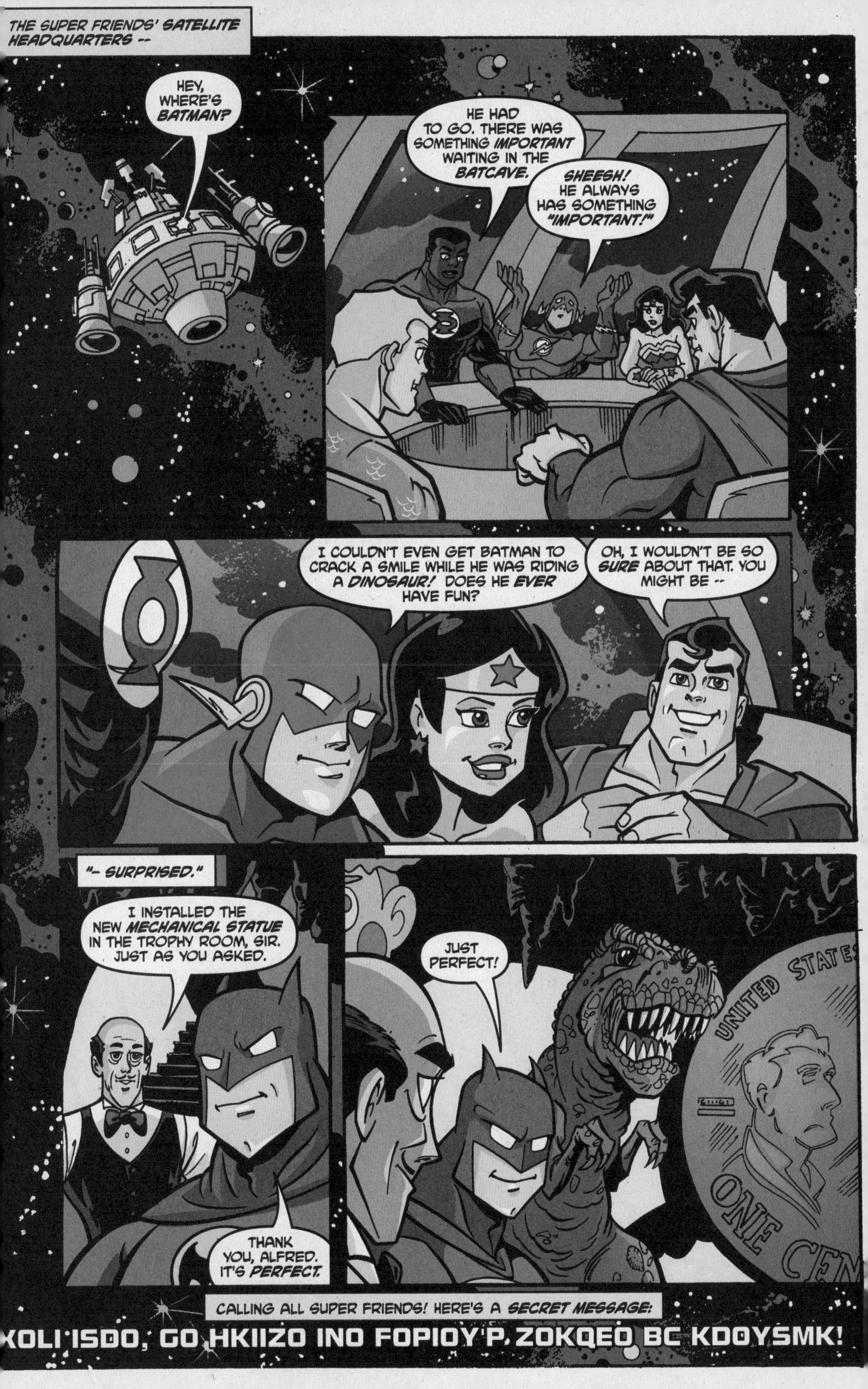
THE SUPER FRIENDS' SATELLITE HEADQUARTERS --
HEY, WHERE'S BATMAN?
HE HAD TO GO. THERE WAS SOMETHING IMPORTANT WAITING IN THE BATCAVE.
SHEESH! HE ALWAYS HAS SOMETHING "IMPORTANT!"
I COULDN'T EVEN GET BATMAN TO CRACK A SMILE WHILE HE WAS RIDING A DINOSAUR! DOES HE EVER HAVE FUN?
OH, I WOULDN'T BE SO SURE ABOUT THAT. YOU MIGHT BE --
"-- SURPRISED."
I INSTALLED THE NEW MECHANICAL STATUE IN THE TROPHY ROOM, SIR. JUST AS YOU ASKED.
THANK YOU, ALFRED. IT'S PERFECT.
JUST PERFECT!
UNITED STATES
ONE CENT
CALLING ALL SUPER FRIENDS! HERE'S A SECRET MESSAGE:
XOLI ISDO, GO HKIIZO INO FOPIOY P, ZOKQEO BC KDOYSMK!

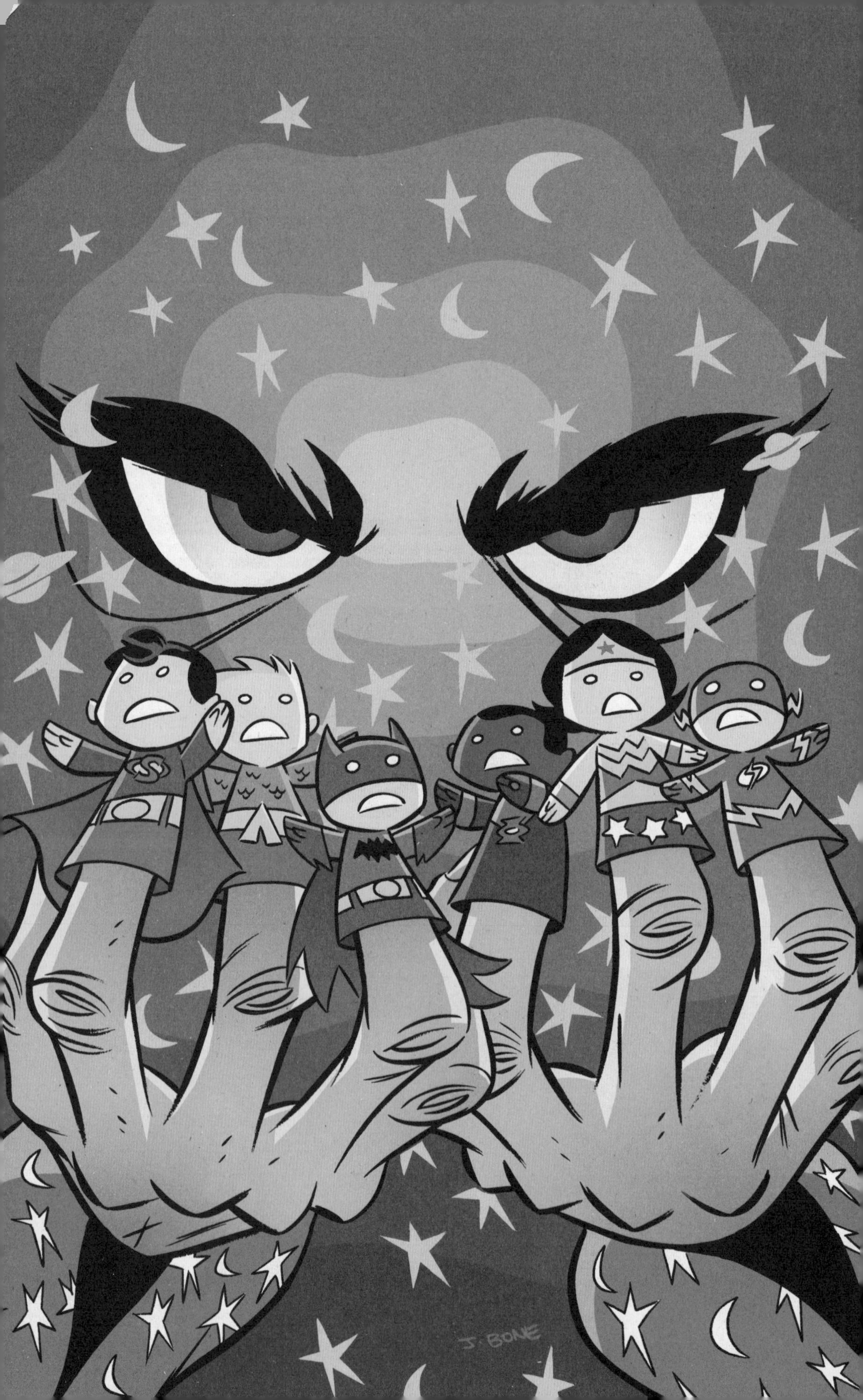
J. BONE

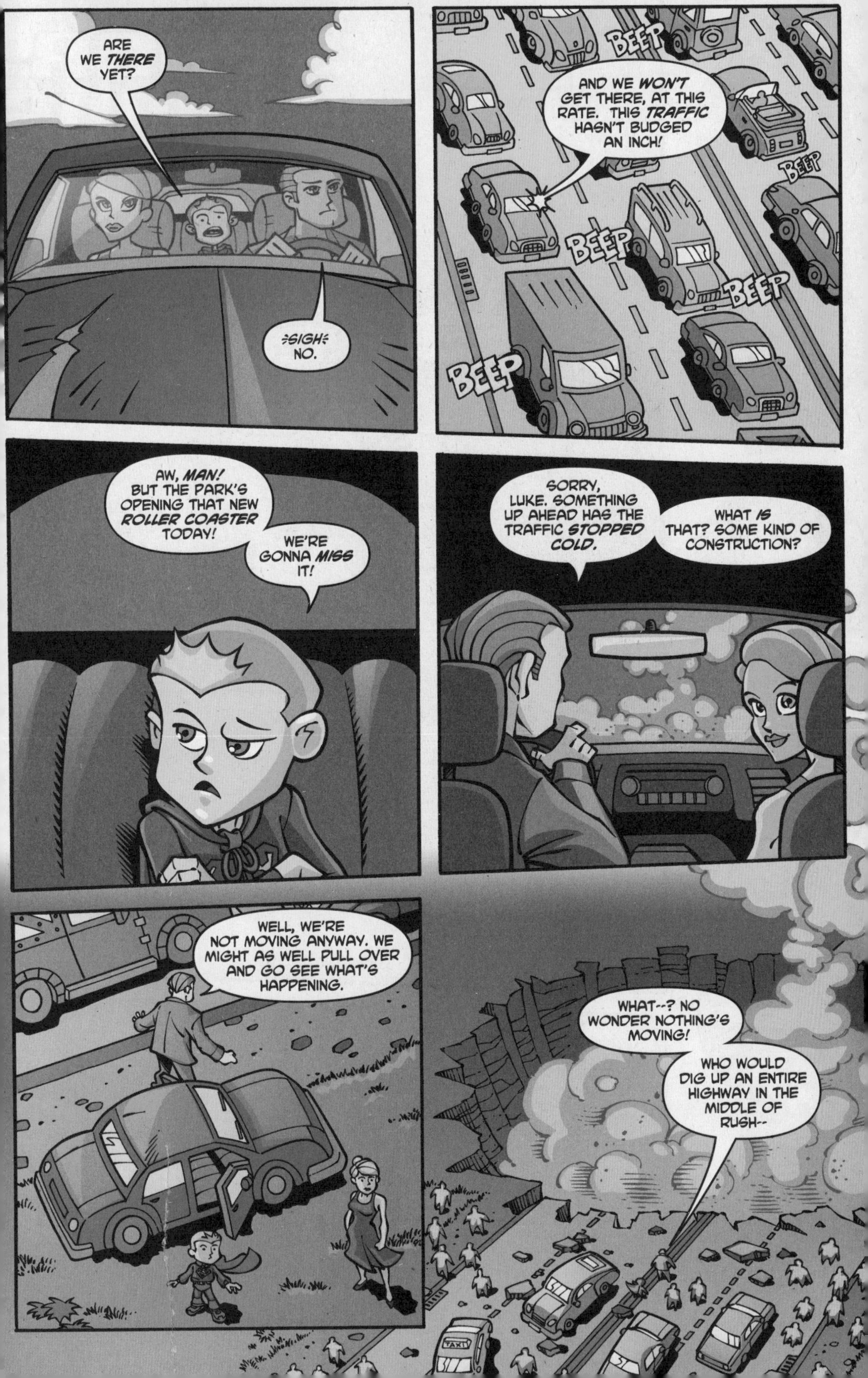
ARE WE *THERE* YET?
SIGH NO.
BEEP
AND WE *WON'T* GET THERE, AT THIS RATE. THIS *TRAFFIC* HASN'T BUDGED AN INCH!
BEEP
BEEP
BEEP
BEEP
AW, *MAN!* BUT THE PARK'S OPENING THAT NEW *ROLLER COASTER* TODAY!
WE'RE GONNA *MISS* IT!
SORRY, LUKE. SOMETHING UP AHEAD HAS THE TRAFFIC *STOPPED COLD.*
WHAT *IS* THAT? SOME KIND OF CONSTRUCTION?
WELL, WE'RE NOT MOVING ANYWAY. WE MIGHT AS WELL PULL OVER AND GO SEE WHAT'S HAPPENING.
WHAT--? NO WONDER NOTHING'S MOVING!
WHO WOULD DIG UP AN ENTIRE HIGHWAY IN THE MIDDLE OF RUSH--
TAXI

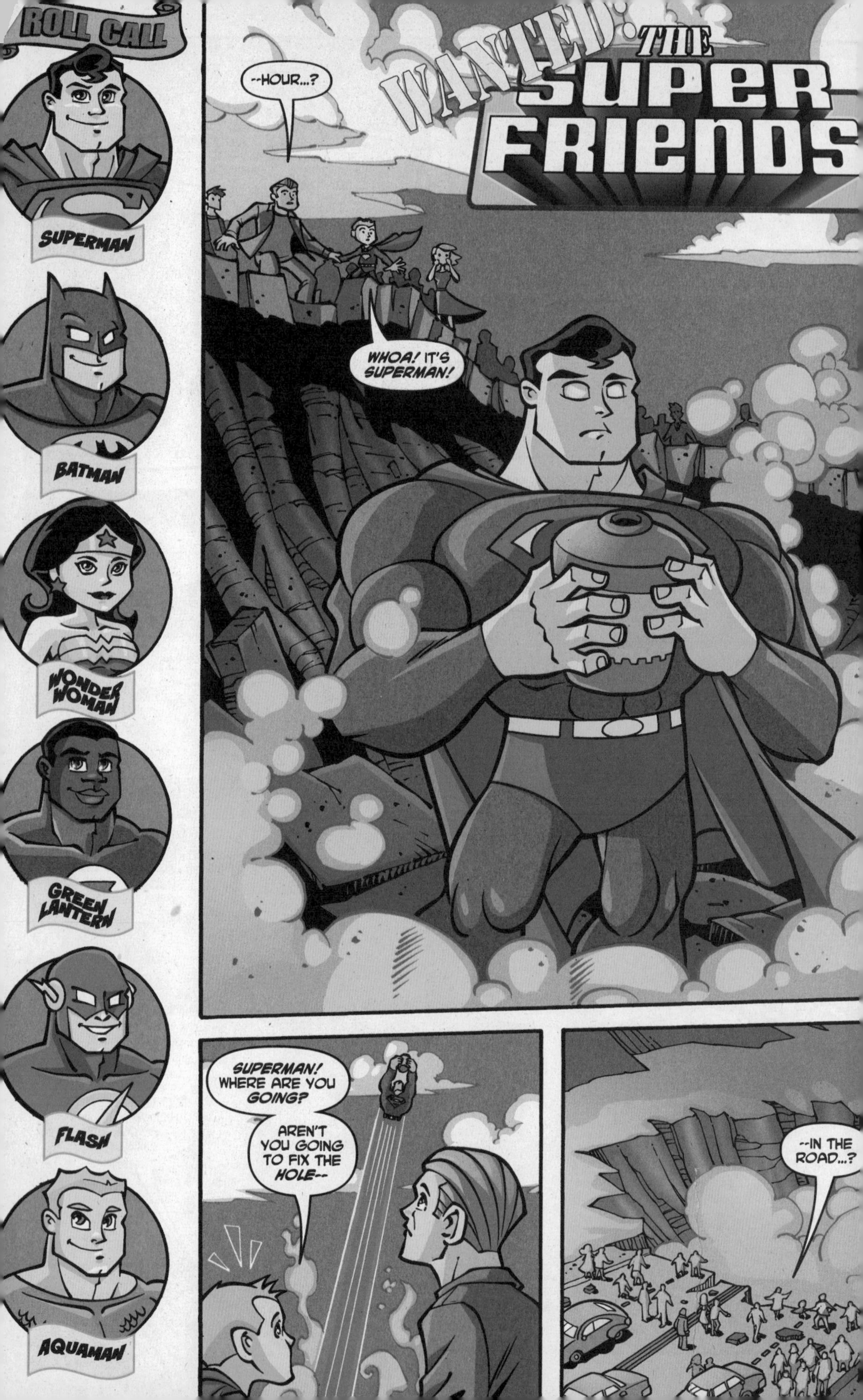
ROLL CALL
SUPERMAN
BATMAN
WONDER WOMAN
GREEN LANTERN
FLASH
AQUAMAN
WANTED: THE SUPER FRIENDS
--HOUR...?
WHOA! IT'S SUPERMAN!
SUPERMAN! WHERE ARE YOU GOING?
AREN'T YOU GOING TO FIX THE HOLE--
--IN THE ROAD...?

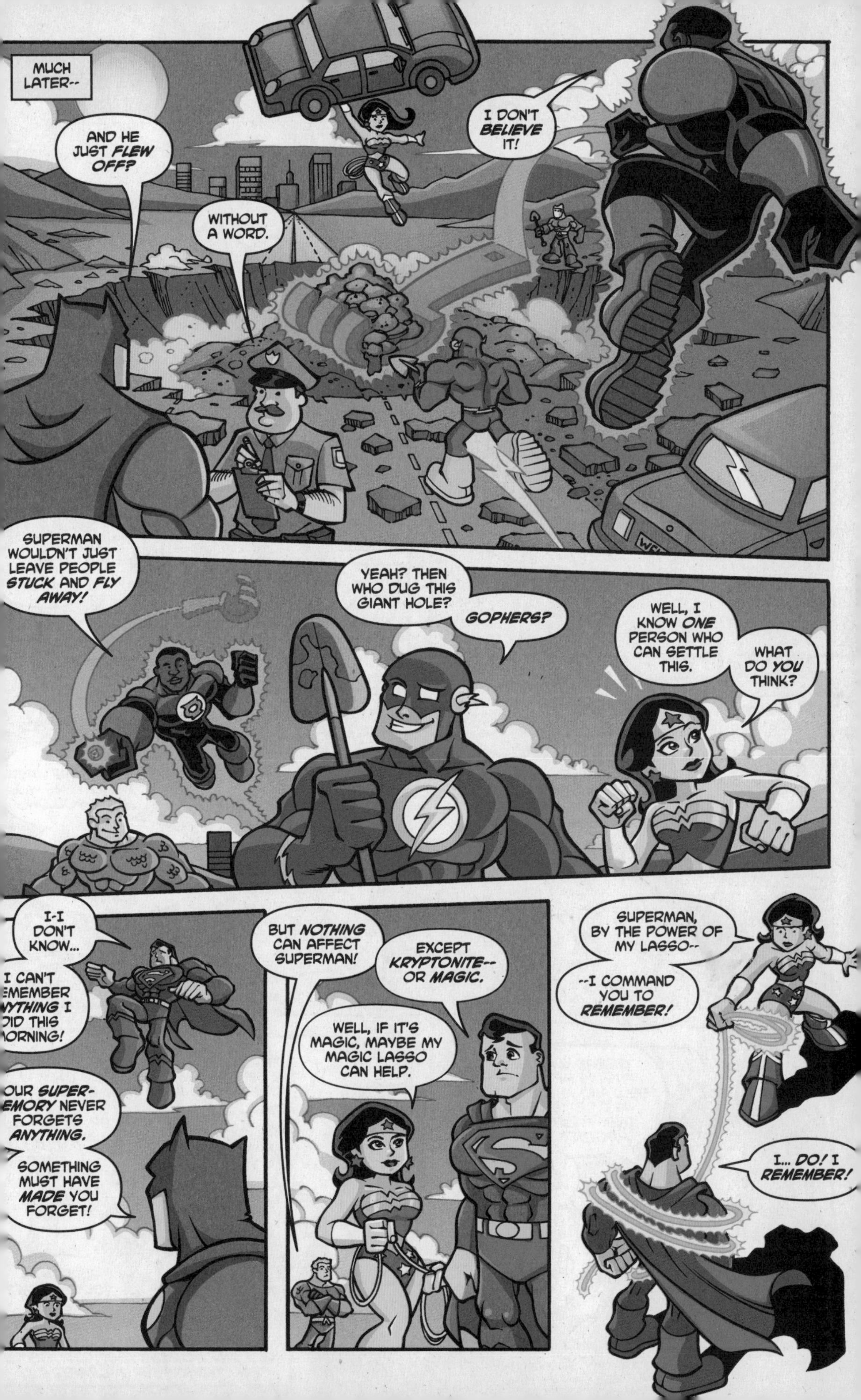
MUCH LATER--
AND HE JUST FLEW OFF?
WITHOUT A WORD.
I DON'T BELIEVE IT!
SUPERMAN WOULDN'T JUST LEAVE PEOPLE STUCK AND FLY AWAY!
YEAH? THEN WHO DUG THIS GIANT HOLE?
GOPHERS?
WELL, I KNOW ONE PERSON WHO CAN SETTLE THIS.
WHAT DO YOU THINK?
I-I DON'T KNOW...
I CAN'T EMEMBER NYTHING I DID THIS ORNING!
OUR SUPER-EMORY NEVER FORGETS ANYTHING.
SOMETHING MUST HAVE MADE YOU FORGET!
BUT NOTHING CAN AFFECT SUPERMAN!
EXCEPT KRYPTONITE-- OR MAGIC.
WELL, IF IT'S MAGIC, MAYBE MY MAGIC LASSO CAN HELP.
SUPERMAN, BY THE POWER OF MY LASSO--
--I COMMAND YOU TO REMEMBER!
I... DO! I REMEMBER!

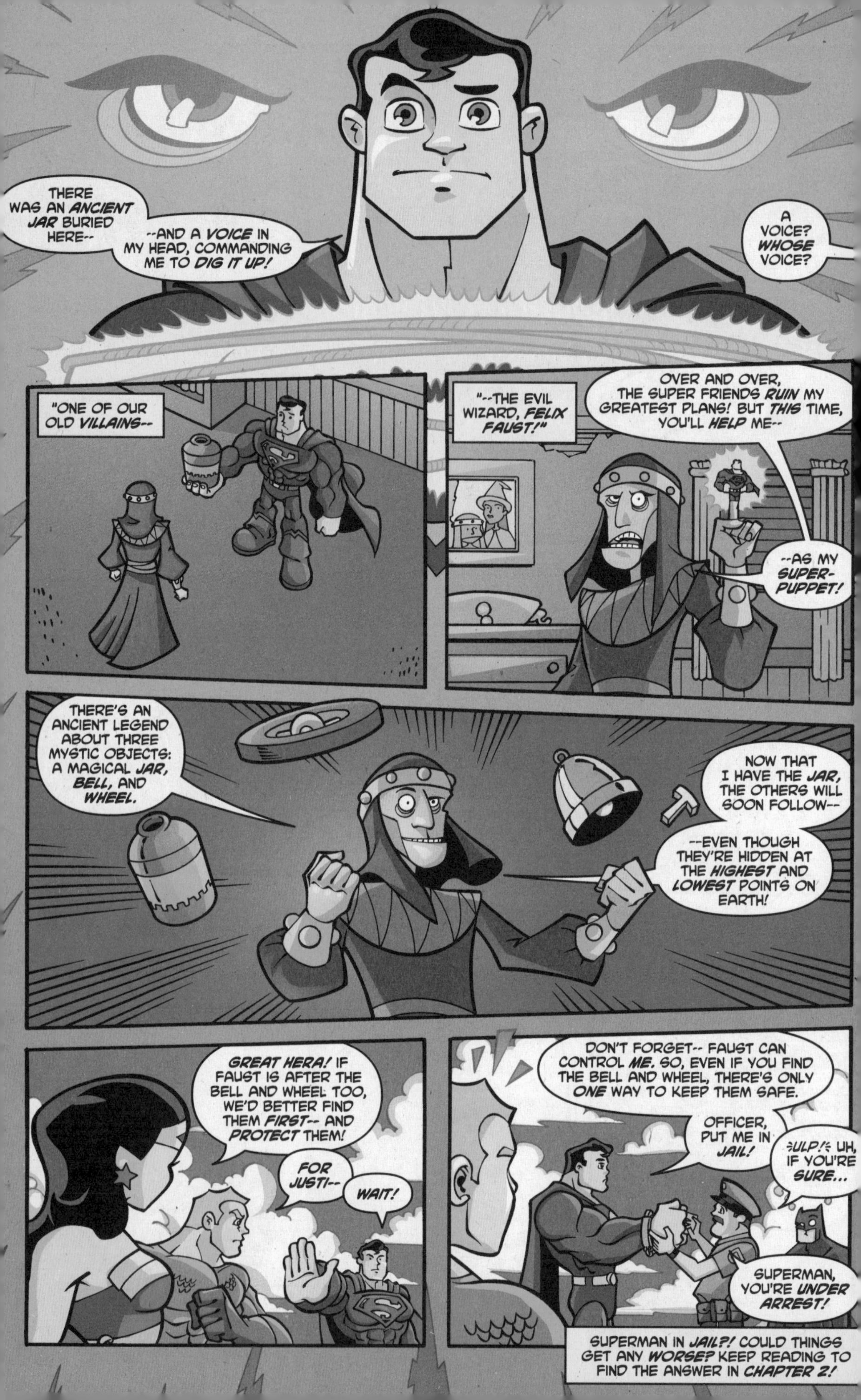
THERE WAS AN ANCIENT JAR BURIED HERE--
--AND A VOICE IN MY HEAD, COMMANDING ME TO DIG IT UP!
A VOICE? WHOSE VOICE?
"ONE OF OUR OLD VILLAINS--
"--THE EVIL WIZARD, FELIX FAUST!"
OVER AND OVER, THE SUPER FRIENDS RUIN MY GREATEST PLANS! BUT THIS TIME, YOU'LL HELP ME--
--AS MY SUPER-PUPPET!
THERE'S AN ANCIENT LEGEND ABOUT THREE MYSTIC OBJECTS: A MAGICAL JAR, BELL, AND WHEEL.
NOW THAT I HAVE THE JAR, THE OTHERS WILL SOON FOLLOW--
--EVEN THOUGH THEY'RE HIDDEN AT THE HIGHEST AND LOWEST POINTS ON EARTH!
GREAT HERA! IF FAUST IS AFTER THE BELL AND WHEEL TOO, WE'D BETTER FIND THEM FIRST-- AND PROTECT THEM!
FOR JUSTI--
WAIT!
DON'T FORGET-- FAUST CAN CONTROL ME. SO, EVEN IF YOU FIND THE BELL AND WHEEL, THERE'S ONLY ONE WAY TO KEEP THEM SAFE.
OFFICER, PUT ME IN JAIL!
GULP! UH, IF YOU'RE SURE...
SUPERMAN, YOU'RE UNDER ARREST!
SUPERMAN IN JAIL?! COULD THINGS GET ANY WORSE? KEEP READING TO FIND THE ANSWER IN CHAPTER 2!

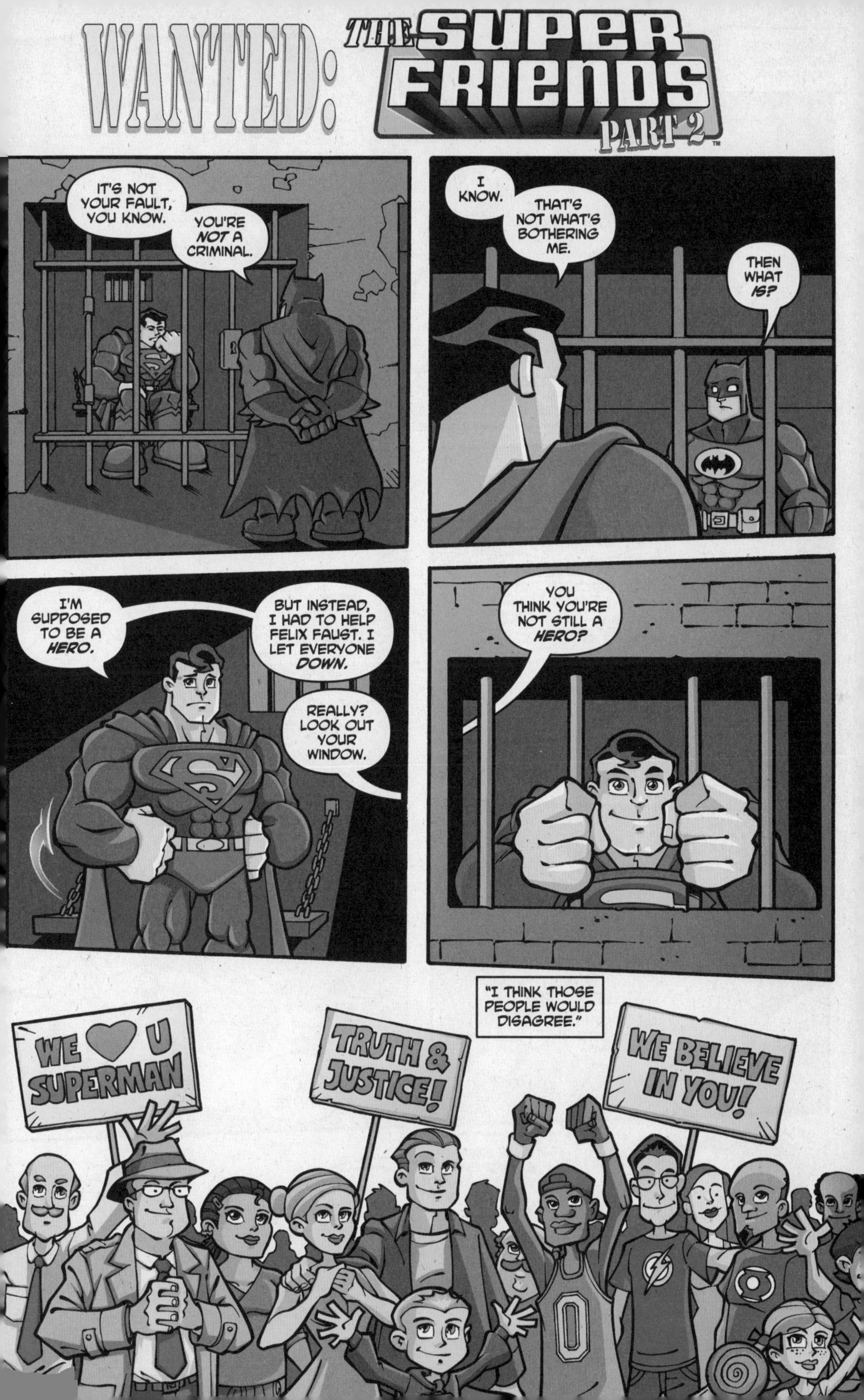
WANTED: THE SUPER FRIENDS PART 2
IT'S NOT YOUR FAULT, YOU KNOW.
YOU'RE NOT A CRIMINAL.
I KNOW.
THAT'S NOT WHAT'S BOTHERING ME.
THEN WHAT IS?
I'M SUPPOSED TO BE A HERO.
BUT INSTEAD, I HAD TO HELP FELIX FAUST. I LET EVERYONE DOWN.
REALLY? LOOK OUT YOUR WINDOW.
YOU THINK YOU'RE NOT STILL A HERO?
"I THINK THOSE PEOPLE WOULD DISAGREE."
WE ♥ U SUPERMAN
TRUTH & JUSTICE!
WE BELIEVE IN YOU!

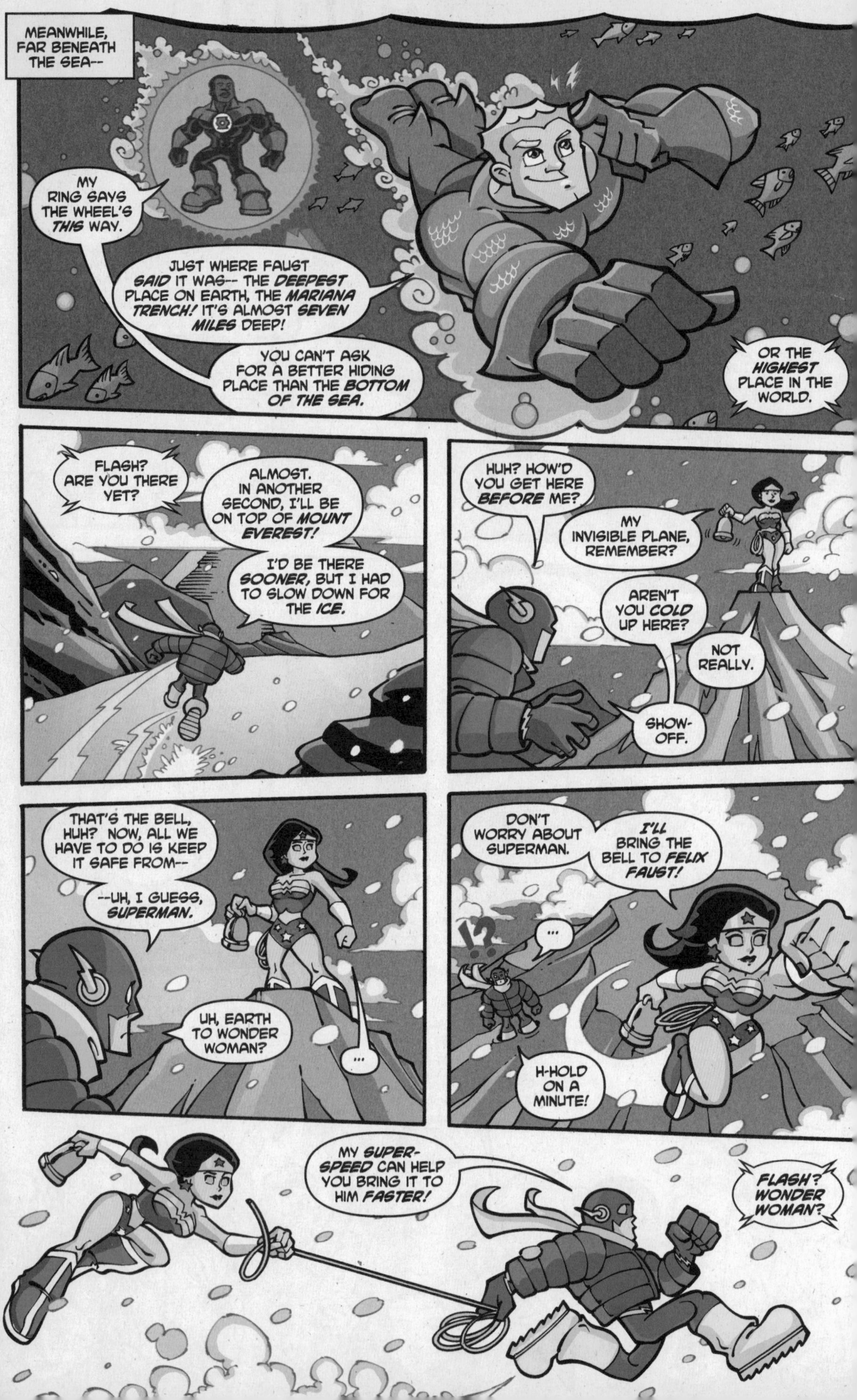
MEANWHILE, FAR BENEATH THE SEA--
MY RING SAYS THE WHEEL'S *THIS* WAY.
JUST WHERE FAUST *SAID* IT WAS-- THE *DEEPEST* PLACE ON EARTH, THE *MARIANA TRENCH!* IT'S ALMOST *SEVEN MILES* DEEP!
YOU CAN'T ASK FOR A BETTER HIDING PLACE THAN THE *BOTTOM OF THE SEA.*
OR THE *HIGHEST* PLACE IN THE WORLD.
FLASH? ARE YOU THERE YET?
ALMOST. IN ANOTHER SECOND, I'LL BE ON TOP OF *MOUNT EVEREST!*
I'D BE THERE *SOONER*, BUT I HAD TO SLOW DOWN FOR THE *ICE.*
HUH? HOW'D YOU GET HERE *BEFORE* ME?
MY INVISIBLE PLANE, REMEMBER?
AREN'T YOU *COLD* UP HERE?
NOT REALLY.
SHOW-OFF.
THAT'S THE BELL, HUH? NOW, ALL WE HAVE TO DO IS KEEP IT SAFE FROM--
--UH, I GUESS, *SUPERMAN.*
UH, EARTH TO WONDER WOMAN?
...
DON'T WORRY ABOUT SUPERMAN.
I'LL BRING THE BELL TO *FELIX FAUST!*
!?
...
H-HOLD ON A MINUTE!
MY *SUPER-SPEED* CAN HELP YOU BRING IT TO HIM *FASTER!*
FLASH? WONDER WOMAN?

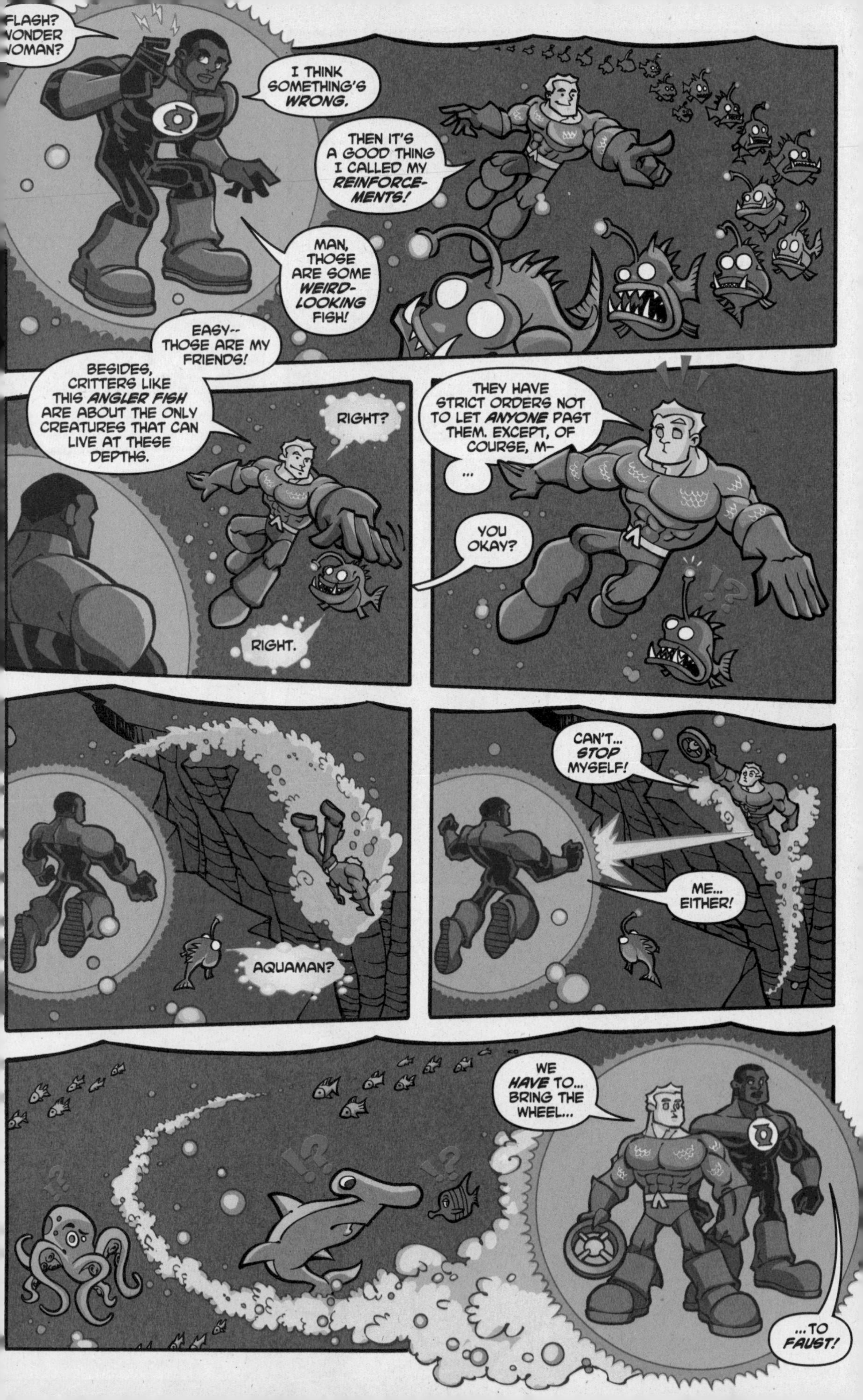
FLASH? WONDER WOMAN?
I THINK SOMETHING'S WRONG.
THEN IT'S A GOOD THING I CALLED MY REINFORCE-MENTS!
MAN, THOSE ARE SOME WEIRD-LOOKING FISH!
EASY-- THOSE ARE MY FRIENDS!
BESIDES, CRITTERS LIKE THIS ANGLER FISH ARE ABOUT THE ONLY CREATURES THAT CAN LIVE AT THESE DEPTHS.
RIGHT?
RIGHT.
THEY HAVE STRICT ORDERS NOT TO LET ANYONE PAST THEM. EXCEPT, OF COURSE, M–
...
YOU OKAY?
AQUAMAN?
CAN'T... STOP MYSELF!
ME... EITHER!
WE HAVE TO... BRING THE WHEEL...
...TO FAUST!

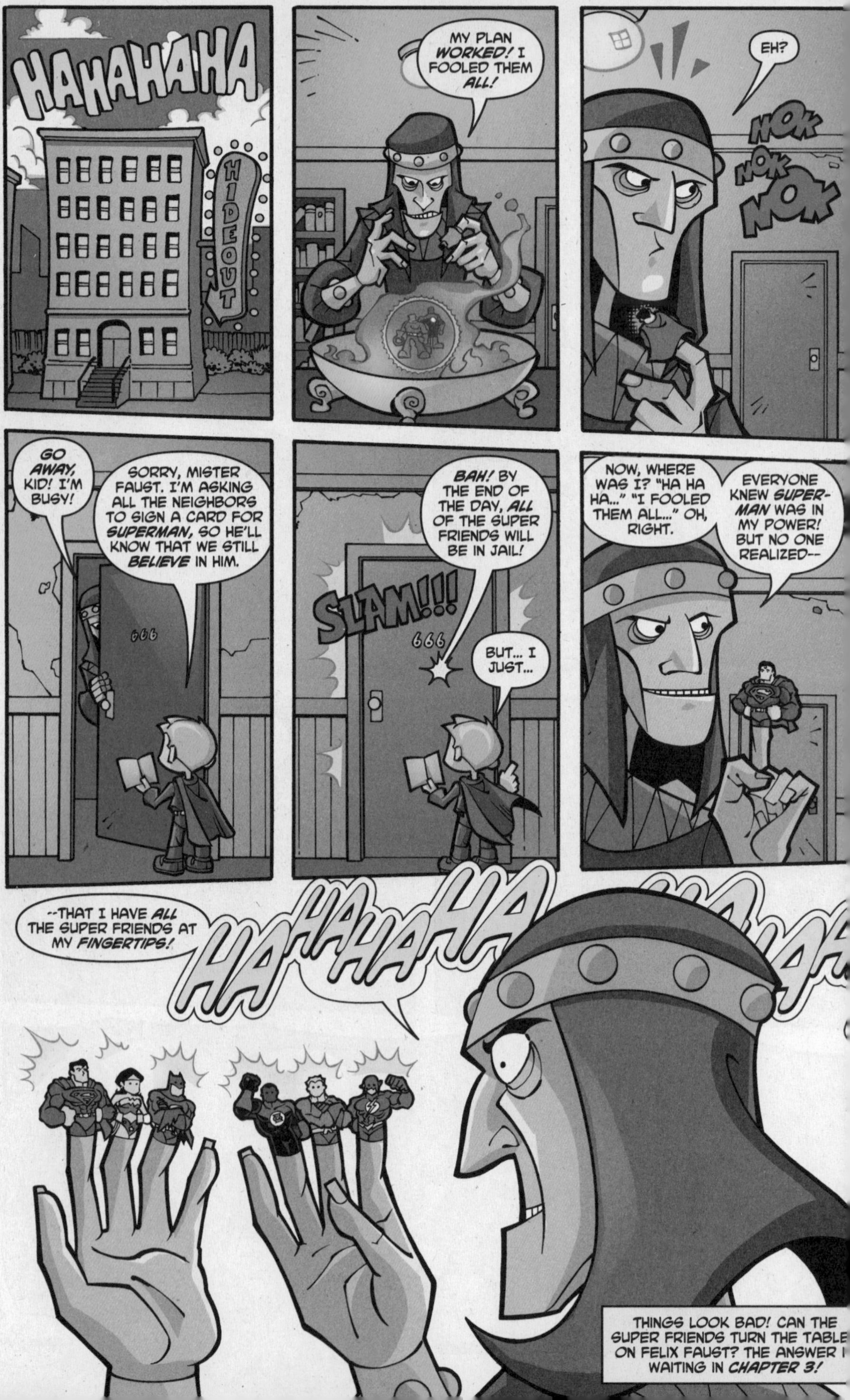
HAHAHAHA
HIDEOUT
MY PLAN WORKED! I FOOLED THEM ALL!
EH?
NOK NOK NOK
GO AWAY, KID! I'M BUSY!
SORRY, MISTER FAUST. I'M ASKING ALL THE NEIGHBORS TO SIGN A CARD FOR SUPERMAN, SO HE'LL KNOW THAT WE STILL BELIEVE IN HIM.
666
BAH! BY THE END OF THE DAY, ALL OF THE SUPER FRIENDS WILL BE IN JAIL!
SLAM!!!
666
BUT... I JUST...
NOW, WHERE WAS I? "HA HA HA..." "I FOOLED THEM ALL..." OH, RIGHT.
EVERYONE KNEW SUPERMAN WAS IN MY POWER! BUT NO ONE REALIZED--
--THAT I HAVE ALL THE SUPER FRIENDS AT MY FINGERTIPS!
HAHAHAHA
THINGS LOOK BAD! CAN THE SUPER FRIENDS TURN THE TABLE ON FELIX FAUST? THE ANSWER I WAITING IN CHAPTER 3!

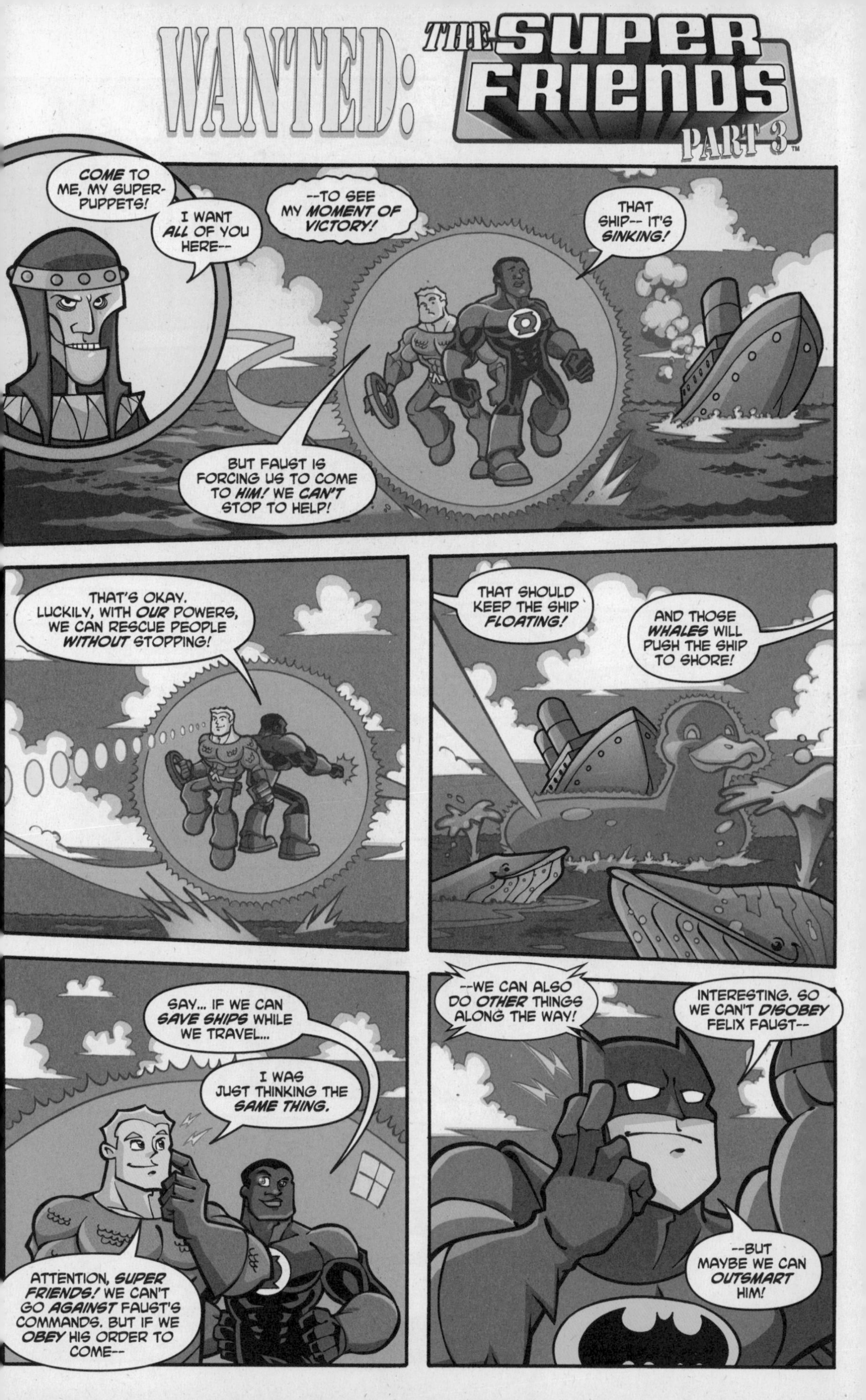
WANTED: THE SUPER FRIENDS PART 3
COME TO ME, MY SUPER-PUPPETS!
I WANT ALL OF YOU HERE--
--TO SEE MY MOMENT OF VICTORY!
THAT SHIP-- IT'S SINKING!
BUT FAUST IS FORCING US TO COME TO HIM! WE CAN'T STOP TO HELP!
THAT'S OKAY. LUCKILY, WITH OUR POWERS, WE CAN RESCUE PEOPLE WITHOUT STOPPING!
THAT SHOULD KEEP THE SHIP FLOATING!
AND THOSE WHALES WILL PUSH THE SHIP TO SHORE!
SAY... IF WE CAN SAVE SHIPS WHILE WE TRAVEL...
I WAS JUST THINKING THE SAME THING.
ATTENTION, SUPER FRIENDS! WE CAN'T GO AGAINST FAUST'S COMMANDS. BUT IF WE OBEY HIS ORDER TO COME--
--WE CAN ALSO DO OTHER THINGS ALONG THE WAY!
INTERESTING. SO WE CAN'T DISOBEY FELIX FAUST--
--BUT MAYBE WE CAN OUTSMART HIM!

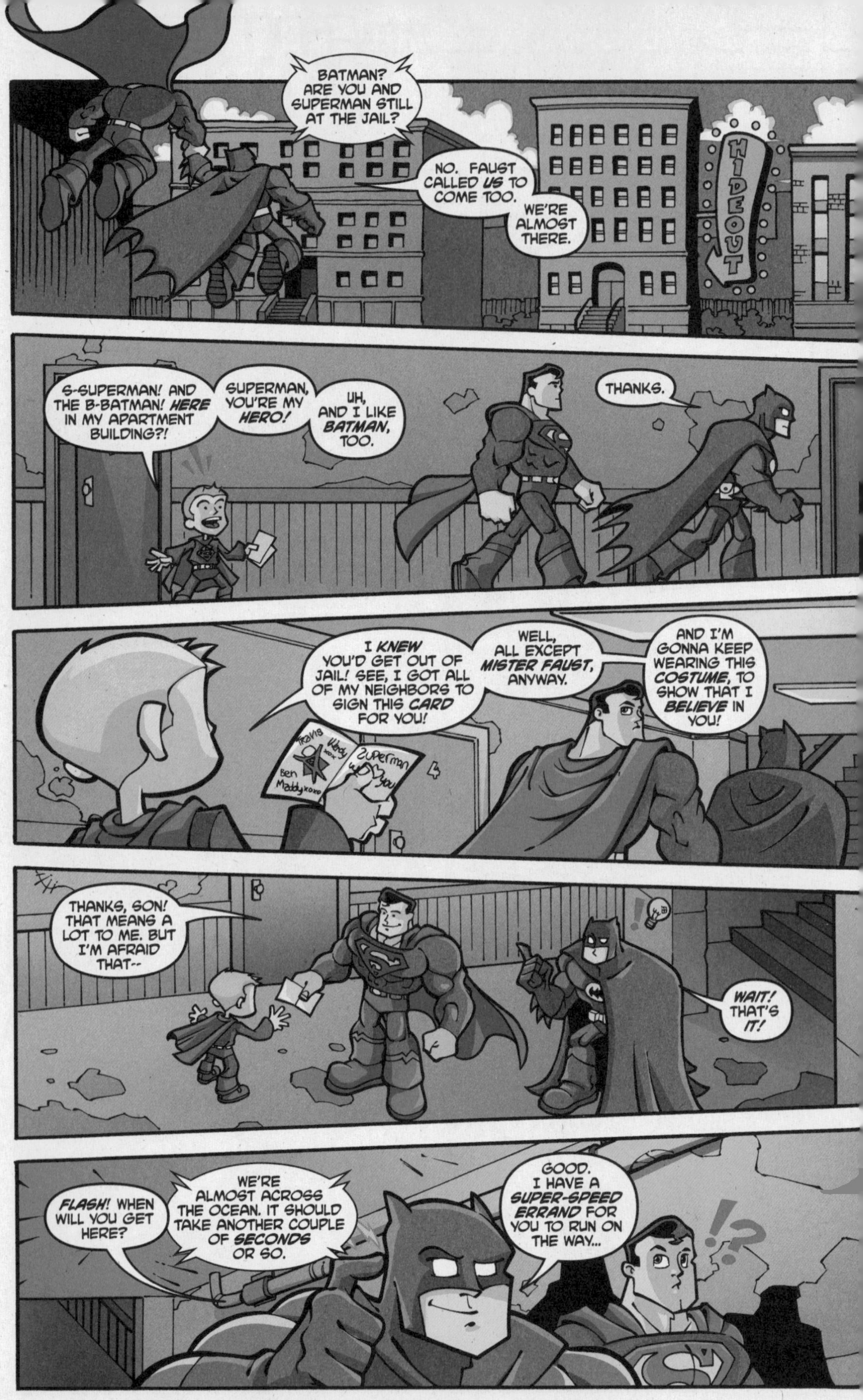
BATMAN? ARE YOU AND SUPERMAN STILL AT THE JAIL?
NO. FAUST CALLED *US* TO COME TOO.
WE'RE ALMOST THERE.
HIDEOUT
S-SUPERMAN! AND THE B-BATMAN! *HERE* IN MY APARTMENT BUILDING?!
SUPERMAN, YOU'RE MY *HERO!*
UH, AND I LIKE *BATMAN,* TOO.
THANKS.
I *KNEW* YOU'D GET OUT OF JAIL! SEE, I GOT ALL OF MY NEIGHBORS TO SIGN THIS *CARD* FOR YOU!
WELL, ALL EXCEPT *MISTER FAUST,* ANYWAY.
AND I'M GONNA KEEP WEARING THIS *COSTUME,* TO SHOW THAT I *BELIEVE* IN YOU!
Travis
Wendy xoxo
Ben
Maddy xoxo
Superman
you
THANKS, SON! THAT MEANS A LOT TO ME. BUT I'M AFRAID THAT--
WAIT! THAT'S *IT!*
FLASH! WHEN WILL YOU GET HERE?
WE'RE ALMOST ACROSS THE OCEAN. IT SHOULD TAKE ANOTHER COUPLE OF *SECONDS* OR SO.
GOOD. I HAVE A *SUPER-SPEED ERRAND* FOR YOU TO RUN ON THE WAY...

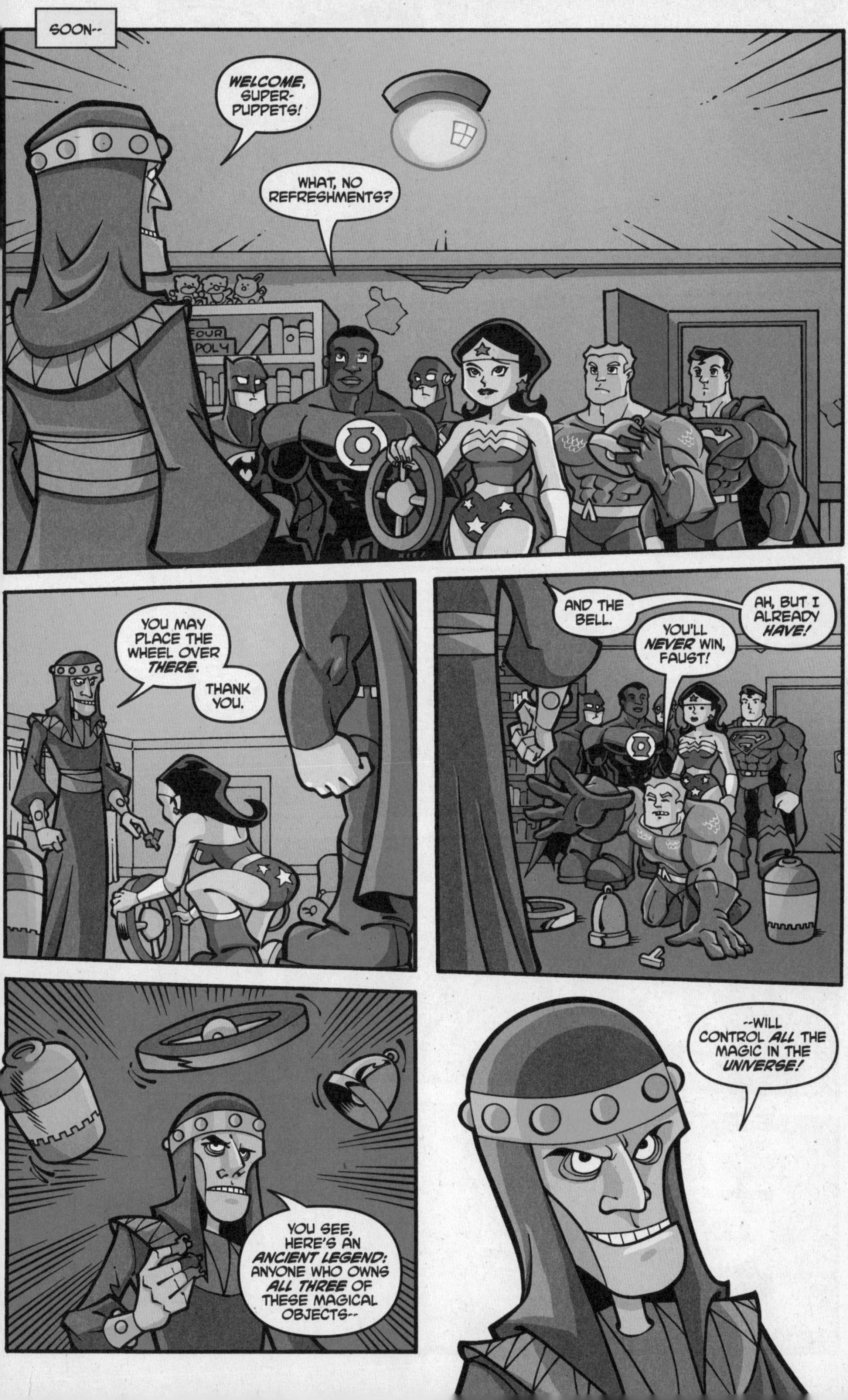
SOON--
WELCOME, SUPER-PUPPETS!
WHAT, NO REFRESHMENTS?
FOUR
POLY
YOU MAY PLACE THE WHEEL OVER THERE.
THANK YOU.
AND THE BELL.
YOU'LL NEVER WIN, FAUST!
AH, BUT I ALREADY HAVE!
YOU SEE, HERE'S AN ANCIENT LEGEND: ANYONE WHO OWNS ALL THREE OF THESE MAGICAL OBJECTS--
--WILL CONTROL ALL THE MAGIC IN THE UNIVERSE!

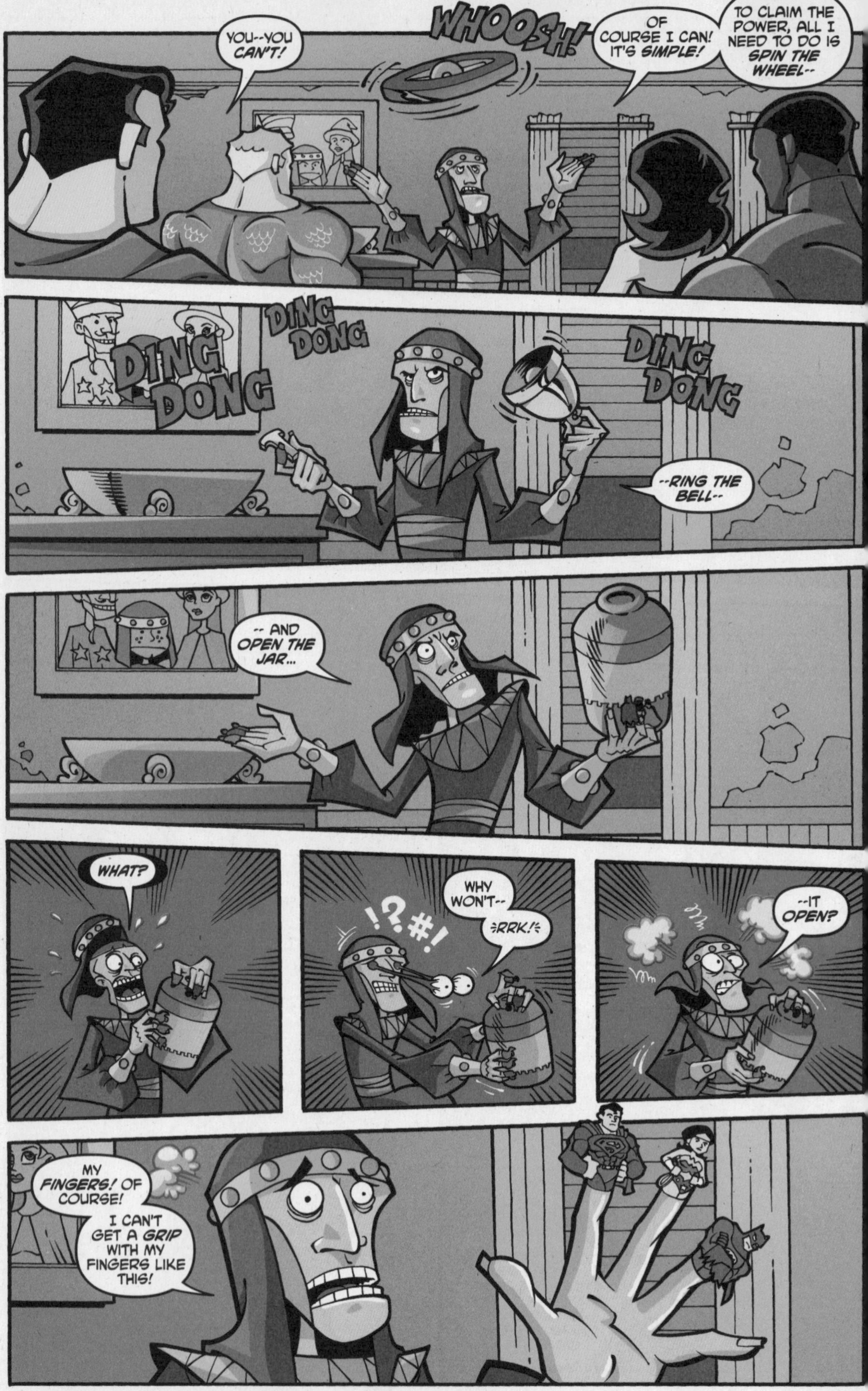
YOU--YOU CAN'T!
WHOOSH!
OF COURSE I CAN! IT'S SIMPLE!
TO CLAIM THE POWER, ALL I NEED TO DO IS SPIN THE WHEEL--
DING DONG
DING DONG
DING DONG
--RING THE BELL--
-- AND OPEN THE JAR...
WHAT?
!?#!
WHY WON'T--
RRK!
--IT OPEN?
MY FINGERS! OF COURSE!
I CAN'T GET A GRIP WITH MY FINGERS LIKE THIS!

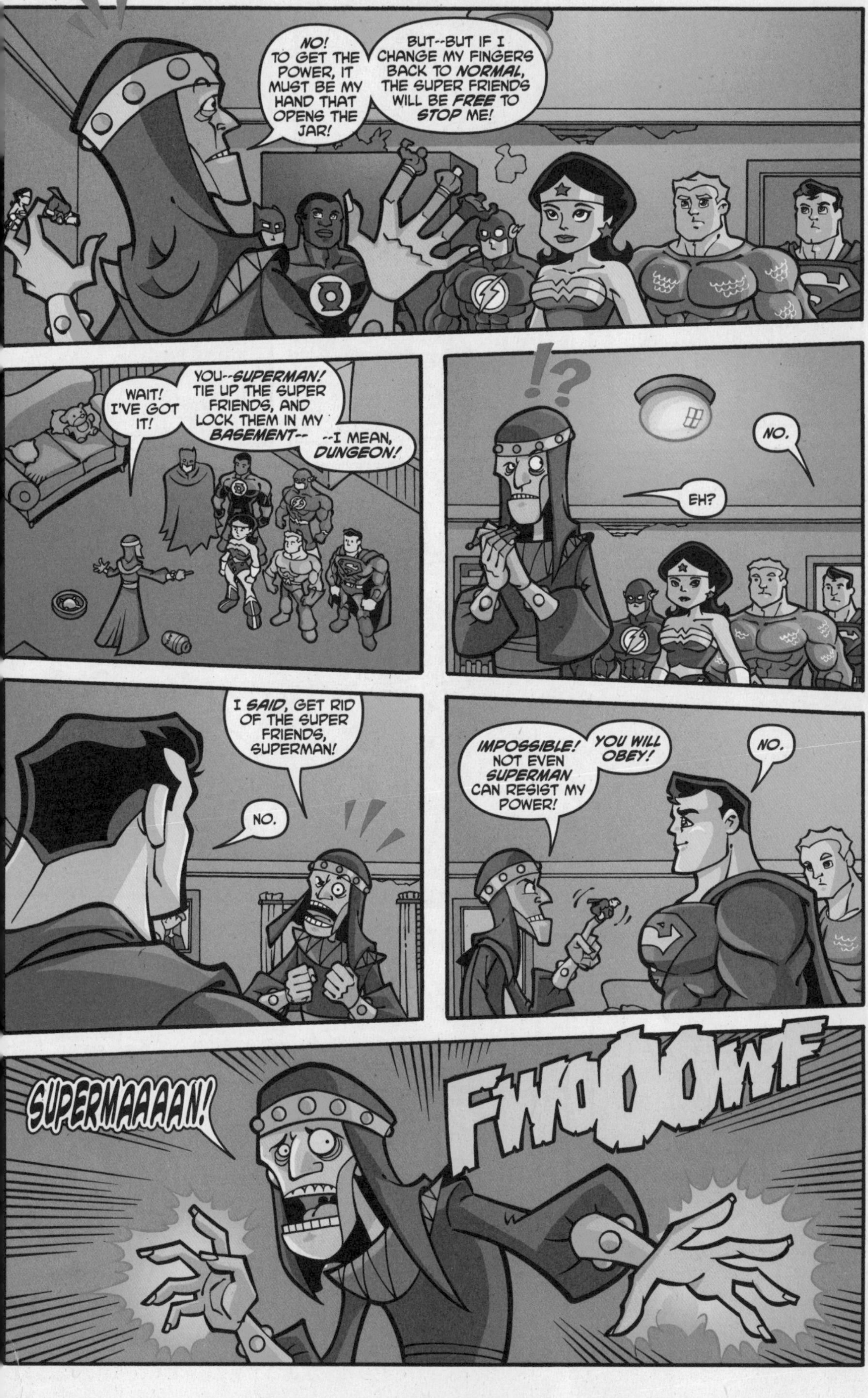
NO! TO GET THE POWER, IT MUST BE MY HAND THAT OPENS THE JAR!
BUT--BUT IF I CHANGE MY FINGERS BACK TO NORMAL, THE SUPER FRIENDS WILL BE FREE TO STOP ME!
WAIT! I'VE GOT IT!
YOU--SUPERMAN! TIE UP THE SUPER FRIENDS, AND LOCK THEM IN MY BASEMENT--
--I MEAN, DUNGEON!
NO.
EH?
I SAID, GET RID OF THE SUPER FRIENDS, SUPERMAN!
NO.
IMPOSSIBLE! NOT EVEN SUPERMAN CAN RESIST MY POWER!
YOU WILL OBEY!
NO.
SUPERMAAAAAN!
FWOOOWF

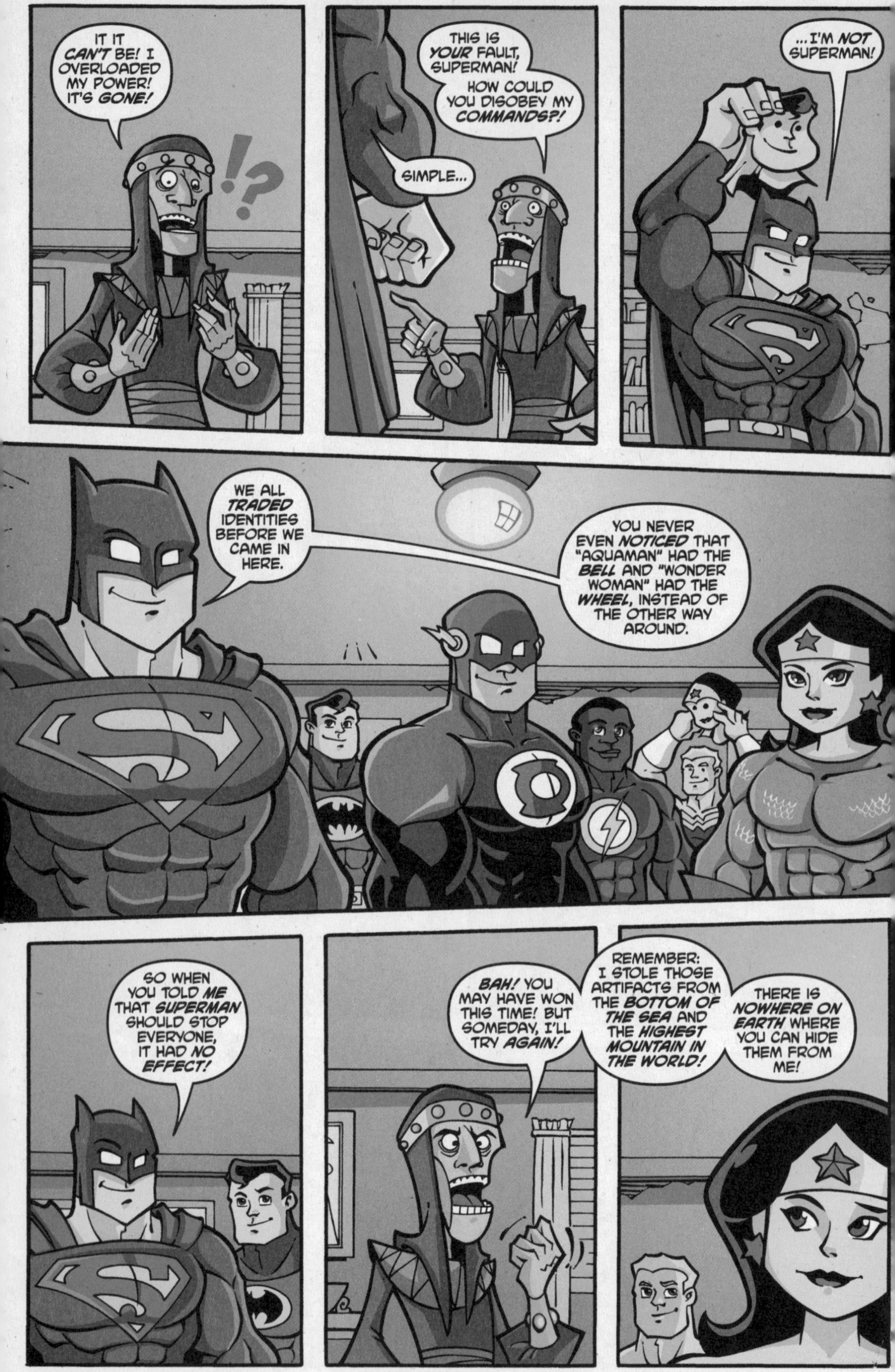
IT IT CAN'T BE! I OVERLOADED MY POWER! IT'S GONE!
!?
THIS IS YOUR FAULT, SUPERMAN!
HOW COULD YOU DISOBEY MY COMMANDS?!
SIMPLE...
...I'M NOT SUPERMAN!
WE ALL TRADED IDENTITIES BEFORE WE CAME IN HERE.
YOU NEVER EVEN NOTICED THAT "AQUAMAN" HAD THE BELL AND "WONDER WOMAN" HAD THE WHEEL, INSTEAD OF THE OTHER WAY AROUND.
SO WHEN YOU TOLD ME THAT SUPERMAN SHOULD STOP EVERYONE, IT HAD NO EFFECT!
BAH! YOU MAY HAVE WON THIS TIME! BUT SOMEDAY, I'LL TRY AGAIN!
REMEMBER: I STOLE THOSE ARTIFACTS FROM THE BOTTOM OF THE SEA AND THE HIGHEST MOUNTAIN IN THE WORLD!
THERE IS NOWHERE ON EARTH WHERE YOU CAN HIDE THEM FROM ME!

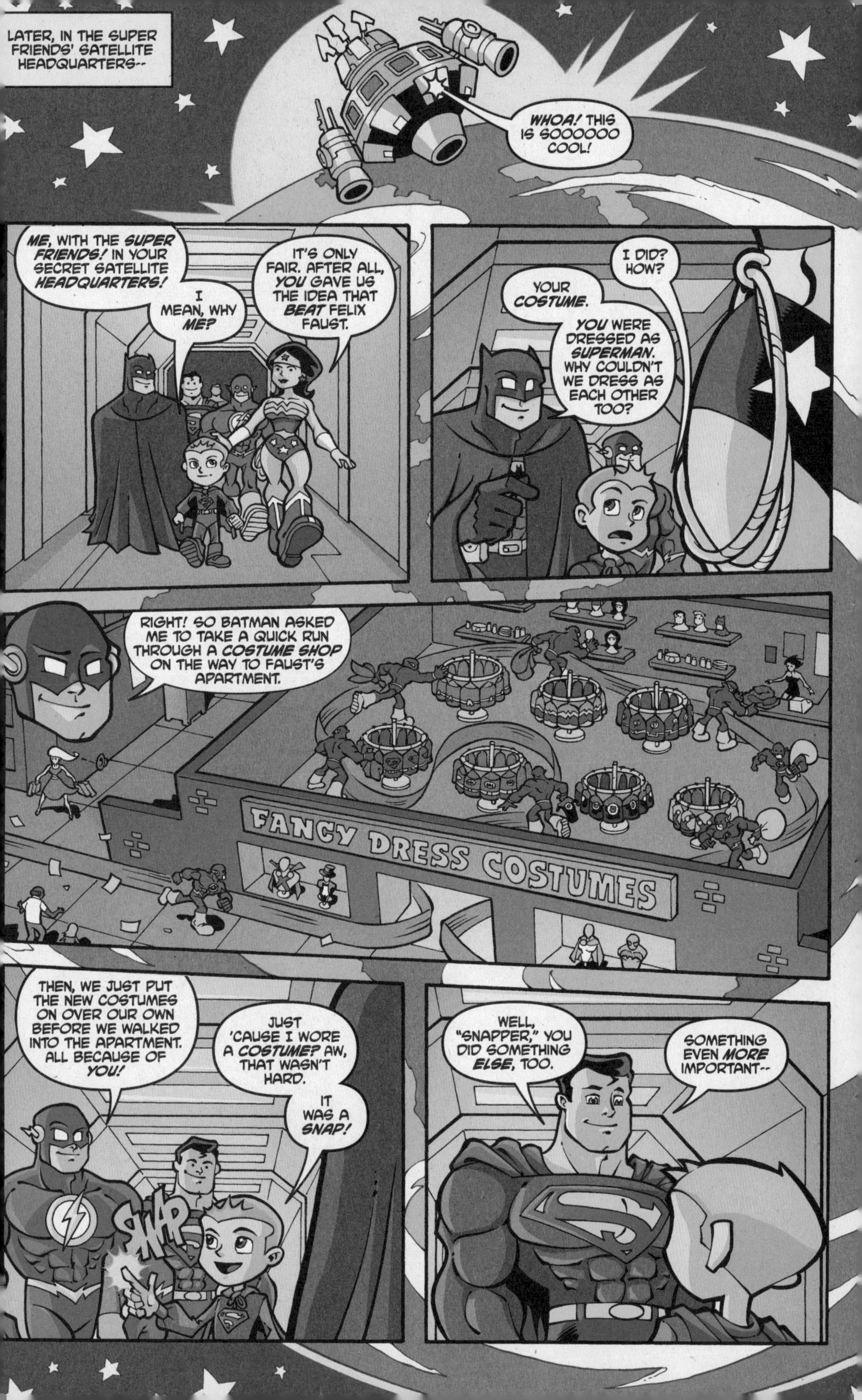
LATER, IN THE SUPER FRIENDS' SATELLITE HEADQUARTERS--
WHOA! THIS IS SOOOOOO COOL!
ME, WITH THE SUPER FRIENDS! IN YOUR SECRET SATELLITE HEADQUARTERS!
I MEAN, WHY ME?
IT'S ONLY FAIR. AFTER ALL, YOU GAVE US THE IDEA THAT BEAT FELIX FAUST.
I DID? HOW?
YOUR COSTUME.
YOU WERE DRESSED AS SUPERMAN. WHY COULDN'T WE DRESS AS EACH OTHER TOO?
RIGHT! SO BATMAN ASKED ME TO TAKE A QUICK RUN THROUGH A COSTUME SHOP ON THE WAY TO FAUST'S APARTMENT.
FANCY DRESS COSTUMES
THEN, WE JUST PUT THE NEW COSTUMES ON OVER OUR OWN BEFORE WE WALKED INTO THE APARTMENT. ALL BECAUSE OF YOU!
JUST 'CAUSE I WORE A COSTUME? AW, THAT WASN'T HARD.
IT WAS A SNAP!
SNAP
WELL, "SNAPPER," YOU DID SOMETHING ELSE, TOO.
SOMETHING EVEN MORE IMPORTANT--

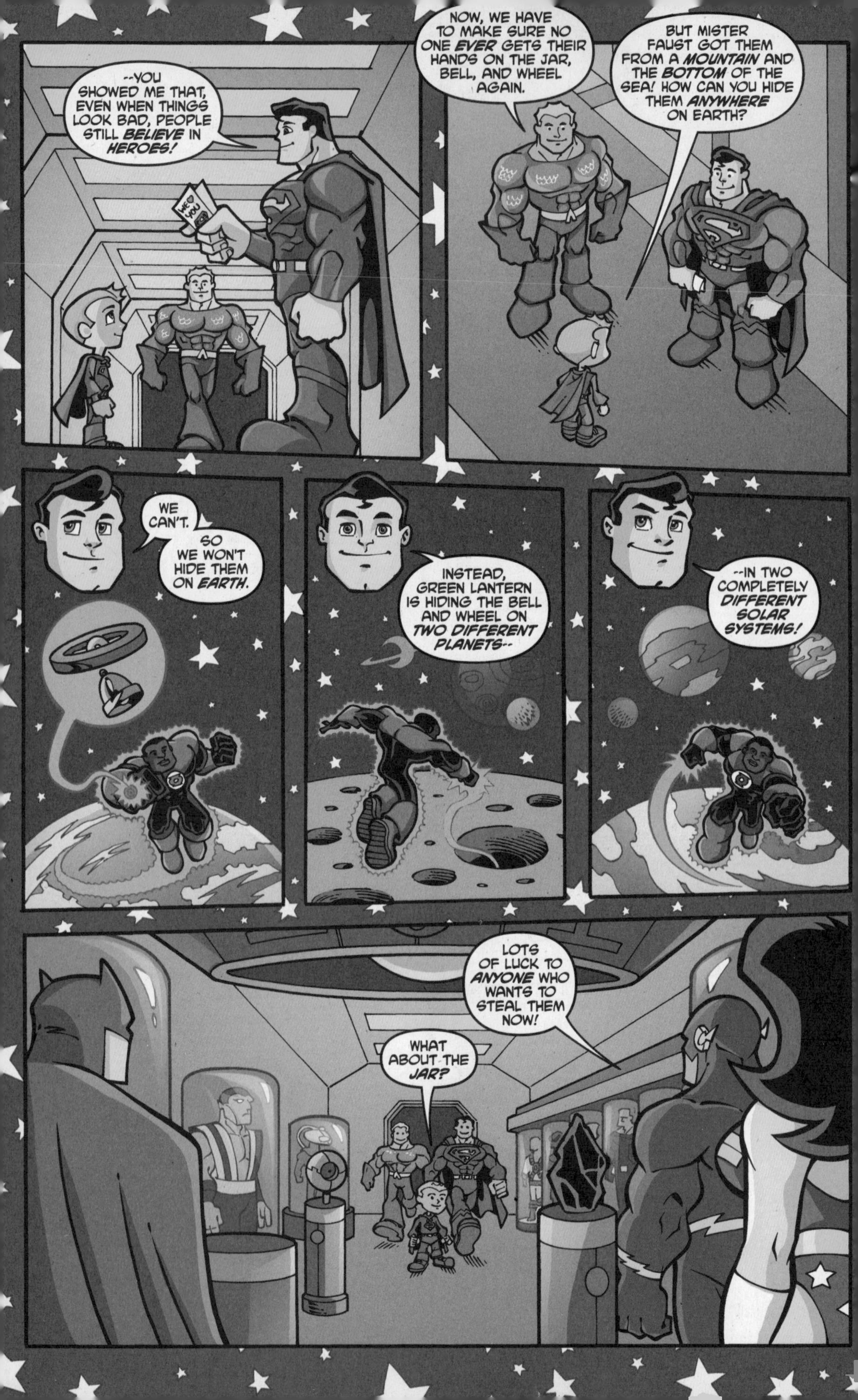
--YOU SHOWED ME THAT, EVEN WHEN THINGS LOOK BAD, PEOPLE STILL *BELIEVE* IN *HEROES!*
NOW, WE HAVE TO MAKE SURE NO ONE *EVER* GETS THEIR HANDS ON THE JAR, BELL, AND WHEEL AGAIN.
BUT MISTER FAUST GOT THEM FROM A *MOUNTAIN* AND THE *BOTTOM* OF THE SEA! HOW CAN YOU HIDE THEM *ANYWHERE* ON EARTH?
WE CAN'T.
SO WE WON'T HIDE THEM ON *EARTH*.
INSTEAD, GREEN LANTERN IS HIDING THE BELL AND WHEEL ON *TWO DIFFERENT PLANETS--*
--IN TWO COMPLETELY *DIFFERENT SOLAR SYSTEMS!*
LOTS OF LUCK TO *ANYONE* WHO WANTS TO STEAL THEM NOW!
WHAT ABOUT THE *JAR?*

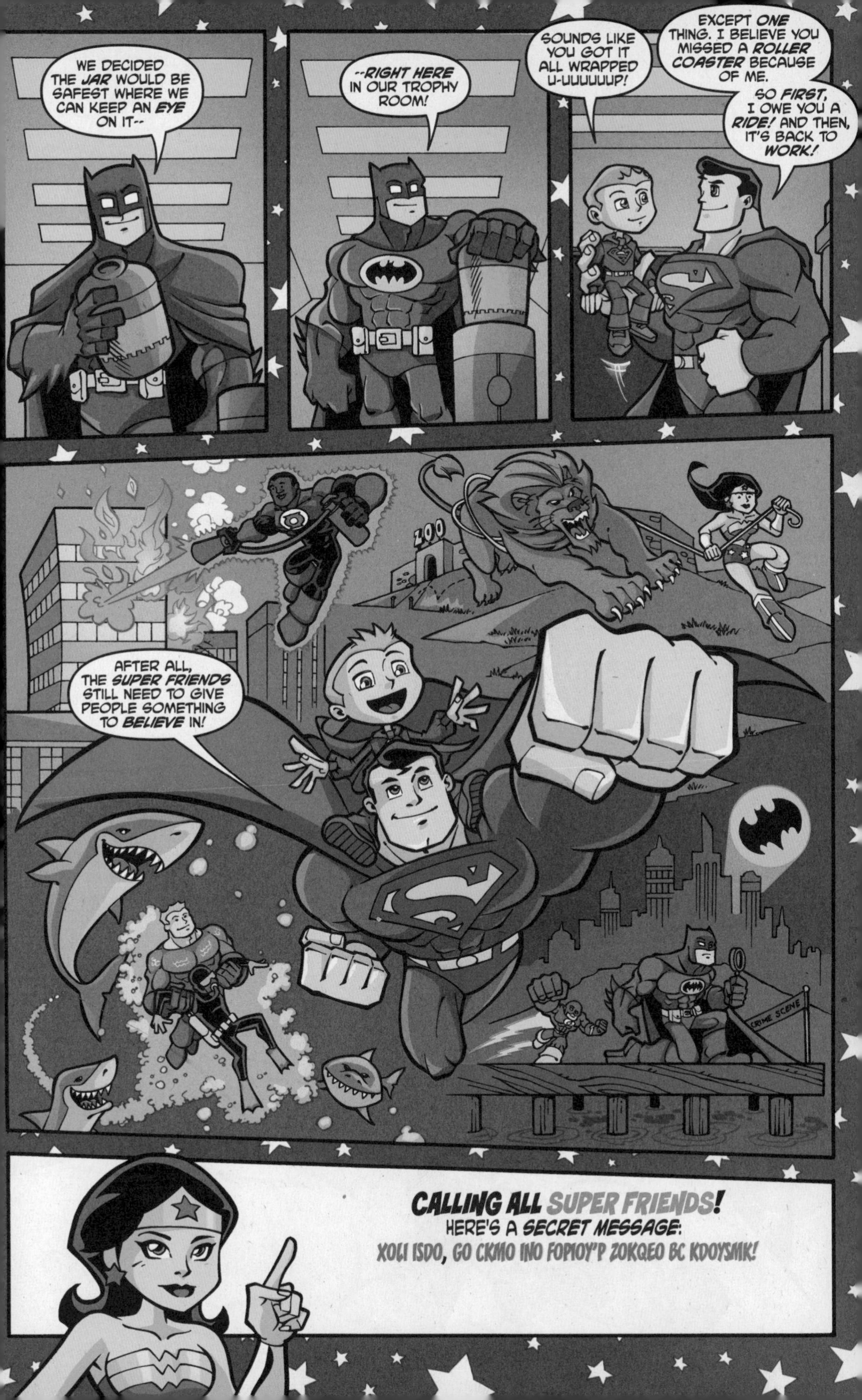
WE DECIDED THE JAR WOULD BE SAFEST WHERE WE CAN KEEP AN EYE ON IT--
--RIGHT HERE IN OUR TROPHY ROOM!
SOUNDS LIKE YOU GOT IT ALL WRAPPED U-UUUUUUP!
EXCEPT ONE THING. I BELIEVE YOU MISSED A ROLLER COASTER BECAUSE OF ME.
SO FIRST, I OWE YOU A RIDE! AND THEN, IT'S BACK TO WORK!
ZOO
AFTER ALL, THE SUPER FRIENDS STILL NEED TO GIVE PEOPLE SOMETHING TO BELIEVE IN!
CRIME SCENE
CALLING ALL SUPER FRIENDS!
HERE'S A SECRET MESSAGE:
XOLI ISDO, GO CKMO INO FOPIOY'P ZOKQEO BC KDOYSMK!

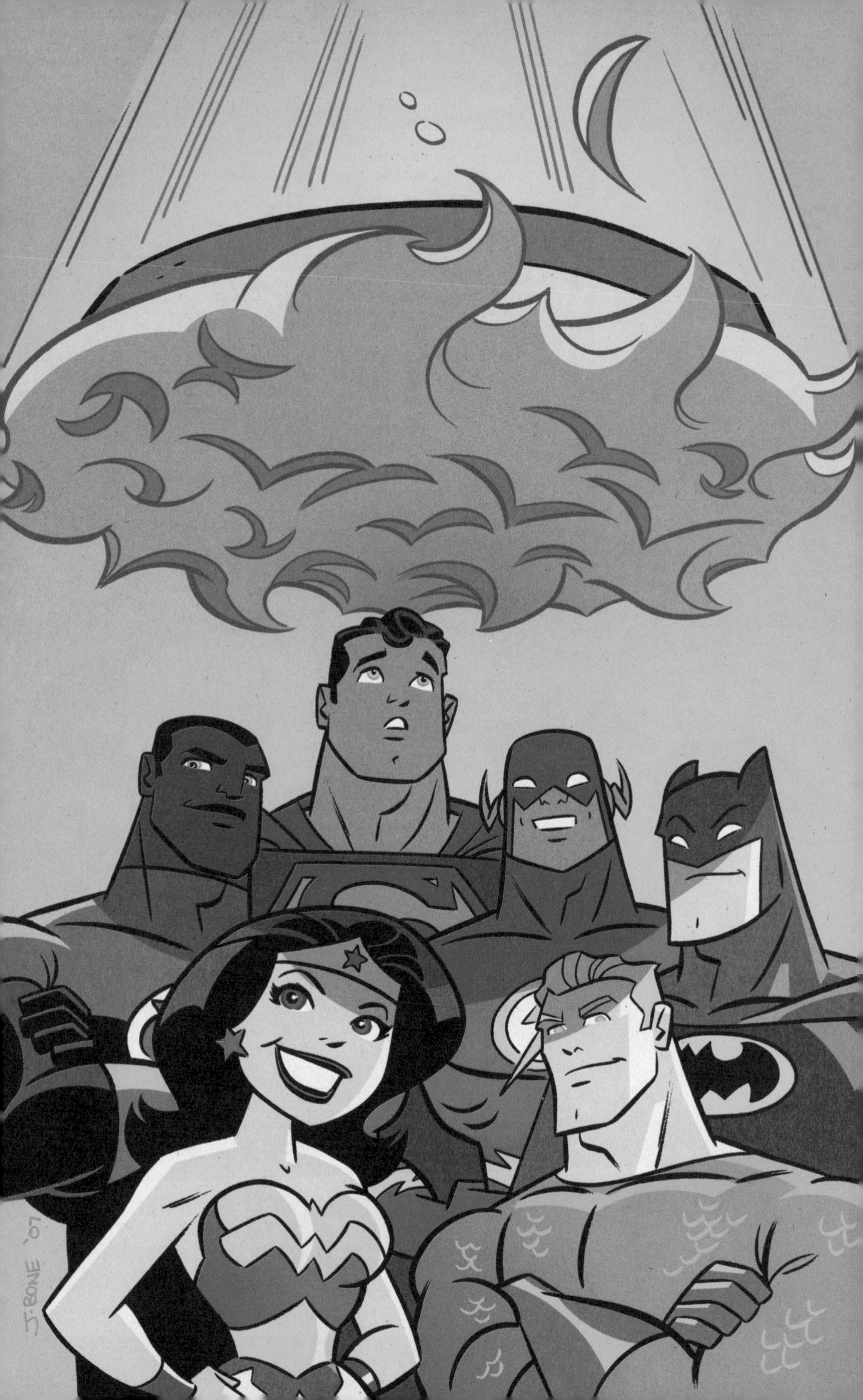
J. BONE '07

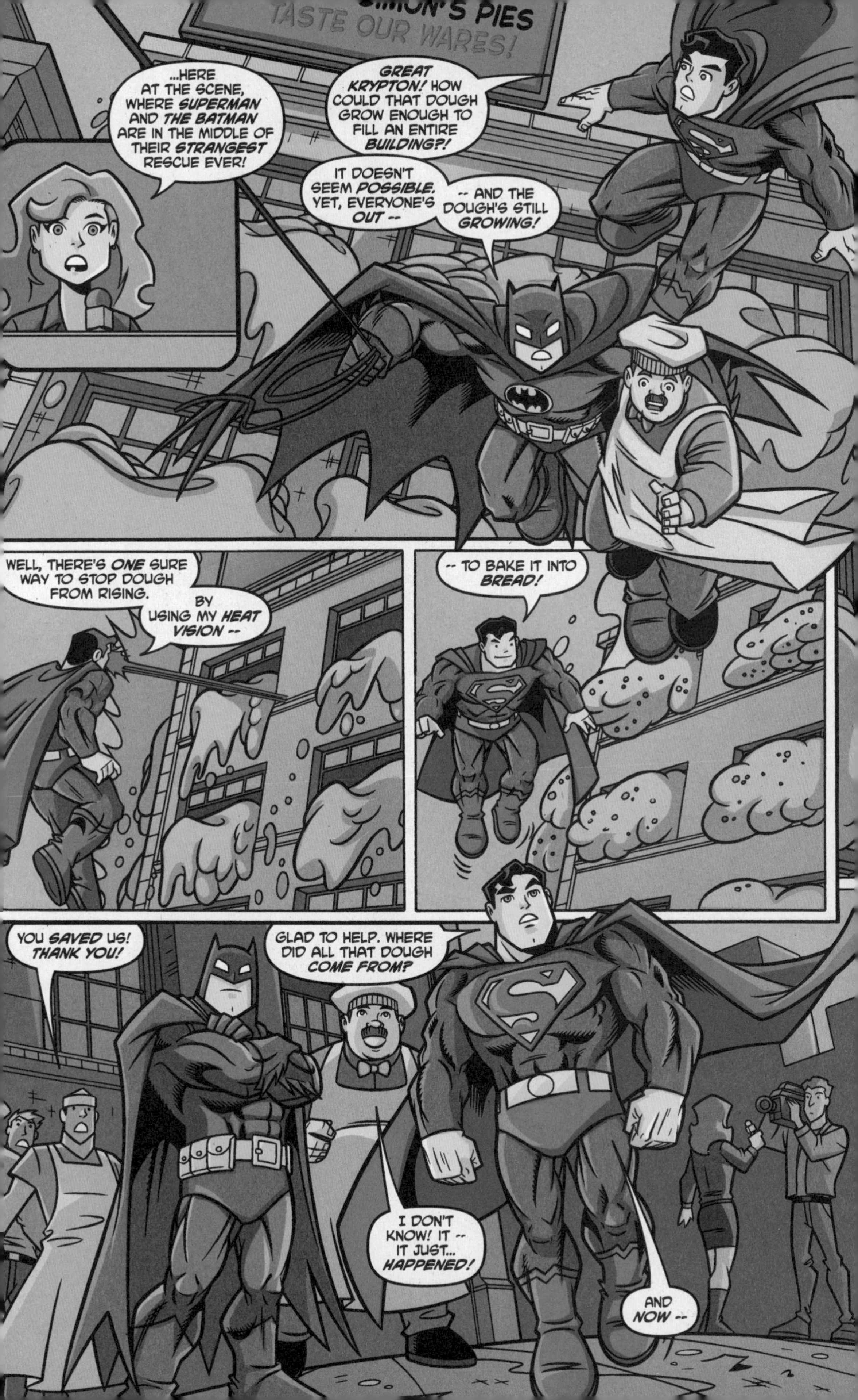

...ON'S PIES
TASTE OUR WARES!
...HERE AT THE SCENE, WHERE SUPERMAN AND THE BATMAN ARE IN THE MIDDLE OF THEIR STRANGEST RESCUE EVER!
GREAT KRYPTON! HOW COULD THAT DOUGH GROW ENOUGH TO FILL AN ENTIRE BUILDING?!
IT DOESN'T SEEM POSSIBLE. YET, EVERYONE'S OUT --
-- AND THE DOUGH'S STILL GROWING!
WELL, THERE'S ONE SURE WAY TO STOP DOUGH FROM RISING.
BY USING MY HEAT VISION --
-- TO BAKE IT INTO BREAD!
YOU SAVED US! THANK YOU!
GLAD TO HELP. WHERE DID ALL THAT DOUGH COME FROM?
I DON'T KNOW! IT -- IT JUST... HAPPENED!
AND NOW --

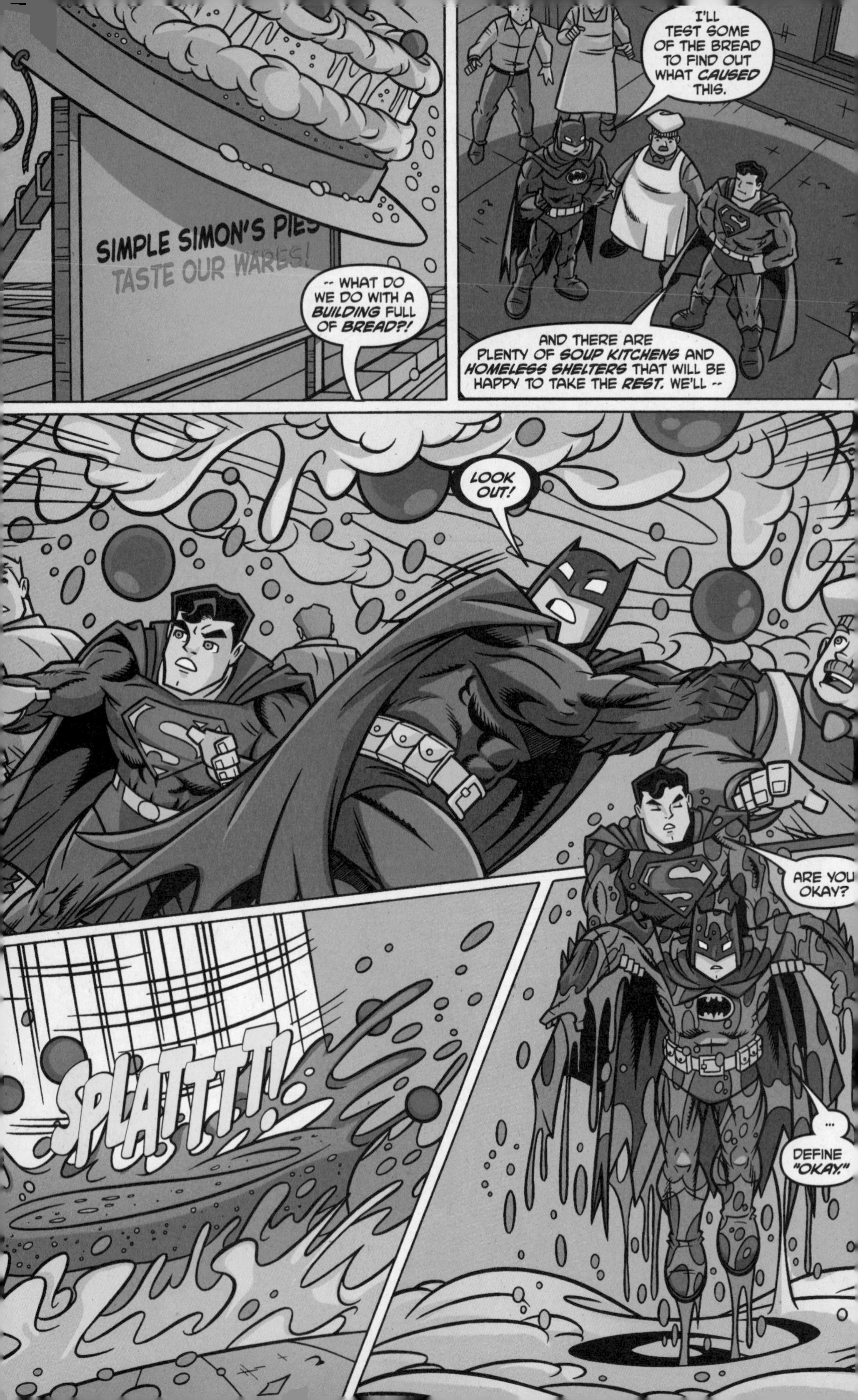
SIMPLE SIMON'S PIES
TASTE OUR WARES!
-- WHAT DO WE DO WITH A BUILDING FULL OF BREAD?!
I'LL TEST SOME OF THE BREAD TO FIND OUT WHAT CAUSED THIS.
AND THERE ARE PLENTY OF SOUP KITCHENS AND HOMELESS SHELTERS THAT WILL BE HAPPY TO TAKE THE REST. WE'LL --
LOOK OUT!
SPLATTTT!
ARE YOU OKAY?
...
DEFINE "OKAY."

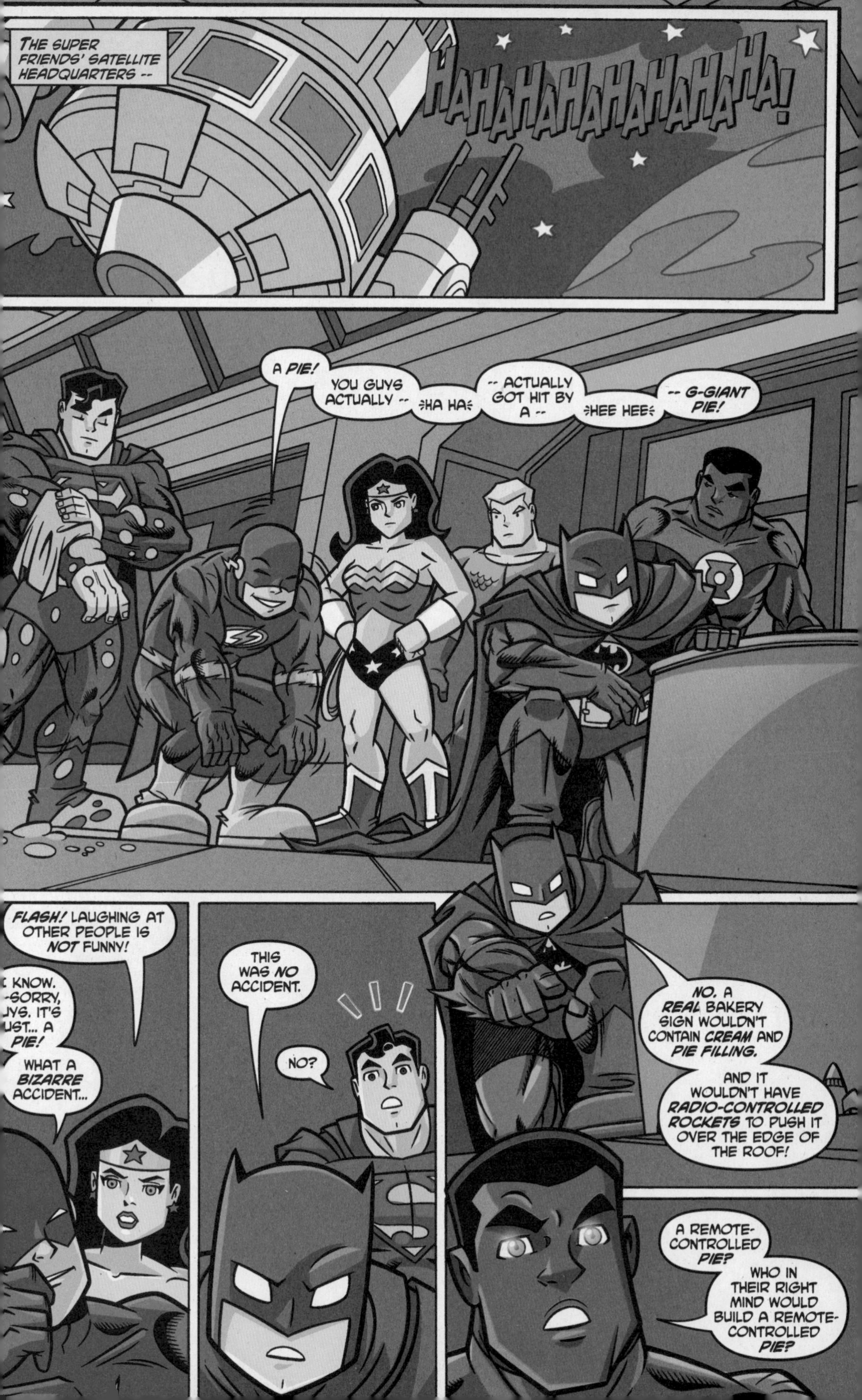
THE SUPER FRIENDS' SATELLITE HEADQUARTERS --
HAHAHAHAHAHAHAHAHA!
A PIE!
YOU GUYS ACTUALLY --
HA HA
-- ACTUALLY GOT HIT BY A --
HEE HEE
-- G-GIANT PIE!
FLASH! LAUGHING AT OTHER PEOPLE IS NOT FUNNY!
I KNOW. I-SORRY, GUYS. IT'S JUST... A PIE!
WHAT A BIZARRE ACCIDENT...
THIS WAS NO ACCIDENT.
NO?
NO. A REAL BAKERY SIGN WOULDN'T CONTAIN CREAM AND PIE FILLING.
AND IT WOULDN'T HAVE RADIO-CONTROLLED ROCKETS TO PUSH IT OVER THE EDGE OF THE ROOF!
A REMOTE-CONTROLLED PIE?
WHO IN THEIR RIGHT MIND WOULD BUILD A REMOTE-CONTROLLED PIE?

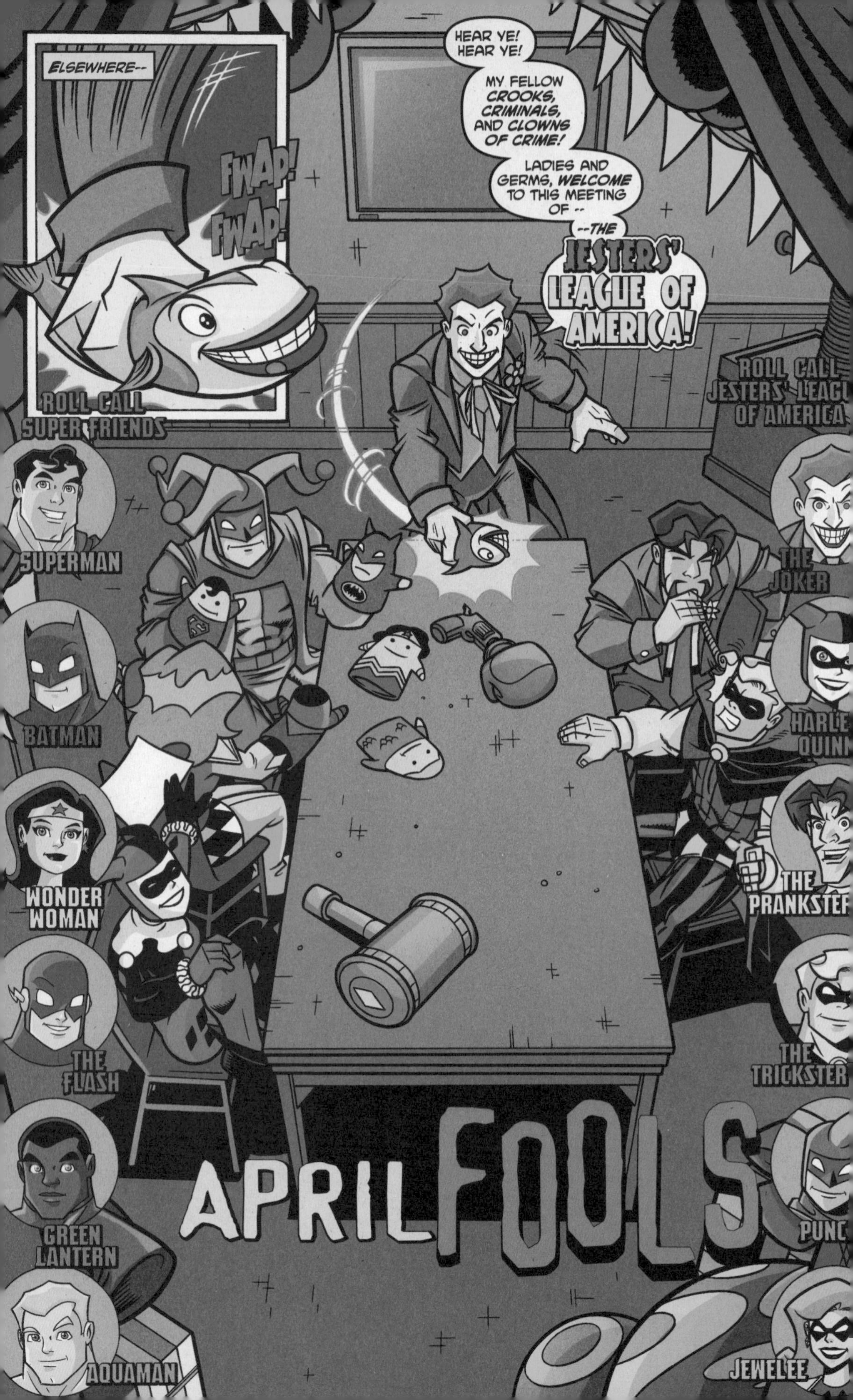

ELSEWHERE--
FWAP! FWAP!
HEAR YE! HEAR YE!
MY FELLOW CROOKS, CRIMINALS, AND CLOWNS OF CRIME!
LADIES AND GERMS, WELCOME TO THIS MEETING OF --
--THE JESTERS' LEAGUE OF AMERICA!
ROLL CALL SUPER FRIENDS
SUPERMAN
BATMAN
WONDER WOMAN
THE FLASH
GREEN LANTERN
AQUAMAN
ROLL CALL JESTERS' LEAGU OF AMERICA
THE JOKER
HARLE QUINN
THE PRANKSTER
THE TRICKSTER
PUNC
JEWELEE
APRIL FOOLS

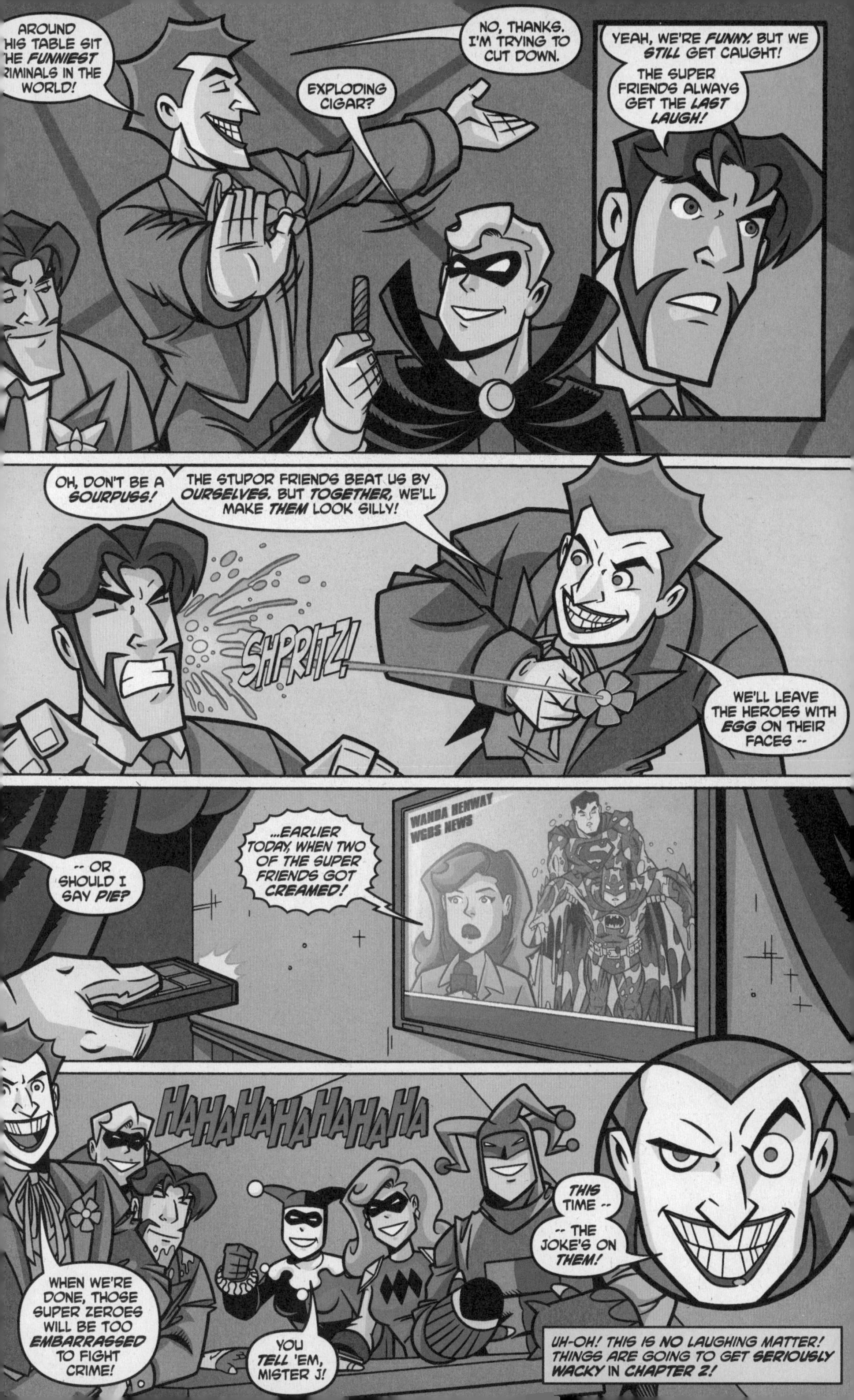

AROUND HIS TABLE SIT THE FUNNIEST CRIMINALS IN THE WORLD!
EXPLODING CIGAR?
NO, THANKS. I'M TRYING TO CUT DOWN.
YEAH, WE'RE FUNNY. BUT WE STILL GET CAUGHT!
THE SUPER FRIENDS ALWAYS GET THE LAST LAUGH!
OH, DON'T BE A SOURPUSS!
THE STUPOR FRIENDS BEAT US BY OURSELVES. BUT TOGETHER, WE'LL MAKE THEM LOOK SILLY!
SHPRITZ!
WE'LL LEAVE THE HEROES WITH EGG ON THEIR FACES --
-- OR SHOULD I SAY PIE?
WANDA HENWAY WGBS NEWS
...EARLIER TODAY, WHEN TWO OF THE SUPER FRIENDS GOT CREAMED!
HAHAHAHAHAHAHAHA
THIS TIME --
-- THE JOKE'S ON THEM!
WHEN WE'RE DONE, THOSE SUPER ZEROES WILL BE TOO EMBARRASSED TO FIGHT CRIME!
YOU TELL 'EM, MISTER J!
UH-OH! THIS IS NO LAUGHING MATTER! THINGS ARE GOING TO GET SERIOUSLY WACKY IN CHAPTER 2!

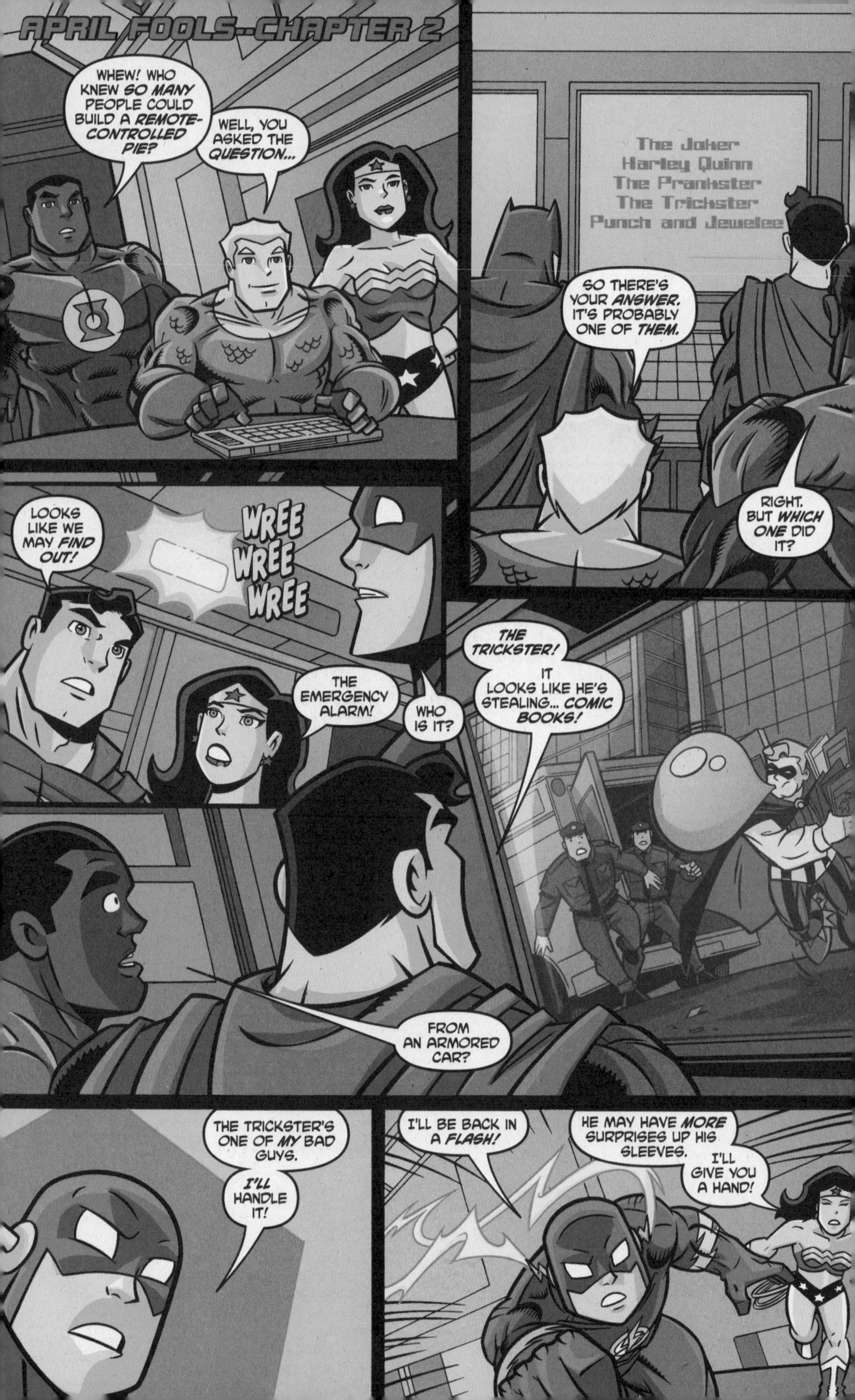
APRIL FOOLS--CHAPTER 2
WHEW! WHO KNEW SO MANY PEOPLE COULD BUILD A REMOTE-CONTROLLED PIE?
WELL, YOU ASKED THE QUESTION...
The Joker
Harley Quinn
The Prankster
The Trickster
Punch and Jewelee
SO THERE'S YOUR ANSWER. IT'S PROBABLY ONE OF THEM.
RIGHT. BUT WHICH ONE DID IT?
LOOKS LIKE WE MAY FIND OUT!
WREE WREE WREE
THE EMERGENCY ALARM!
WHO IS IT?
THE TRICKSTER!
IT LOOKS LIKE HE'S STEALING... COMIC BOOKS!
FROM AN ARMORED CAR?
THE TRICKSTER'S ONE OF MY BAD GUYS.
I'LL HANDLE IT!
I'LL BE BACK IN A FLASH!
HE MAY HAVE MORE SURPRISES UP HIS SLEEVES.
I'LL GIVE YOU A HAND!

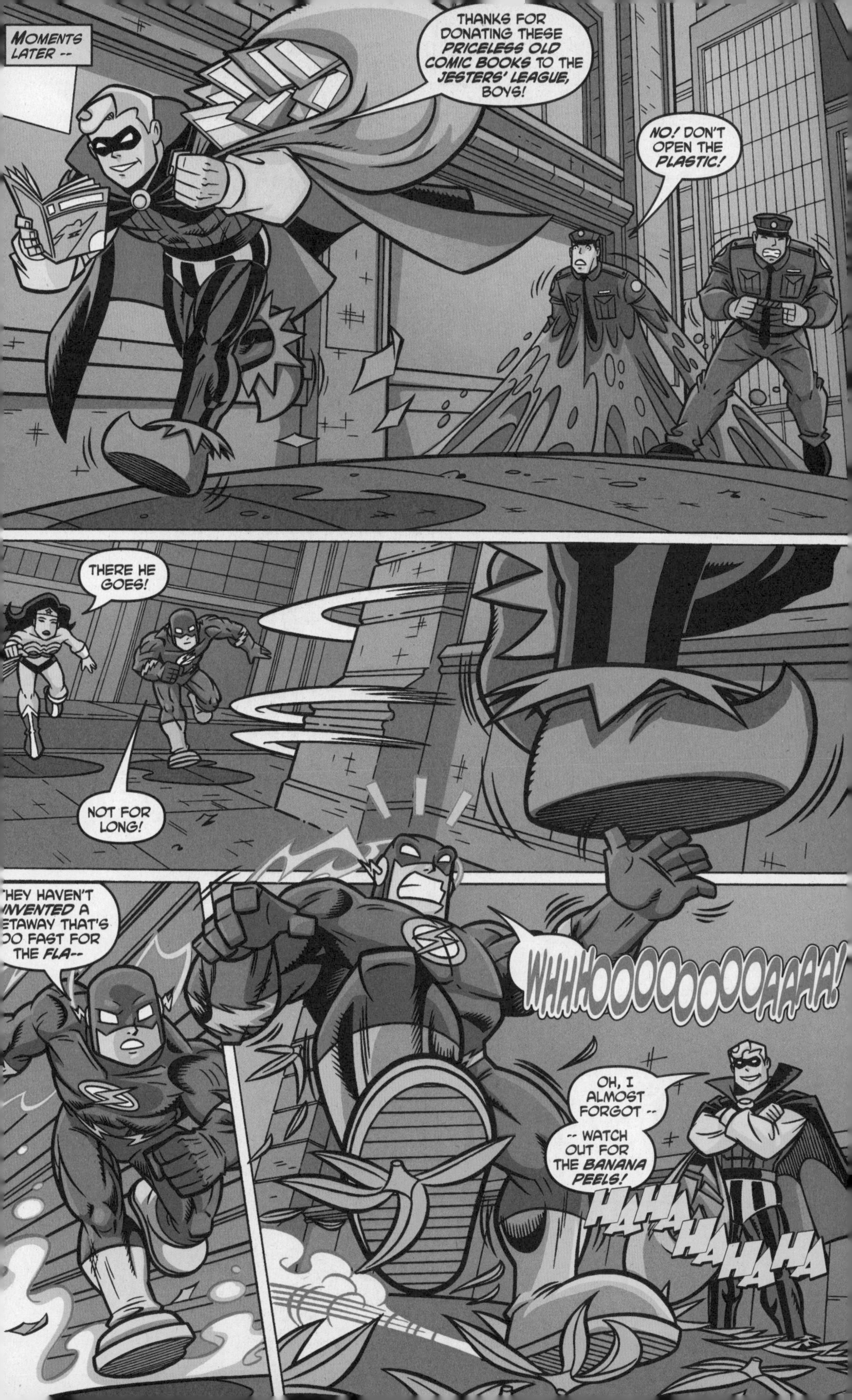
MOMENTS LATER --
THANKS FOR DONATING THESE PRICELESS OLD COMIC BOOKS TO THE JESTERS' LEAGUE, BOYS!
NO! DON'T OPEN THE PLASTIC!
THERE HE GOES!
NOT FOR LONG!
THEY HAVEN'T INVENTED A ETAWAY THAT'S OO FAST FOR THE FLA--
WHHHOOOOOOOOOAAAA!
OH, I ALMOST FORGOT --
-- WATCH OUT FOR THE BANANA PEELS!
HAHAHAHAHAHA

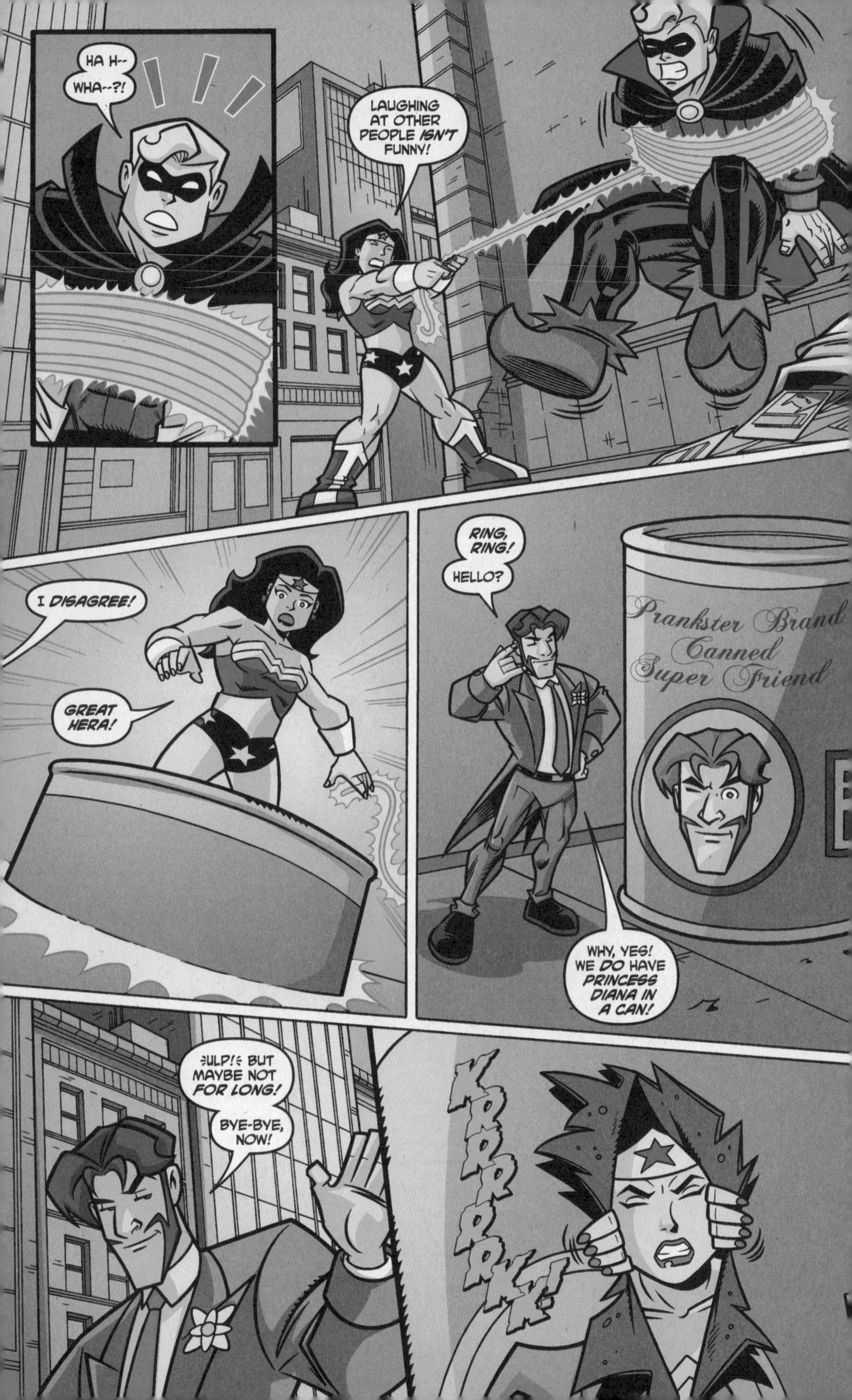
HA H--
WHA--?!
LAUGHING AT OTHER PEOPLE ISN'T FUNNY!
I DISAGREE!
GREAT HERA!
RING, RING!
HELLO?
Prankster Brand Canned Super Friend
WHY, YES! WE DO HAVE PRINCESS DIANA IN A CAN!
ULP! BUT MAYBE NOT FOR LONG!
BYE-BYE, NOW!
KRRRRRKK!

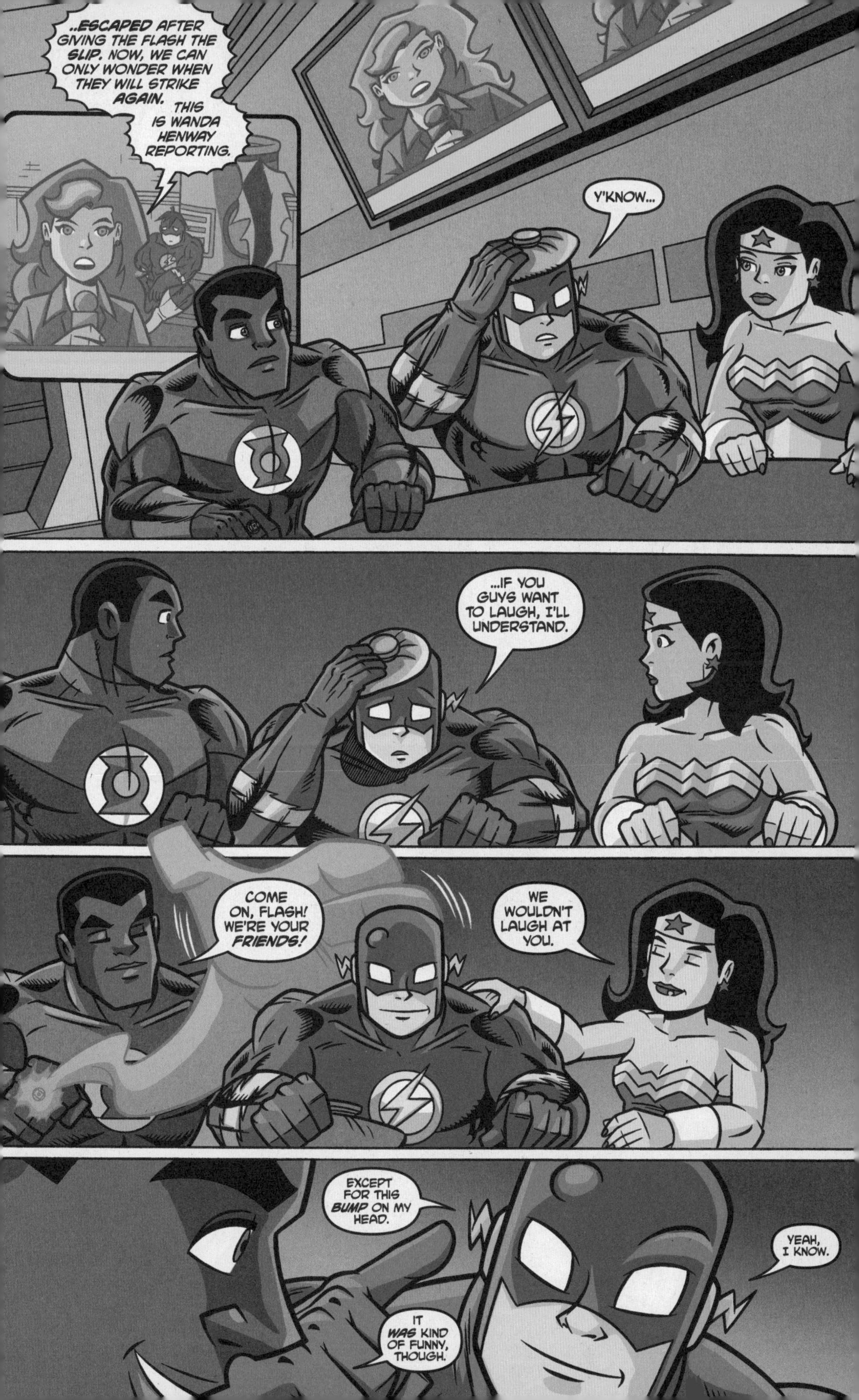
..ESCAPED AFTER GIVING THE FLASH THE SLIP. NOW, WE CAN ONLY WONDER WHEN THEY WILL STRIKE AGAIN.
THIS IS WANDA HENWAY REPORTING.
Y'KNOW...
...IF YOU GUYS WANT TO LAUGH, I'LL UNDERSTAND.
COME ON, FLASH! WE'RE YOUR FRIENDS!
WE WOULDN'T LAUGH AT YOU.
EXCEPT FOR THIS BUMP ON MY HEAD.
IT WAS KIND OF FUNNY, THOUGH.
YEAH, I KNOW.

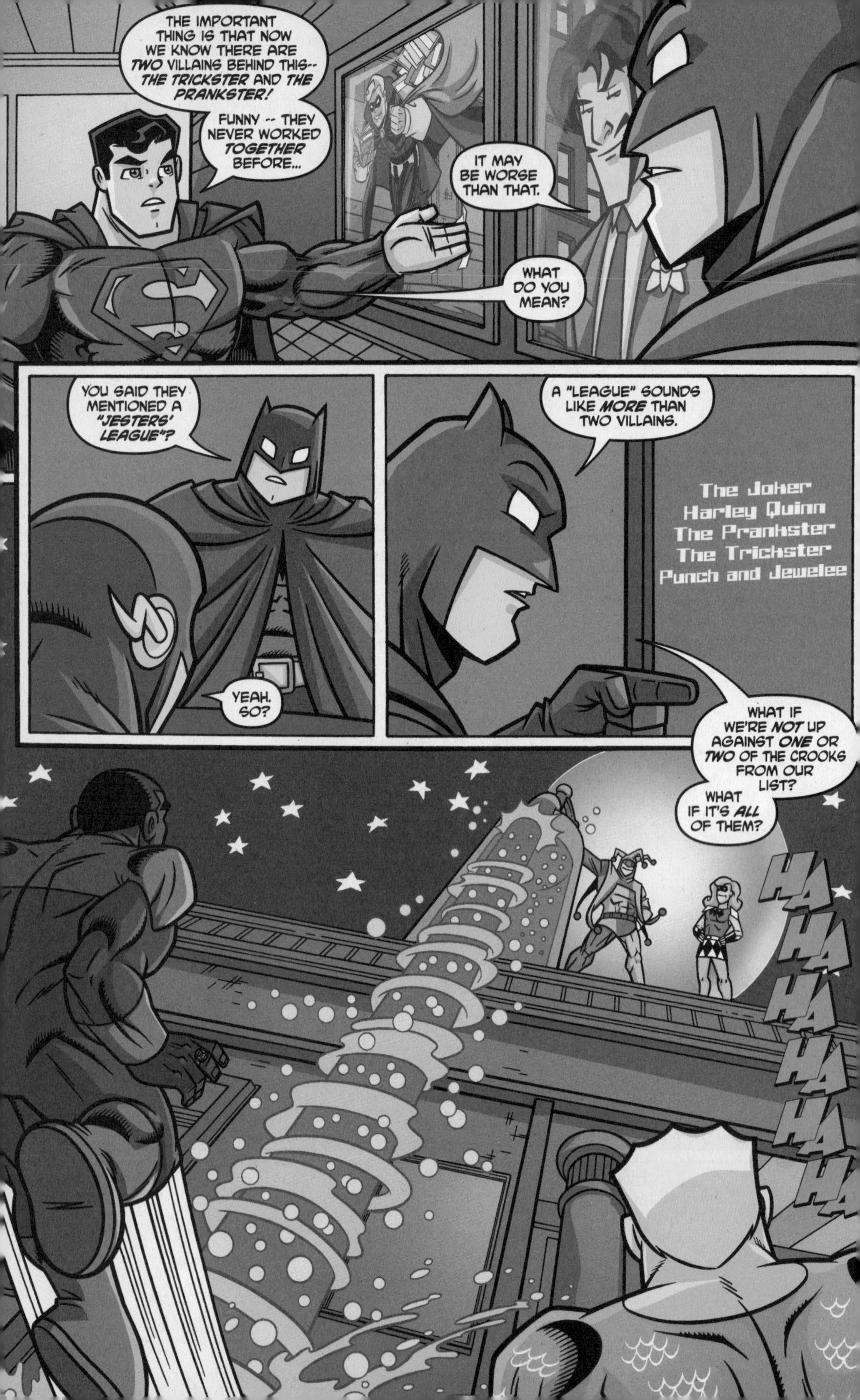
THE IMPORTANT THING IS THAT NOW WE KNOW THERE ARE *TWO* VILLAINS BEHIND THIS-- *THE TRICKSTER* AND *THE PRANKSTER!*
FUNNY -- THEY NEVER WORKED *TOGETHER* BEFORE...
IT MAY BE WORSE THAN THAT.
WHAT DO YOU MEAN?
YOU SAID THEY MENTIONED A *"JESTERS' LEAGUE"*?
YEAH. SO?
A "LEAGUE" SOUNDS LIKE *MORE* THAN TWO VILLAINS.
The Joker
Harley Quinn
The Prankster
The Trickster
Punch and Jewelee
WHAT IF WE'RE *NOT* UP AGAINST *ONE* OR *TWO* OF THE CROOKS FROM OUR LIST?
WHAT IF IT'S *ALL* OF THEM?
HAHAHAHAHAHAHA

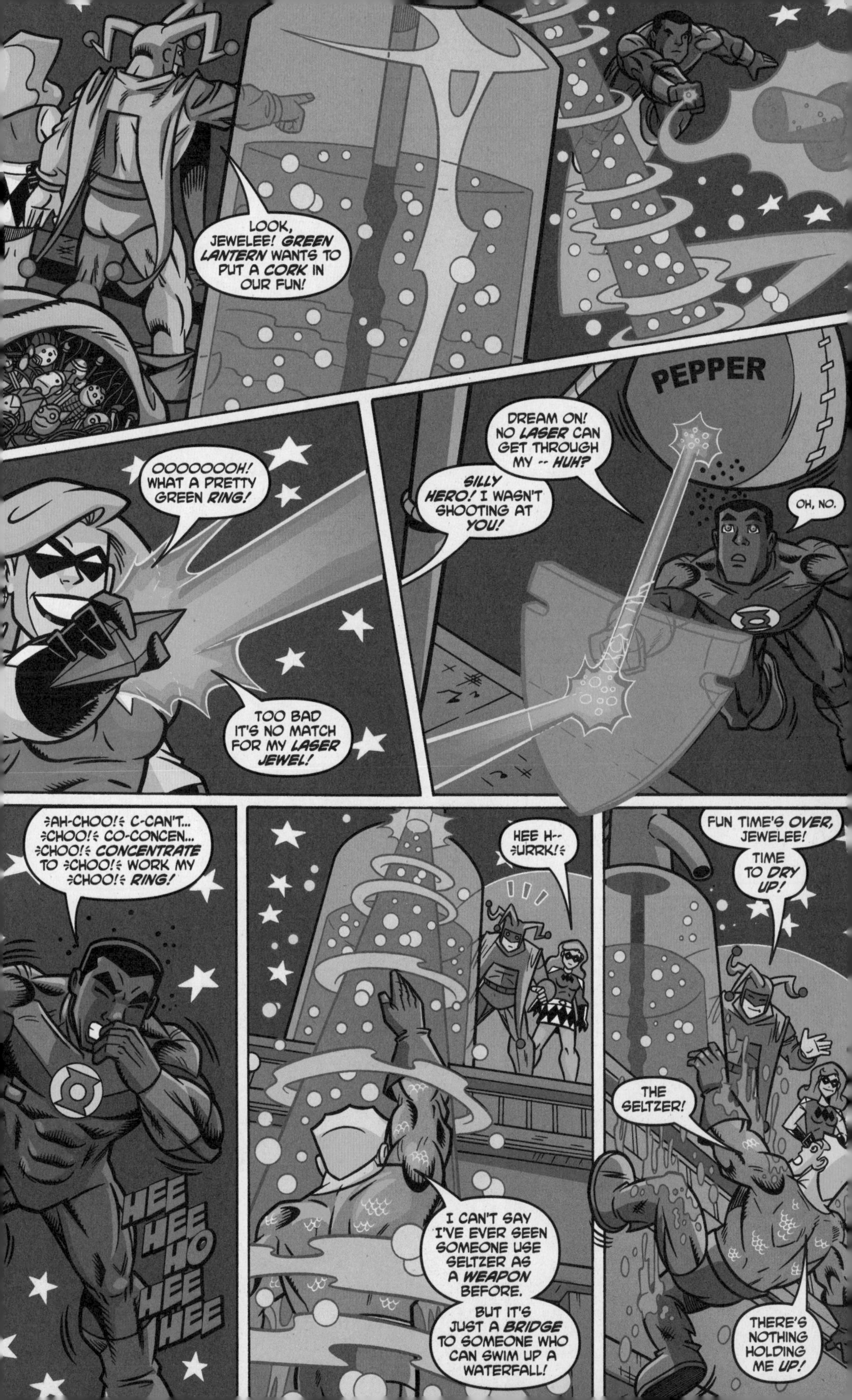
LOOK, JEWELEE! GREEN LANTERN WANTS TO PUT A CORK IN OUR FUN!
PEPPER
OOOOOOOH! WHAT A PRETTY GREEN RING!
TOO BAD IT'S NO MATCH FOR MY LASER JEWEL!
DREAM ON! NO LASER CAN GET THROUGH MY -- HUH?
SILLY HERO! I WASN'T SHOOTING AT YOU!
OH, NO.
AH-CHOO! C-CAN'T... CHOO! CO-CONCEN... CHOO! CONCENTRATE TO CHOO! WORK MY CHOO! RING!
HEE HEE HO HEE HEE
HEE H-- URRK!
I CAN'T SAY I'VE EVER SEEN SOMEONE USE SELTZER AS A WEAPON BEFORE.
BUT IT'S JUST A BRIDGE TO SOMEONE WHO CAN SWIM UP A WATERFALL!
FUN TIME'S OVER, JEWELEE!
TIME TO DRY UP!
THE SELTZER!
THERE'S NOTHING HOLDING ME UP!

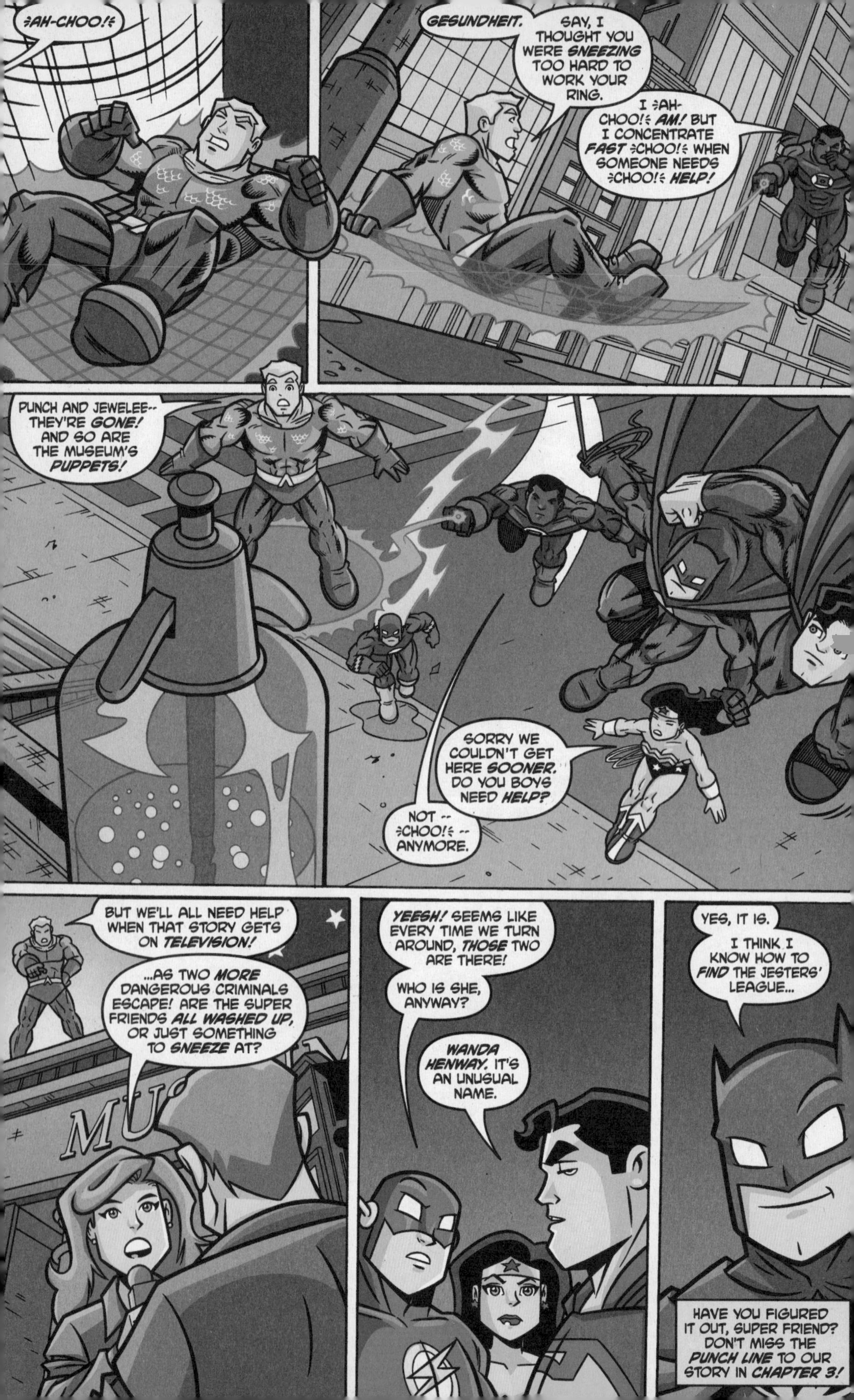

AH-CHOO!
GESUNDHEIT.
SAY, I THOUGHT YOU WERE SNEEZING TOO HARD TO WORK YOUR RING.
I AH-CHOO! AM! BUT I CONCENTRATE FAST CHOO! WHEN SOMEONE NEEDS CHOO! HELP!
PUNCH AND JEWELEE-- THEY'RE GONE! AND SO ARE THE MUSEUM'S PUPPETS!
SORRY WE COULDN'T GET HERE SOONER. DO YOU BOYS NEED HELP?
NOT -- CHOO! -- ANYMORE.
BUT WE'LL ALL NEED HELP WHEN THAT STORY GETS ON TELEVISION!
...AS TWO MORE DANGEROUS CRIMINALS ESCAPE! ARE THE SUPER FRIENDS ALL WASHED UP, OR JUST SOMETHING TO SNEEZE AT?
MU
YEESH! SEEMS LIKE EVERY TIME WE TURN AROUND, THOSE TWO ARE THERE!
WHO IS SHE, ANYWAY?
WANDA HENWAY. IT'S AN UNUSUAL NAME.
YES, IT IS.
I THINK I KNOW HOW TO FIND THE JESTERS' LEAGUE...
HAVE YOU FIGURED IT OUT, SUPER FRIEND? DON'T MISS THE PUNCH LINE TO OUR STORY IN CHAPTER 3!

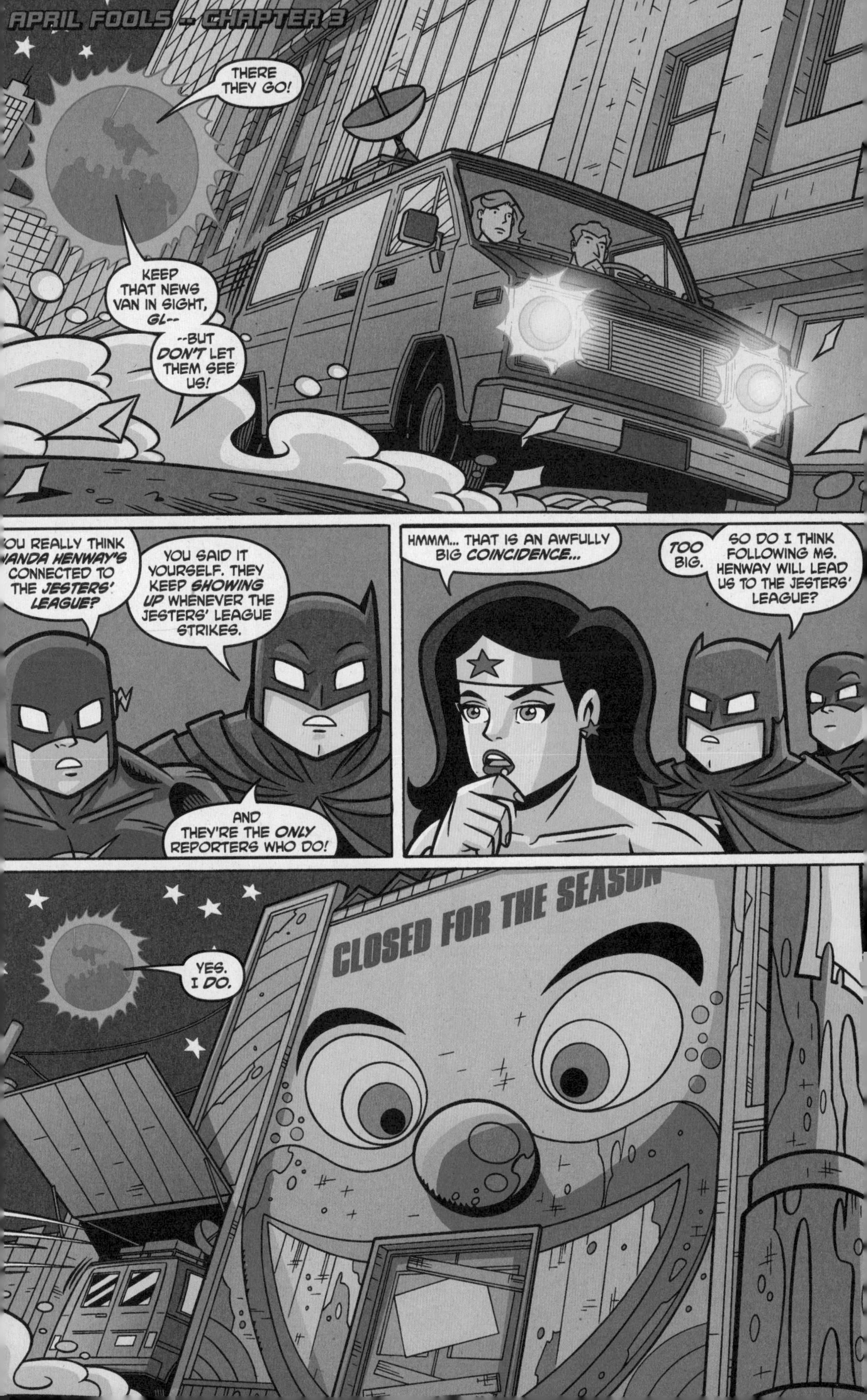
THERE THEY GO!
KEEP THAT NEWS VAN IN SIGHT, GL--
--BUT DON'T LET THEM SEE US!
YOU REALLY THINK WANDA HENWAY'S CONNECTED TO THE JESTERS' LEAGUE?
YOU SAID IT YOURSELF. THEY KEEP SHOWING UP WHENEVER THE JESTERS' LEAGUE STRIKES.
AND THEY'RE THE ONLY REPORTERS WHO DO!
HMMM... THAT IS AN AWFULLY BIG COINCIDENCE...
TOO BIG.
SO DO I THINK FOLLOWING MS. HENWAY WILL LEAD US TO THE JESTERS' LEAGUE?
YES. I DO.
CLOSED FOR THE SEASON

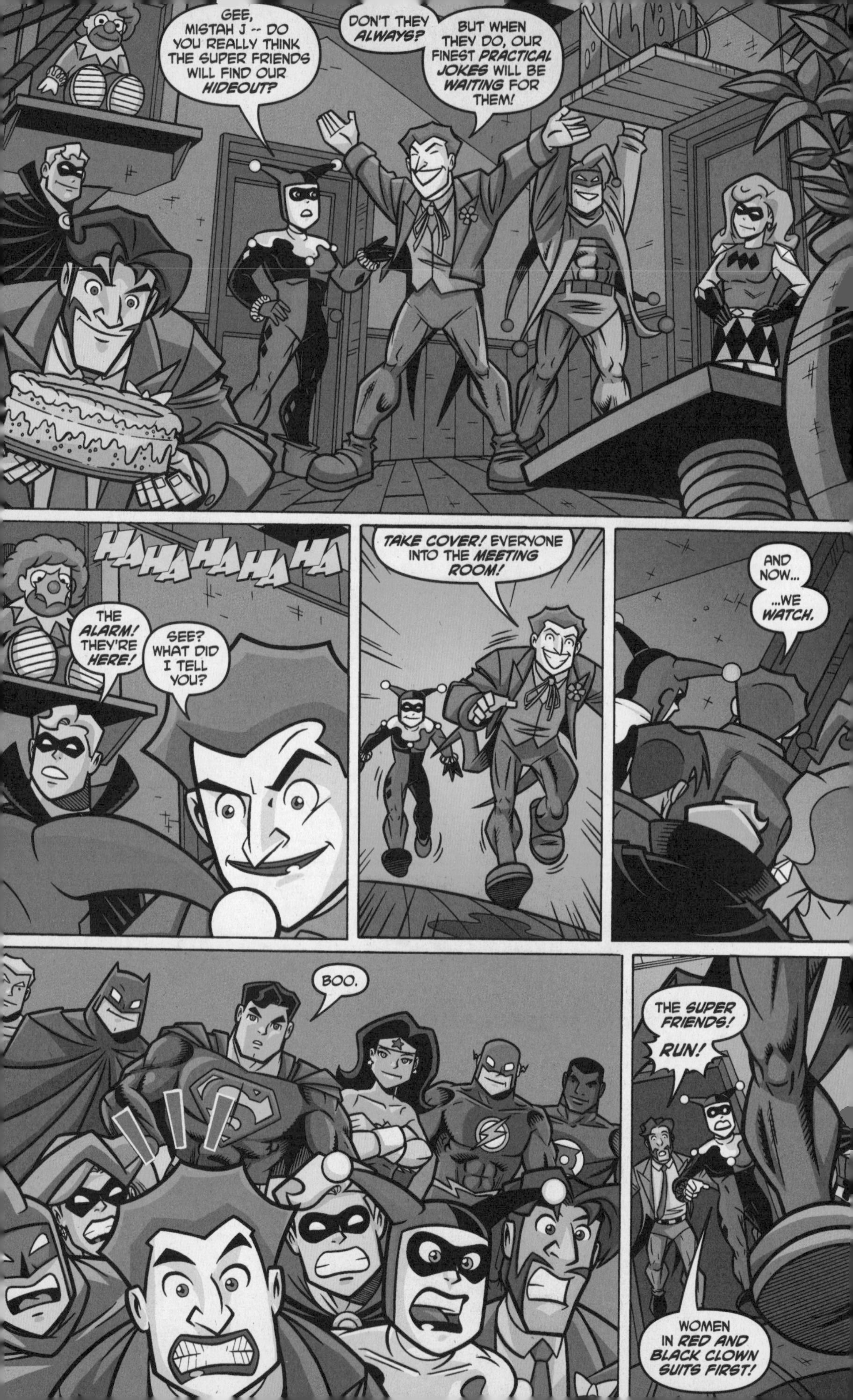
GEE, MISTAH J -- DO YOU REALLY THINK THE SUPER FRIENDS WILL FIND OUR *HIDEOUT?*
DON'T THEY *ALWAYS?*
BUT WHEN THEY DO, OUR FINEST *PRACTICAL JOKES* WILL BE *WAITING* FOR THEM!
HAHAHAHAHAHA
THE *ALARM!* THEY'RE *HERE!*
SEE? WHAT DID I TELL YOU?
TAKE COVER! EVERYONE INTO THE *MEETING ROOM!*
AND NOW...
...WE *WATCH.*
BOO.
!!!
THE *SUPER FRIENDS!*
RUN!
WOMEN IN *RED AND BLACK CLOWN SUITS FIRST!*

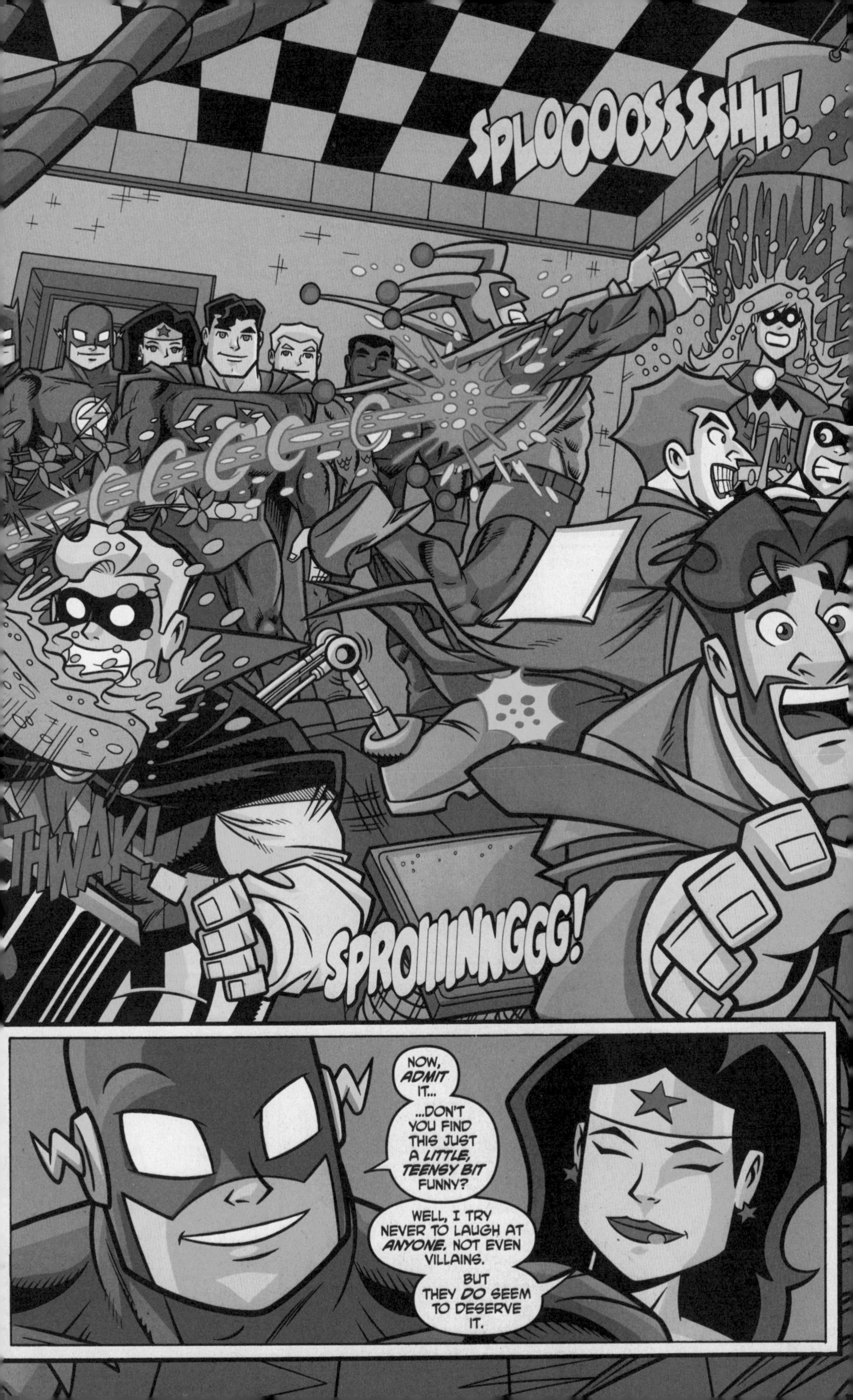
SPLOOOOSSSSHH!
THWAK!
SPROIIIINNGGG!
NOW, ADMIT IT...
...DON'T YOU FIND THIS JUST A LITTLE, TEENSY BIT FUNNY?
WELL, I TRY NEVER TO LAUGH AT ANYONE. NOT EVEN VILLAINS.
BUT THEY DO SEEM TO DESERVE IT.

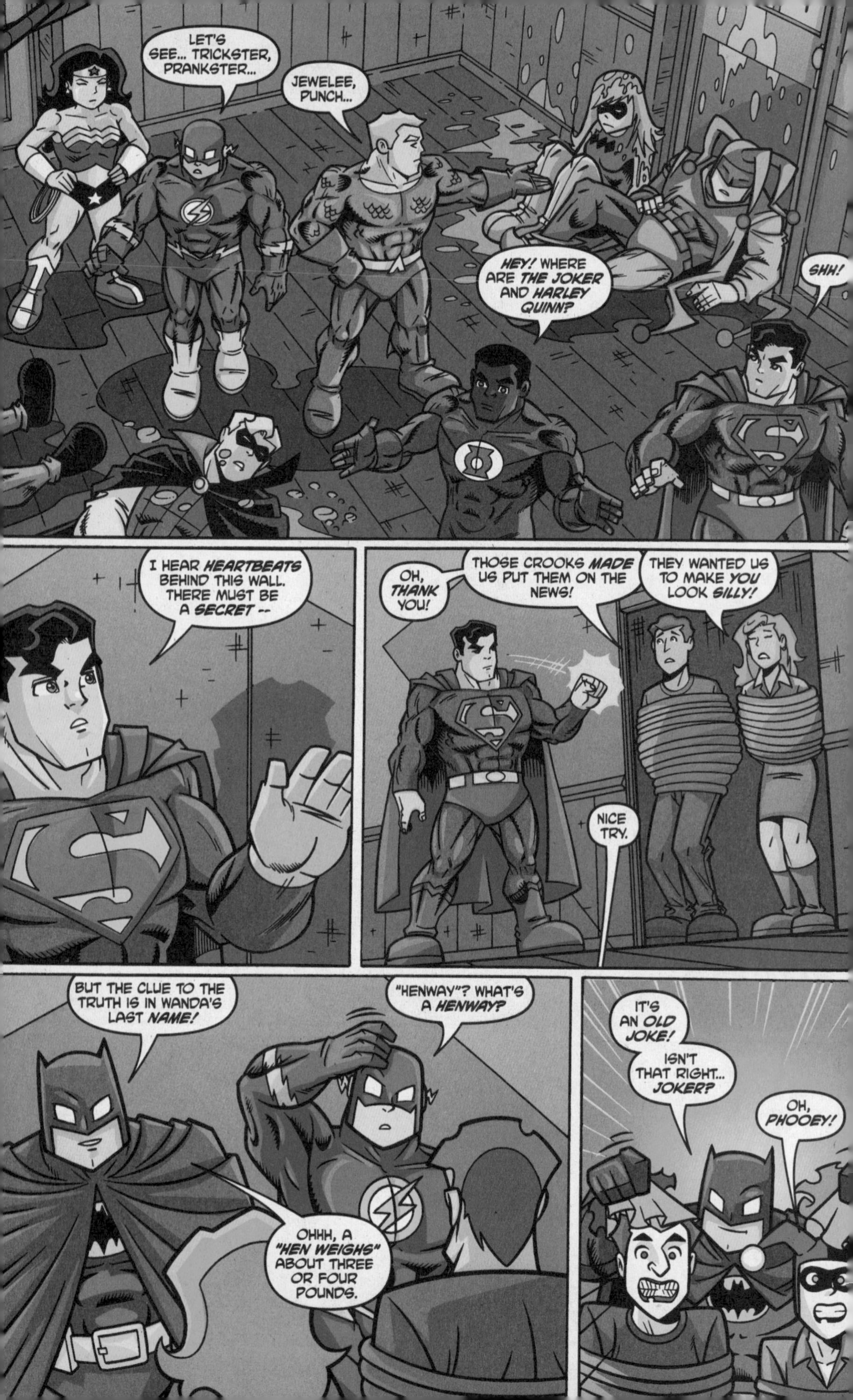
LET'S SEE... TRICKSTER, PRANKSTER...
JEWELEE, PUNCH...
HEY! WHERE ARE THE JOKER AND HARLEY QUINN?
SHH!
I HEAR HEARTBEATS BEHIND THIS WALL. THERE MUST BE A SECRET --
OH, THANK YOU!
THOSE CROOKS MADE US PUT THEM ON THE NEWS!
THEY WANTED US TO MAKE YOU LOOK SILLY!
NICE TRY.
BUT THE CLUE TO THE TRUTH IS IN WANDA'S LAST NAME!
"HENWAY"? WHAT'S A HENWAY?
OHHH, A "HEN WEIGHS" ABOUT THREE OR FOUR POUNDS.
IT'S AN OLD JOKE!
ISN'T THAT RIGHT... JOKER?
OH, PHOOEY!

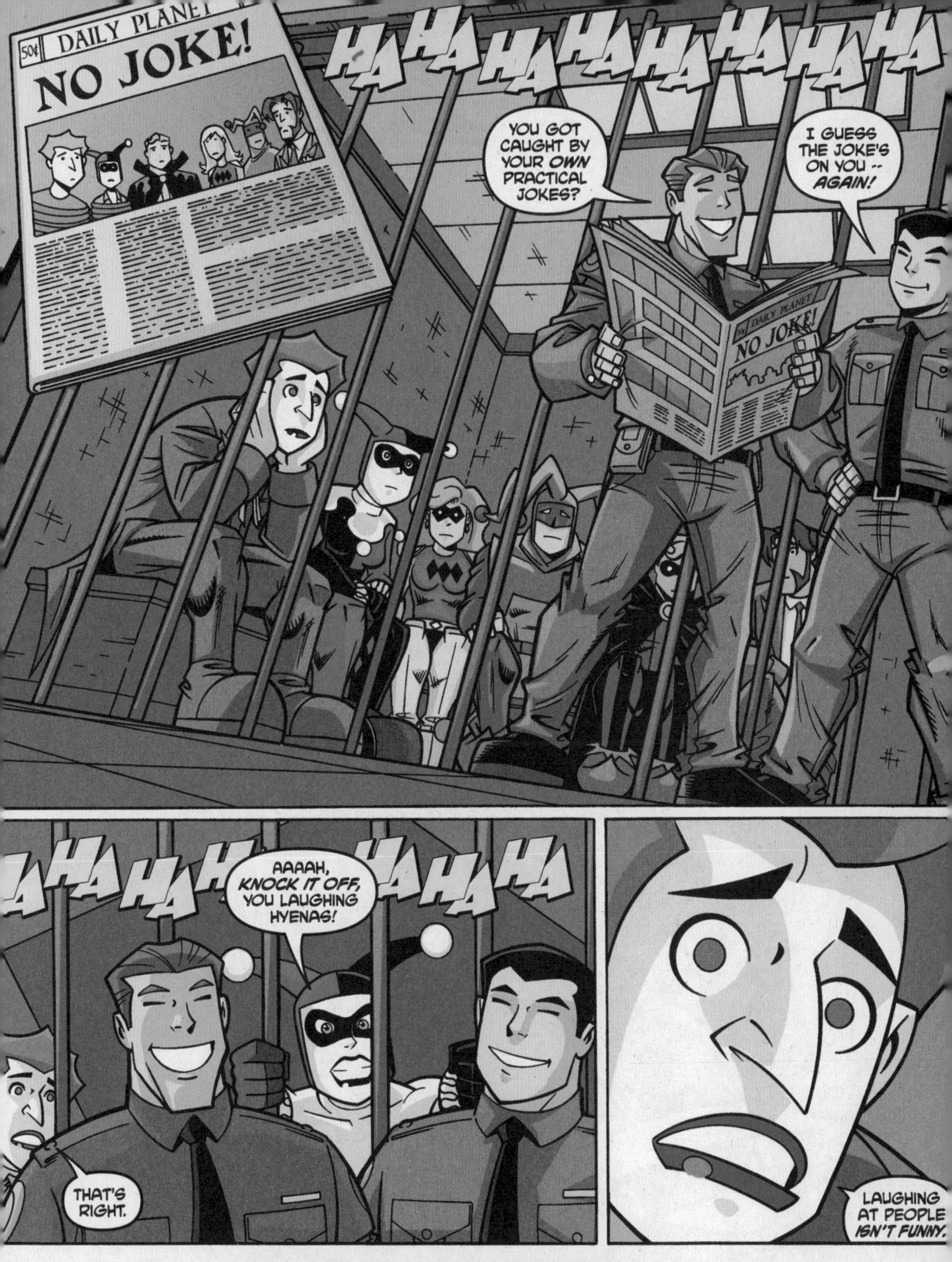
DAILY PLANET
50¢
NO JOKE!
HA HA HA HA HA HA HA HA HA HA
YOU GOT CAUGHT BY YOUR *OWN* PRACTICAL JOKES?
I GUESS THE JOKE'S ON YOU -- *AGAIN!*
NO JOKE!
HA HA HA HA HA HA HA HA
AAAAH, *KNOCK IT OFF,* YOU LAUGHING HYENAS!
THAT'S RIGHT.
LAUGHING AT PEOPLE *ISN'T FUNNY.*

ATTENTION, SUPER FRIENDS!

Here's another secret message:

XOLI DBXIN, INO PEVOY CYSOXRP TSPSI
QBYSZZK MSIW CBY PBDO "DBXUOW HEPSXOPP!"

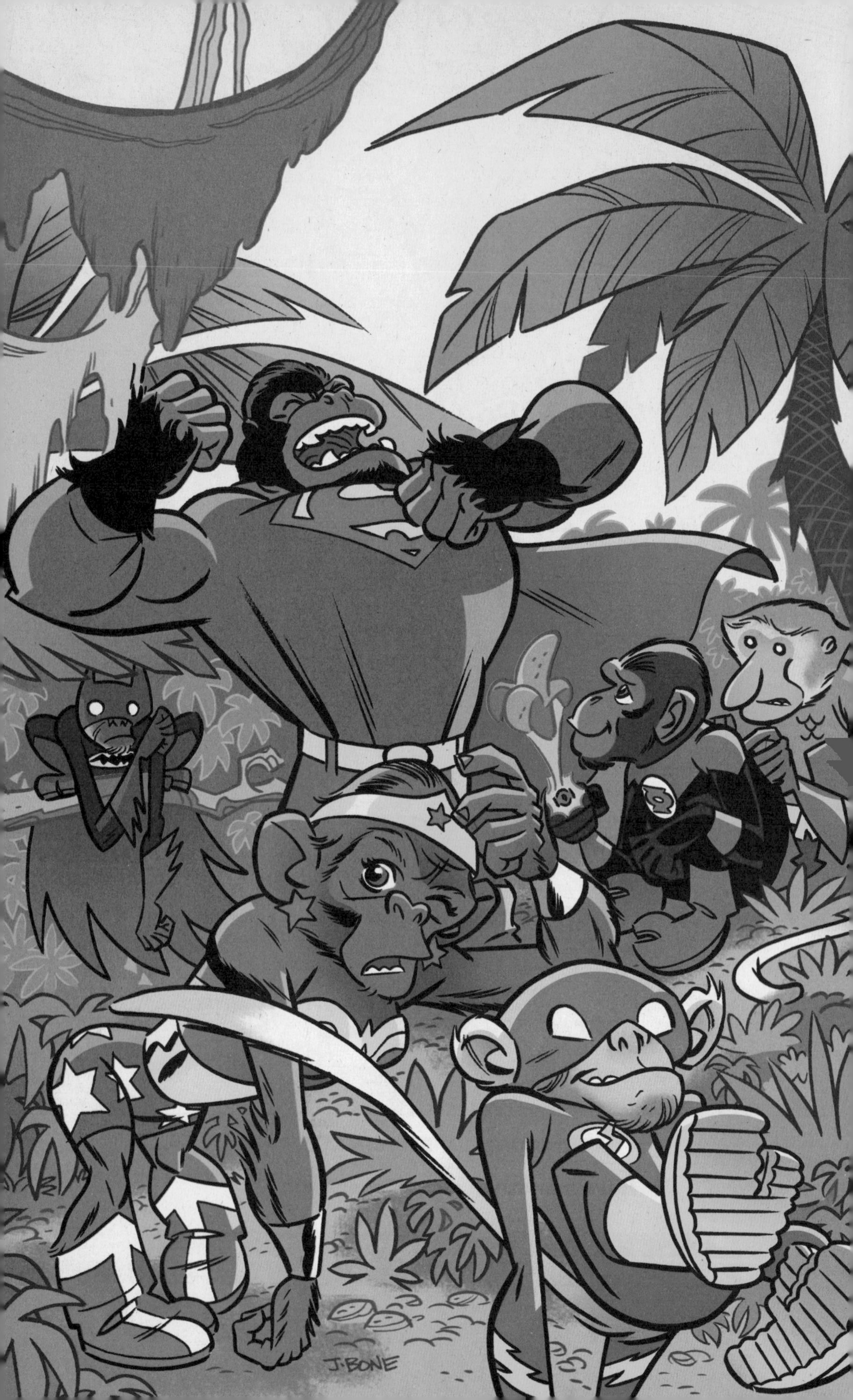
J.BONE

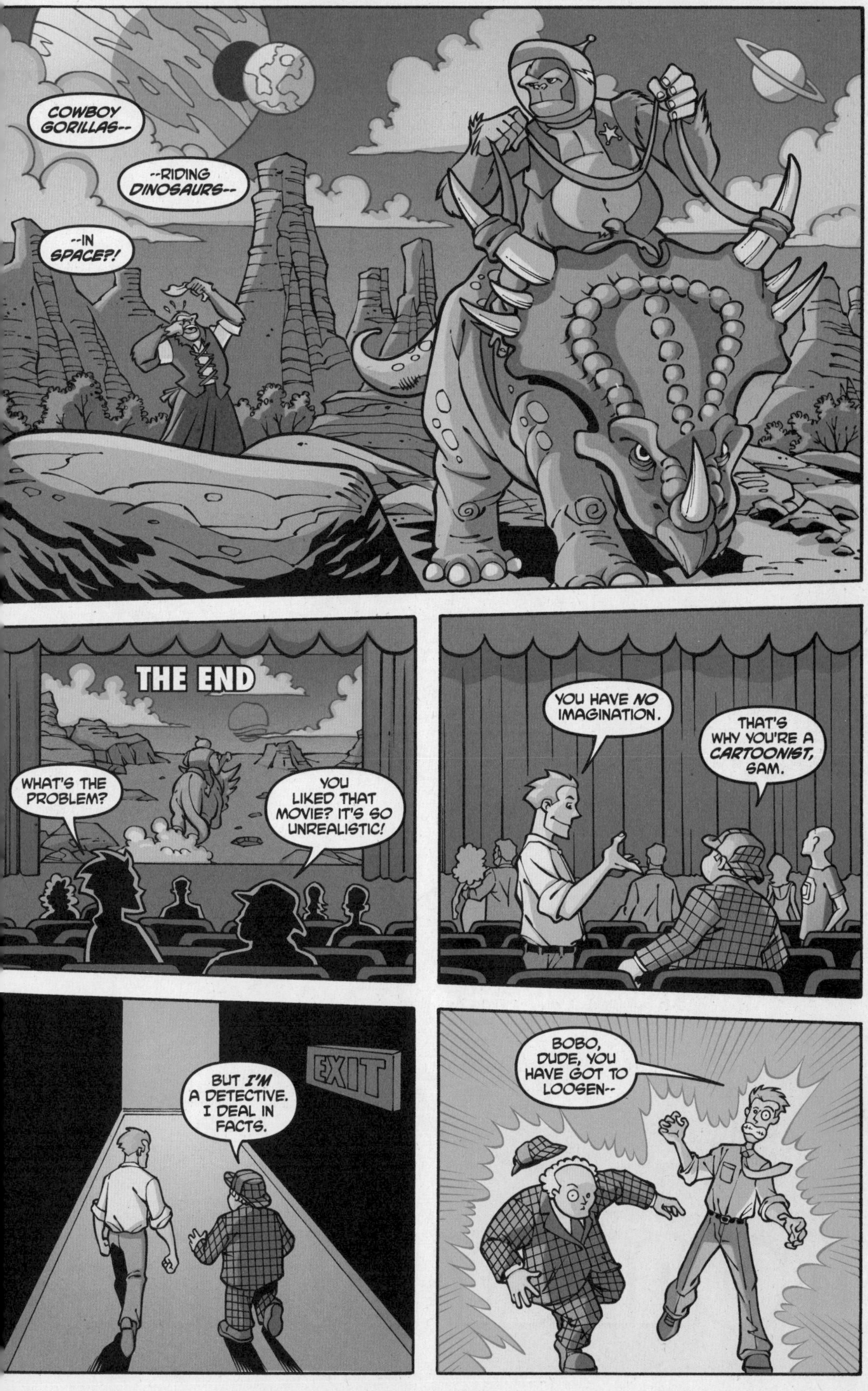
COWBOY GORILLAS--
--RIDING DINOSAURS--
--IN SPACE?!
THE END
WHAT'S THE PROBLEM?
YOU LIKED THAT MOVIE? IT'S SO UNREALISTIC!
YOU HAVE NO IMAGINATION.
THAT'S WHY YOU'RE A CARTOONIST, SAM.
BUT I'M A DETECTIVE. I DEAL IN FACTS.
EXIT
BOBO, DUDE, YOU HAVE GOT TO LOOSEN--

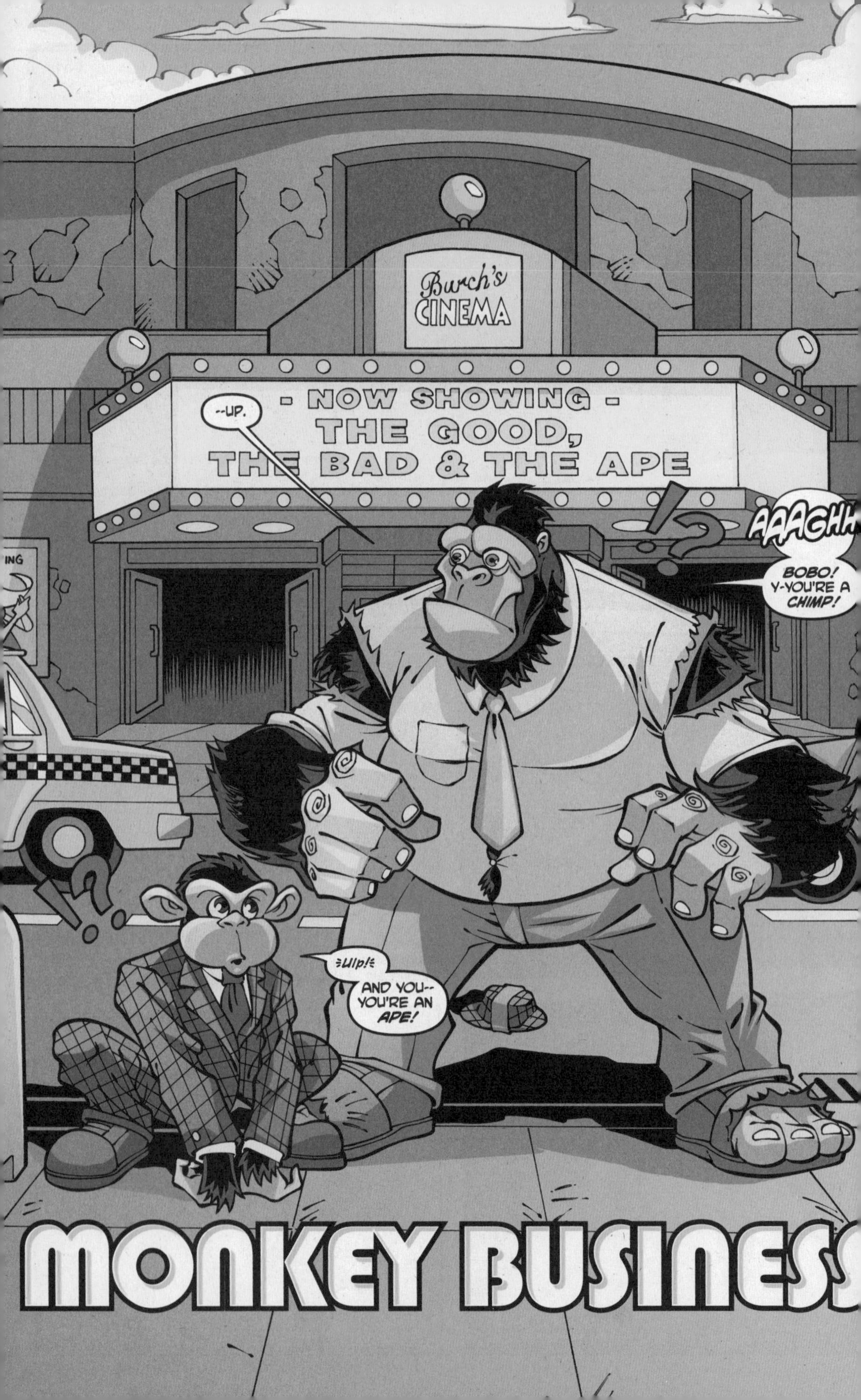
Burch's CINEMA
- NOW SHOWING -
THE GOOD, THE BAD & THE APE
--UP.
!?
AAAGHH
BOBO! Y-YOU'RE A CHIMP!
!?
ULP!
AND YOU-- YOU'RE AN APE!
MONKEY BUSINESS

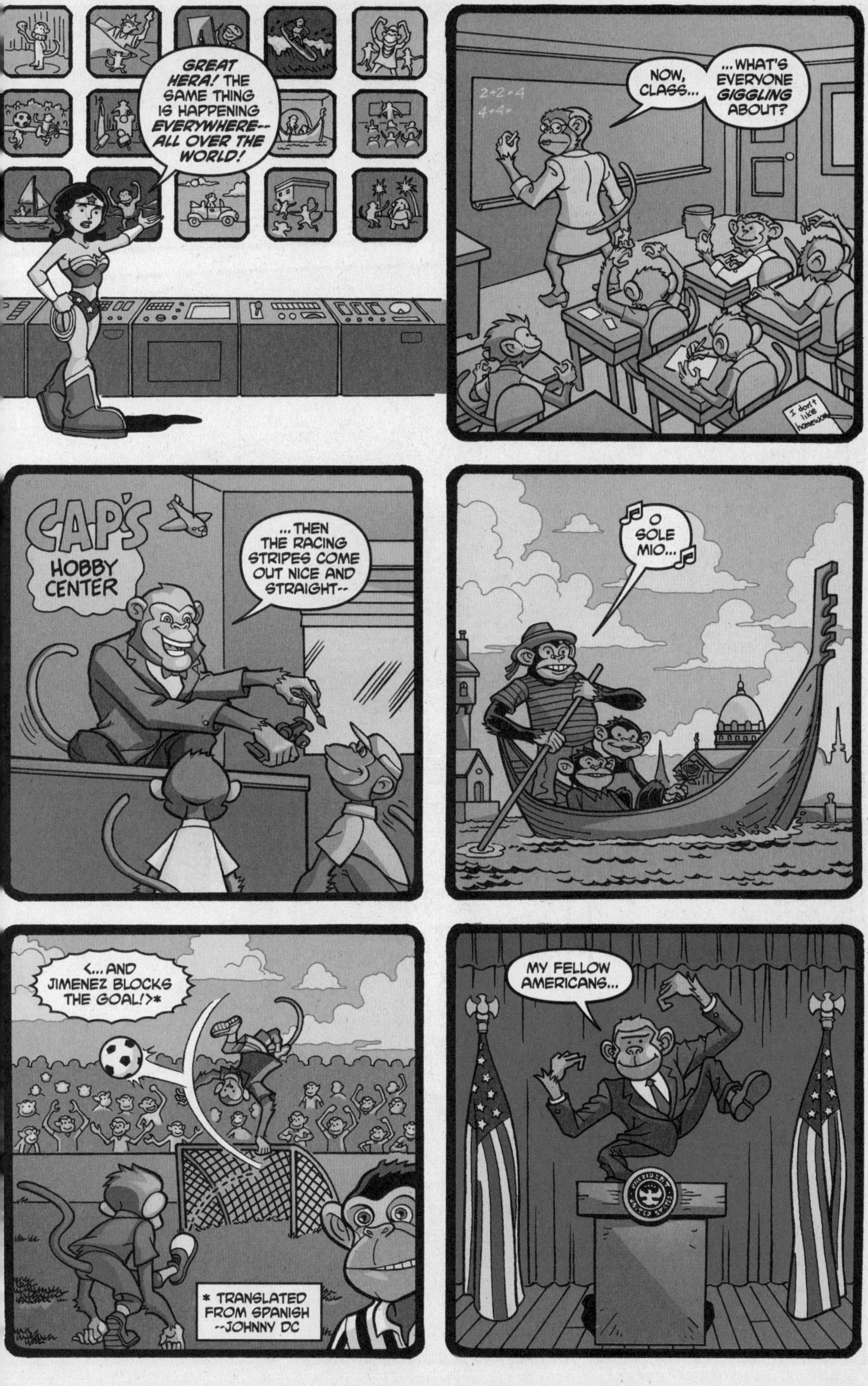
GREAT HERA! THE SAME THING IS HAPPENING EVERYWHERE-- ALL OVER THE WORLD!
2+2=4
4+4=
NOW, CLASS...
...WHAT'S EVERYONE GIGGLING ABOUT?
I don't like
CAP'S HOBBY CENTER
...THEN THE RACING STRIPES COME OUT NICE AND STRAIGHT--
O SOLE MIO...
<...AND JIMENEZ BLOCKS THE GOAL!>*
* TRANSLATED FROM SPANISH --JOHNNY DC
MY FELLOW AMERICANS...

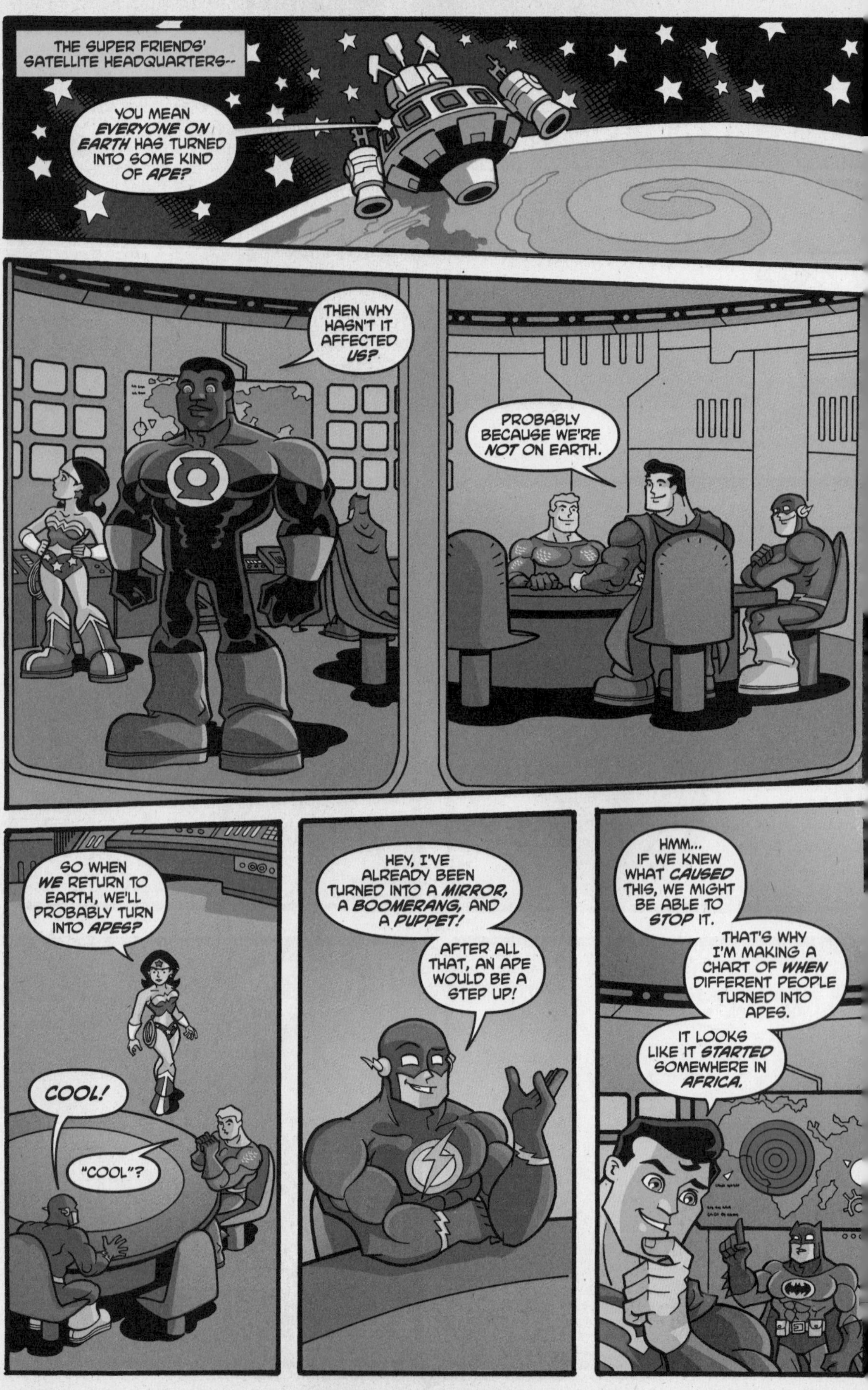
THE SUPER FRIENDS' SATELLITE HEADQUARTERS--
YOU MEAN EVERYONE ON EARTH HAS TURNED INTO SOME KIND OF APE?
THEN WHY HASN'T IT AFFECTED US?
PROBABLY BECAUSE WE'RE NOT ON EARTH.
SO WHEN WE RETURN TO EARTH, WE'LL PROBABLY TURN INTO APES?
COOL!
"COOL"?
HEY, I'VE ALREADY BEEN TURNED INTO A MIRROR, A BOOMERANG, AND A PUPPET!
AFTER ALL THAT, AN APE WOULD BE A STEP UP!
HMM... IF WE KNEW WHAT CAUSED THIS, WE MIGHT BE ABLE TO STOP IT.
THAT'S WHY I'M MAKING A CHART OF WHEN DIFFERENT PEOPLE TURNED INTO APES.
IT LOOKS LIKE IT STARTED SOMEWHERE IN AFRICA.

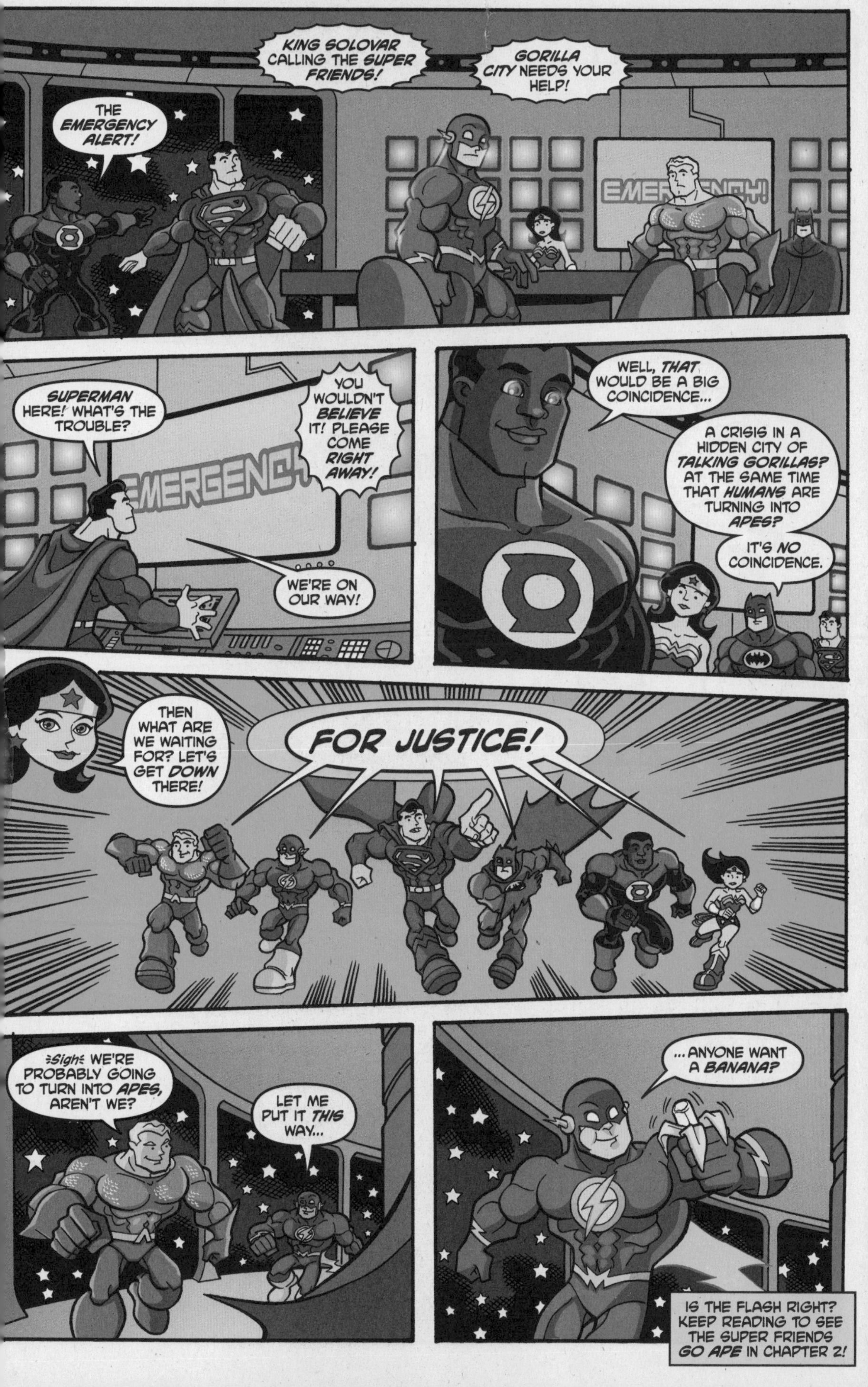
KING SOLOVAR CALLING THE SUPER FRIENDS!
GORILLA CITY NEEDS YOUR HELP!
THE EMERGENCY ALERT!
EMERGENCY!
SUPERMAN HERE! WHAT'S THE TROUBLE?
YOU WOULDN'T BELIEVE IT! PLEASE COME RIGHT AWAY!
WE'RE ON OUR WAY!
WELL, THAT WOULD BE A BIG COINCIDENCE...
A CRISIS IN A HIDDEN CITY OF TALKING GORILLAS? AT THE SAME TIME THAT HUMANS ARE TURNING INTO APES?
IT'S NO COINCIDENCE.
THEN WHAT ARE WE WAITING FOR? LET'S GET DOWN THERE!
FOR JUSTICE!
Sigh WE'RE PROBABLY GOING TO TURN INTO APES, AREN'T WE?
LET ME PUT IT THIS WAY...
...ANYONE WANT A BANANA?
IS THE FLASH RIGHT? KEEP READING TO SEE THE SUPER FRIENDS GO APE IN CHAPTER 2!

MONKEY BUSINESS CHAPTER 2

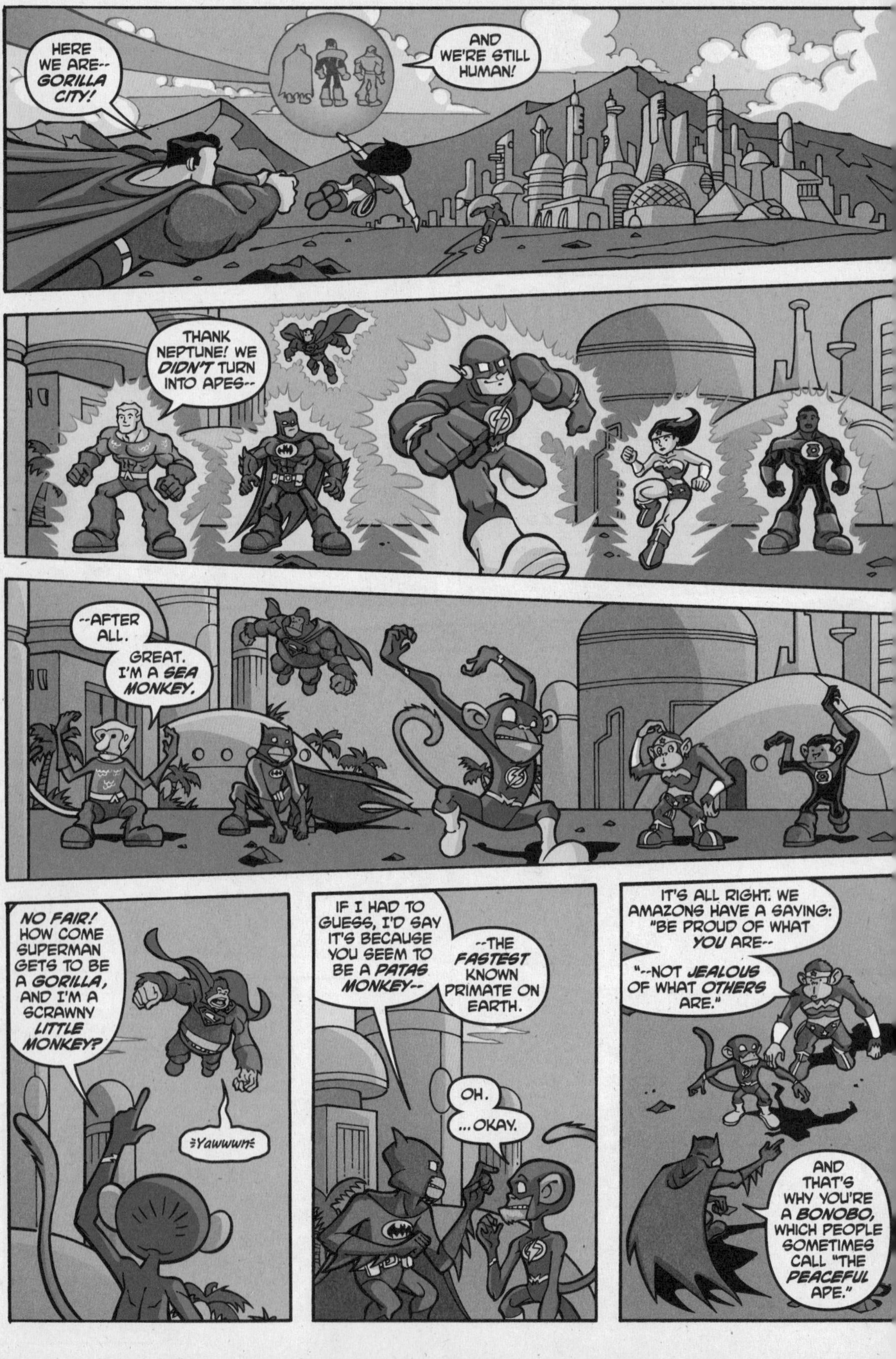

HERE WE ARE-- GORILLA CITY!
AND WE'RE STILL HUMAN!
THANK NEPTUNE! WE DIDN'T TURN INTO APES--
--AFTER ALL.
GREAT. I'M A SEA MONKEY.
NO FAIR! HOW COME SUPERMAN GETS TO BE A GORILLA, AND I'M A SCRAWNY LITTLE MONKEY?
Yawwwn
IF I HAD TO GUESS, I'D SAY IT'S BECAUSE YOU SEEM TO BE A PATAS MONKEY--
--THE FASTEST KNOWN PRIMATE ON EARTH.
OH.
...OKAY.
IT'S ALL RIGHT. WE AMAZONS HAVE A SAYING: "BE PROUD OF WHAT YOU ARE--
"--NOT JEALOUS OF WHAT OTHERS ARE."
AND THAT'S WHY YOU'RE A BONOBO, WHICH PEOPLE SOMETIMES CALL "THE PEACEFUL APE."

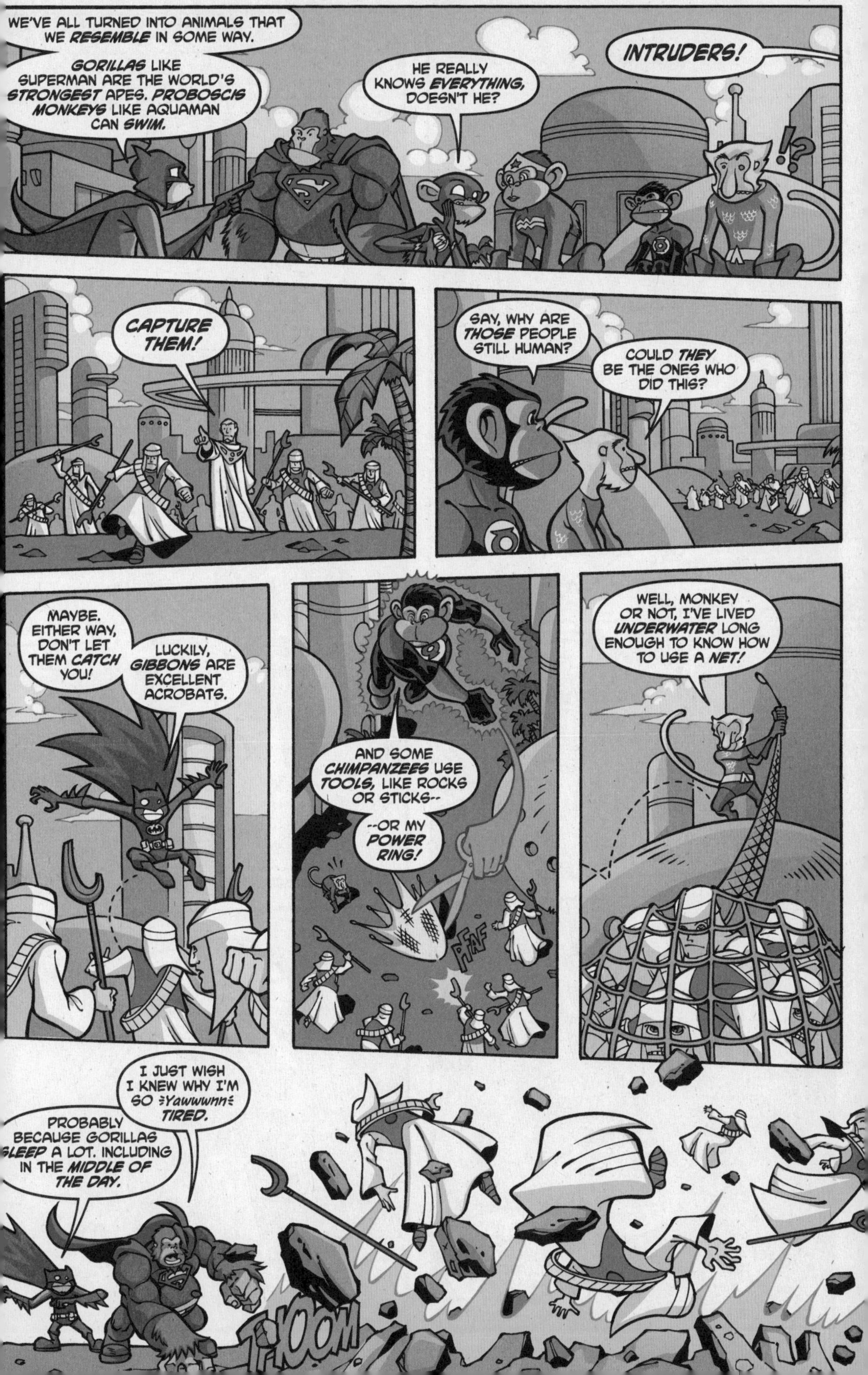

WE'VE ALL TURNED INTO ANIMALS THAT WE *RESEMBLE* IN SOME WAY.
GORILLAS LIKE SUPERMAN ARE THE WORLD'S *STRONGEST* APES. *PROBOSCIS MONKEYS* LIKE AQUAMAN CAN *SWIM.*
HE REALLY KNOWS *EVERYTHING,* DOESN'T HE?
INTRUDERS!
!?
CAPTURE THEM!
SAY, WHY ARE *THOSE* PEOPLE STILL HUMAN?
COULD *THEY* BE THE ONES WHO DID THIS?
MAYBE. EITHER WAY, DON'T LET THEM *CATCH* YOU!
LUCKILY, *GIBBONS* ARE EXCELLENT ACROBATS.
AND SOME *CHIMPANZEES* USE *TOOLS,* LIKE ROCKS OR STICKS--
--OR MY *POWER RING!*
FFAF
WELL, MONKEY OR NOT, I'VE LIVED *UNDERWATER* LONG ENOUGH TO KNOW HOW TO USE A *NET!*
I JUST WISH I KNEW WHY I'M SO *Yawwwnn* *TIRED.*
PROBABLY BECAUSE GORILLAS *SLEEP* A LOT. INCLUDING IN THE *MIDDLE OF THE DAY.*
THOOM

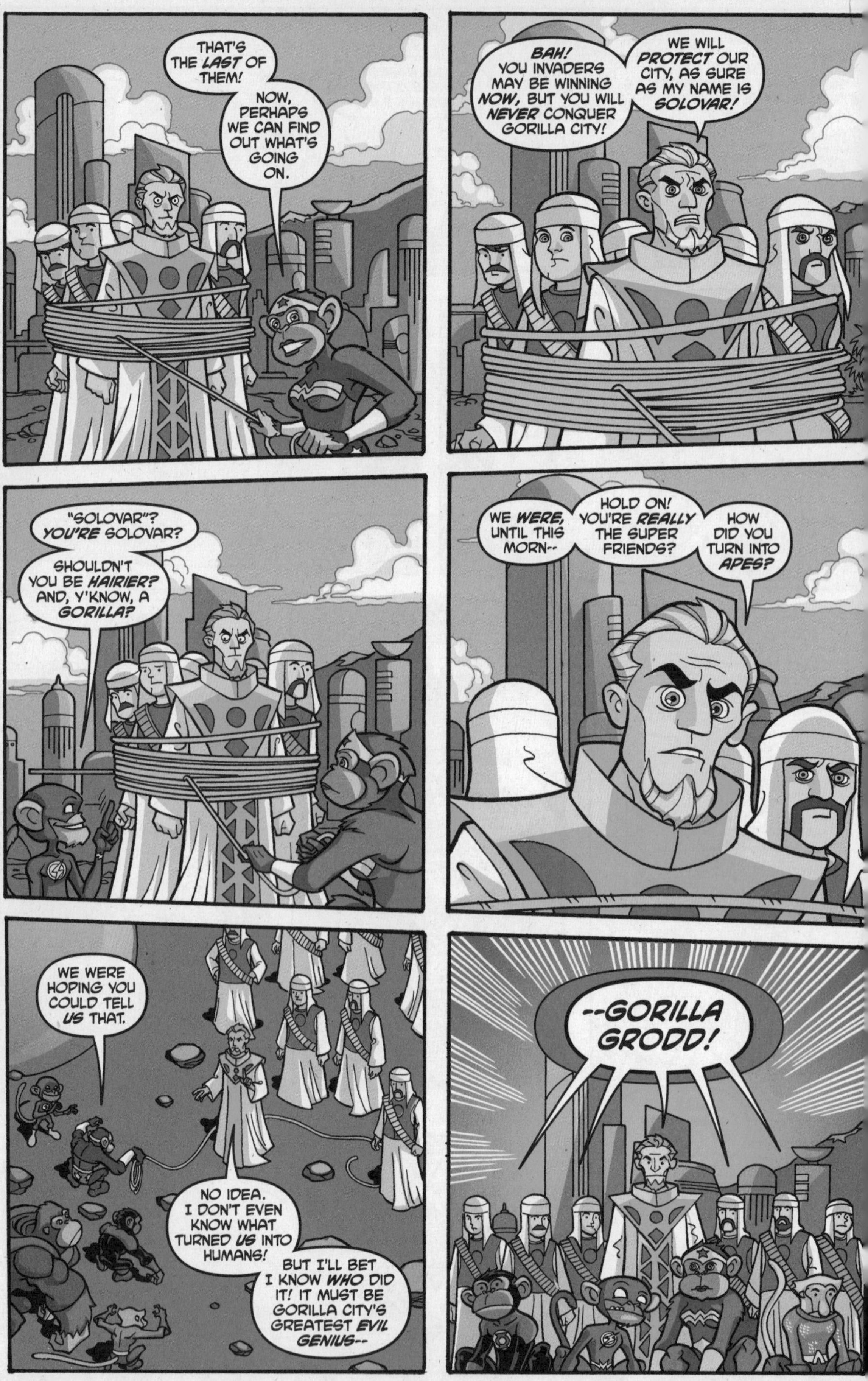
THAT'S THE LAST OF THEM!
NOW, PERHAPS WE CAN FIND OUT WHAT'S GOING ON.
BAH! YOU INVADERS MAY BE WINNING NOW, BUT YOU WILL NEVER CONQUER GORILLA CITY!
WE WILL PROTECT OUR CITY, AS SURE AS MY NAME IS SOLOVAR!
"SOLOVAR"? YOU'RE SOLOVAR?
SHOULDN'T YOU BE HAIRIER? AND, Y'KNOW, A GORILLA?
WE WERE, UNTIL THIS MORN--
HOLD ON! YOU'RE REALLY THE SUPER FRIENDS?
HOW DID YOU TURN INTO APES?
WE WERE HOPING YOU COULD TELL US THAT.
NO IDEA. I DON'T EVEN KNOW WHAT TURNED US INTO HUMANS!
BUT I'LL BET I KNOW WHO DID IT! IT MUST BE GORILLA CITY'S GREATEST EVIL GENIUS--
--GORILLA GRODD!

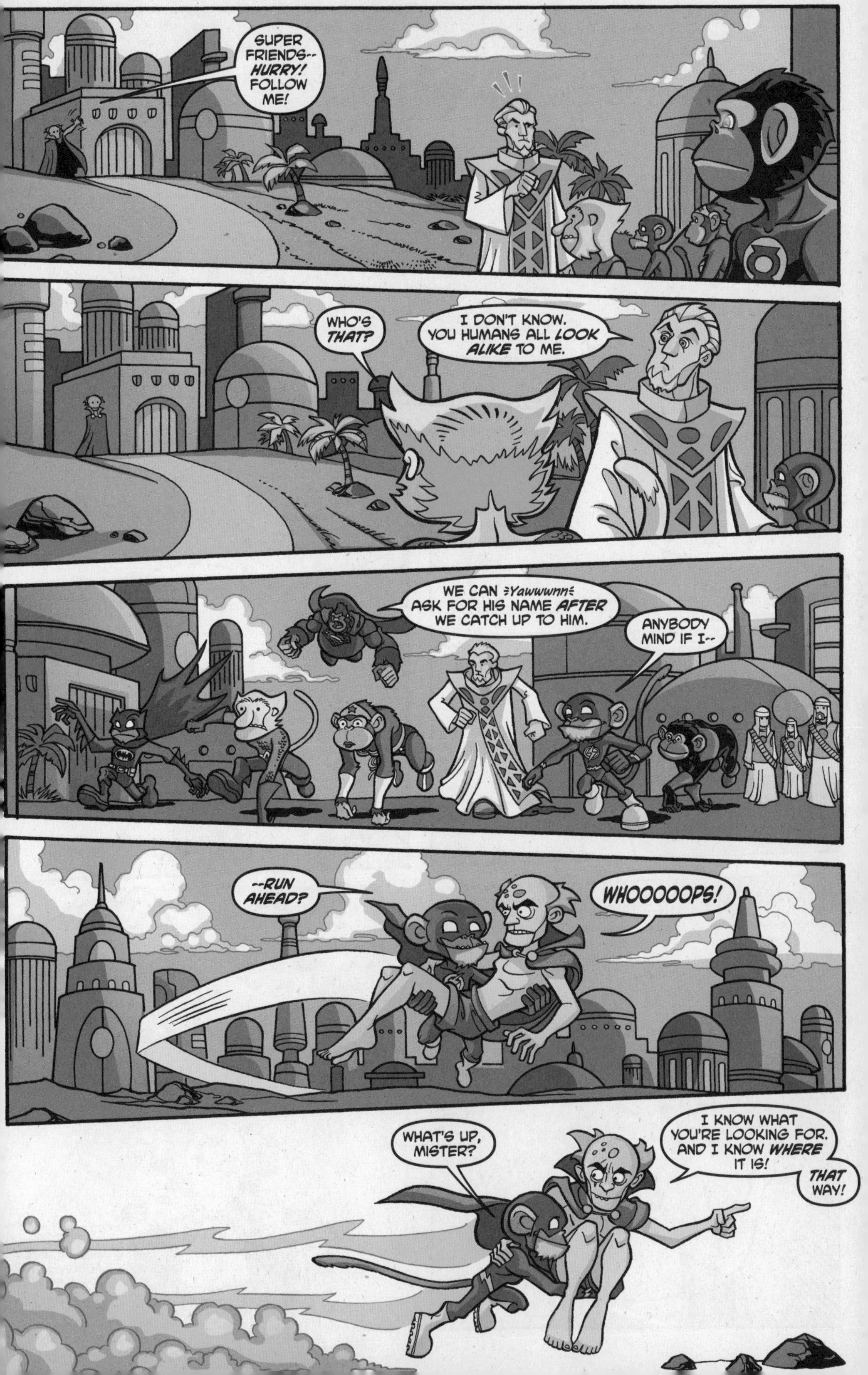
SUPER FRIENDS-- HURRY! FOLLOW ME!
WHO'S THAT?
I DON'T KNOW. YOU HUMANS ALL LOOK ALIKE TO ME.
WE CAN ≷Yawwwnn≷ ASK FOR HIS NAME AFTER WE CATCH UP TO HIM.
ANYBODY MIND IF I--
--RUN AHEAD?
WHOOOOOPS!
WHAT'S UP, MISTER?
I KNOW WHAT YOU'RE LOOKING FOR. AND I KNOW WHERE IT IS!
THAT WAY!

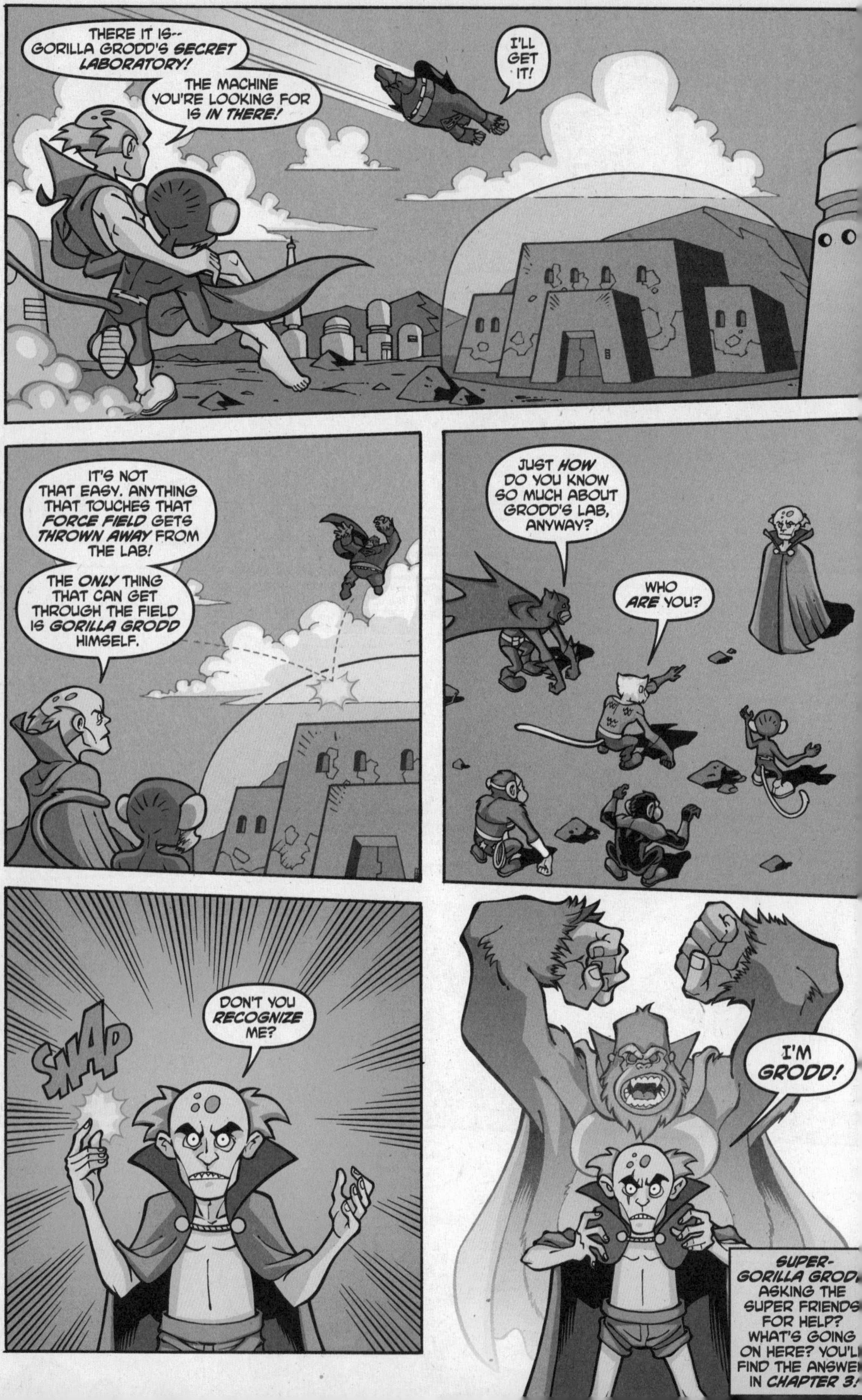
THERE IT IS-- GORILLA GRODD'S SECRET LABORATORY!
THE MACHINE YOU'RE LOOKING FOR IS IN THERE!
I'LL GET IT!
IT'S NOT THAT EASY. ANYTHING THAT TOUCHES THAT FORCE FIELD GETS THROWN AWAY FROM THE LAB!
THE ONLY THING THAT CAN GET THROUGH THE FIELD IS GORILLA GRODD HIMSELF.
JUST HOW DO YOU KNOW SO MUCH ABOUT GRODD'S LAB, ANYWAY?
WHO ARE YOU?
SNAP
DON'T YOU RECOGNIZE ME?
I'M GRODD!
SUPER-GORILLA GROD, ASKING THE SUPER FRIENDS FOR HELP? WHAT'S GOING ON HERE? YOU'L FIND THE ANSWE IN CHAPTER 3!

MONKEY BUSINESS CHAPTER 3

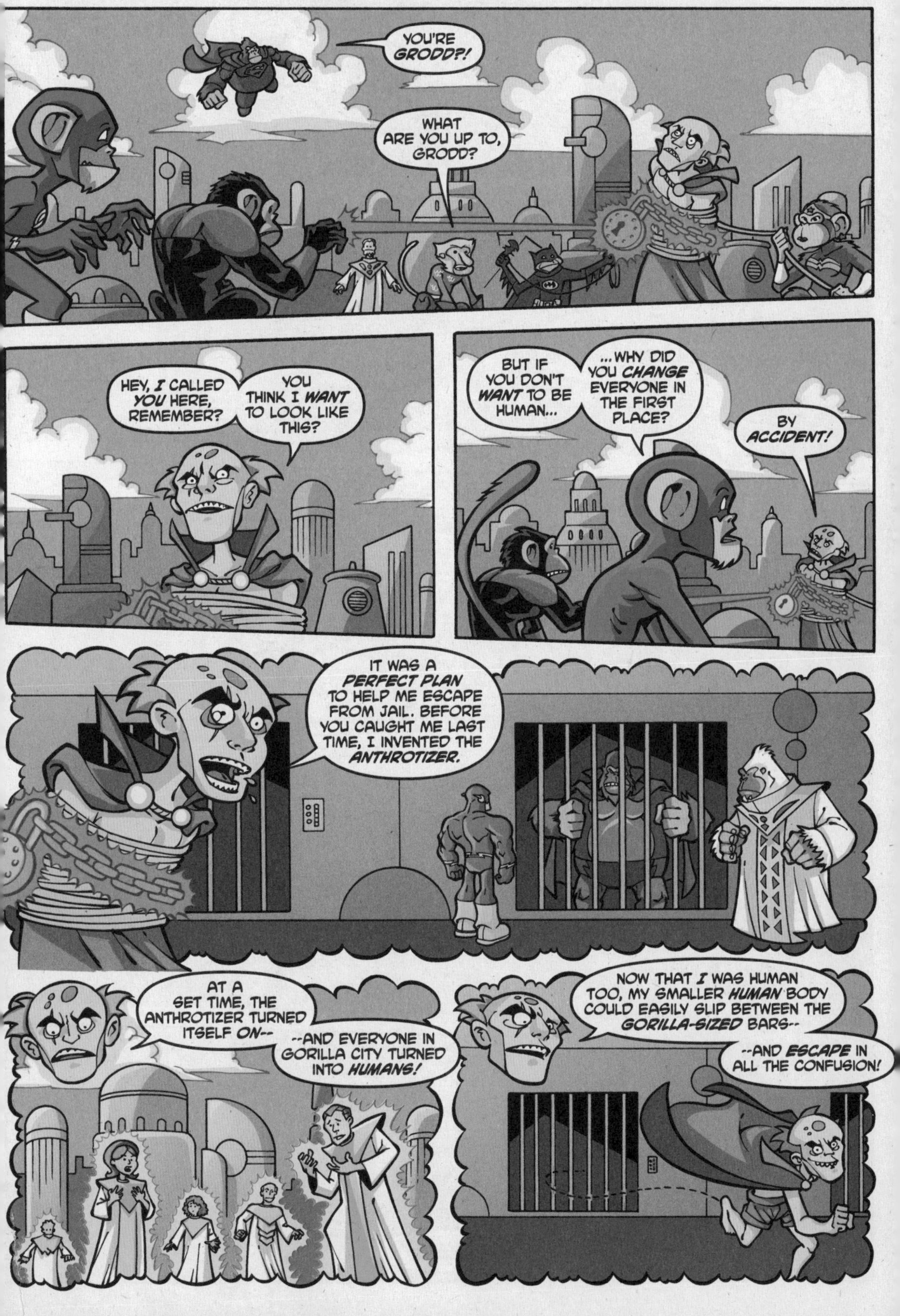
YOU'RE GRODD?!
WHAT ARE YOU UP TO, GRODD?
HEY, I CALLED YOU HERE, REMEMBER?
YOU THINK I WANT TO LOOK LIKE THIS?
BUT IF YOU DON'T WANT TO BE HUMAN...
...WHY DID YOU CHANGE EVERYONE IN THE FIRST PLACE?
BY ACCIDENT!
IT WAS A PERFECT PLAN TO HELP ME ESCAPE FROM JAIL. BEFORE YOU CAUGHT ME LAST TIME, I INVENTED THE ANTHROTIZER.
AT A SET TIME, THE ANTHROTIZER TURNED ITSELF ON--
--AND EVERYONE IN GORILLA CITY TURNED INTO HUMANS!
NOW THAT I WAS HUMAN TOO, MY SMALLER HUMAN BODY COULD EASILY SLIP BETWEEN THE GORILLA-SIZED BARS--
--AND ESCAPE IN ALL THE CONFUSION!

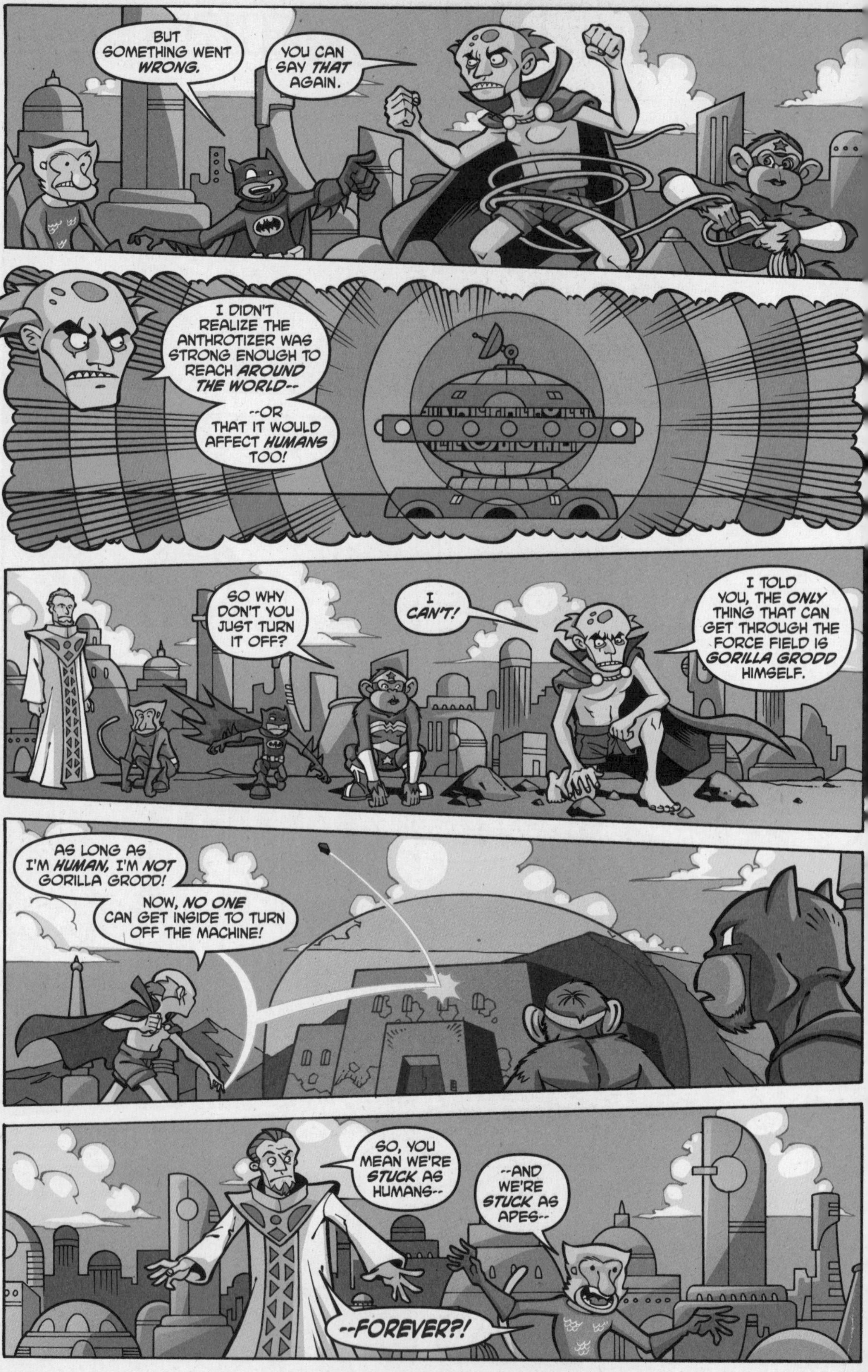

BUT SOMETHING WENT WRONG.
YOU CAN SAY THAT AGAIN.
I DIDN'T REALIZE THE ANTHROTIZER WAS STRONG ENOUGH TO REACH AROUND THE WORLD--
--OR THAT IT WOULD AFFECT HUMANS TOO!
SO WHY DON'T YOU JUST TURN IT OFF?
I CAN'T!
I TOLD YOU, THE ONLY THING THAT CAN GET THROUGH THE FORCE FIELD IS GORILLA GRODD HIMSELF.
AS LONG AS I'M HUMAN, I'M NOT GORILLA GRODD!
NOW, NO ONE CAN GET INSIDE TO TURN OFF THE MACHINE!
SO, YOU MEAN WE'RE STUCK AS HUMANS--
--AND WE'RE STUCK AS APES--
--FOREVER?!

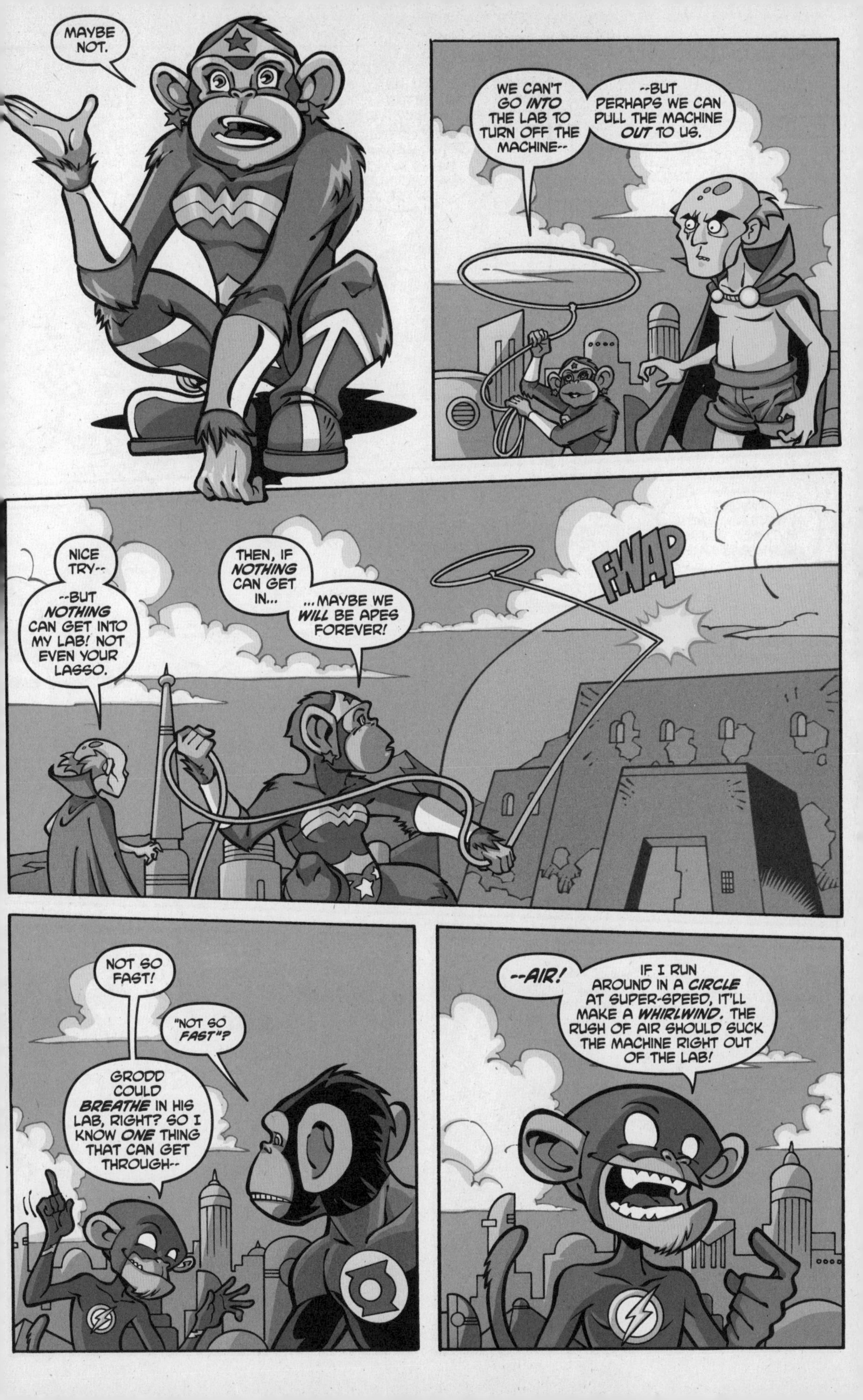

MAYBE NOT.
WE CAN'T GO INTO THE LAB TO TURN OFF THE MACHINE--
--BUT PERHAPS WE CAN PULL THE MACHINE OUT TO US.
NICE TRY--
--BUT NOTHING CAN GET INTO MY LAB! NOT EVEN YOUR LASSO.
THEN, IF NOTHING CAN GET IN...
...MAYBE WE WILL BE APES FOREVER!
FWAP
NOT SO FAST!
"NOT SO FAST"?
GRODD COULD BREATHE IN HIS LAB, RIGHT? SO I KNOW ONE THING THAT CAN GET THROUGH--
--AIR!
IF I RUN AROUND IN A CIRCLE AT SUPER-SPEED, IT'LL MAKE A WHIRLWIND. THE RUSH OF AIR SHOULD SUCK THE MACHINE RIGHT OUT OF THE LAB!

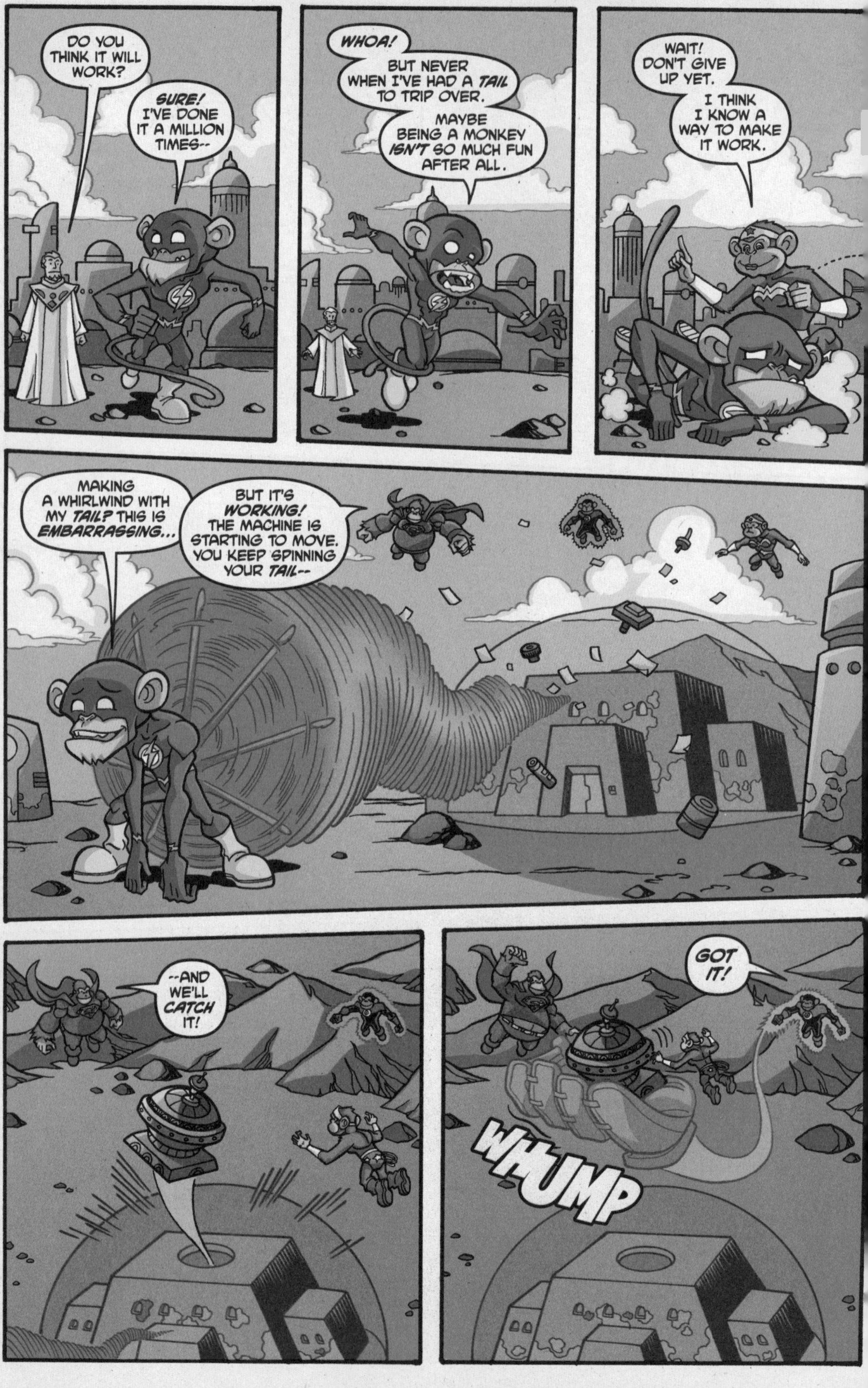
DO YOU THINK IT WILL WORK?
SURE! I'VE DONE IT A MILLION TIMES--
WHOA!
BUT NEVER WHEN I'VE HAD A TAIL TO TRIP OVER.
MAYBE BEING A MONKEY ISN'T SO MUCH FUN AFTER ALL.
WAIT! DON'T GIVE UP YET.
I THINK I KNOW A WAY TO MAKE IT WORK.
MAKING A WHIRLWIND WITH MY TAIL? THIS IS EMBARRASSING...
BUT IT'S WORKING! THE MACHINE IS STARTING TO MOVE. YOU KEEP SPINNING YOUR TAIL--
--AND WE'LL CATCH IT!
GOT IT!
WHUMP

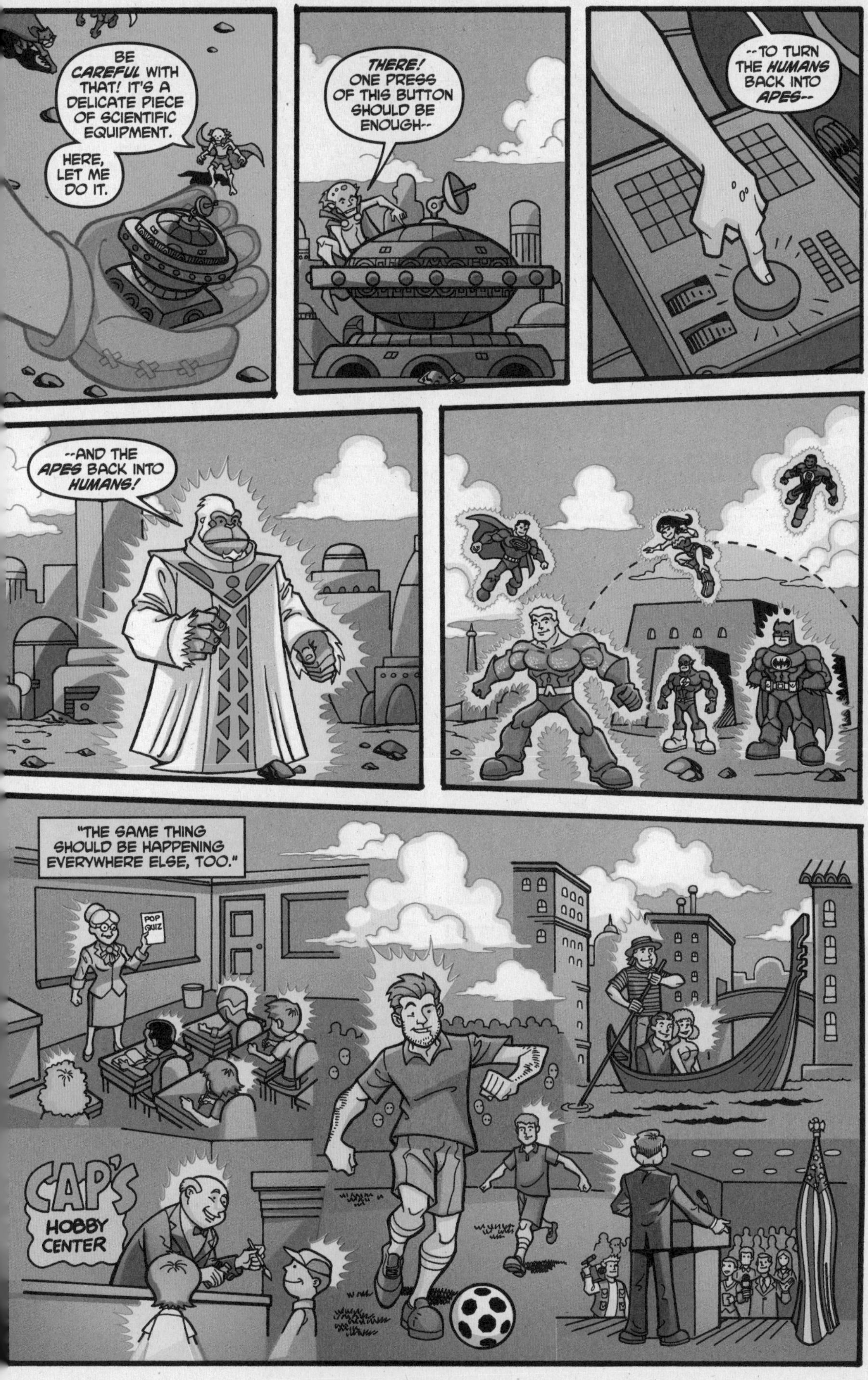
BE CAREFUL WITH THAT! IT'S A DELICATE PIECE OF SCIENTIFIC EQUIPMENT.
HERE, LET ME DO IT.
THERE! ONE PRESS OF THIS BUTTON SHOULD BE ENOUGH--
--TO TURN THE HUMANS BACK INTO APES--
--AND THE APES BACK INTO HUMANS!
"THE SAME THING SHOULD BE HAPPENING EVERYWHERE ELSE, TOO."
POP QUIZ
CAP'S HOBBY CENTER

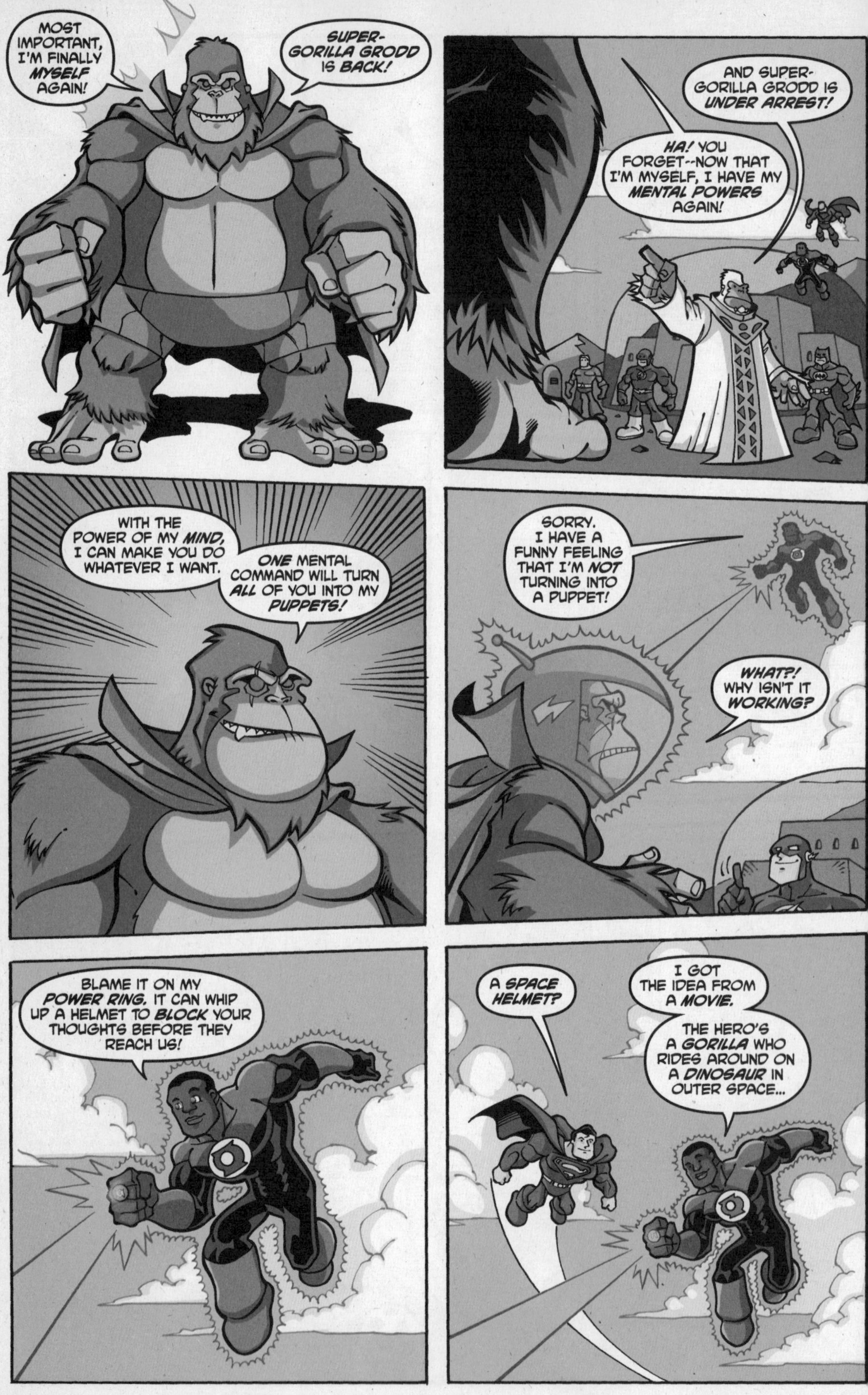
MOST IMPORTANT, I'M FINALLY MYSELF AGAIN!
SUPER-GORILLA GRODD IS BACK!
AND SUPER-GORILLA GRODD IS UNDER ARREST!
HA! YOU FORGET--NOW THAT I'M MYSELF, I HAVE MY MENTAL POWERS AGAIN!
WITH THE POWER OF MY MIND, I CAN MAKE YOU DO WHATEVER I WANT.
ONE MENTAL COMMAND WILL TURN ALL OF YOU INTO MY PUPPETS!
SORRY. I HAVE A FUNNY FEELING THAT I'M NOT TURNING INTO A PUPPET!
WHAT?! WHY ISN'T IT WORKING?
BLAME IT ON MY POWER RING. IT CAN WHIP UP A HELMET TO BLOCK YOUR THOUGHTS BEFORE THEY REACH US!
A SPACE HELMET?
I GOT THE IDEA FROM A MOVIE.
THE HERO'S A GORILLA WHO RIDES AROUND ON A DINOSAUR IN OUTER SPACE...

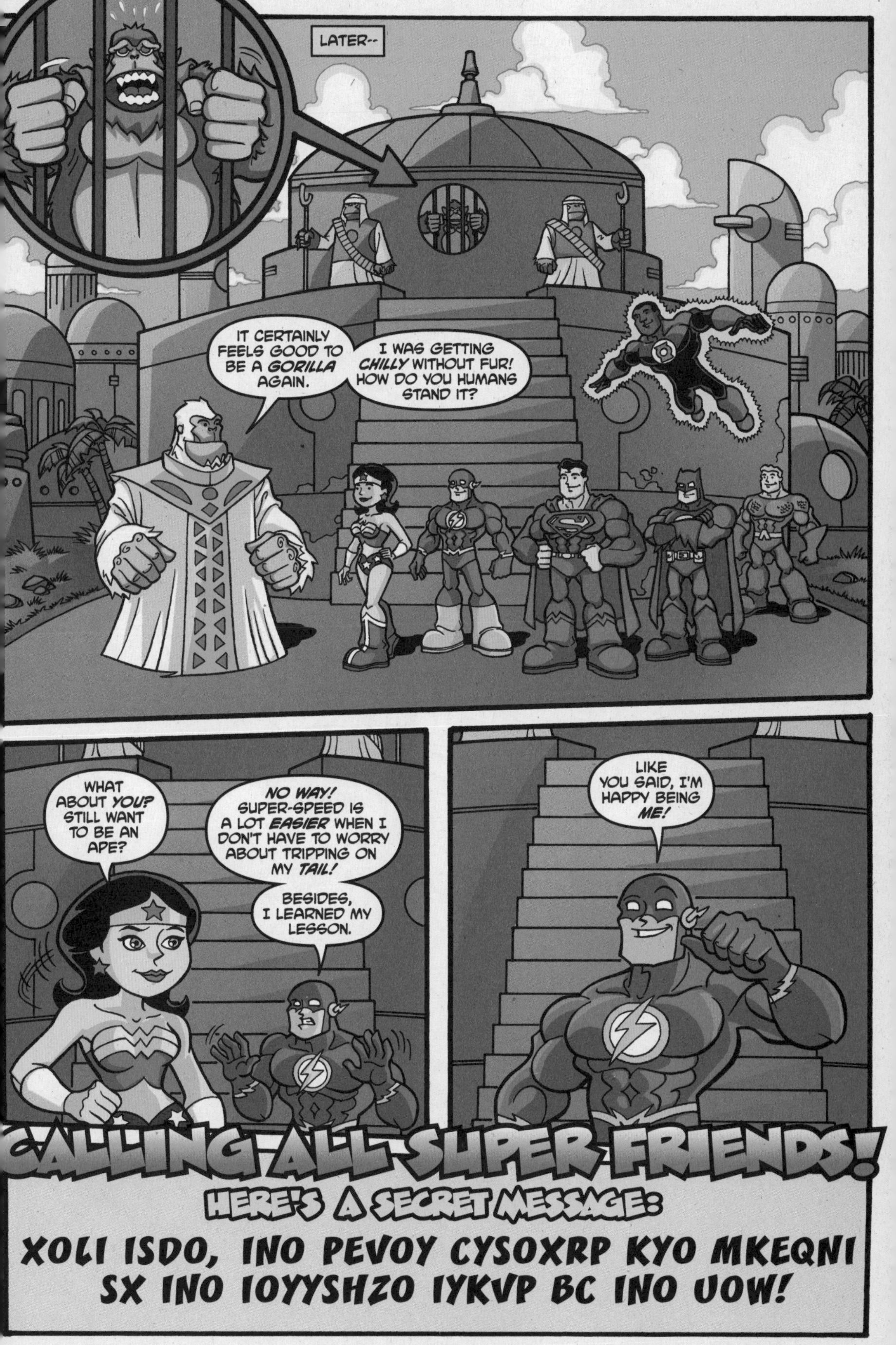
LATER--
IT CERTAINLY FEELS GOOD TO BE A *GORILLA* AGAIN.
I WAS GETTING *CHILLY* WITHOUT FUR! HOW DO YOU HUMANS STAND IT?
WHAT ABOUT *YOU?* STILL WANT TO BE AN APE?
NO WAY! SUPER-SPEED IS A LOT *EASIER* WHEN I DON'T HAVE TO WORRY ABOUT TRIPPING ON MY *TAIL!*
BESIDES, I LEARNED MY LESSON.
LIKE YOU SAID, I'M HAPPY BEING *ME!*

CALLING ALL SUPER FRIENDS!

HERE'S A SECRET MESSAGE:

XOLI ISDO, INO PEVOY CYSOXRP KYO MKEQNI SX INO IOYYSHZO IYKVP BC INO UOW!

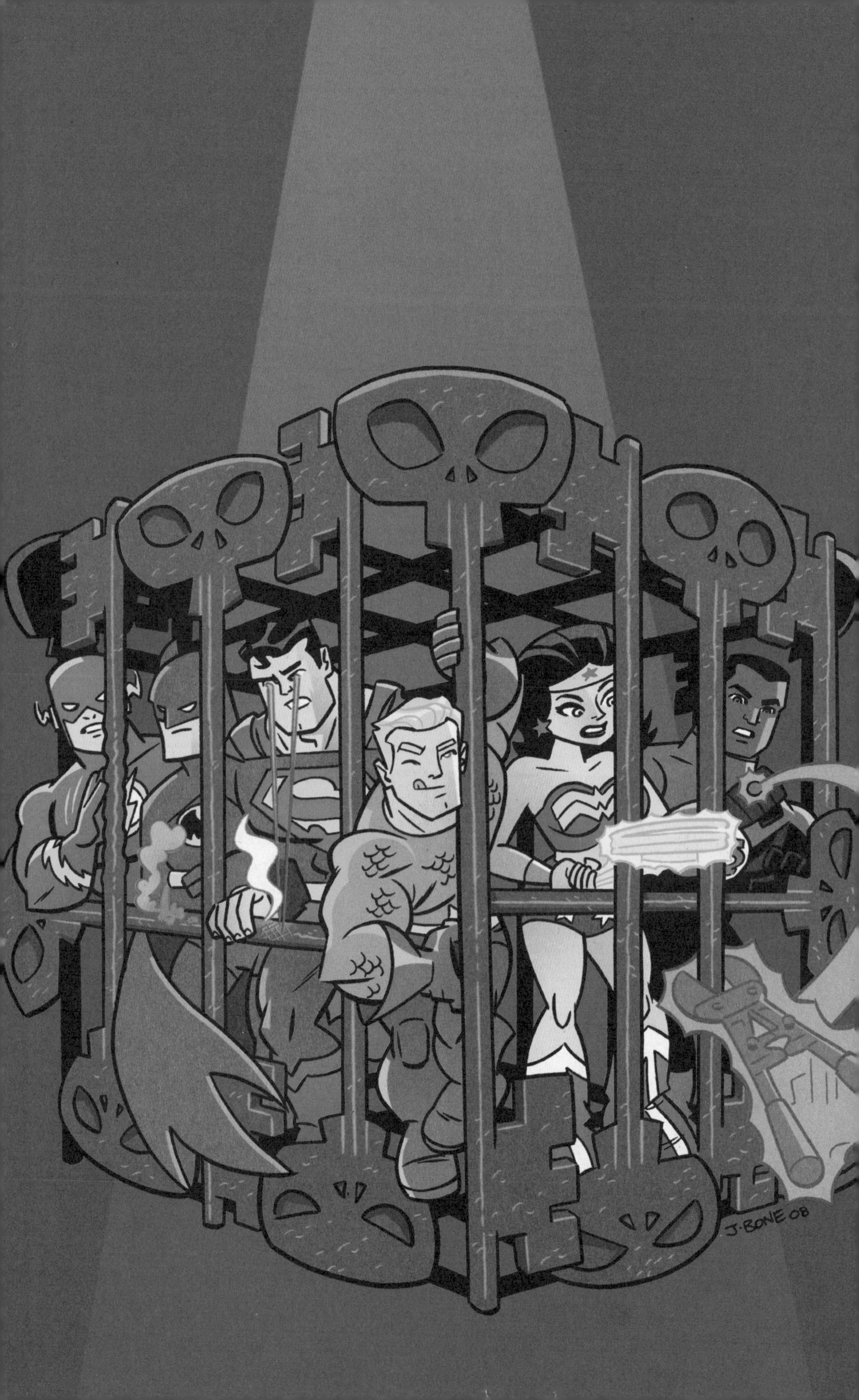
J-BONE '08

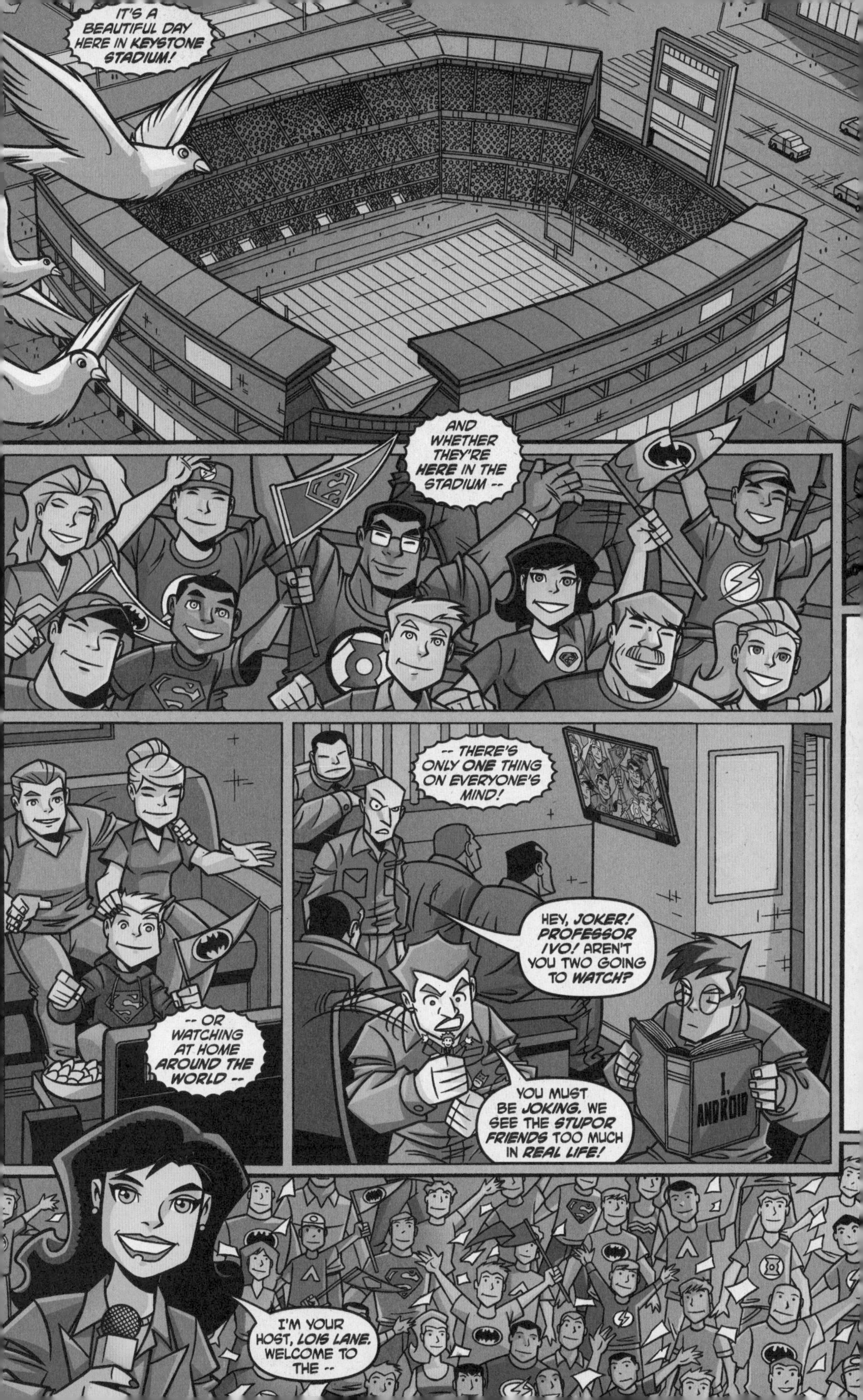
IT'S A BEAUTIFUL DAY HERE IN KEYSTONE STADIUM!
AND WHETHER THEY'RE HERE IN THE STADIUM --
-- OR WATCHING AT HOME AROUND THE WORLD --
-- THERE'S ONLY ONE THING ON EVERYONE'S MIND!
HEY, JOKER! PROFESSOR IVO! AREN'T YOU TWO GOING TO WATCH?
YOU MUST BE JOKING. WE SEE THE STUPOR FRIENDS TOO MUCH IN REAL LIFE!
I, ANDROID
I'M YOUR HOST, LOIS LANE. WELCOME TO THE --

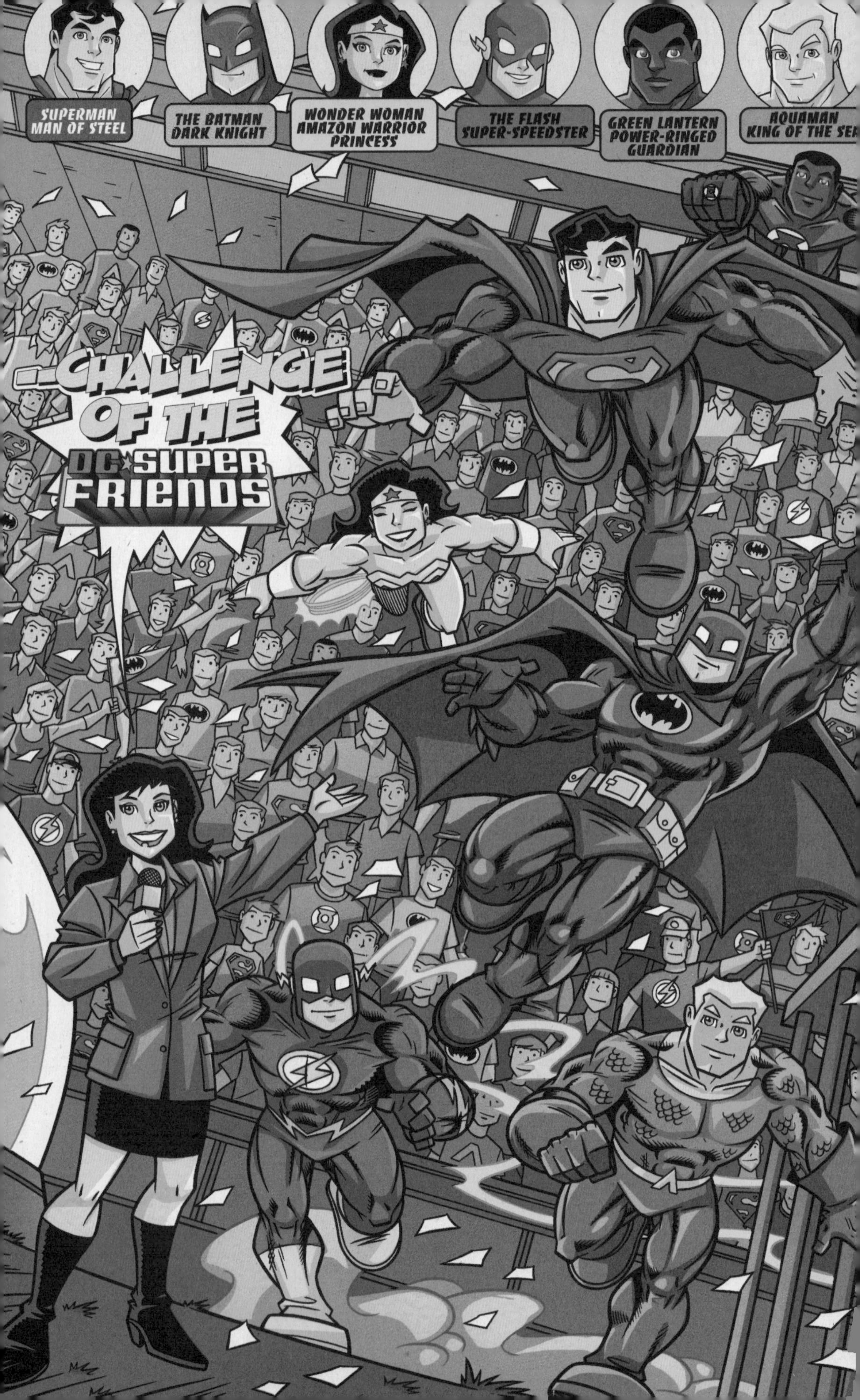

SUPERMAN MAN OF STEEL
THE BATMAN DARK KNIGHT
WONDER WOMAN AMAZON WARRIOR PRINCESS
THE FLASH SUPER-SPEEDSTER
GREEN LANTERN POWER-RINGED GUARDIAN
AQUAMAN KING OF THE SEA
CHALLENGE OF THE DC SUPER FRIENDS

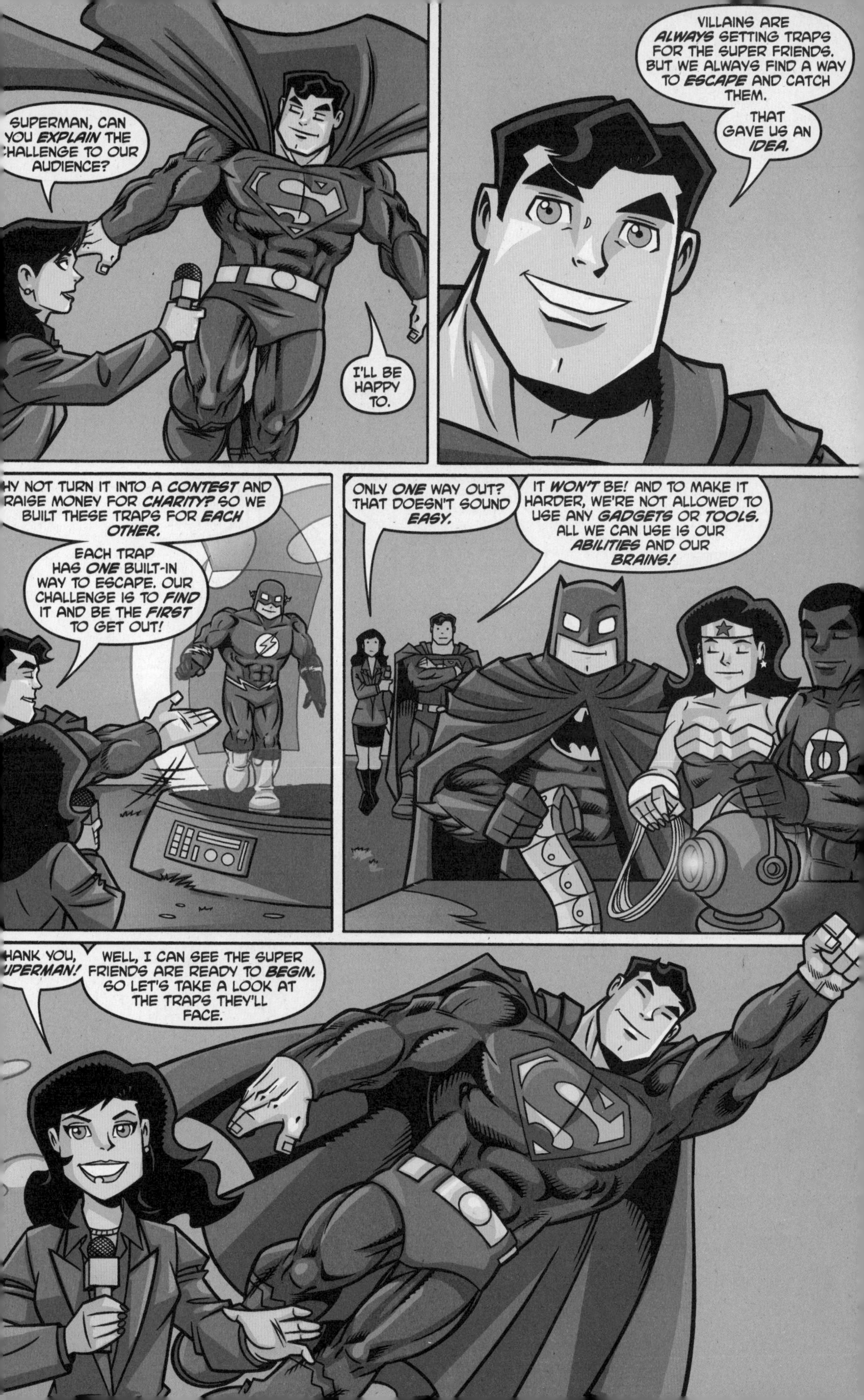
SUPERMAN, CAN YOU EXPLAIN THE CHALLENGE TO OUR AUDIENCE?
I'LL BE HAPPY TO.
VILLAINS ARE ALWAYS SETTING TRAPS FOR THE SUPER FRIENDS. BUT WE ALWAYS FIND A WAY TO ESCAPE AND CATCH THEM.
THAT GAVE US AN IDEA.
HY NOT TURN IT INTO A CONTEST AND RAISE MONEY FOR CHARITY? SO WE BUILT THESE TRAPS FOR EACH OTHER.
EACH TRAP HAS ONE BUILT-IN WAY TO ESCAPE. OUR CHALLENGE IS TO FIND IT AND BE THE FIRST TO GET OUT!
ONLY ONE WAY OUT? THAT DOESN'T SOUND EASY.
IT WON'T BE! AND TO MAKE IT HARDER, WE'RE NOT ALLOWED TO USE ANY GADGETS OR TOOLS. ALL WE CAN USE IS OUR ABILITIES AND OUR BRAINS!
HANK YOU, UPERMAN!
WELL, I CAN SEE THE SUPER FRIENDS ARE READY TO BEGIN. SO LET'S TAKE A LOOK AT THE TRAPS THEY'LL FACE.

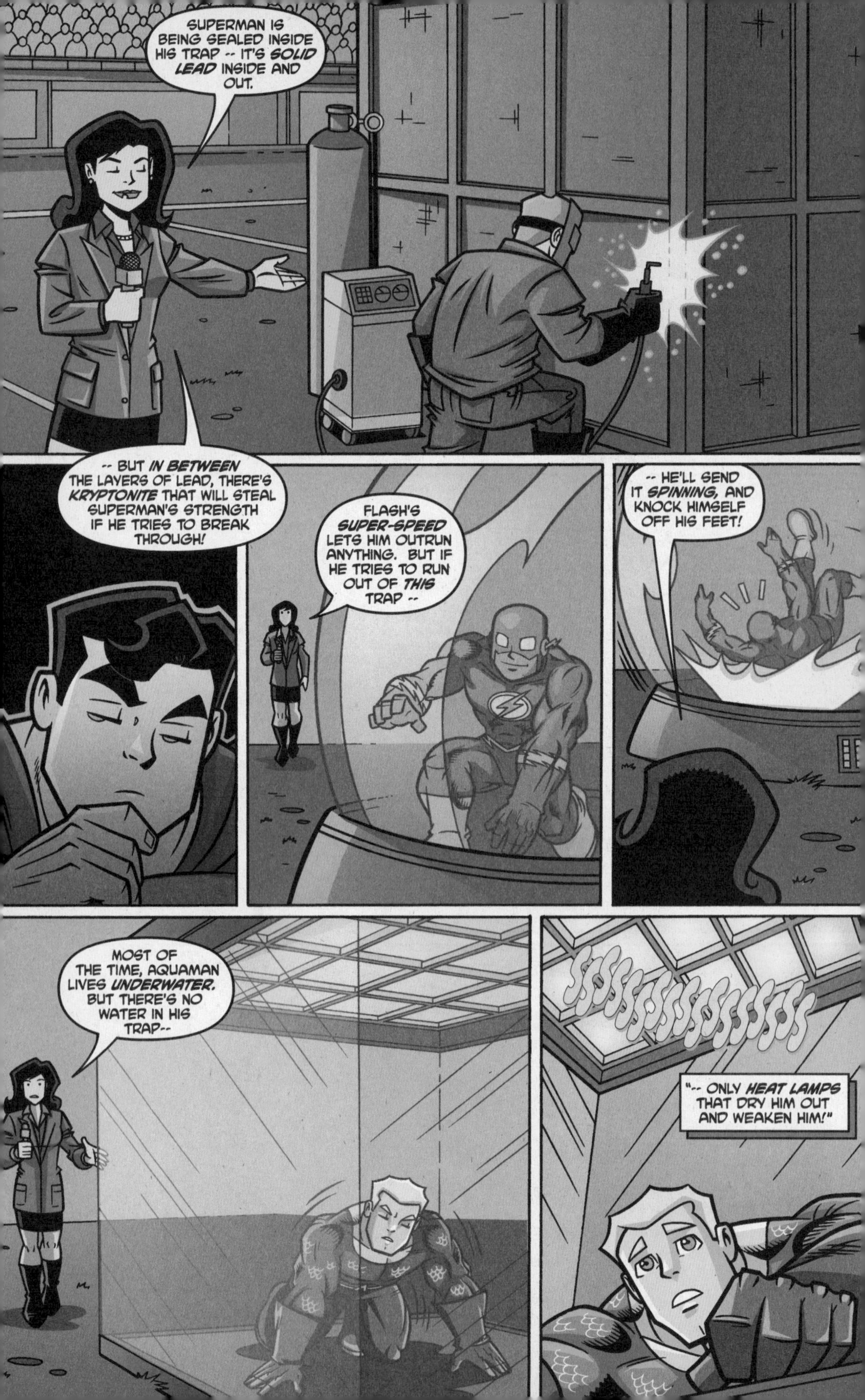
SUPERMAN IS BEING SEALED INSIDE HIS TRAP -- IT'S *SOLID LEAD* INSIDE AND OUT.
-- BUT *IN BETWEEN* THE LAYERS OF LEAD, THERE'S *KRYPTONITE* THAT WILL STEAL SUPERMAN'S STRENGTH IF HE TRIES TO BREAK THROUGH!
FLASH'S *SUPER-SPEED* LETS HIM OUTRUN ANYTHING. BUT IF HE TRIES TO RUN OUT OF *THIS* TRAP --
-- HE'LL SEND IT *SPINNING,* AND KNOCK HIMSELF OFF HIS FEET!
MOST OF THE TIME, AQUAMAN LIVES *UNDERWATER.* BUT THERE'S NO WATER IN HIS TRAP--
SSSSSSSSSSSSSSSSSSSS
"-- ONLY *HEAT LAMPS* THAT DRY HIM OUT AND WEAKEN HIM!"

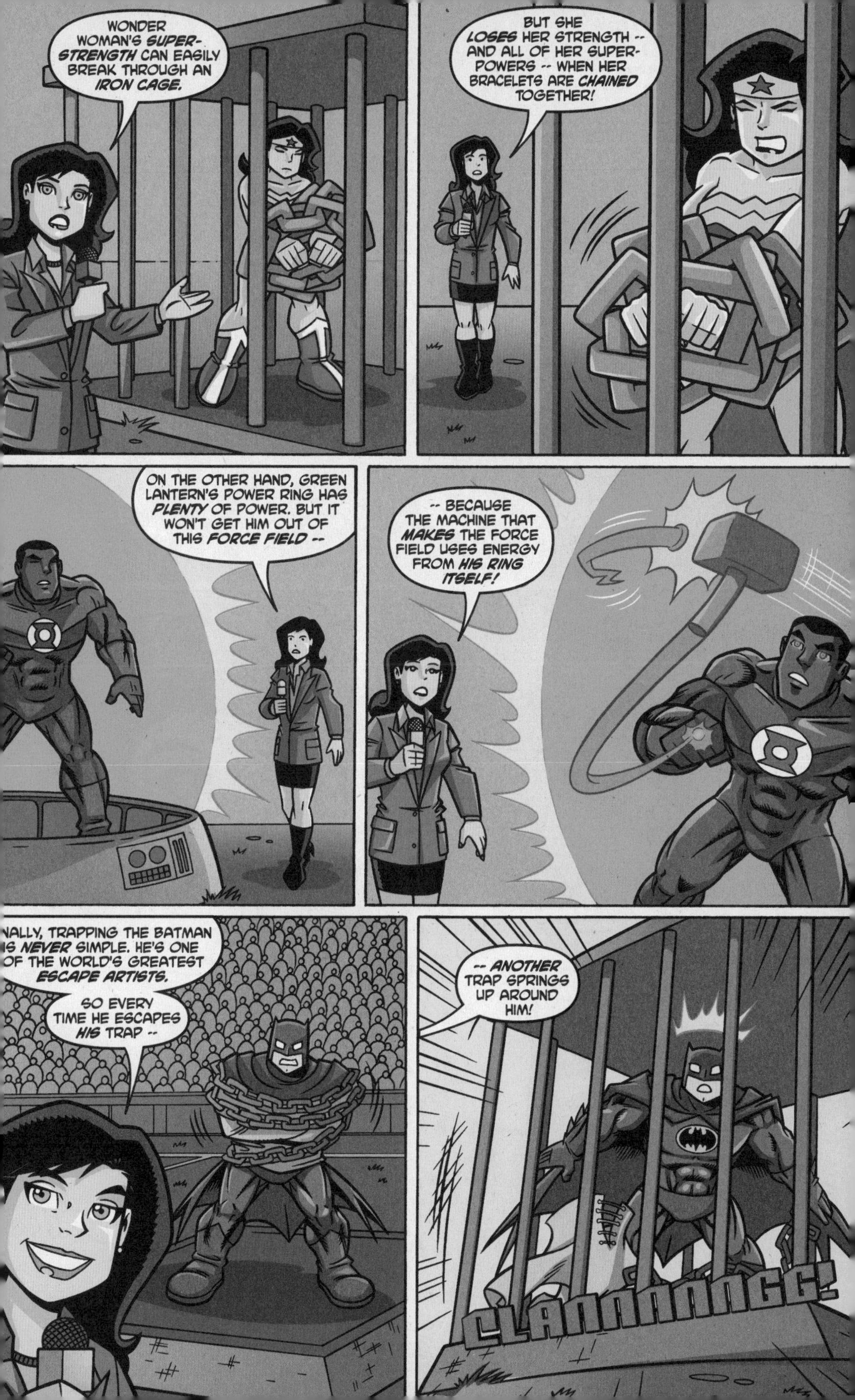
WONDER WOMAN'S SUPER-STRENGTH CAN EASILY BREAK THROUGH AN IRON CAGE.
BUT SHE LOSES HER STRENGTH -- AND ALL OF HER SUPER-POWERS -- WHEN HER BRACELETS ARE CHAINED TOGETHER!
ON THE OTHER HAND, GREEN LANTERN'S POWER RING HAS PLENTY OF POWER. BUT IT WON'T GET HIM OUT OF THIS FORCE FIELD --
-- BECAUSE THE MACHINE THAT MAKES THE FORCE FIELD USES ENERGY FROM HIS RING ITSELF!
NALLY, TRAPPING THE BATMAN IS NEVER SIMPLE. HE'S ONE OF THE WORLD'S GREATEST ESCAPE ARTISTS.
SO EVERY TIME HE ESCAPES HIS TRAP --
-- ANOTHER TRAP SPRINGS UP AROUND HIM!
CLANNNNNNGG!

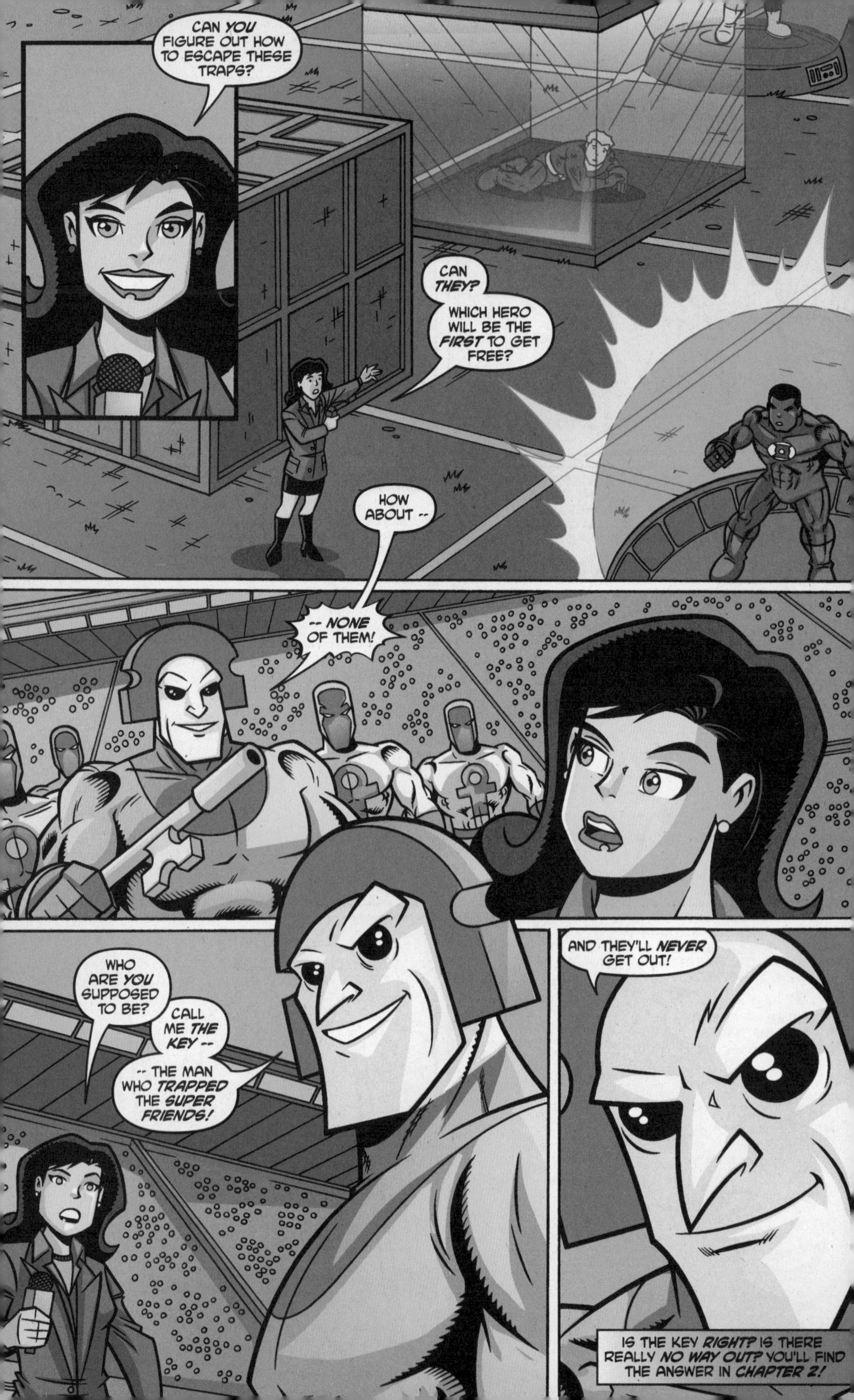
CAN YOU FIGURE OUT HOW TO ESCAPE THESE TRAPS?
CAN THEY?
WHICH HERO WILL BE THE FIRST TO GET FREE?
HOW ABOUT --
-- NONE OF THEM!
WHO ARE YOU SUPPOSED TO BE?
CALL ME THE KEY --
-- THE MAN WHO TRAPPED THE SUPER FRIENDS!
AND THEY'LL NEVER GET OUT!
IS THE KEY RIGHT? IS THERE REALLY NO WAY OUT? YOU'LL FIND THE ANSWER IN CHAPTER 2!

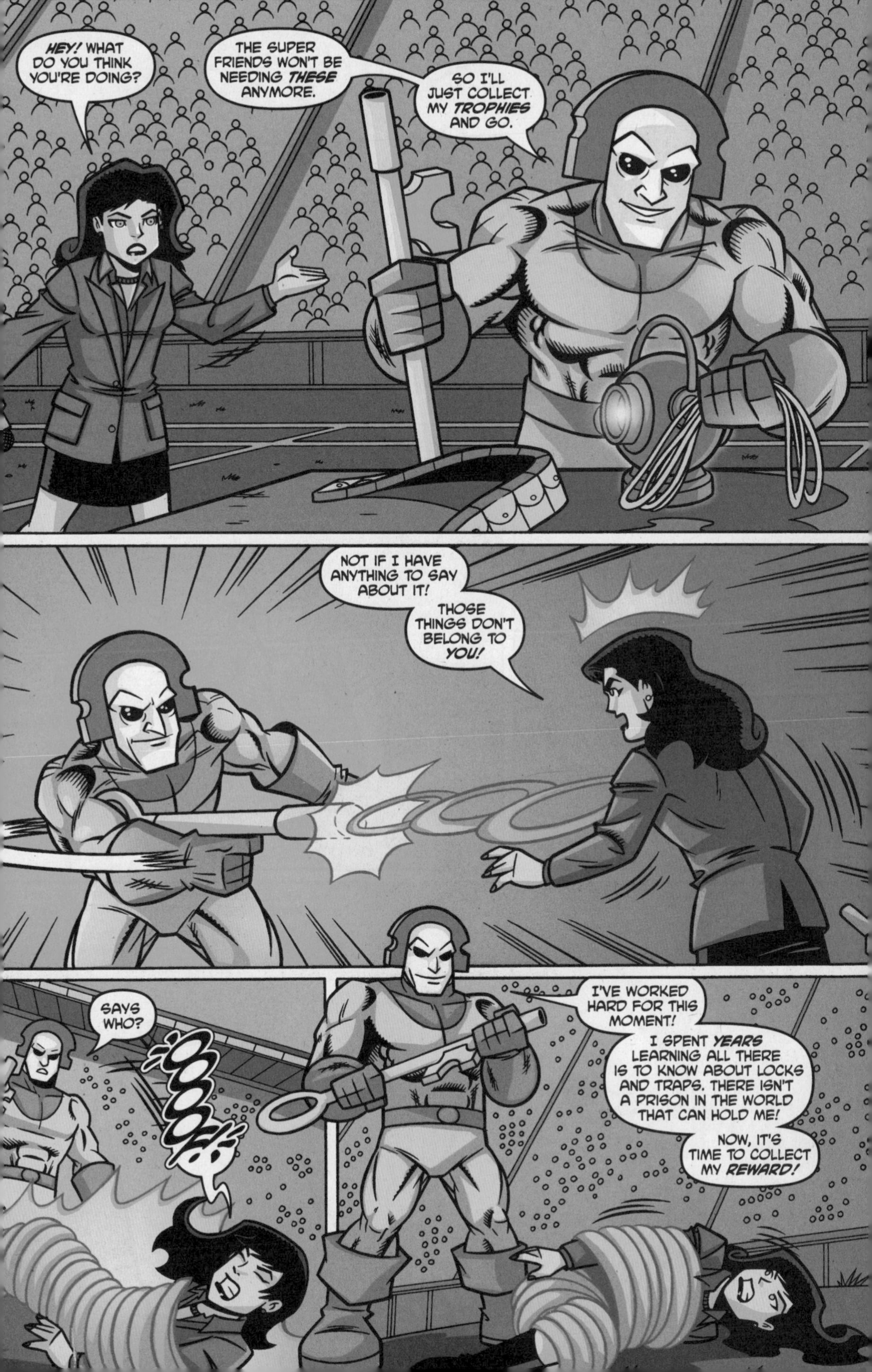
HEY! WHAT DO YOU THINK YOU'RE DOING?
THE SUPER FRIENDS WON'T BE NEEDING THESE ANYMORE.
SO I'LL JUST COLLECT MY TROPHIES AND GO.
NOT IF I HAVE ANYTHING TO SAY ABOUT IT!
THOSE THINGS DON'T BELONG TO YOU!
SAYS WHO?
OOOF!
I'VE WORKED HARD FOR THIS MOMENT!
I SPENT YEARS LEARNING ALL THERE IS TO KNOW ABOUT LOCKS AND TRAPS. THERE ISN'T A PRISON IN THE WORLD THAT CAN HOLD ME!
NOW, IT'S TIME TO COLLECT MY REWARD!

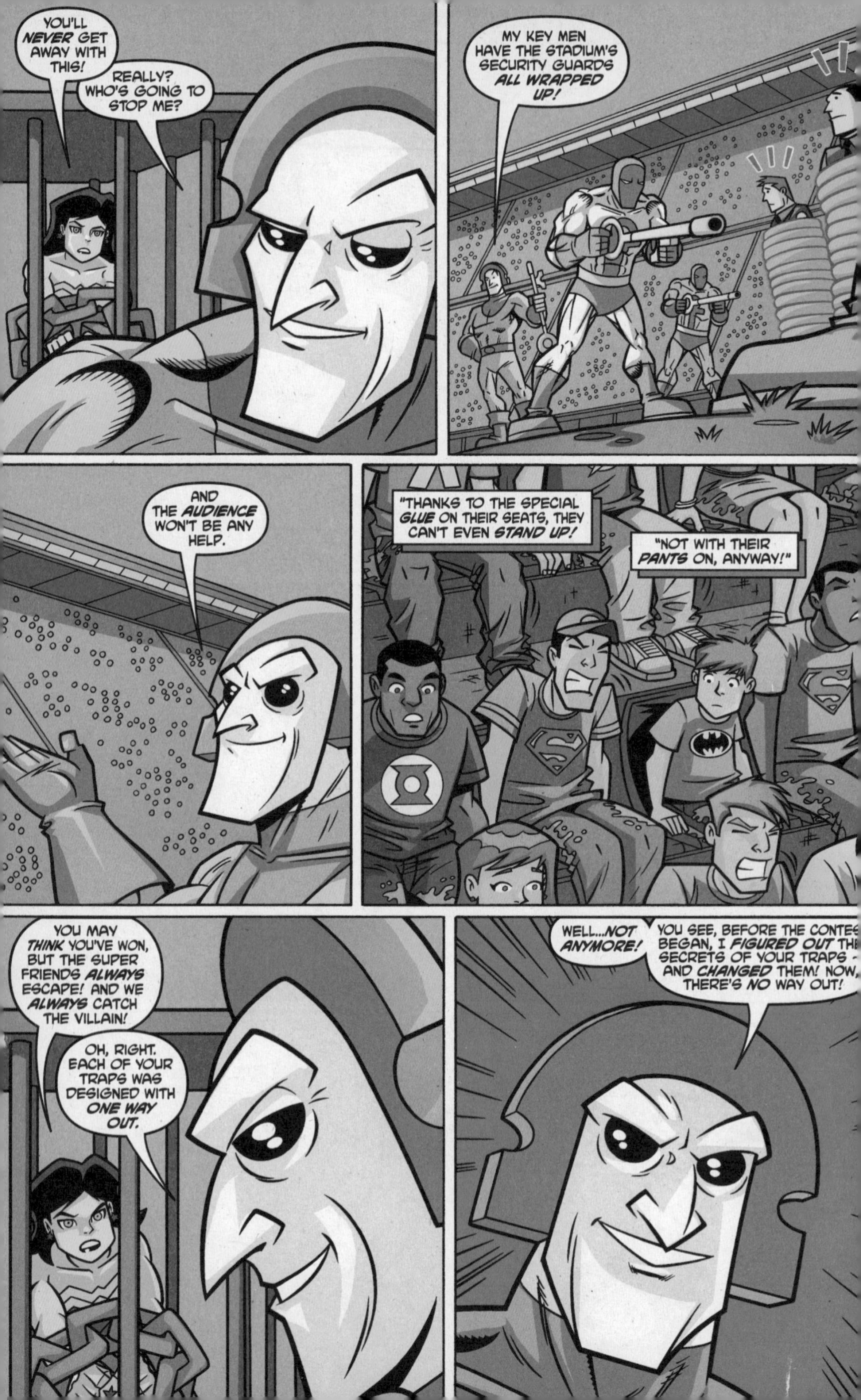
YOU'LL NEVER GET AWAY WITH THIS!
REALLY? WHO'S GOING TO STOP ME?
MY KEY MEN HAVE THE STADIUM'S SECURITY GUARDS ALL WRAPPED UP!
AND THE AUDIENCE WON'T BE ANY HELP.
"THANKS TO THE SPECIAL GLUE ON THEIR SEATS, THEY CAN'T EVEN STAND UP!
"NOT WITH THEIR PANTS ON, ANYWAY!"
YOU MAY THINK YOU'VE WON, BUT THE SUPER FRIENDS ALWAYS ESCAPE! AND WE ALWAYS CATCH THE VILLAIN!
OH, RIGHT. EACH OF YOUR TRAPS WAS DESIGNED WITH ONE WAY OUT.
WELL...NOT ANYMORE!
YOU SEE, BEFORE THE CONTES BEGAN, I FIGURED OUT TH SECRETS OF YOUR TRAPS - AND CHANGED THEM! NOW, THERE'S NO WAY OUT!

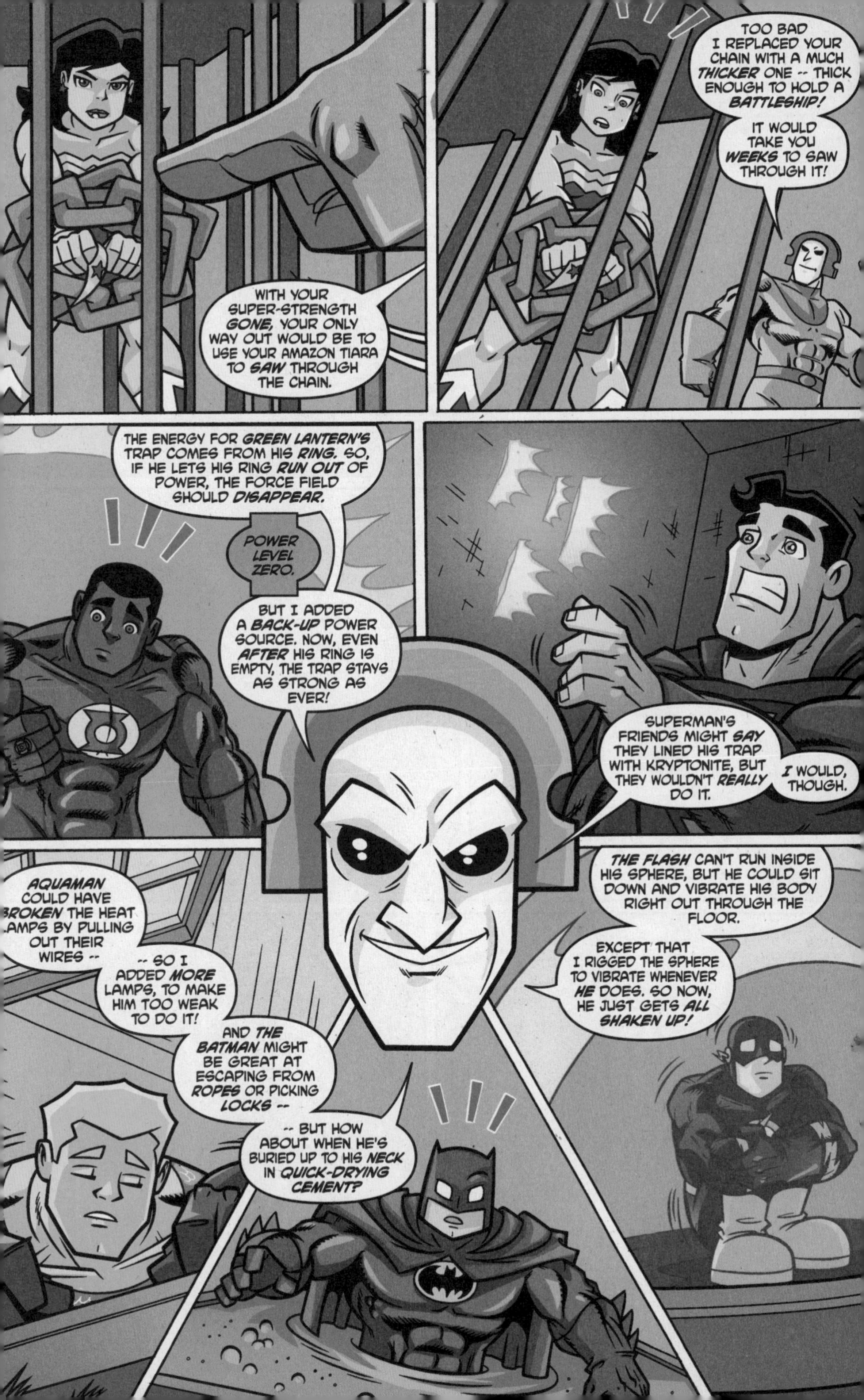
WITH YOUR SUPER-STRENGTH GONE, YOUR ONLY WAY OUT WOULD BE TO USE YOUR AMAZON TIARA TO SAW THROUGH THE CHAIN.
TOO BAD I REPLACED YOUR CHAIN WITH A MUCH THICKER ONE -- THICK ENOUGH TO HOLD A BATTLESHIP!
IT WOULD TAKE YOU WEEKS TO SAW THROUGH IT!
THE ENERGY FOR GREEN LANTERN'S TRAP COMES FROM HIS RING. SO, IF HE LETS HIS RING RUN OUT OF POWER, THE FORCE FIELD SHOULD DISAPPEAR.
POWER LEVEL ZERO.
BUT I ADDED A BACK-UP POWER SOURCE. NOW, EVEN AFTER HIS RING IS EMPTY, THE TRAP STAYS AS STRONG AS EVER!
SUPERMAN'S FRIENDS MIGHT SAY THEY LINED HIS TRAP WITH KRYPTONITE, BUT THEY WOULDN'T REALLY DO IT.
I WOULD, THOUGH.
AQUAMAN COULD HAVE BROKEN THE HEAT LAMPS BY PULLING OUT THEIR WIRES --
-- SO I ADDED MORE LAMPS, TO MAKE HIM TOO WEAK TO DO IT!
AND THE BATMAN MIGHT BE GREAT AT ESCAPING FROM ROPES OR PICKING LOCKS --
-- BUT HOW ABOUT WHEN HE'S BURIED UP TO HIS NECK IN QUICK-DRYING CEMENT?
THE FLASH CAN'T RUN INSIDE HIS SPHERE, BUT HE COULD SIT DOWN AND VIBRATE HIS BODY RIGHT OUT THROUGH THE FLOOR.
EXCEPT THAT I RIGGED THE SPHERE TO VIBRATE WHENEVER HE DOES. SO NOW, HE JUST GETS ALL SHAKEN UP!

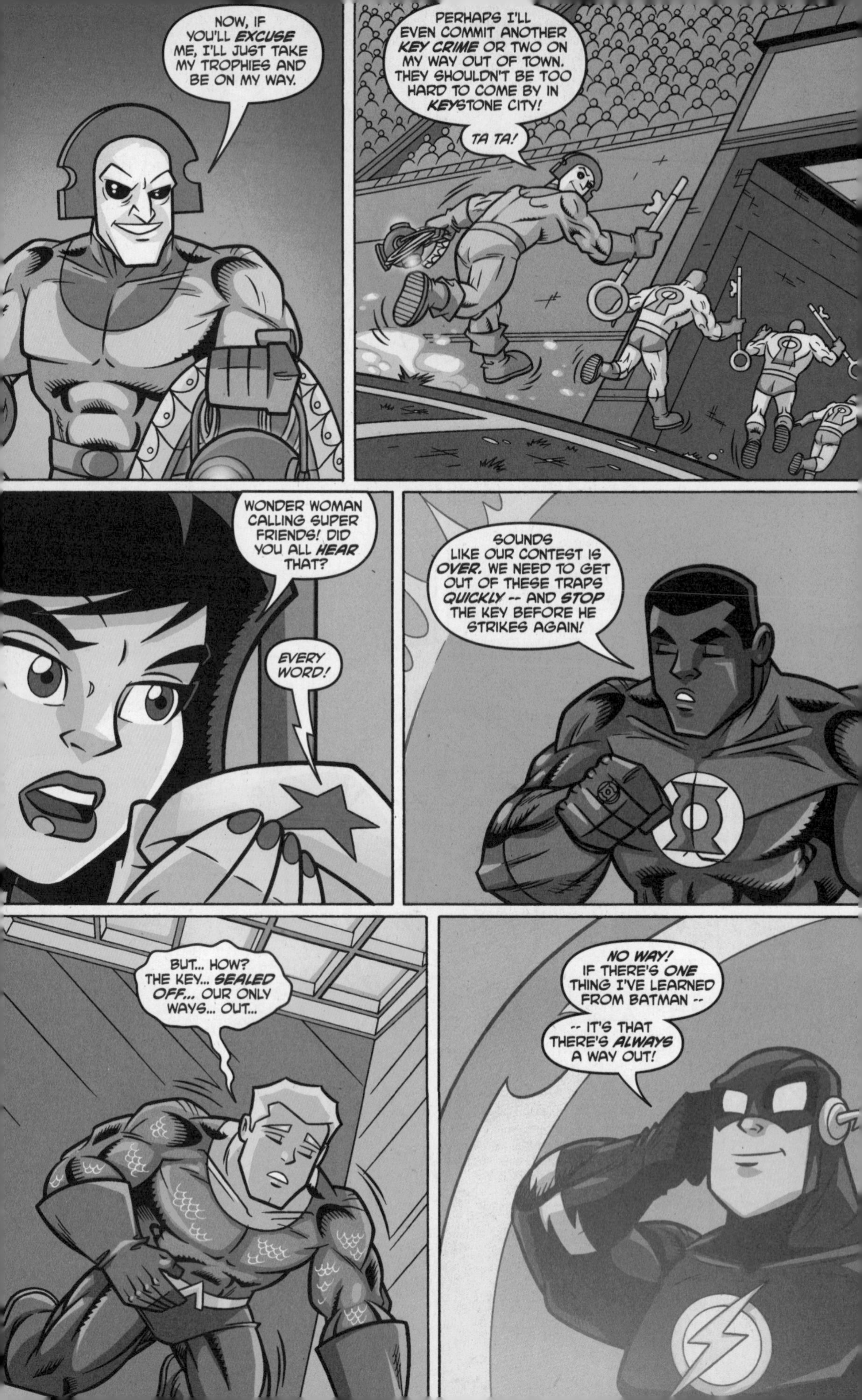
NOW, IF YOU'LL EXCUSE ME, I'LL JUST TAKE MY TROPHIES AND BE ON MY WAY.
PERHAPS I'LL EVEN COMMIT ANOTHER KEY CRIME OR TWO ON MY WAY OUT OF TOWN. THEY SHOULDN'T BE TOO HARD TO COME BY IN KEYSTONE CITY!
TA TA!
WONDER WOMAN CALLING SUPER FRIENDS! DID YOU ALL HEAR THAT?
EVERY WORD!
SOUNDS LIKE OUR CONTEST IS OVER. WE NEED TO GET OUT OF THESE TRAPS QUICKLY -- AND STOP THE KEY BEFORE HE STRIKES AGAIN!
BUT... HOW? THE KEY... SEALED OFF... OUR ONLY WAYS... OUT...
NO WAY! IF THERE'S ONE THING I'VE LEARNED FROM BATMAN --
-- IT'S THAT THERE'S ALWAYS A WAY OUT!

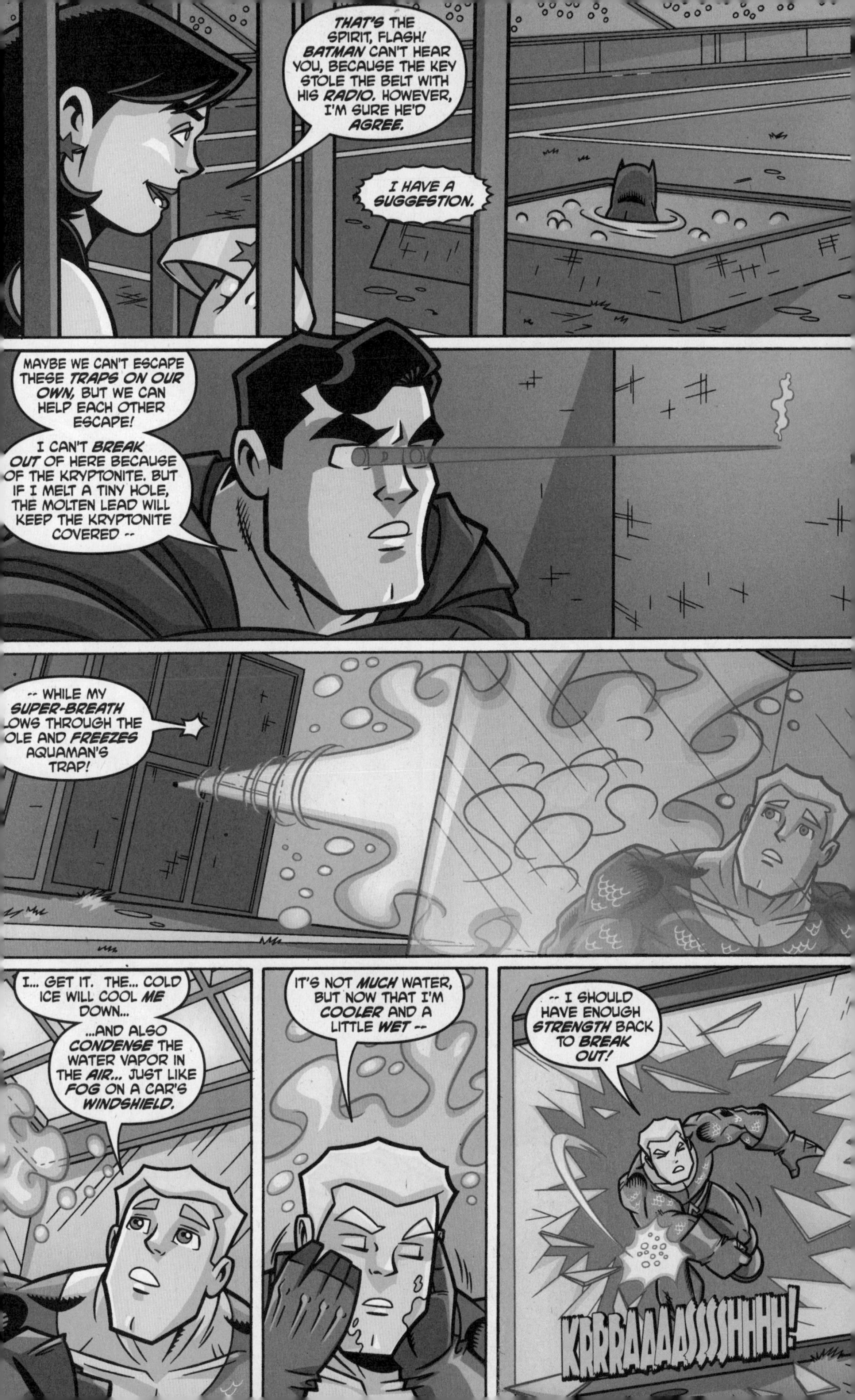
THAT'S THE SPIRIT, FLASH! BATMAN CAN'T HEAR YOU, BECAUSE THE KEY STOLE THE BELT WITH HIS RADIO. HOWEVER, I'M SURE HE'D AGREE.
I HAVE A SUGGESTION.
MAYBE WE CAN'T ESCAPE THESE TRAPS ON OUR OWN, BUT WE CAN HELP EACH OTHER ESCAPE!
I CAN'T BREAK OUT OF HERE BECAUSE OF THE KRYPTONITE. BUT IF I MELT A TINY HOLE, THE MOLTEN LEAD WILL KEEP THE KRYPTONITE COVERED --
-- WHILE MY SUPER-BREATH LOWS THROUGH THE OLE AND FREEZES AQUAMAN'S TRAP!
I... GET IT. THE... COLD ICE WILL COOL ME DOWN...
...AND ALSO CONDENSE THE WATER VAPOR IN THE AIR... JUST LIKE FOG ON A CAR'S WINDSHIELD.
IT'S NOT MUCH WATER, BUT NOW THAT I'M COOLER AND A LITTLE WET --
-- I SHOULD HAVE ENOUGH STRENGTH BACK TO BREAK OUT!
KRRRAAAASSSSHHHH!

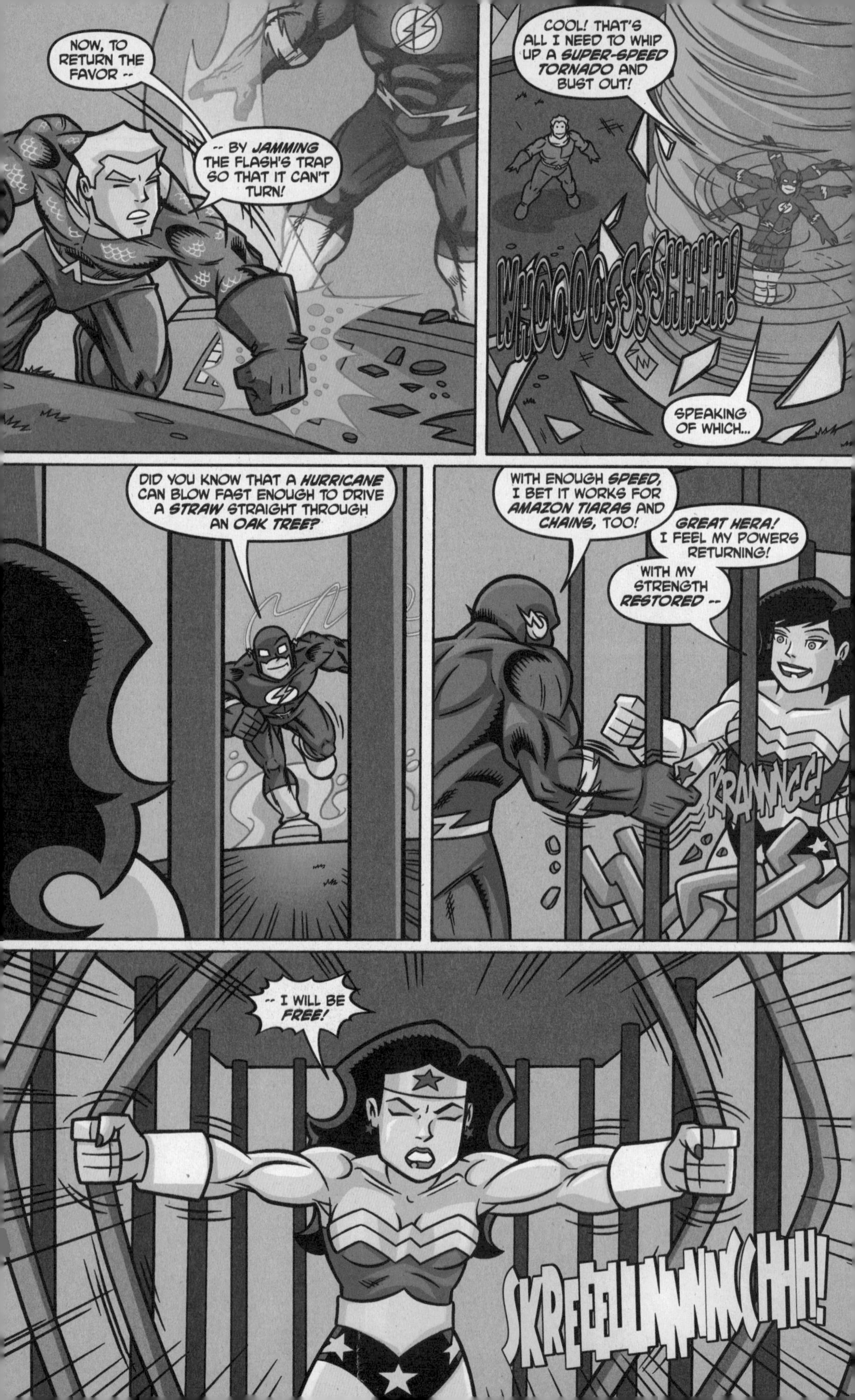
NOW, TO RETURN THE FAVOR --
-- BY JAMMING THE FLASH'S TRAP SO THAT IT CAN'T TURN!
COOL! THAT'S ALL I NEED TO WHIP UP A SUPER-SPEED TORNADO AND BUST OUT!
WHOOOOOSSSSHHHH!
SPEAKING OF WHICH...
DID YOU KNOW THAT A HURRICANE CAN BLOW FAST ENOUGH TO DRIVE A STRAW STRAIGHT THROUGH AN OAK TREE?
WITH ENOUGH SPEED, I BET IT WORKS FOR AMAZON TIARAS AND CHAINS, TOO!
GREAT HERA! I FEEL MY POWERS RETURNING!
WITH MY STRENGTH RESTORED --
KRANNNGG!
-- I WILL BE FREE!
SKREEEUNNNNCHHH!

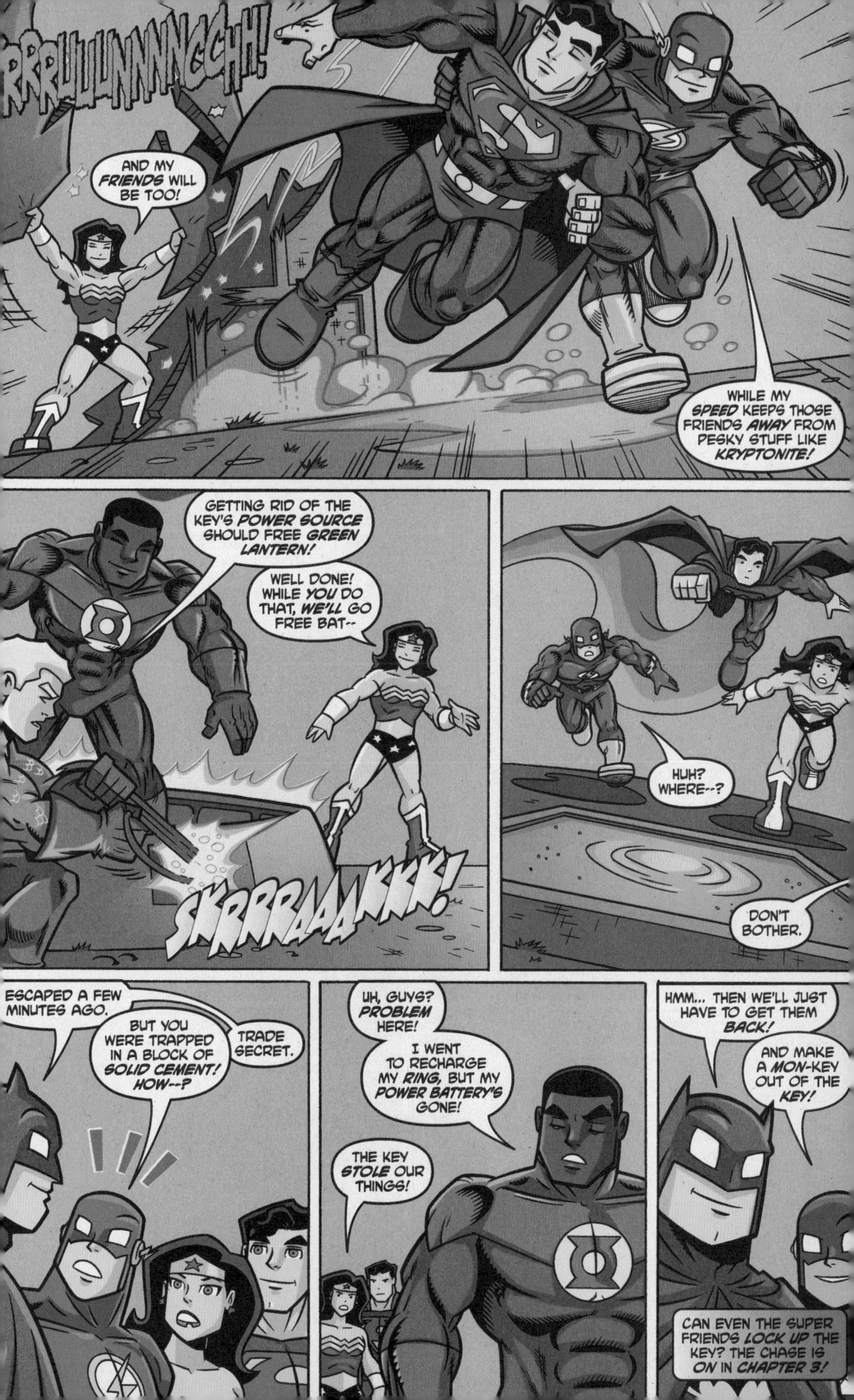

RRRUUUNNNNCCHH!
AND MY FRIENDS WILL BE TOO!
WHILE MY SPEED KEEPS THOSE FRIENDS AWAY FROM PESKY STUFF LIKE KRYPTONITE!
GETTING RID OF THE KEY'S POWER SOURCE SHOULD FREE GREEN LANTERN!
WELL DONE! WHILE YOU DO THAT, WE'LL GO FREE BAT--
SKRRRAAAKKK!
HUH? WHERE--?
DON'T BOTHER.
ESCAPED A FEW MINUTES AGO.
BUT YOU WERE TRAPPED IN A BLOCK OF SOLID CEMENT! HOW--?
TRADE SECRET.
UH, GUYS? PROBLEM HERE!
I WENT TO RECHARGE MY RING, BUT MY POWER BATTERY'S GONE!
THE KEY STOLE OUR THINGS!
HMM... THEN WE'LL JUST HAVE TO GET THEM BACK!
AND MAKE A MON-KEY OUT OF THE KEY!
CAN EVEN THE SUPER FRIENDS LOCK UP THE KEY? THE CHASE IS ON IN CHAPTER 3!

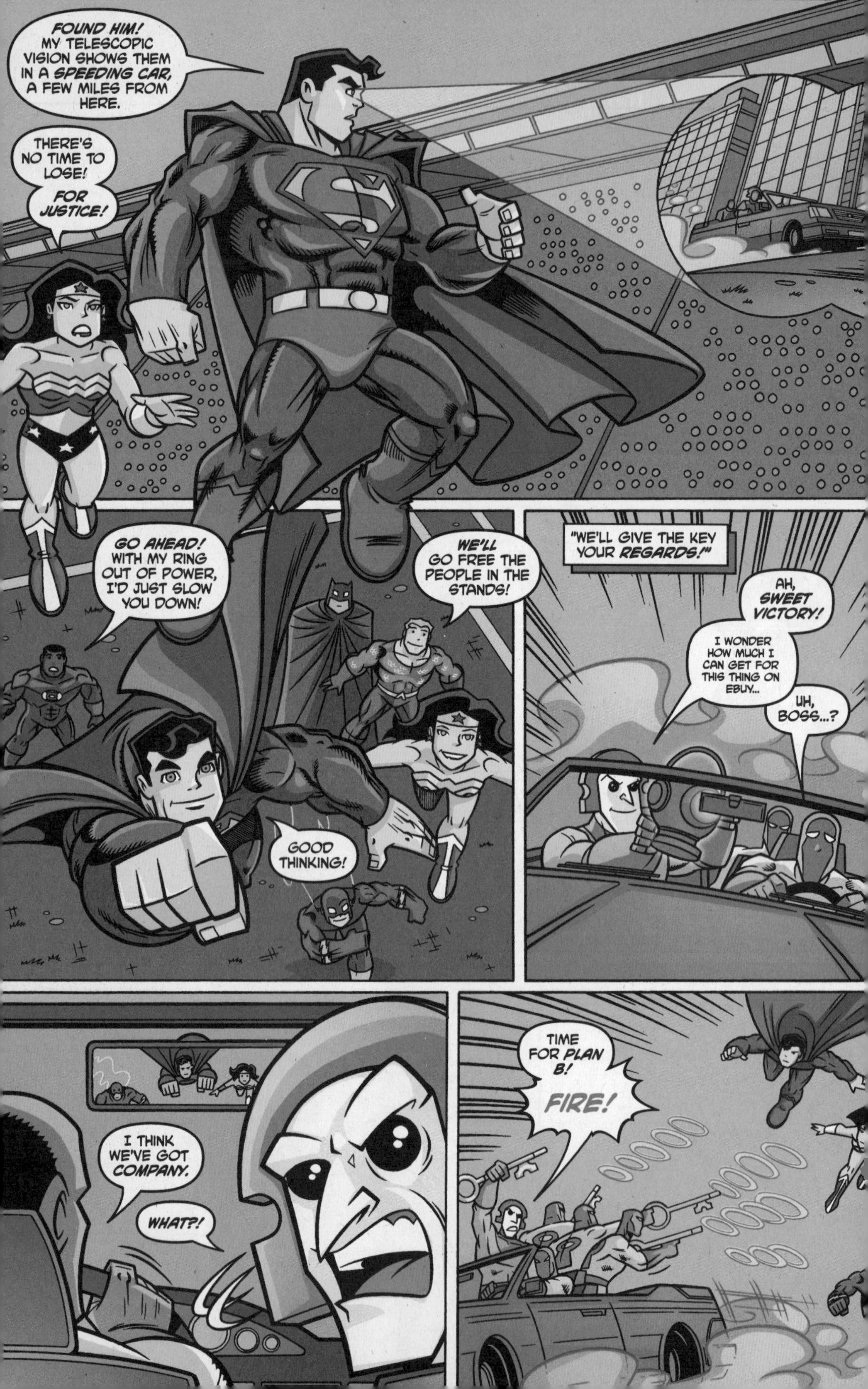
FOUND HIM! MY TELESCOPIC VISION SHOWS THEM IN A SPEEDING CAR, A FEW MILES FROM HERE.
THERE'S NO TIME TO LOSE!
FOR JUSTICE!
GO AHEAD! WITH MY RING OUT OF POWER, I'D JUST SLOW YOU DOWN!
WE'LL GO FREE THE PEOPLE IN THE STANDS!
GOOD THINKING!
"WE'LL GIVE THE KEY YOUR REGARDS!"
AH, SWEET VICTORY!
I WONDER HOW MUCH I CAN GET FOR THIS THING ON EBUY...
UH, BOSS...?
I THINK WE'VE GOT COMPANY.
WHAT?!
TIME FOR PLAN B!
FIRE!

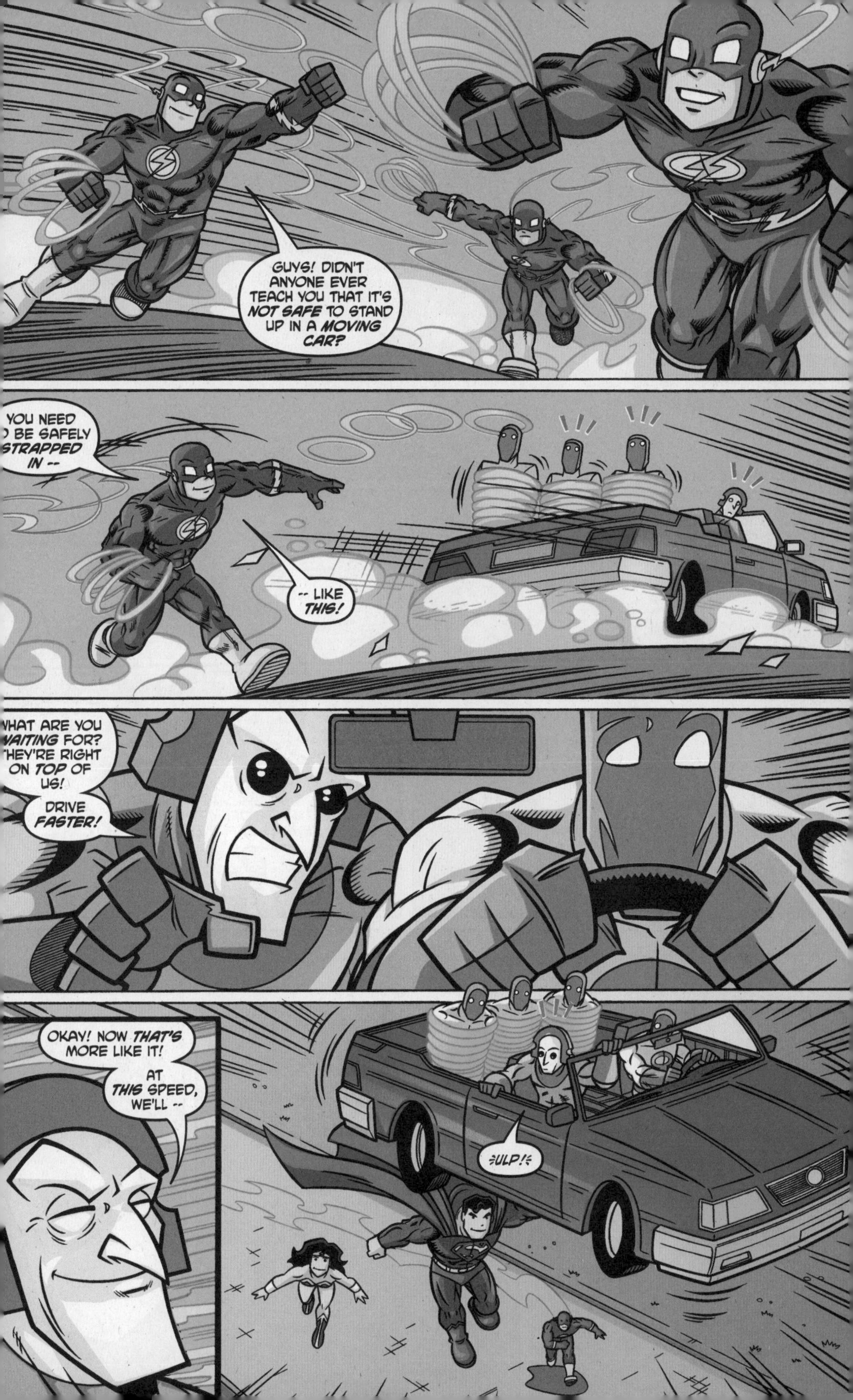
GUYS! DIDN'T ANYONE EVER TEACH YOU THAT IT'S NOT SAFE TO STAND UP IN A MOVING CAR?
YOU NEED TO BE SAFELY STRAPPED IN --
-- LIKE THIS!
WHAT ARE YOU WAITING FOR? THEY'RE RIGHT ON TOP OF US!
DRIVE FASTER!
OKAY! NOW THAT'S MORE LIKE IT!
AT THIS SPEED, WE'LL --
ULP!

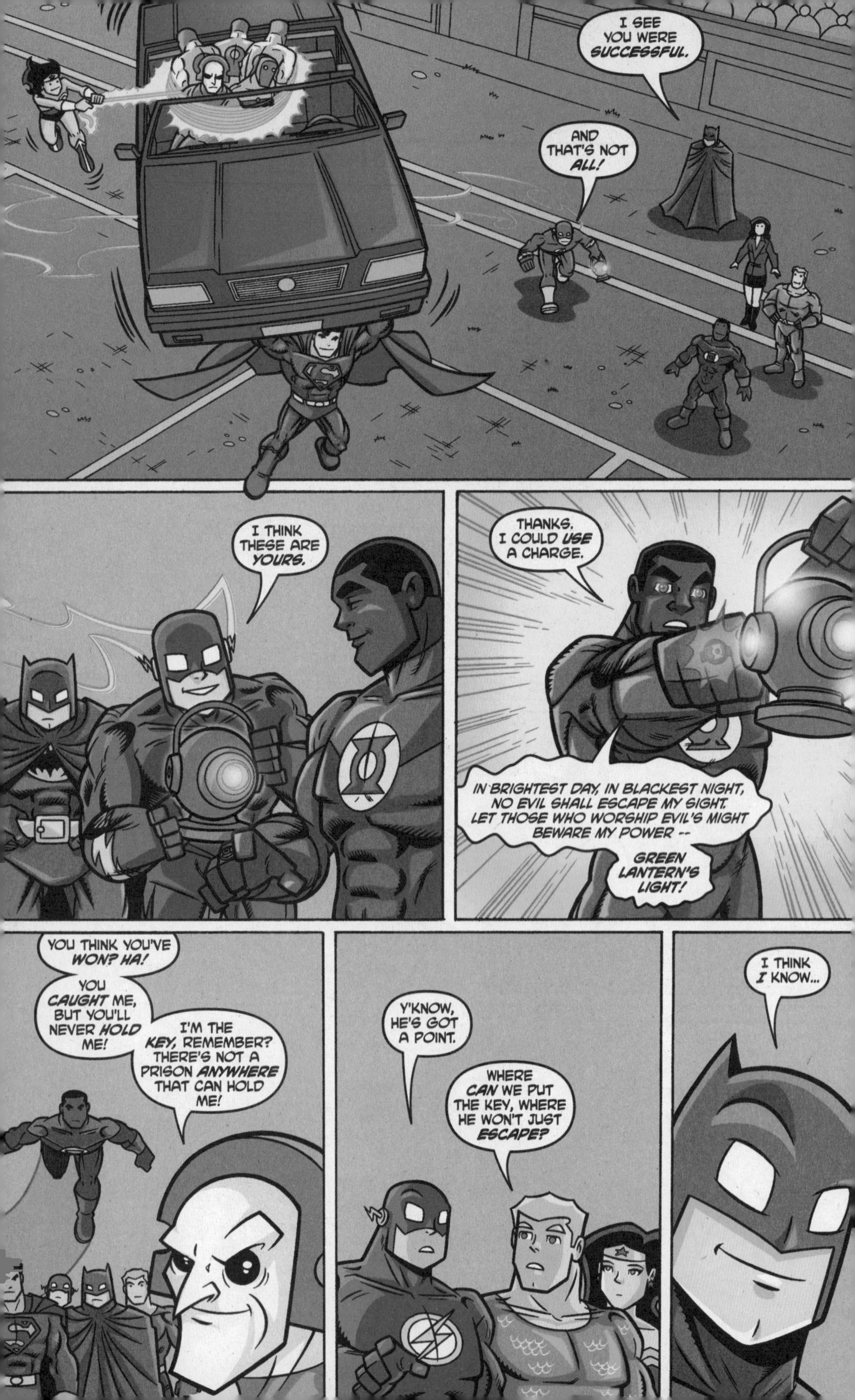
I SEE YOU WERE SUCCESSFUL.
AND THAT'S NOT ALL!
I THINK THESE ARE YOURS.
THANKS. I COULD USE A CHARGE.
IN BRIGHTEST DAY, IN BLACKEST NIGHT, NO EVIL SHALL ESCAPE MY SIGHT. LET THOSE WHO WORSHIP EVIL'S MIGHT BEWARE MY POWER --
GREEN LANTERN'S LIGHT!
YOU THINK YOU'VE WON? HA!
YOU CAUGHT ME, BUT YOU'LL NEVER HOLD ME!
I'M THE KEY, REMEMBER? THERE'S NOT A PRISON ANYWHERE THAT CAN HOLD ME!
Y'KNOW, HE'S GOT A POINT.
WHERE CAN WE PUT THE KEY, WHERE HE WON'T JUST ESCAPE?
I THINK I KNOW...

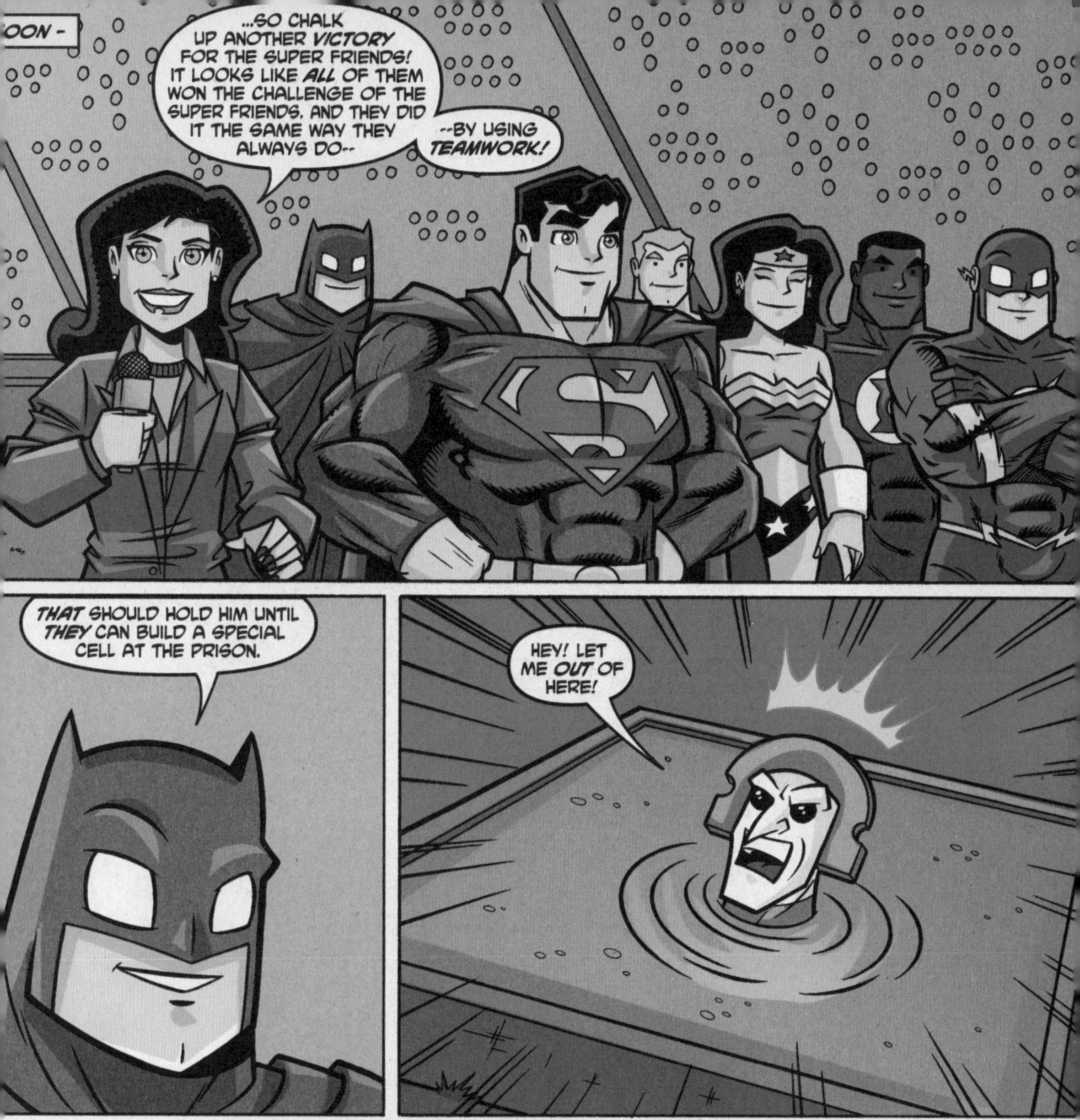
OON -
...SO CHALK UP ANOTHER VICTORY FOR THE SUPER FRIENDS! IT LOOKS LIKE ALL OF THEM WON THE CHALLENGE OF THE SUPER FRIENDS, AND THEY DID IT THE SAME WAY THEY ALWAYS DO--
--BY USING TEAMWORK!
THAT SHOULD HOLD HIM UNTIL THEY CAN BUILD A SPECIAL CELL AT THE PRISON.
HEY! LET ME OUT OF HERE!

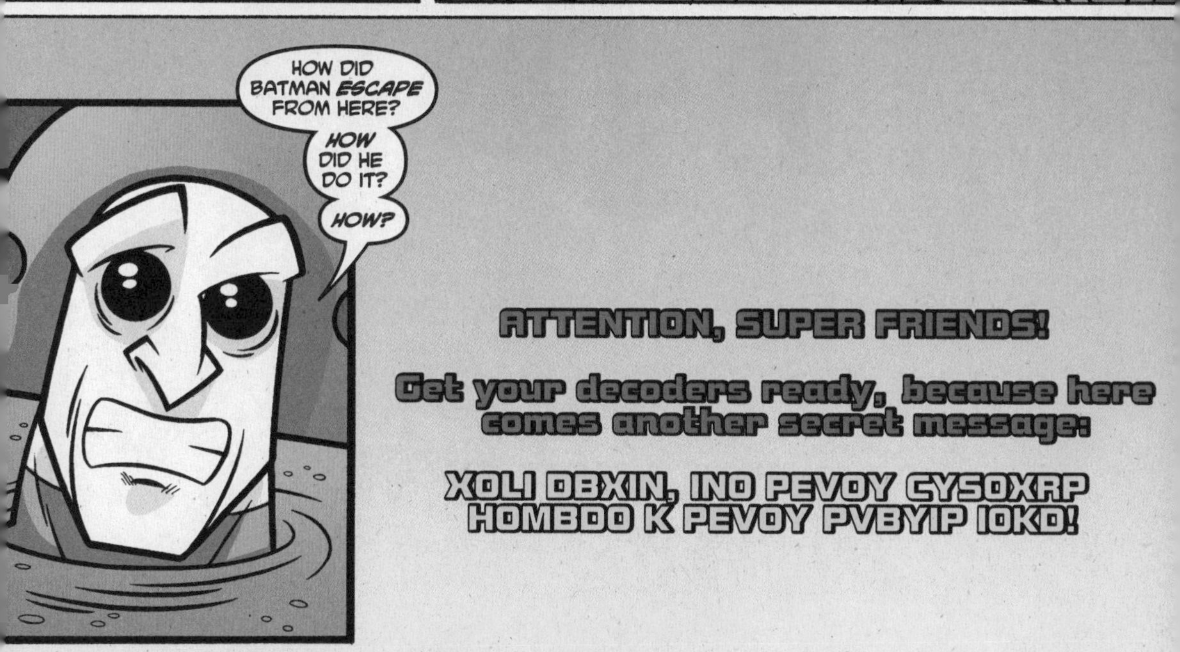
HOW DID BATMAN ESCAPE FROM HERE?
HOW DID HE DO IT?
HOW?

ATTENTION, SUPER FRIENDS!

Get your decoders ready, because here comes another secret message:

XOLI DBXIN, INO PEVOY CYSOXRP HOMBDO K PEVOY PVBYIP IOKD!

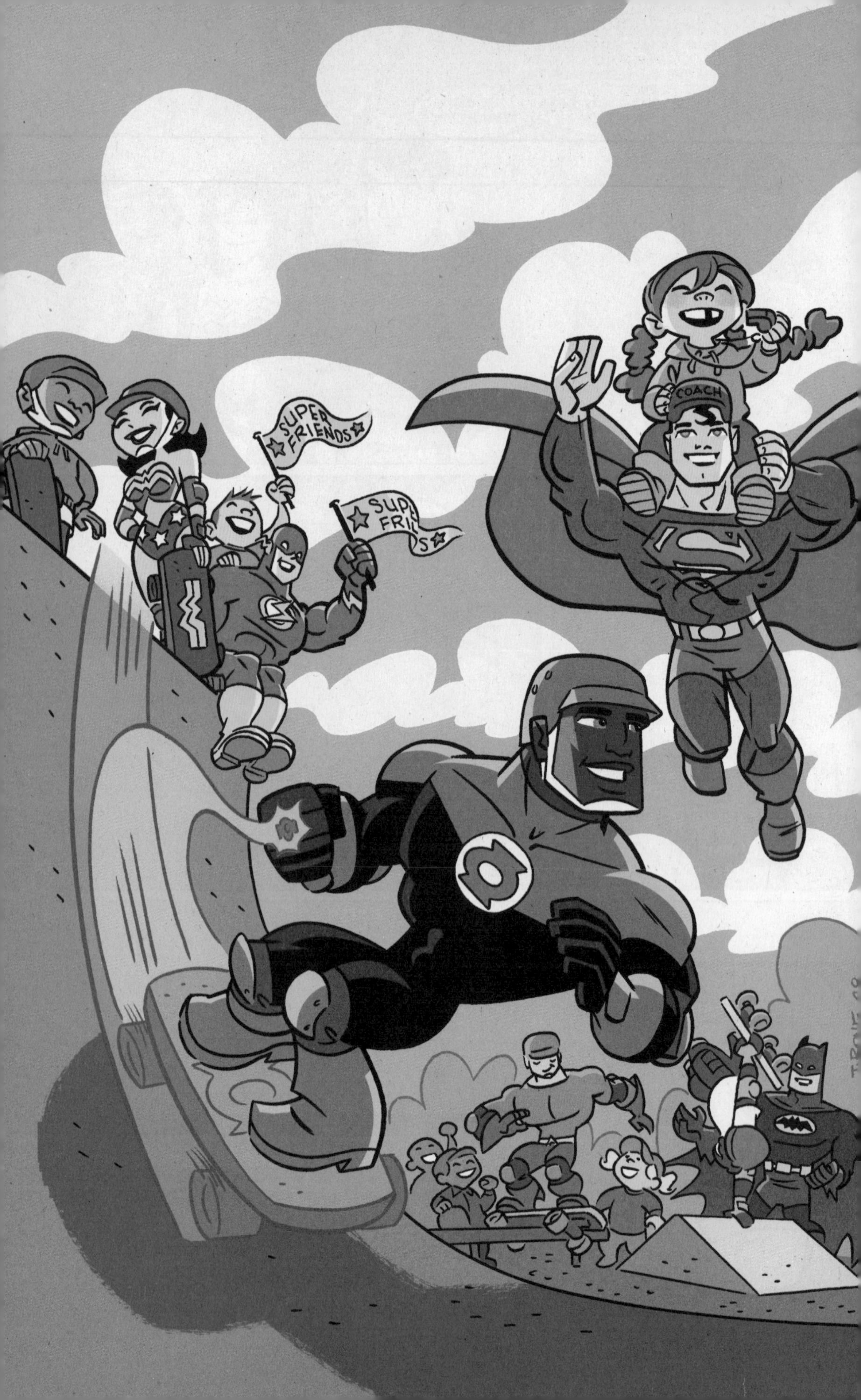
SUPER FRIENDS
COACH

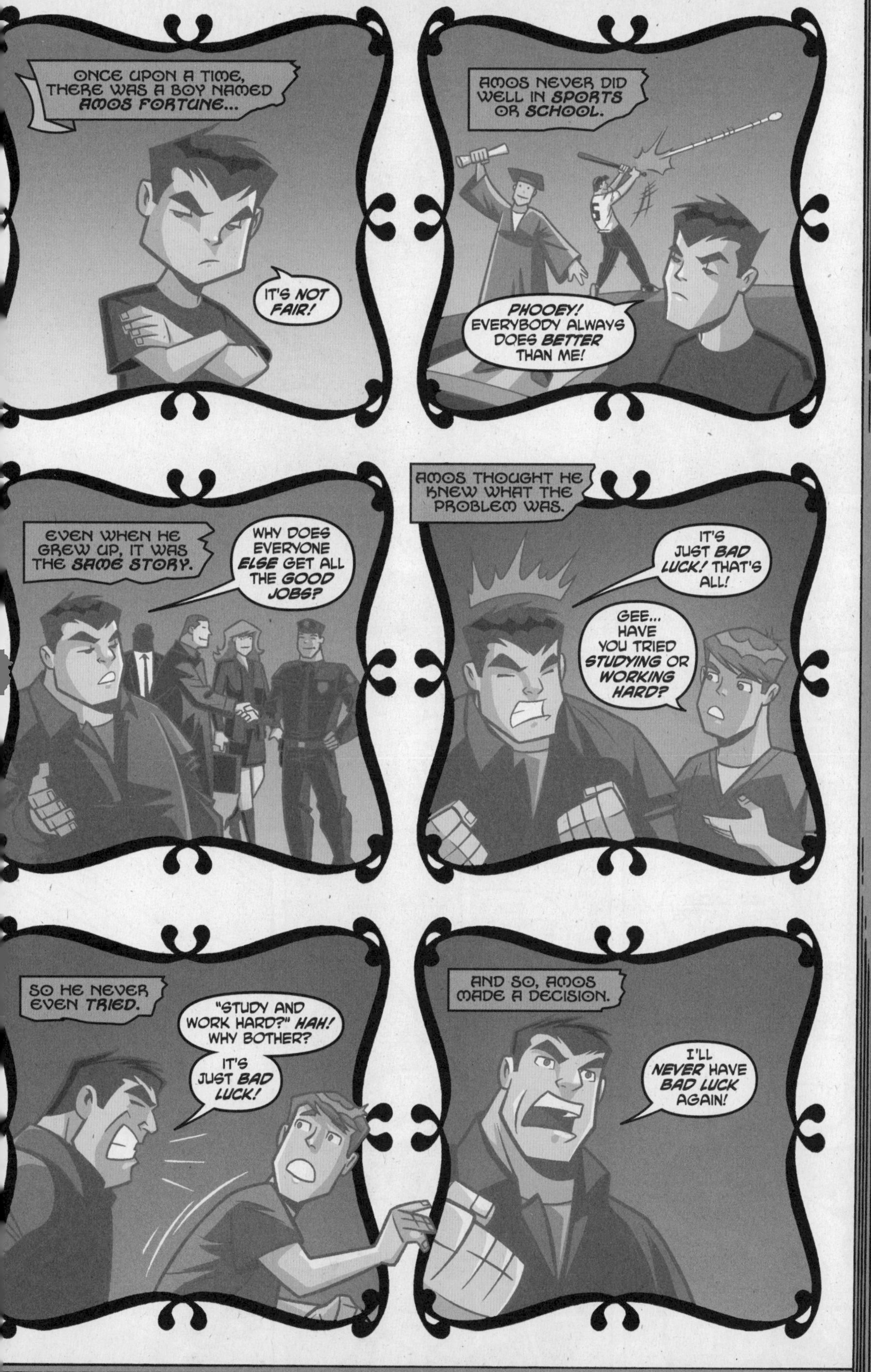
ONCE UPON A TIME, THERE WAS A BOY NAMED AMOS FORTUNE...
IT'S NOT FAIR!
AMOS NEVER DID WELL IN SPORTS OR SCHOOL.
PHOOEY! EVERYBODY ALWAYS DOES BETTER THAN ME!
EVEN WHEN HE GREW UP, IT WAS THE SAME STORY.
WHY DOES EVERYONE ELSE GET ALL THE GOOD JOBS?
AMOS THOUGHT HE KNEW WHAT THE PROBLEM WAS.
IT'S JUST BAD LUCK! THAT'S ALL!
GEE... HAVE YOU TRIED STUDYING OR WORKING HARD?
SO HE NEVER EVEN TRIED.
"STUDY AND WORK HARD?" HAH! WHY BOTHER?
IT'S JUST BAD LUCK!
AND SO, AMOS MADE A DECISION.
I'LL NEVER HAVE BAD LUCK AGAIN!

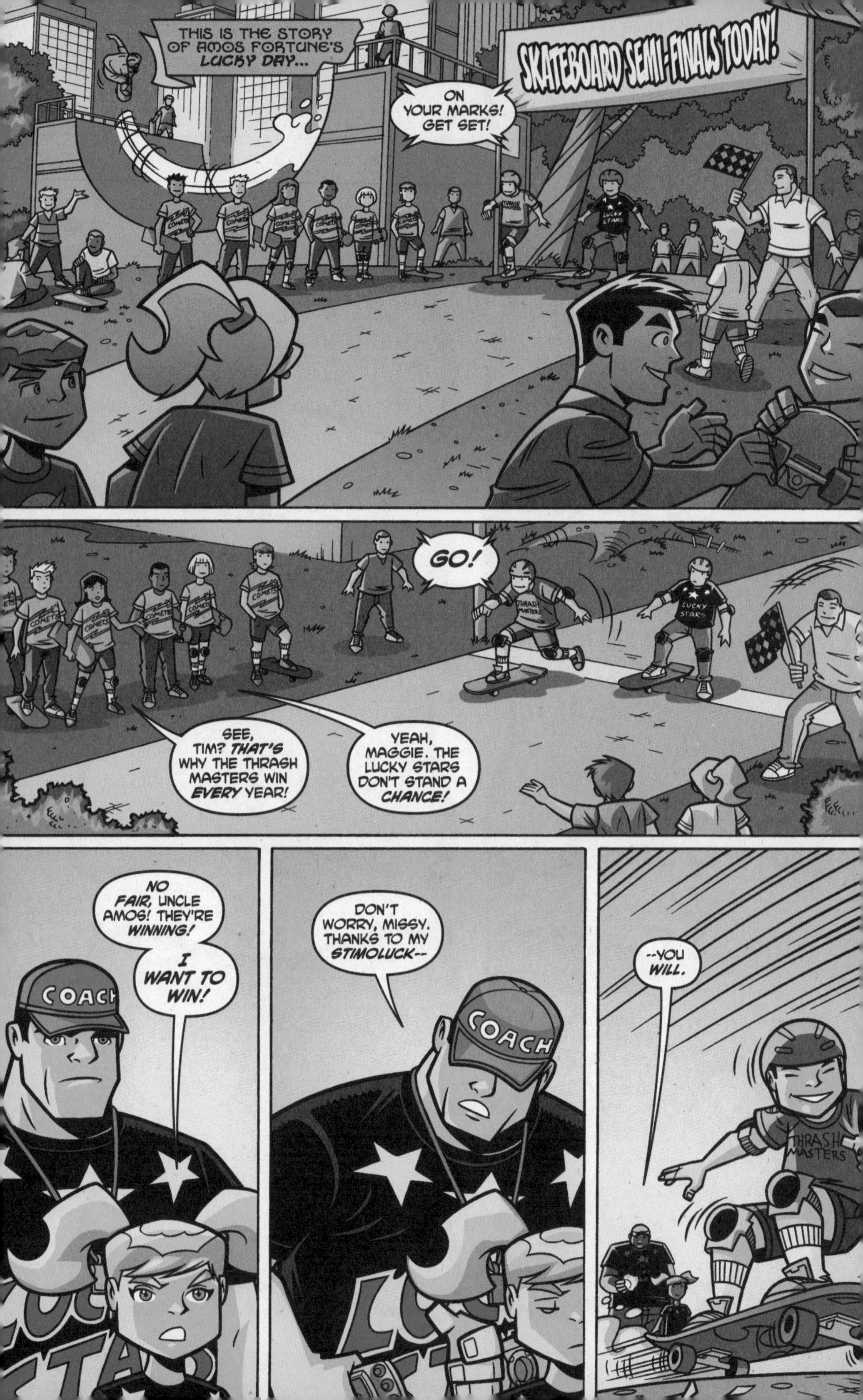
THIS IS THE STORY OF AMOS FORTUNE'S LUCKY DAY...
SKATEBOARD SEMI-FINALS TODAY!
ON YOUR MARKS! GET SET!
COMETS
THRASH MASTERS
LUCKY STARS
GO!
SEE, TIM? THAT'S WHY THE THRASH MASTERS WIN EVERY YEAR!
YEAH, MAGGIE. THE LUCKY STARS DON'T STAND A CHANCE!
NO FAIR, UNCLE AMOS! THEY'RE WINNING!
I WANT TO WIN!
COACH
DON'T WORRY, MISSY. THANKS TO MY STIMOLUCK--
COACH
--YOU WILL.
THRASH MASTERS

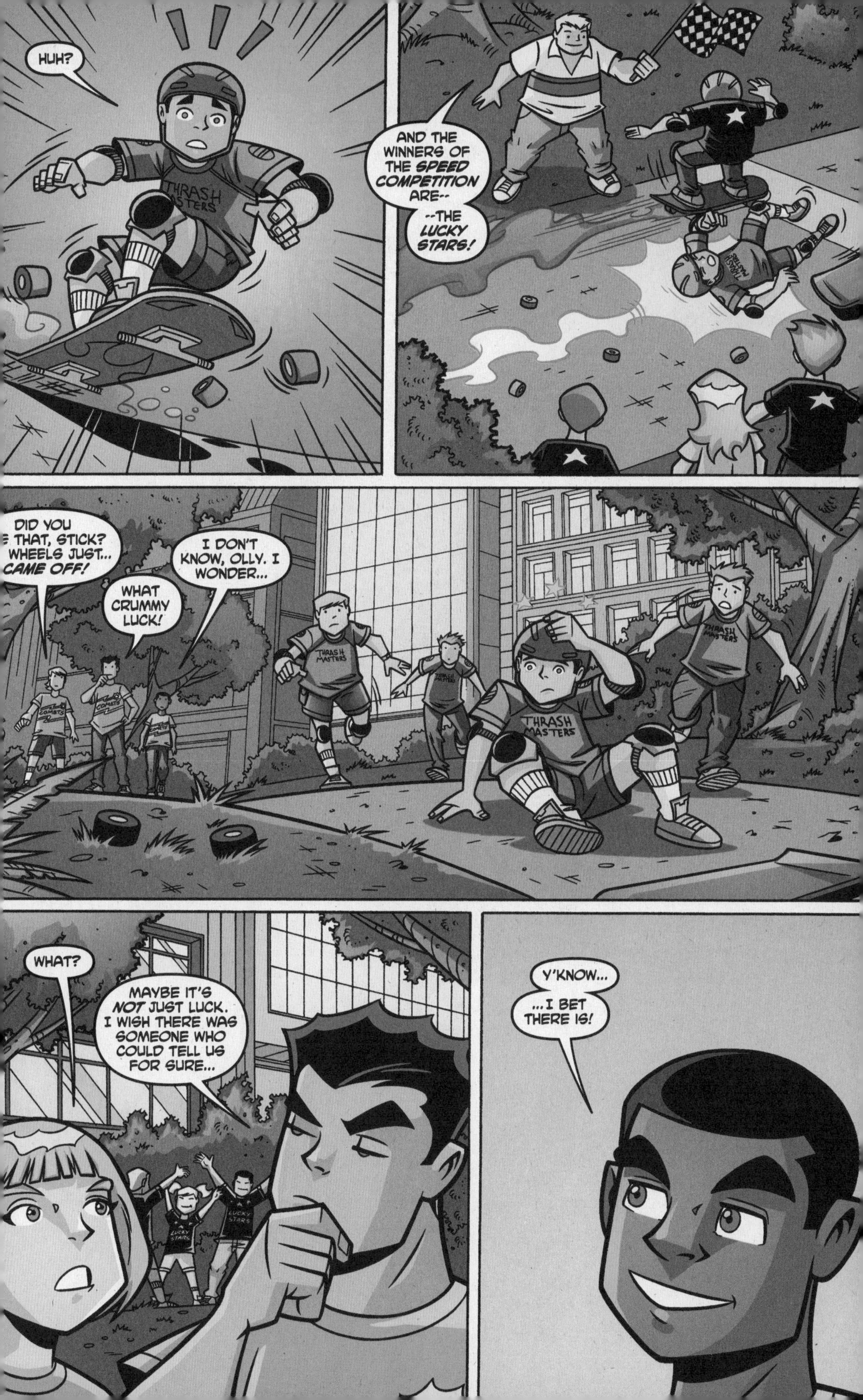
HUH?
AND THE WINNERS OF THE *SPEED COMPETITION* ARE--
--THE *LUCKY STARS!*
DID YOU
E THAT, STICK?
WHEELS JUST...
CAME OFF!
WHAT CRUMMY LUCK!
I DON'T KNOW, OLLY. I WONDER...
WHAT?
MAYBE IT'S *NOT* JUST LUCK. I WISH THERE WAS SOMEONE WHO COULD TELL US FOR SURE...
Y'KNOW...
...I BET THERE IS!

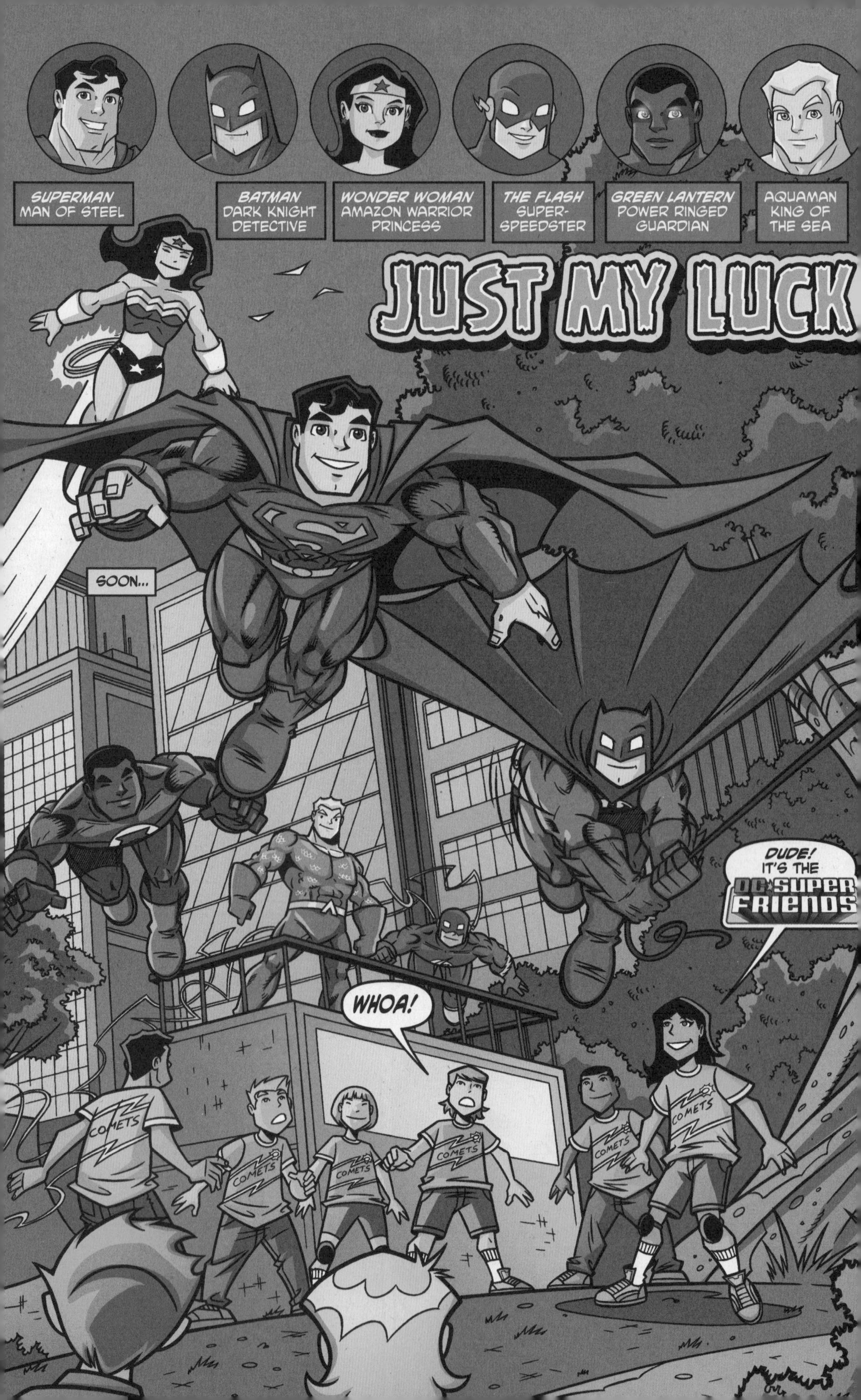
SUPERMAN
MAN OF STEEL
BATMAN
DARK KNIGHT DETECTIVE
WONDER WOMAN
AMAZON WARRIOR PRINCESS
THE FLASH
SUPER-SPEEDSTER
GREEN LANTERN
POWER RINGED GUARDIAN
AQUAMAN
KING OF THE SEA
JUST MY LUCK
SOON...
DUDE! IT'S THE DC SUPER FRIENDS
WHOA!
COMETS

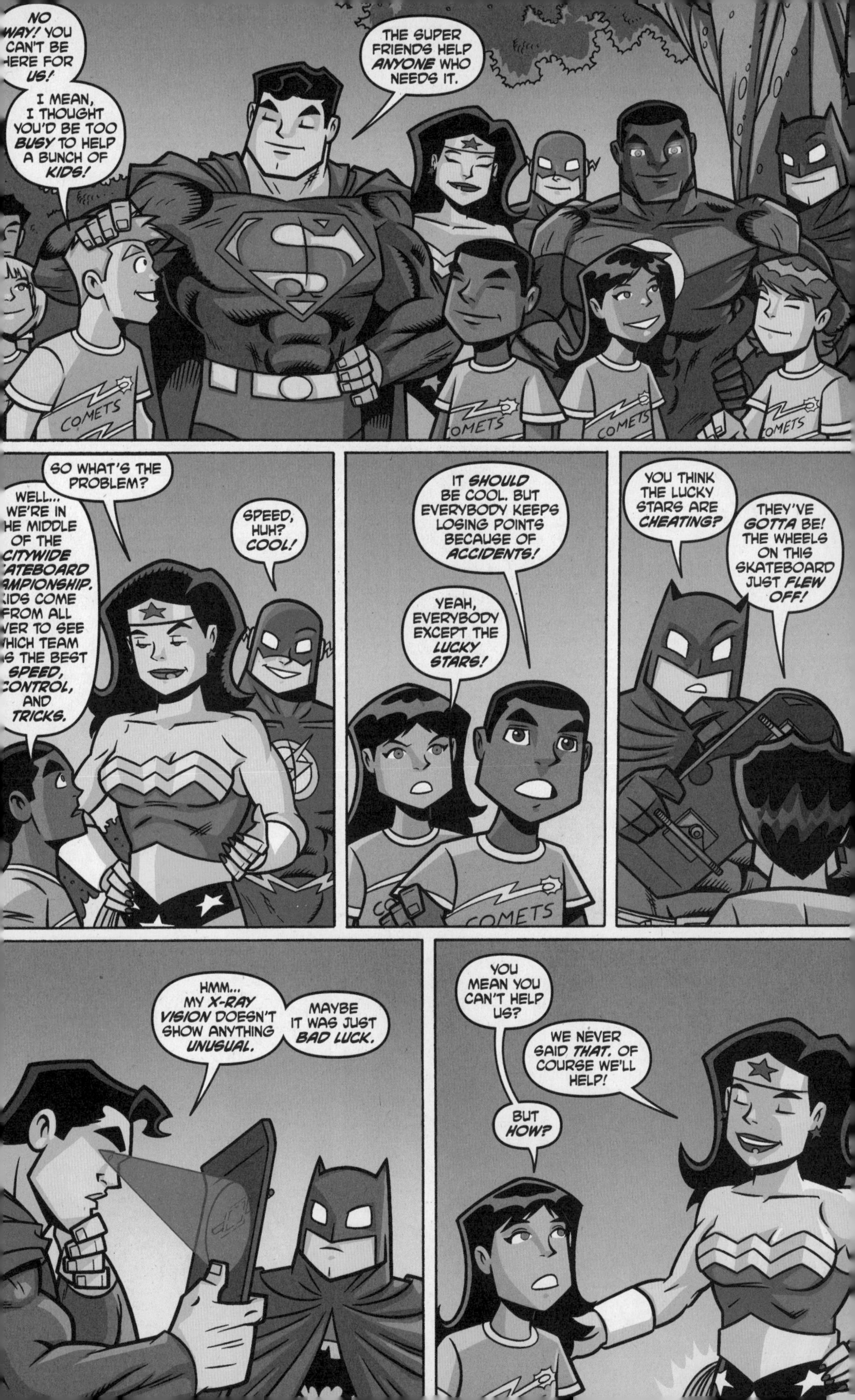
NO WAY! YOU CAN'T BE ERE FOR US!
I MEAN, I THOUGHT YOU'D BE TOO BUSY TO HELP A BUNCH OF KIDS!
THE SUPER FRIENDS HELP ANYONE WHO NEEDS IT.
SO WHAT'S THE PROBLEM?
WELL... WE'RE IN HE MIDDLE OF THE CITYWIDE ATEBOARD AMPIONSHIP. IDS COME FROM ALL VER TO SEE HICH TEAM S THE BEST SPEED, CONTROL, AND TRICKS.
SPEED, HUH? COOL!
IT SHOULD BE COOL. BUT EVERYBODY KEEPS LOSING POINTS BECAUSE OF ACCIDENTS!
YEAH, EVERYBODY EXCEPT THE LUCKY STARS!
YOU THINK THE LUCKY STARS ARE CHEATING?
THEY'VE GOTTA BE! THE WHEELS ON THIS SKATEBOARD JUST FLEW OFF!
HMM... MY X-RAY VISION DOESN'T SHOW ANYTHING UNUSUAL.
MAYBE IT WAS JUST BAD LUCK.
YOU MEAN YOU CAN'T HELP US?
WE NEVER SAID THAT. OF COURSE WE'LL HELP!
BUT HOW?

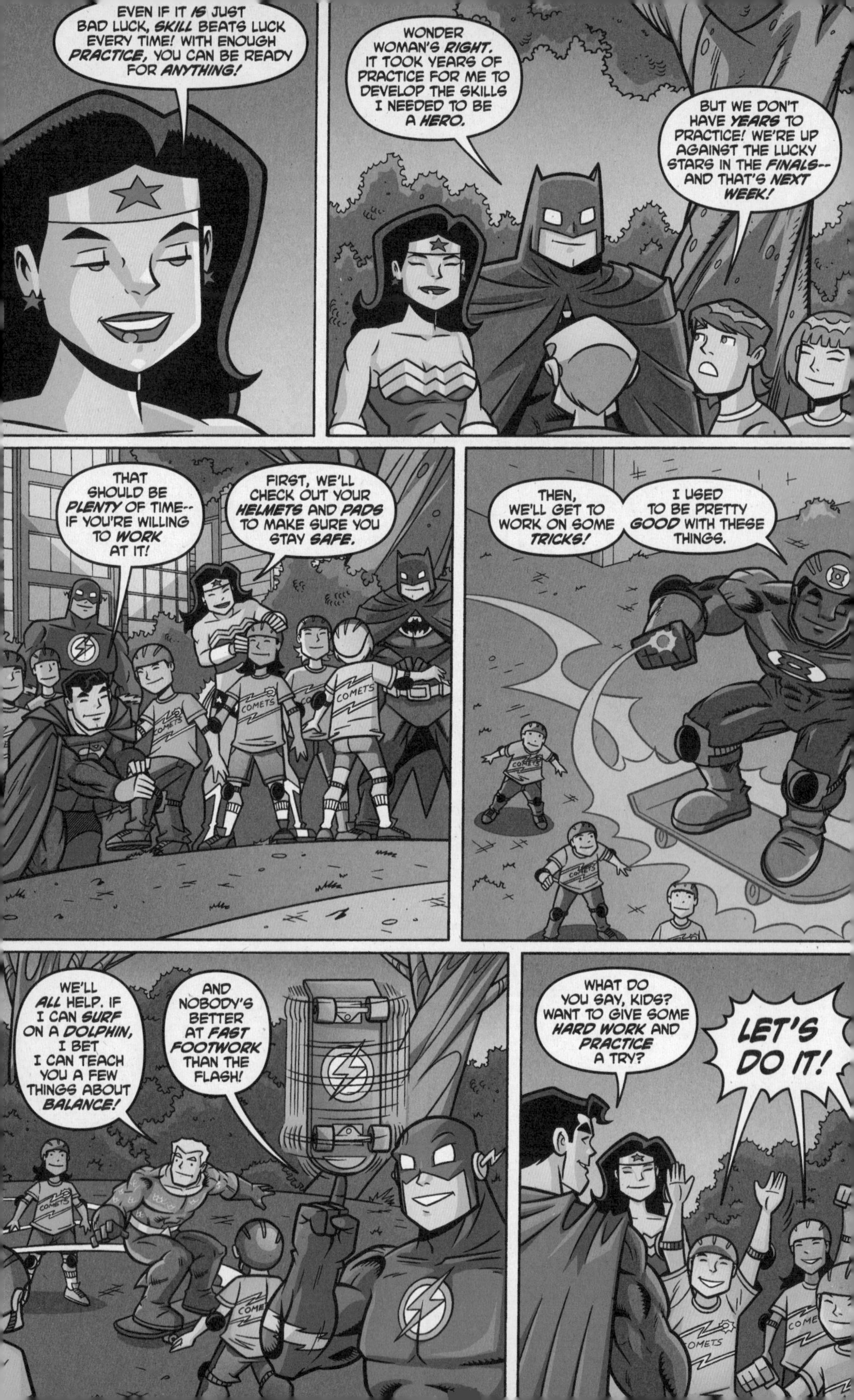
EVEN IF IT IS JUST BAD LUCK, SKILL BEATS LUCK EVERY TIME! WITH ENOUGH PRACTICE, YOU CAN BE READY FOR ANYTHING!
WONDER WOMAN'S RIGHT. IT TOOK YEARS OF PRACTICE FOR ME TO DEVELOP THE SKILLS I NEEDED TO BE A HERO.
BUT WE DON'T HAVE YEARS TO PRACTICE! WE'RE UP AGAINST THE LUCKY STARS IN THE FINALS-- AND THAT'S NEXT WEEK!
THAT SHOULD BE PLENTY OF TIME-- IF YOU'RE WILLING TO WORK AT IT!
FIRST, WE'LL CHECK OUT YOUR HELMETS AND PADS TO MAKE SURE YOU STAY SAFE.
COMETS
THEN, WE'LL GET TO WORK ON SOME TRICKS!
I USED TO BE PRETTY GOOD WITH THESE THINGS.
WE'LL ALL HELP. IF I CAN SURF ON A DOLPHIN, I BET I CAN TEACH YOU A FEW THINGS ABOUT BALANCE!
AND NOBODY'S BETTER AT FAST FOOTWORK THAN THE FLASH!
WHAT DO YOU SAY, KIDS? WANT TO GIVE SOME HARD WORK AND PRACTICE A TRY?
LET'S DO IT!

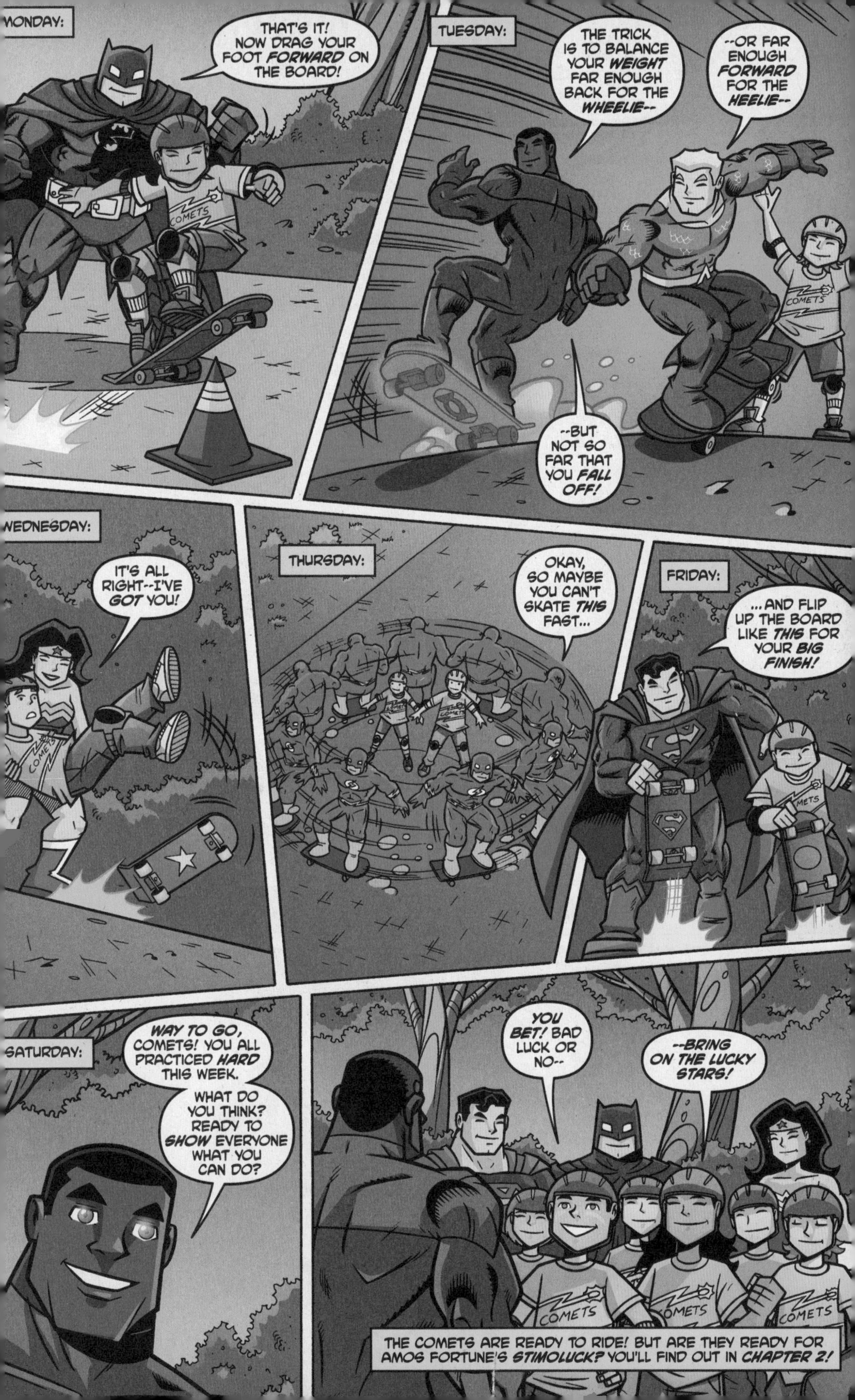
MONDAY:
THAT'S IT! NOW DRAG YOUR FOOT FORWARD ON THE BOARD!
TUESDAY:
THE TRICK IS TO BALANCE YOUR WEIGHT FAR ENOUGH BACK FOR THE WHEELIE--
--OR FAR ENOUGH FORWARD FOR THE HEELIE--
--BUT NOT SO FAR THAT YOU FALL OFF!
WEDNESDAY:
IT'S ALL RIGHT--I'VE GOT YOU!
THURSDAY:
OKAY, SO MAYBE YOU CAN'T SKATE THIS FAST...
FRIDAY:
...AND FLIP UP THE BOARD LIKE THIS FOR YOUR BIG FINISH!
SATURDAY:
WAY TO GO, COMETS! YOU ALL PRACTICED HARD THIS WEEK.
WHAT DO YOU THINK? READY TO SHOW EVERYONE WHAT YOU CAN DO?
YOU BET! BAD LUCK OR NO--
--BRING ON THE LUCKY STARS!
THE COMETS ARE READY TO RIDE! BUT ARE THEY READY FOR AMOS FORTUNE'S STIMOLUCK? YOU'LL FIND OUT IN CHAPTER 2!

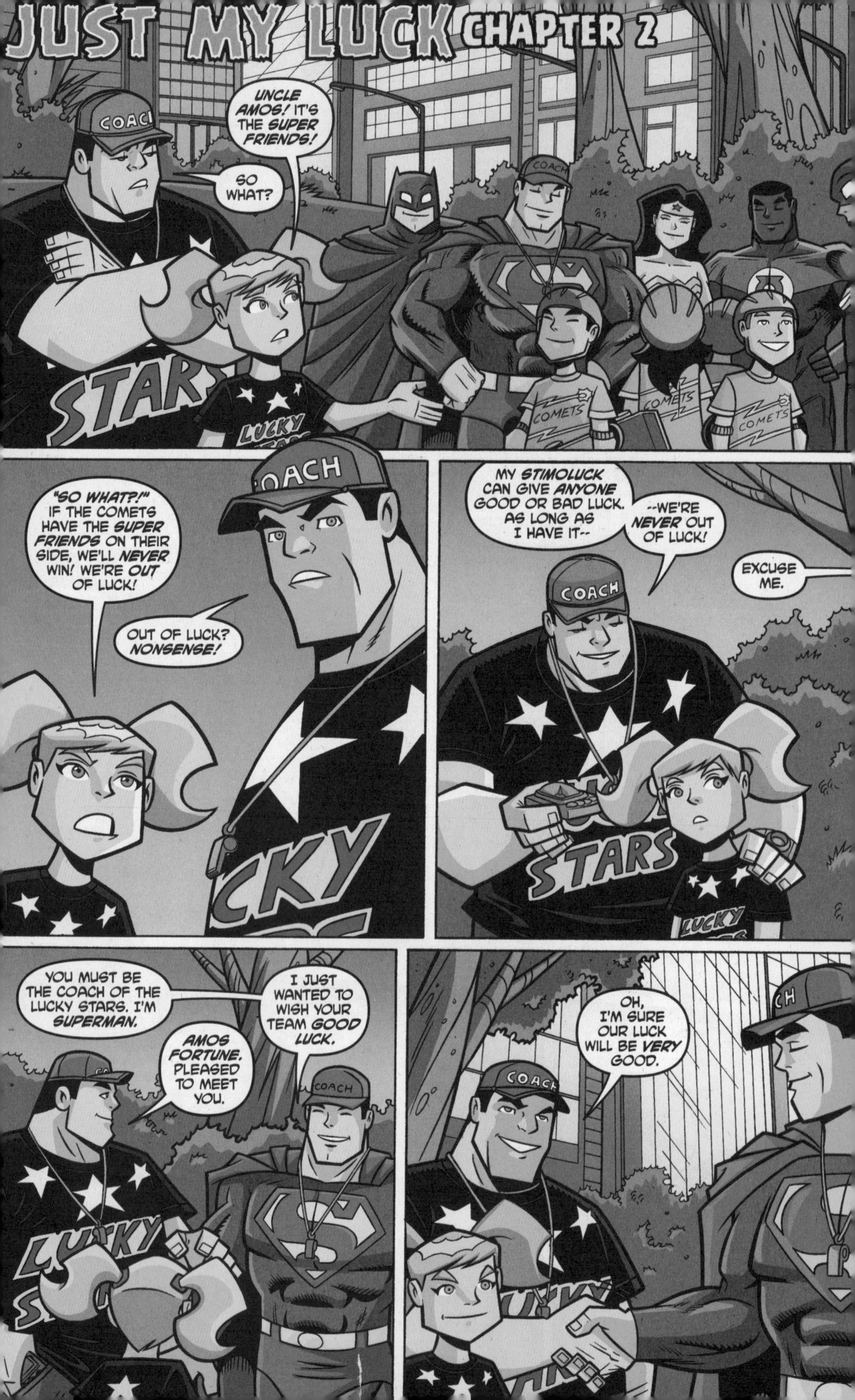
JUST MY LUCK CHAPTER 2
UNCLE AMOS! IT'S THE SUPER FRIENDS!
SO WHAT?
COACH
STARS
LUCKY
COMETS
"SO WHAT?!" IF THE COMETS HAVE THE SUPER FRIENDS ON THEIR SIDE, WE'LL NEVER WIN! WE'RE OUT OF LUCK!
OUT OF LUCK? NONSENSE!
MY STIMOLUCK CAN GIVE ANYONE GOOD OR BAD LUCK. AS LONG AS I HAVE IT--
--WE'RE NEVER OUT OF LUCK!
EXCUSE ME.
YOU MUST BE THE COACH OF THE LUCKY STARS. I'M SUPERMAN.
I JUST WANTED TO WISH YOUR TEAM GOOD LUCK.
AMOS FORTUNE. PLEASED TO MEET YOU.
OH, I'M SURE OUR LUCK WILL BE VERY GOOD.

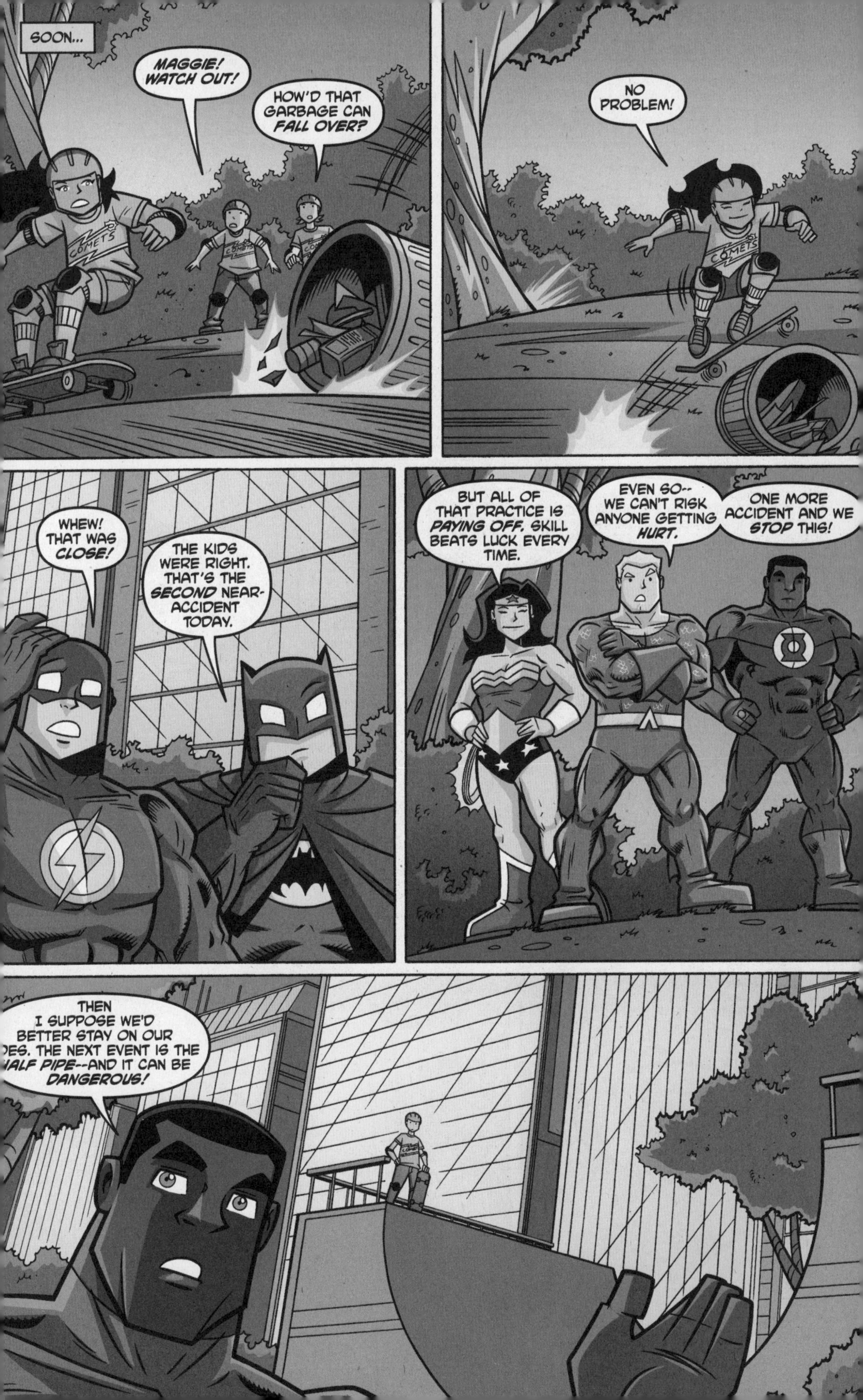
SOON...
MAGGIE! WATCH OUT!
HOW'D THAT GARBAGE CAN FALL OVER?
NO PROBLEM!
WHEW! THAT WAS CLOSE!
THE KIDS WERE RIGHT. THAT'S THE SECOND NEAR-ACCIDENT TODAY.
BUT ALL OF THAT PRACTICE IS PAYING OFF. SKILL BEATS LUCK EVERY TIME.
EVEN SO-- WE CAN'T RISK ANYONE GETTING HURT.
ONE MORE ACCIDENT AND WE STOP THIS!
THEN I SUPPOSE WE'D BETTER STAY ON OUR
DES. THE NEXT EVENT IS THE
ALF PIPE--AND IT CAN BE DANGEROUS!

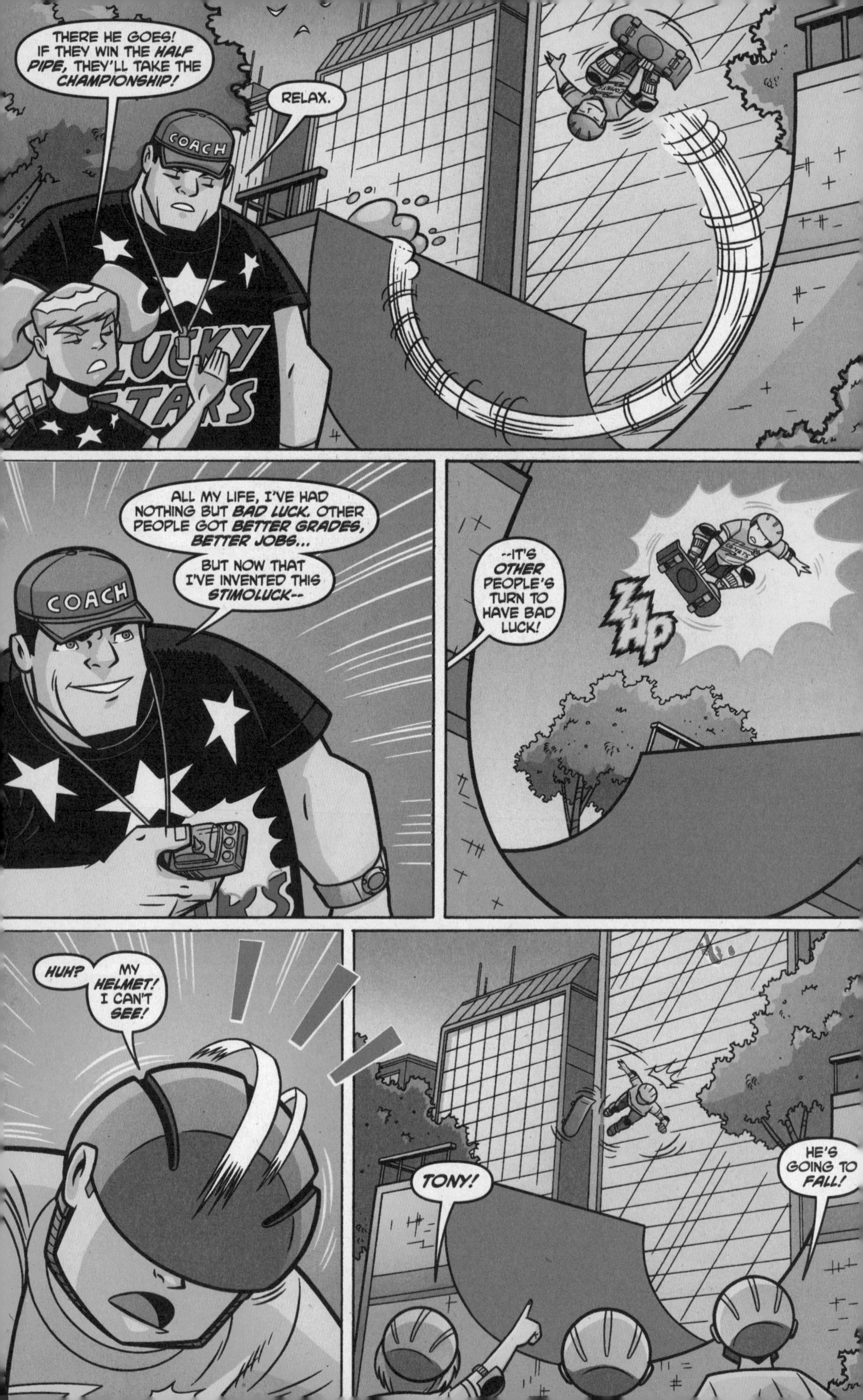
THERE HE GOES! IF THEY WIN THE HALF PIPE, THEY'LL TAKE THE CHAMPIONSHIP!
RELAX.
COACH
LUCKY STARS
ALL MY LIFE, I'VE HAD NOTHING BUT BAD LUCK. OTHER PEOPLE GOT BETTER GRADES, BETTER JOBS...
BUT NOW THAT I'VE INVENTED THIS STIMOLUCK--
COACH
--IT'S OTHER PEOPLE'S TURN TO HAVE BAD LUCK!
ZAP
HUH?
MY HELMET! I CAN'T SEE!
TONY!
HE'S GOING TO FALL!

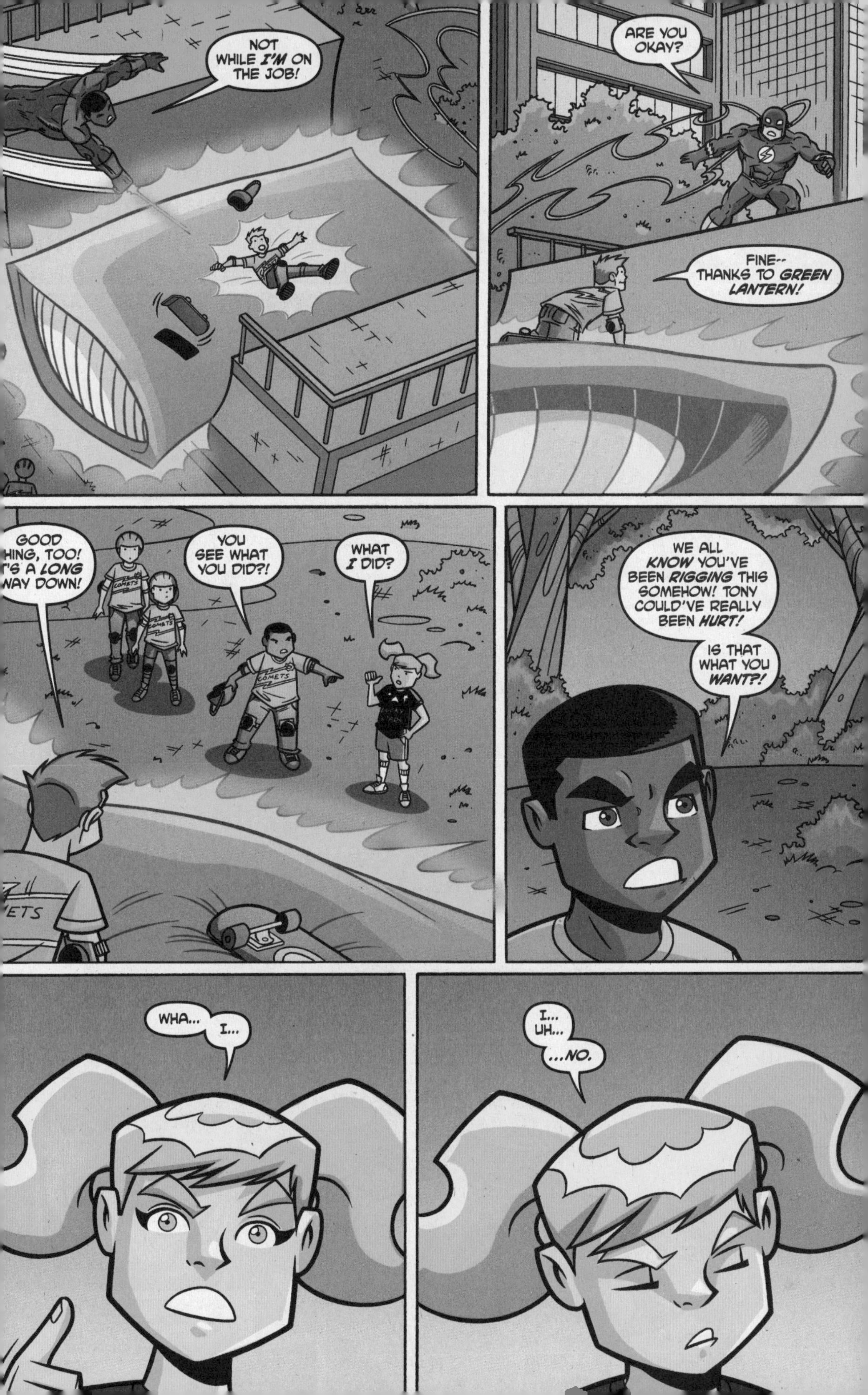
NOT WHILE I'M ON THE JOB!
ARE YOU OKAY?
FINE-- THANKS TO GREEN LANTERN!
GOOD THING, TOO! IT'S A LONG WAY DOWN!
YOU SEE WHAT YOU DID?!
WHAT I DID?
WE ALL KNOW YOU'VE BEEN RIGGING THIS SOMEHOW! TONY COULD'VE REALLY BEEN HURT!
IS THAT WHAT YOU WANT?!
WHA... I...
I... UH... ...NO.

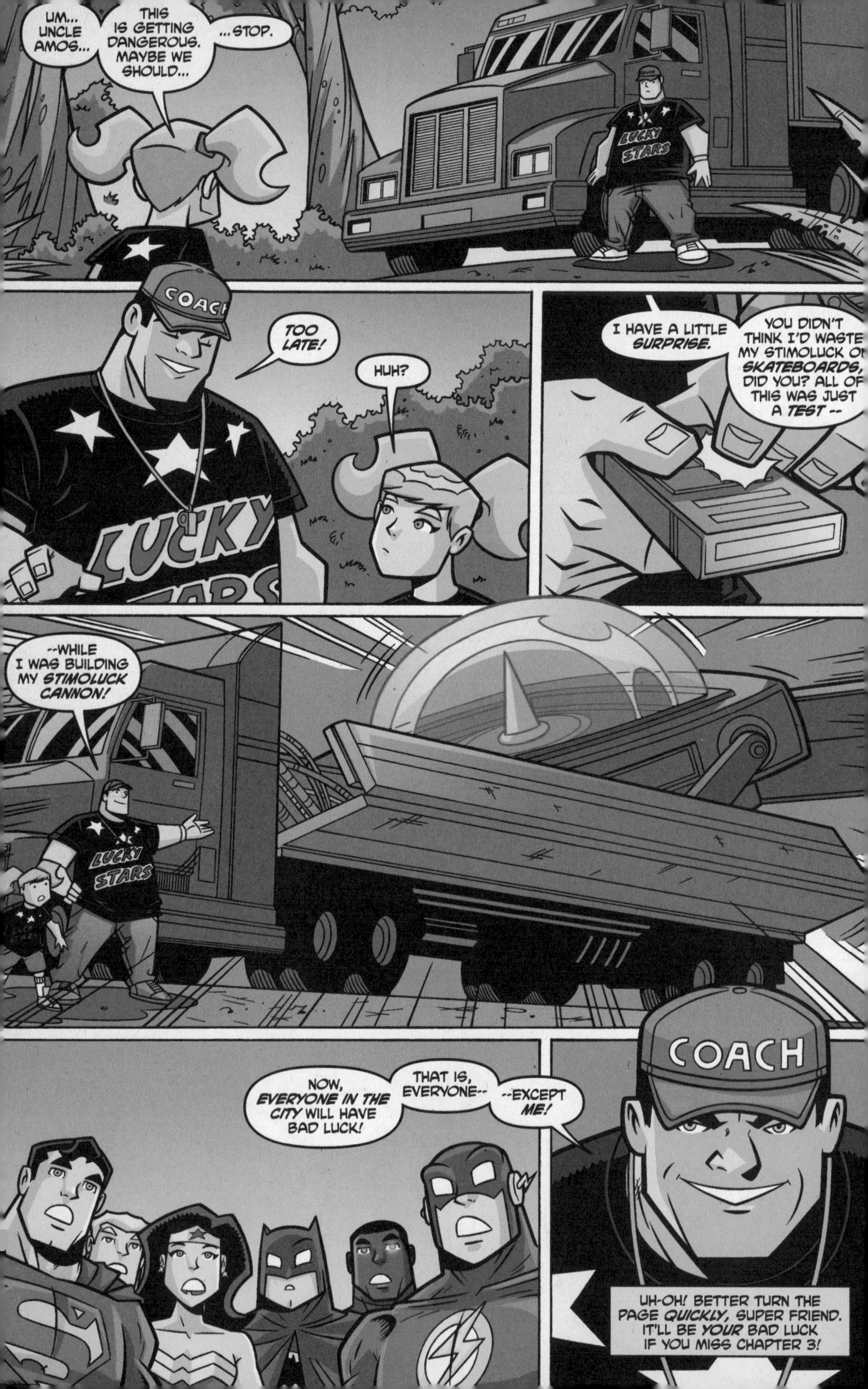
UM... UNCLE AMOS...
THIS IS GETTING DANGEROUS. MAYBE WE SHOULD...
...STOP.
LUCKY STARS
COACH
TOO LATE!
HUH?
I HAVE A LITTLE SURPRISE.
YOU DIDN'T THINK I'D WASTE MY STIMOLUCK ON SKATEBOARDS, DID YOU? ALL OF THIS WAS JUST A TEST --
--WHILE I WAS BUILDING MY STIMOLUCK CANNON!
NOW, EVERYONE IN THE CITY WILL HAVE BAD LUCK!
THAT IS, EVERYONE--
--EXCEPT ME!
COACH
UH-OH! BETTER TURN THE PAGE QUICKLY, SUPER FRIEND. IT'LL BE YOUR BAD LUCK IF YOU MISS CHAPTER 3!

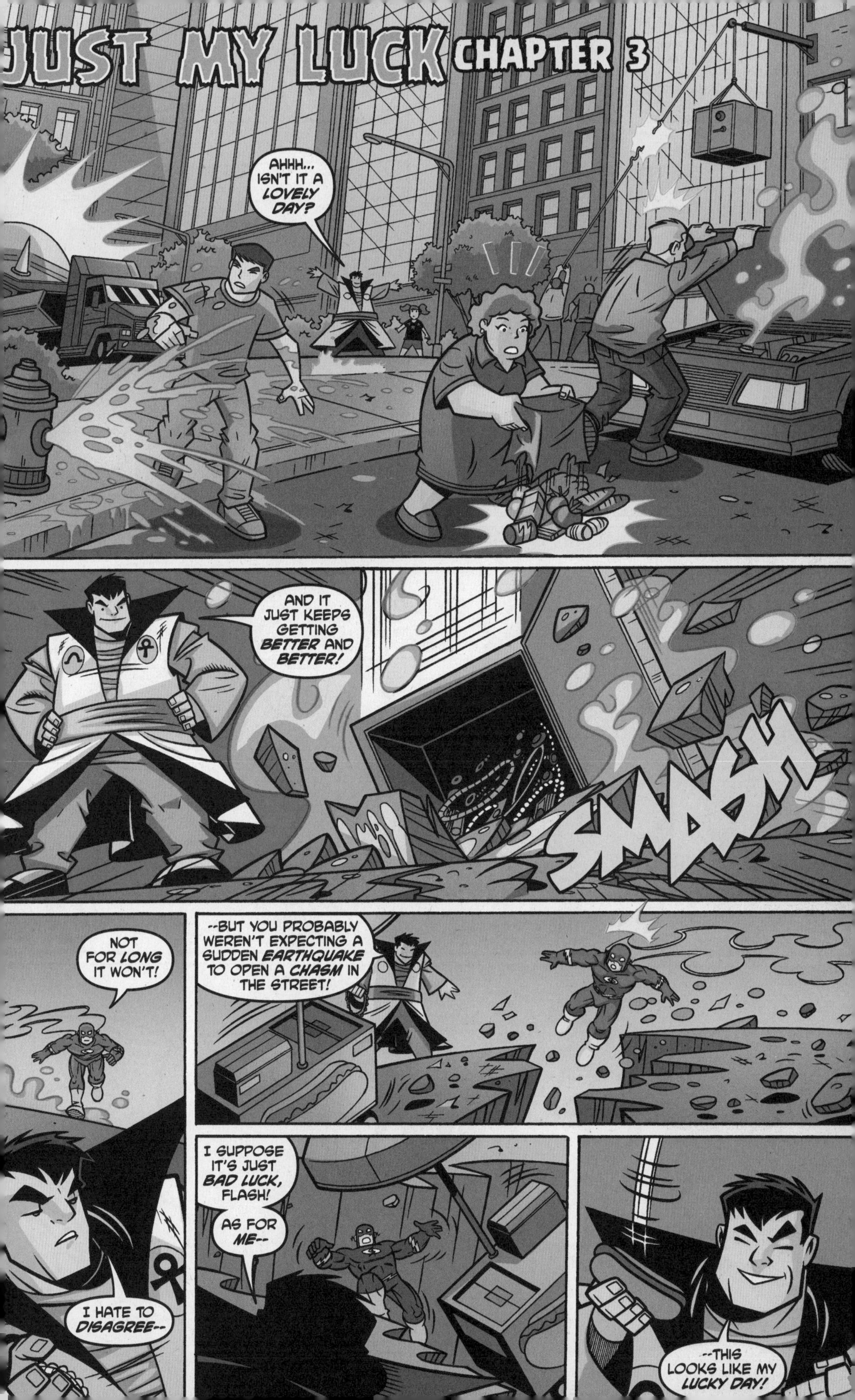
JUST MY LUCK CHAPTER 3
AHHH... ISN'T IT A LOVELY DAY?
AND IT JUST KEEPS GETTING BETTER AND BETTER!
SMASH
NOT FOR LONG IT WON'T!
--BUT YOU PROBABLY WEREN'T EXPECTING A SUDDEN EARTHQUAKE TO OPEN A CHASM IN THE STREET!
I HATE TO DISAGREE--
I SUPPOSE IT'S JUST BAD LUCK, FLASH!
AS FOR ME--
--THIS LOOKS LIKE MY LUCKY DAY!

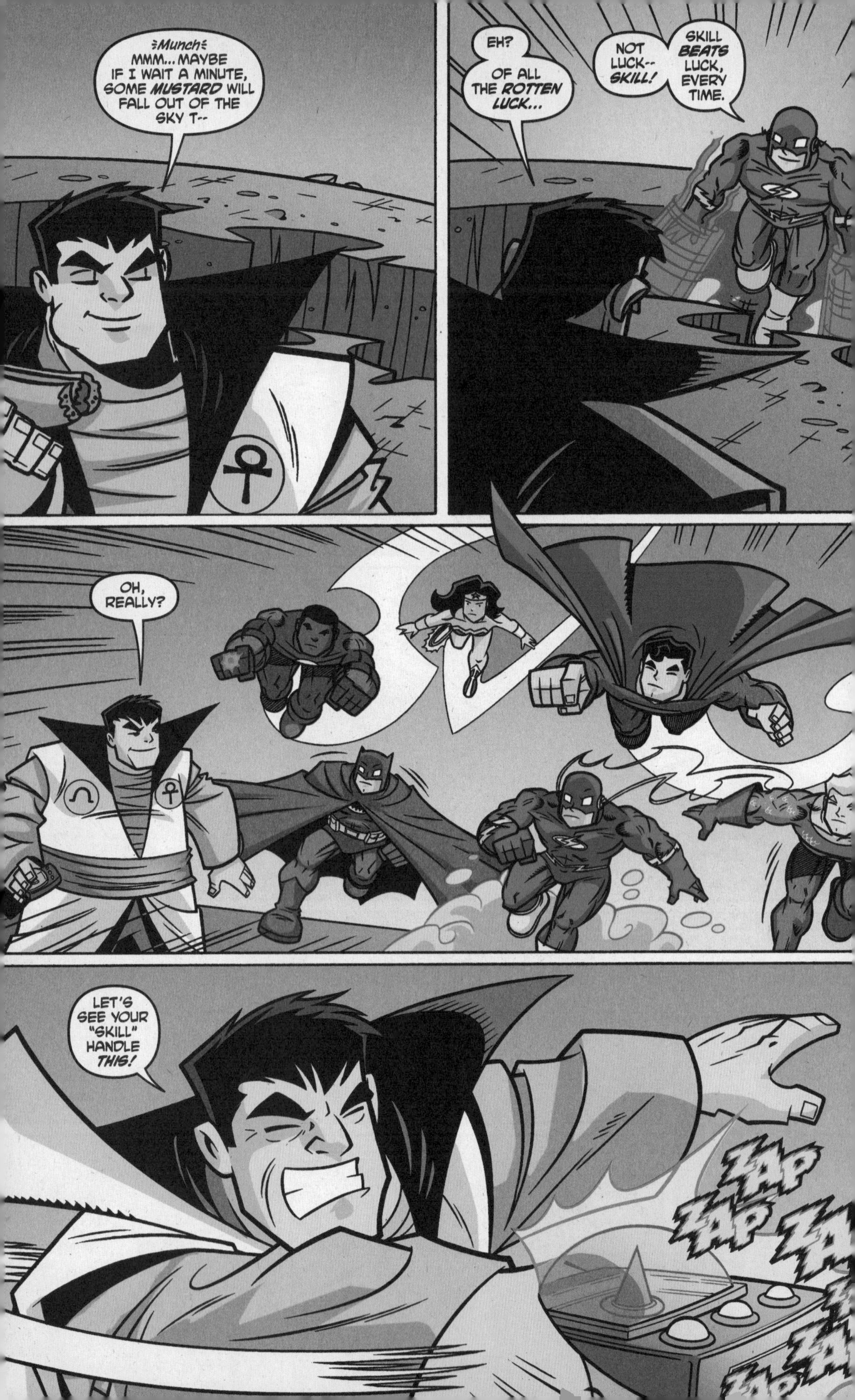

≈Munch≈
MMM... MAYBE IF I WAIT A MINUTE, SOME MUSTARD WILL FALL OUT OF THE SKY T--
EH?
OF ALL THE ROTTEN LUCK...
NOT LUCK-- SKILL!
SKILL BEATS LUCK, EVERY TIME.
OH, REALLY?
LET'S SEE YOUR "SKILL" HANDLE THIS!
ZAP ZAP

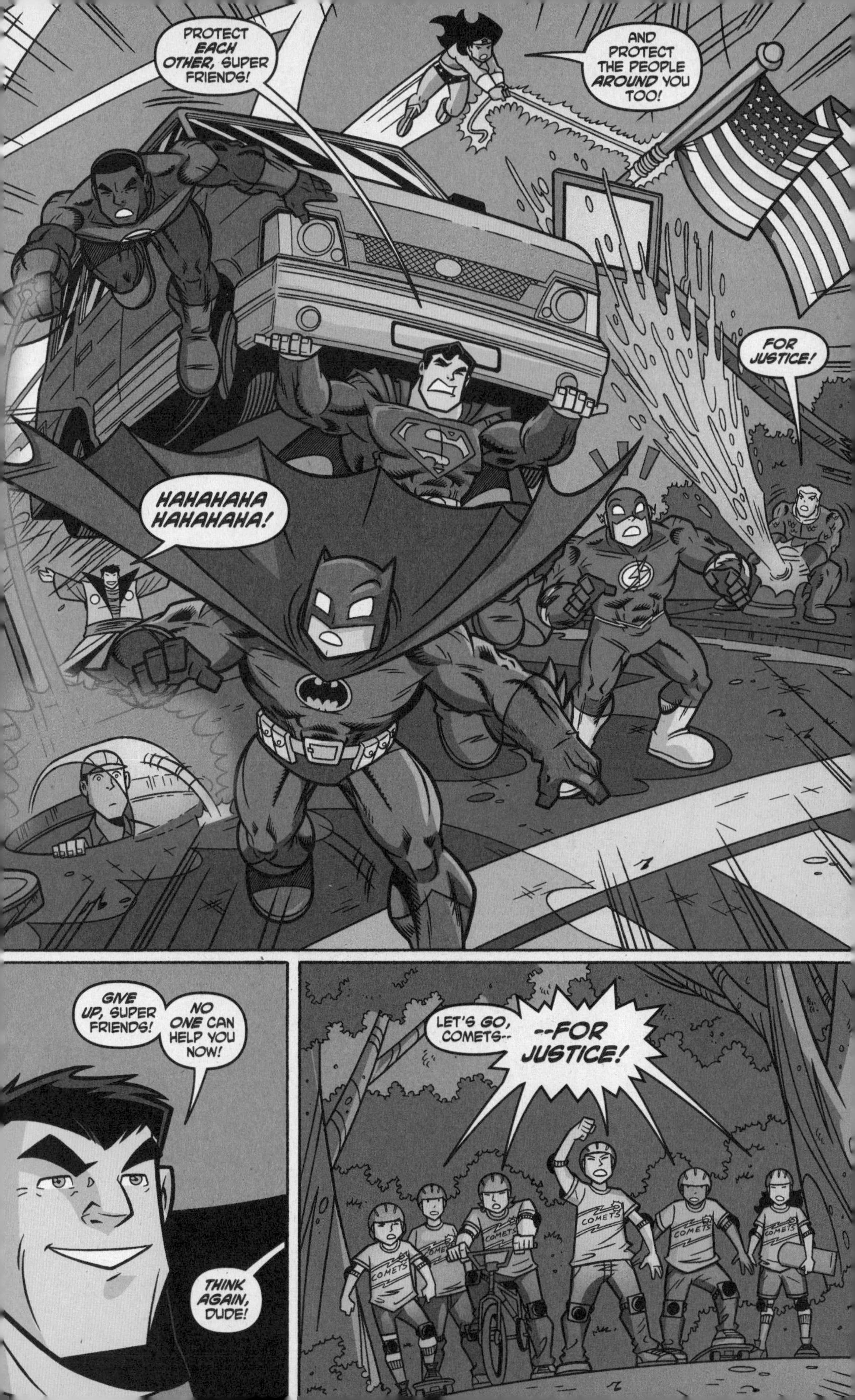
PROTECT EACH OTHER, SUPER FRIENDS!
AND PROTECT THE PEOPLE AROUND YOU TOO!
FOR JUSTICE!
HAHAHAHA HAHAHAHA!
GIVE UP, SUPER FRIENDS!
NO ONE CAN HELP YOU NOW!
THINK AGAIN, DUDE!
LET'S GO, COMETS--
--FOR JUSTICE!
COMETS

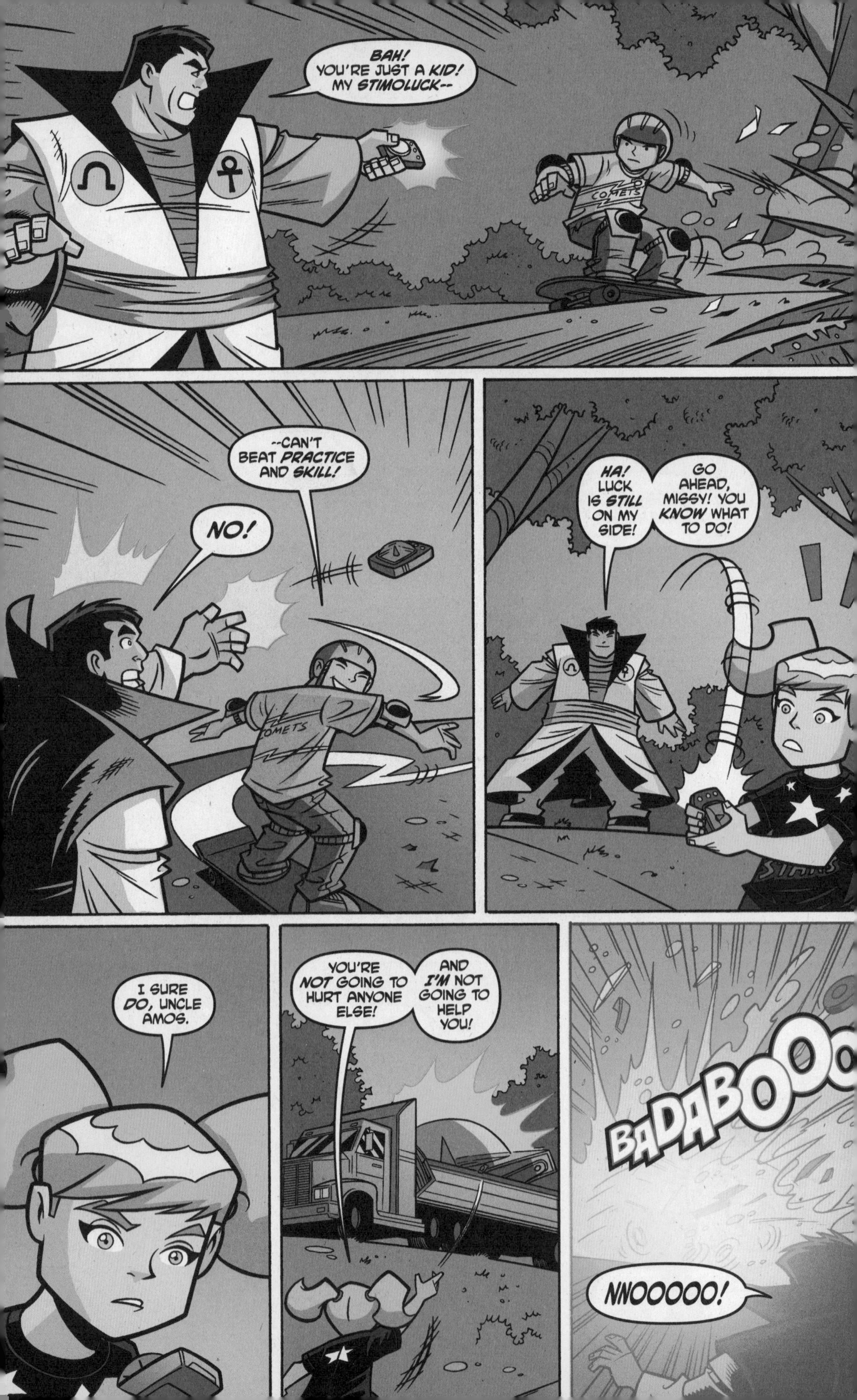
BAH! YOU'RE JUST A KID! MY STIMOLUCK--
COMETS
--CAN'T BEAT PRACTICE AND SKILL!
NO!
COMETS
HA! LUCK IS STILL ON MY SIDE!
GO AHEAD, MISSY! YOU KNOW WHAT TO DO!
I SURE DO, UNCLE AMOS.
YOU'RE NOT GOING TO HURT ANYONE ELSE!
AND I'M NOT GOING TO HELP YOU!
BADABOOO
NNOOOOO!

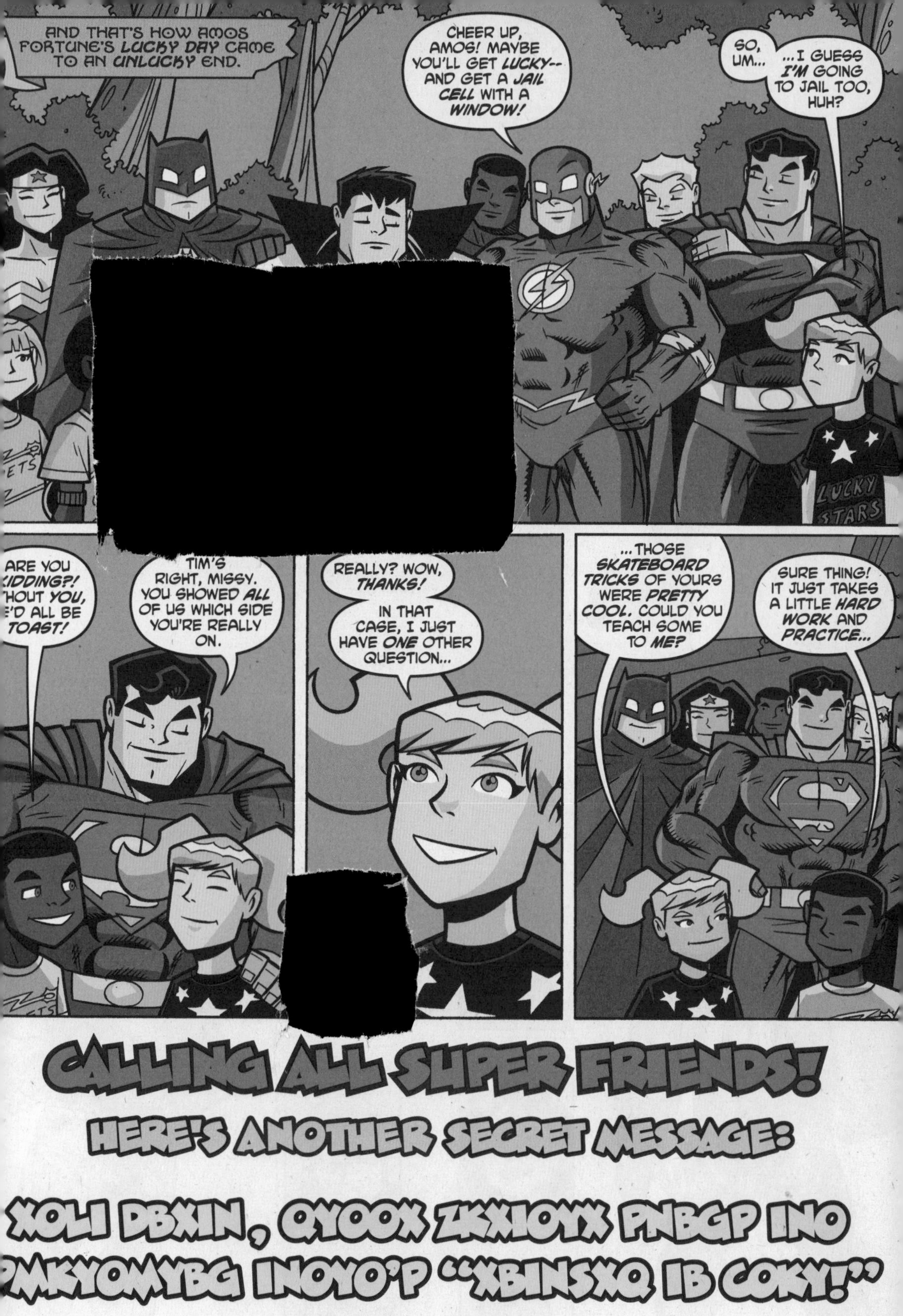
AND THAT'S HOW AMOS FORTUNE'S LUCKY DAY CAME TO AN UNLUCKY END.
CHEER UP, AMOS! MAYBE YOU'LL GET LUCKY-- AND GET A JAIL CELL WITH A WINDOW!
SO, UM...
...I GUESS I'M GOING TO JAIL TOO, HUH?
LUCKY STARS
ARE YOU KIDDING?! THOUT YOU, E'D ALL BE TOAST!
TIM'S RIGHT, MISSY. YOU SHOWED ALL OF US WHICH SIDE YOU'RE REALLY ON.
REALLY? WOW, THANKS!
IN THAT CASE, I JUST HAVE ONE OTHER QUESTION...
...THOSE SKATEBOARD TRICKS OF YOURS WERE PRETTY COOL. COULD YOU TEACH SOME TO ME?
SURE THING! IT JUST TAKES A LITTLE HARD WORK AND PRACTICE...

CALLING ALL SUPER FRIENDS!

HERE'S ANOTHER SECRET MESSAGE:

XOLI DBXIN, QYOOX ZKXIOYX PNBGP INO
PMKYOMYBG INOYO'P "XBINSXQ IB COKY!"

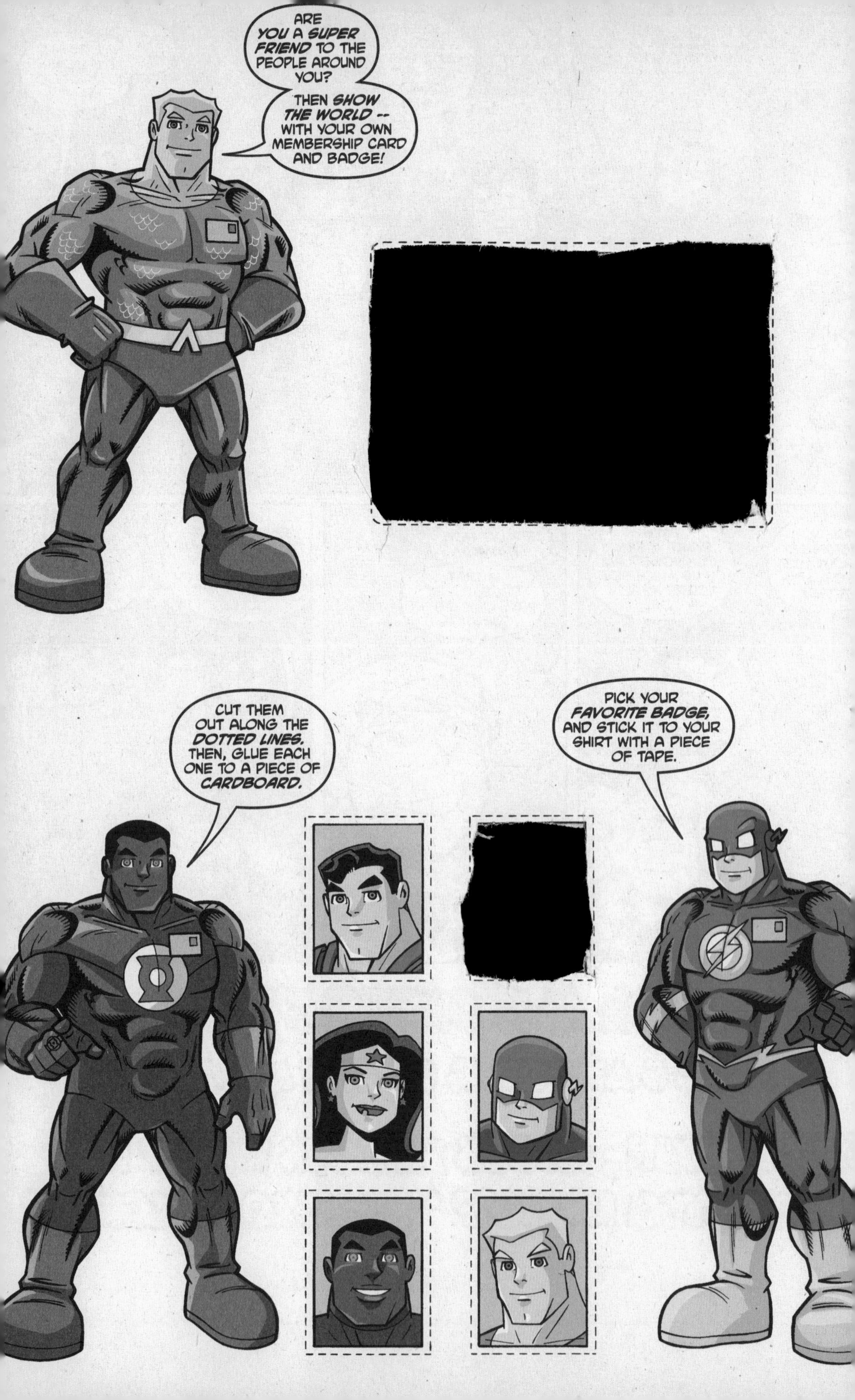
ARE YOU A SUPER FRIEND TO THE PEOPLE AROUND YOU?
THEN SHOW THE WORLD -- WITH YOUR OWN MEMBERSHIP CARD AND BADGE!
CUT THEM OUT ALONG THE DOTTED LINES. THEN, GLUE EACH ONE TO A PIECE OF CARDBOARD.
PICK YOUR FAVORITE BADGE, AND STICK IT TO YOUR SHIRT WITH A PIECE OF TAPE.

DC SUPER FRIENDS
Certificate of Membership

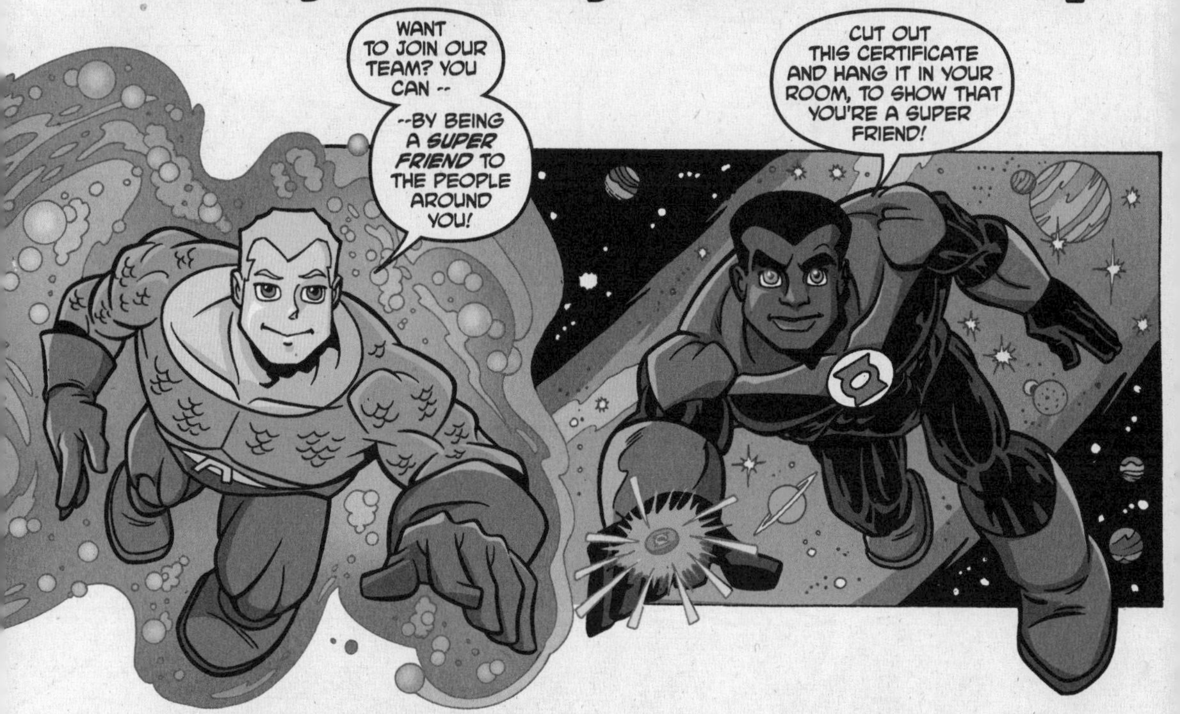
WANT TO JOIN OUR TEAM? YOU CAN --
--BY BEING A *SUPER FRIEND* TO THE PEOPLE AROUND YOU!
CUT OUT THIS CERTIFICATE AND HANG IT IN YOUR ROOM, TO SHOW THAT YOU'RE A SUPER FRIEND!

THIS IS TO CERTIFY THAT

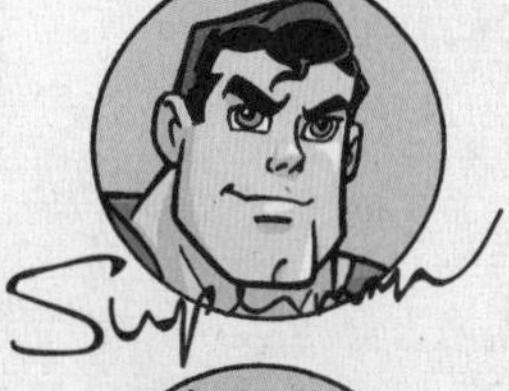
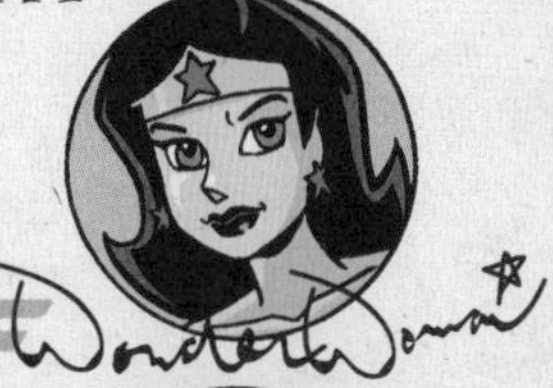

____

(Your name)

is a SUPER FRIEND who upholds the Super Friends code of honor by:

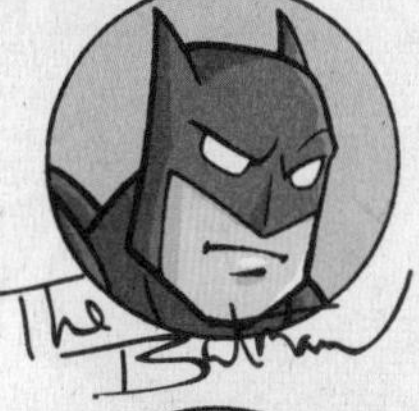
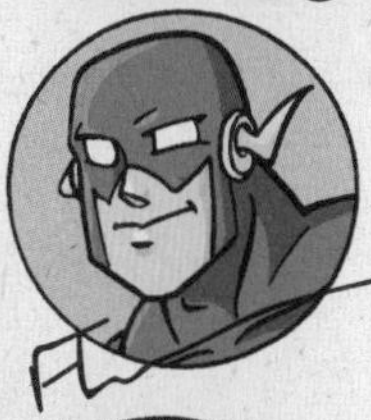

Being kind and polite
Helping other people
Showing respect for others
Doing the right thing

In return, ______________ is entitled to all of the privileges of membership, including the use of the Super Friends' secret code.

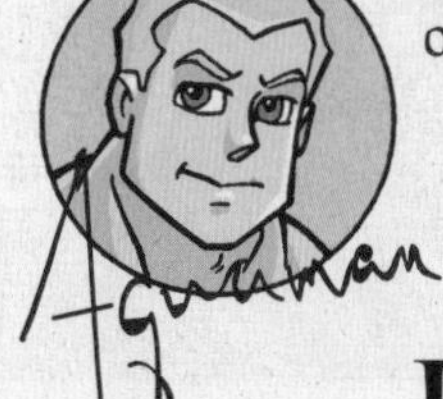
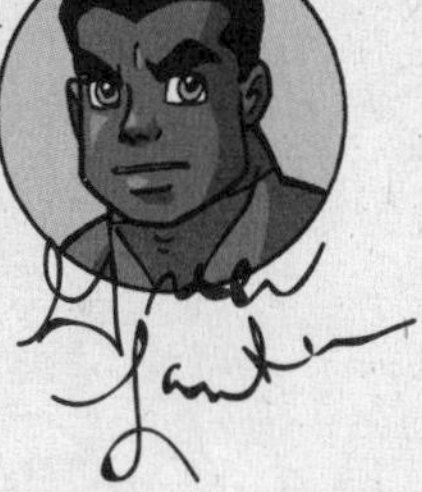

FOR JUSTICE!

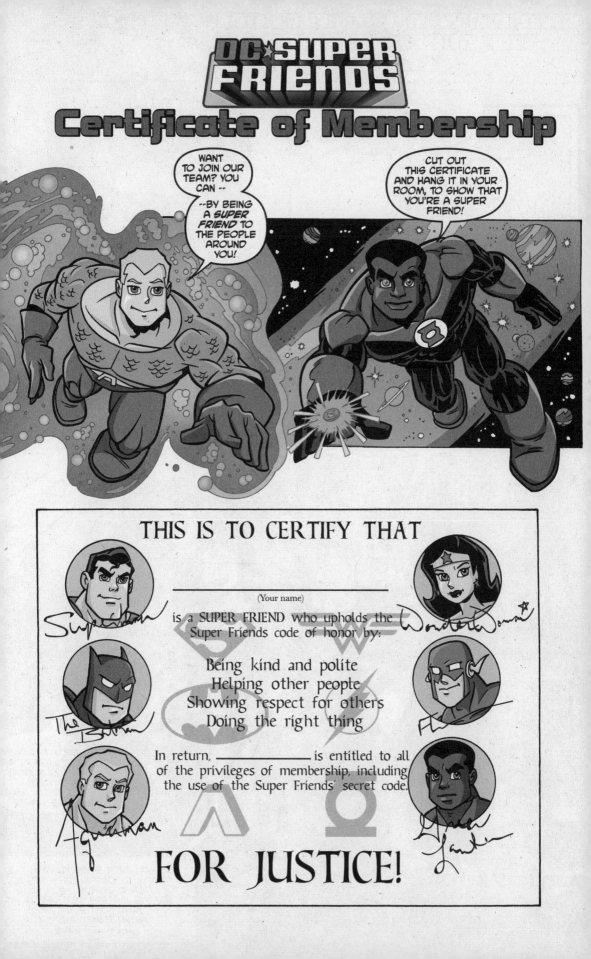

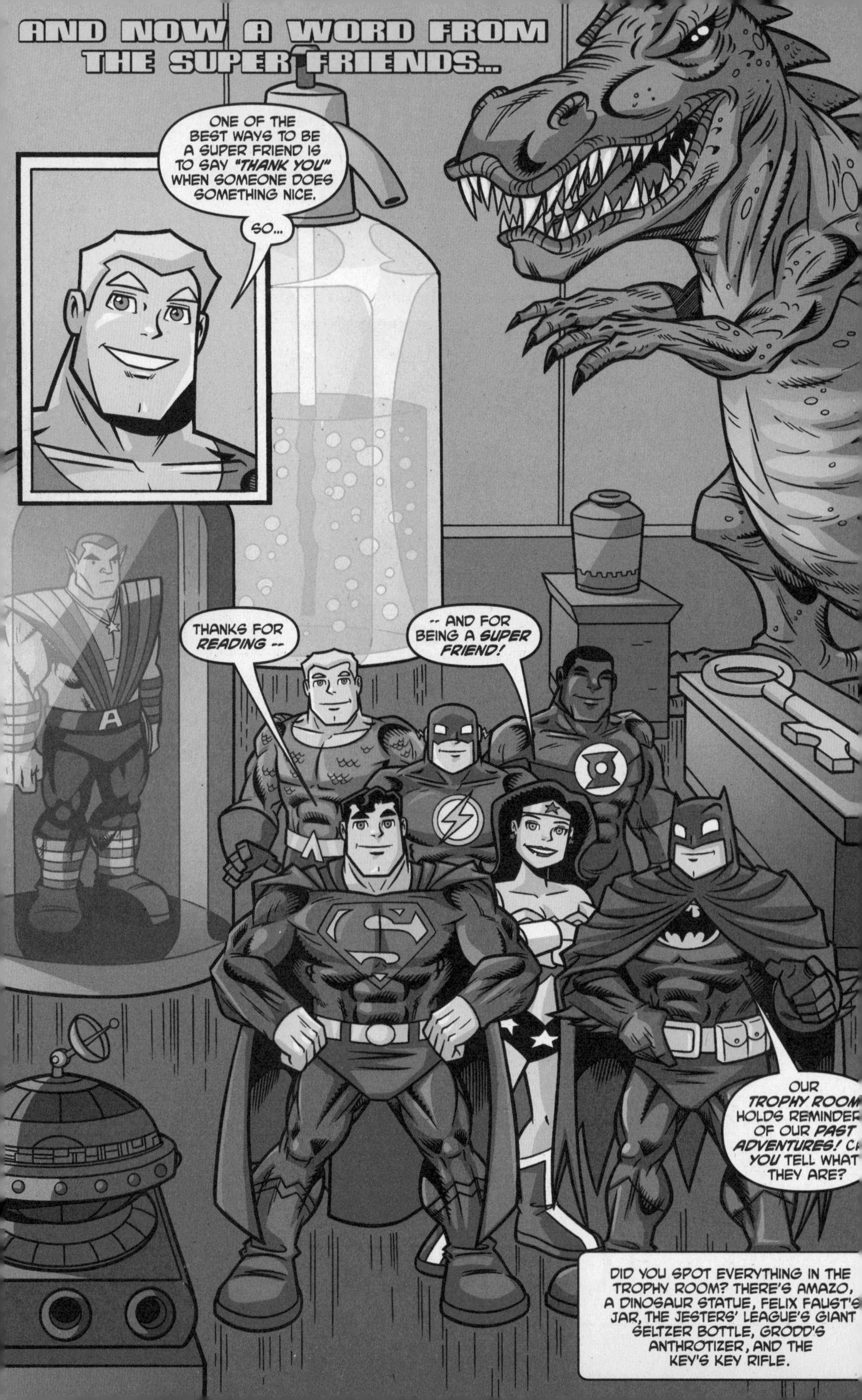
AND NOW A WORD FROM THE SUPER FRIENDS...
ONE OF THE BEST WAYS TO BE A SUPER FRIEND IS TO SAY *"THANK YOU"* WHEN SOMEONE DOES SOMETHING NICE.
SO...
THANKS FOR *READING* --
-- AND FOR BEING A *SUPER FRIEND!*
OUR *TROPHY ROOM* HOLDS REMINDER OF OUR *PAST ADVENTURES!* *YOU* TELL WHAT THEY ARE?
DID YOU SPOT EVERYTHING IN THE TROPHY ROOM? THERE'S AMAZO, A DINOSAUR STATUE, FELIX FAUST'S JAR, THE JESTERS' LEAGUE'S GIANT SELTZER BOTTLE, GRODD'S ANTHROTIZER, AND THE KEY'S KEY RIFLE.

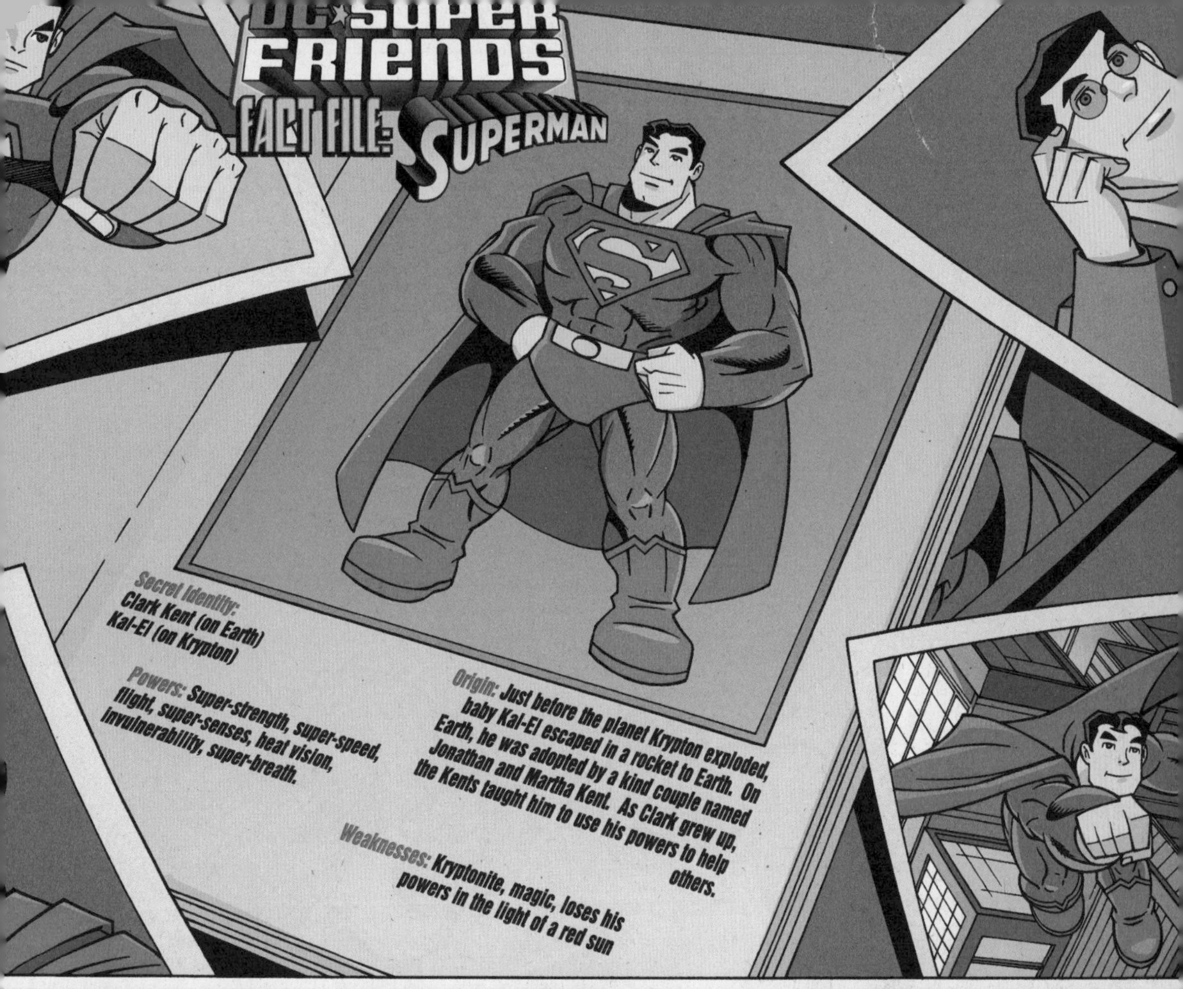
DC SUPER FRIENDS
FACT FILE: SUPERMAN
Secret Identity:
Clark Kent (on Earth)
Kal-El (on Krypton)
Powers: Super-strength, super-speed, flight, super-senses, heat vision, invulnerability, super-breath.
Origin: Just before the planet Krypton exploded, baby Kal-El escaped in a rocket to Earth. On Earth, he was adopted by a kind couple named Jonathan and Martha Kent. As Clark grew up, the Kents taught him to use his powers to help others.
Weaknesses: Kryptonite, magic, loses his powers in the light of a red sun

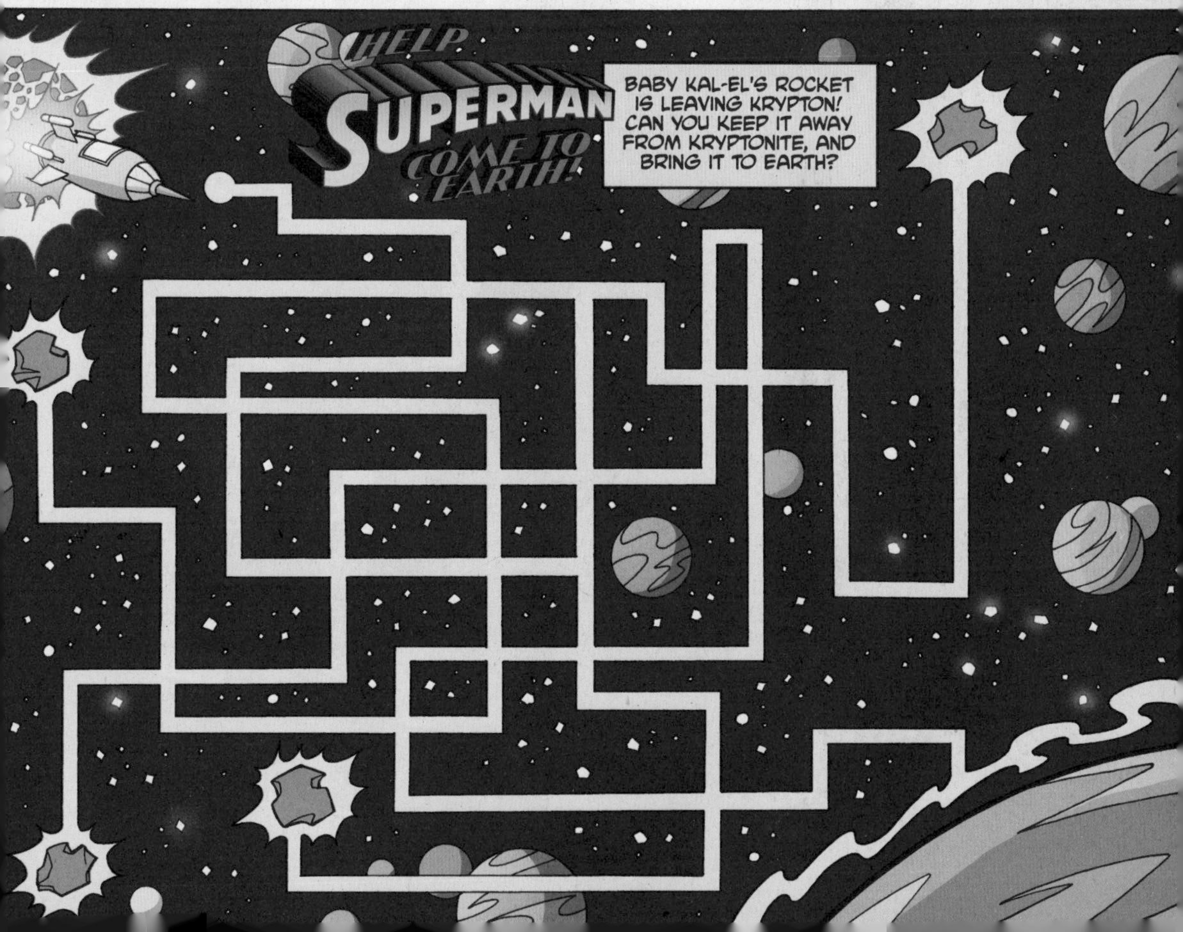
HELP SUPERMAN COME TO EARTH!
BABY KAL-EL'S ROCKET IS LEAVING KRYPTON! CAN YOU KEEP IT AWAY FROM KRYPTONITE, AND BRING IT TO EARTH?

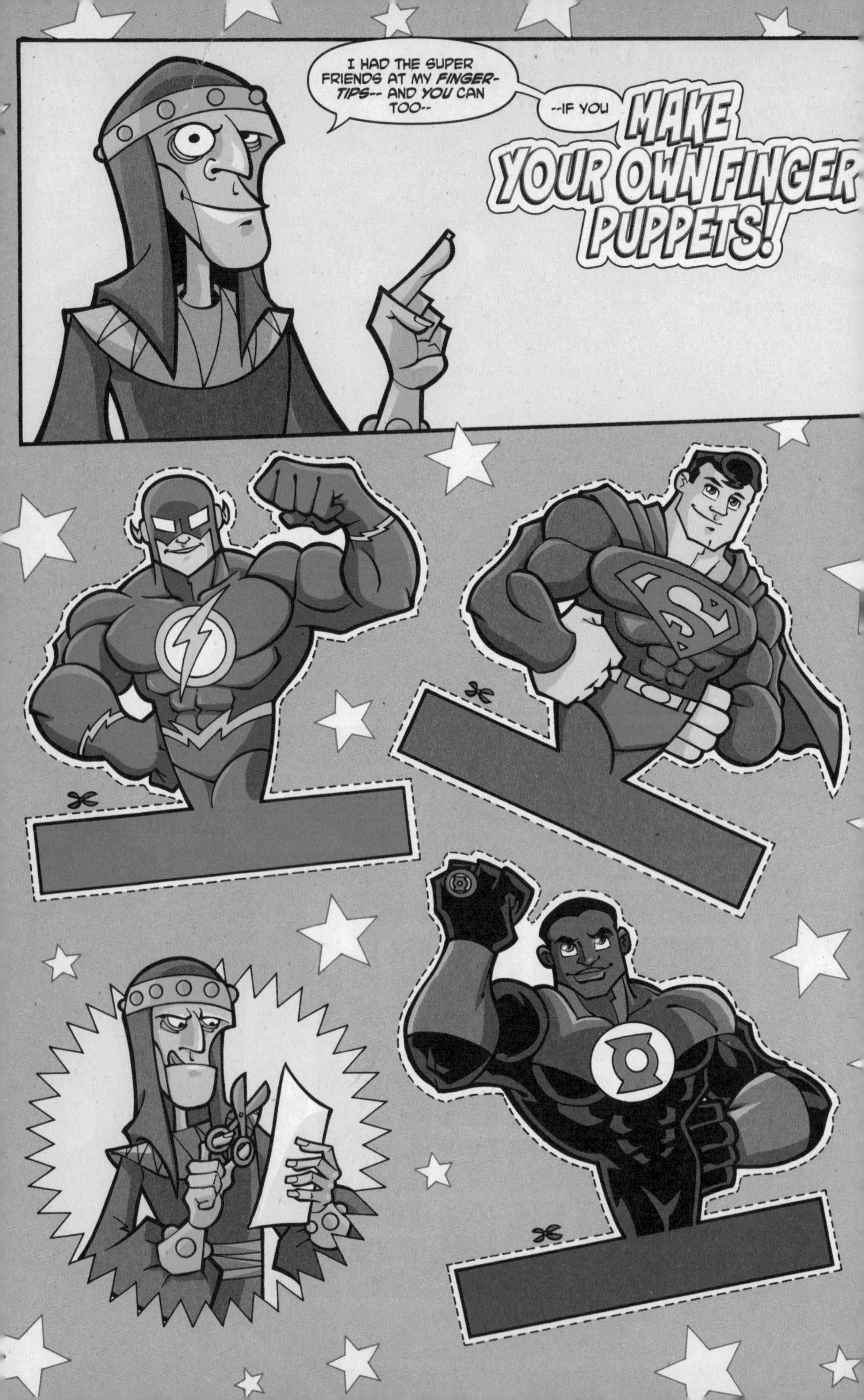
I HAD THE SUPER FRIENDS AT MY *FINGER-TIPS*-- AND *YOU* CAN TOO--
--IF YOU
MAKE YOUR OWN FINGER PUPPETS!

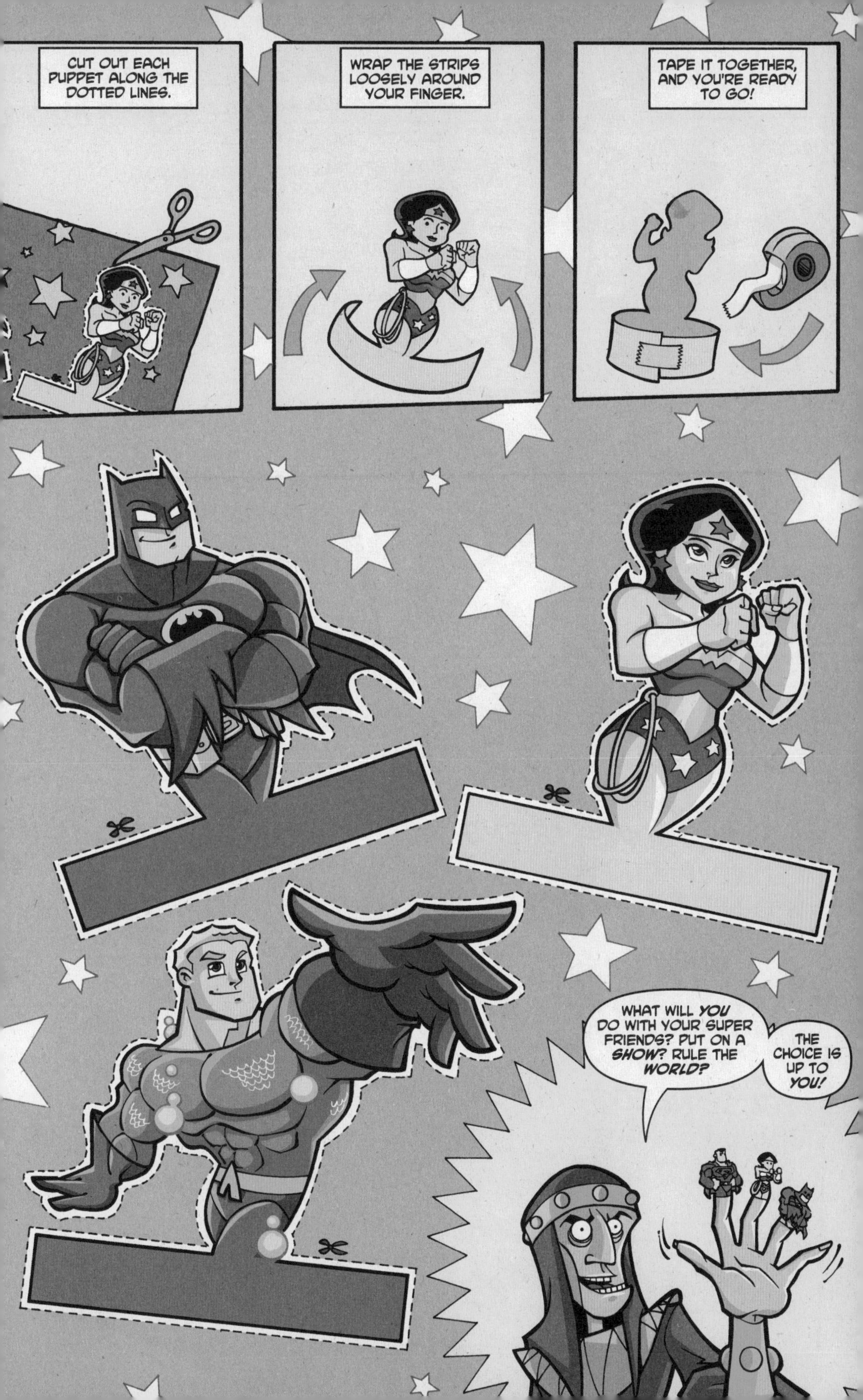
CUT OUT EACH PUPPET ALONG THE DOTTED LINES.
WRAP THE STRIPS LOOSELY AROUND YOUR FINGER.
TAPE IT TOGETHER, AND YOU'RE READY TO GO!
WHAT WILL YOU DO WITH YOUR SUPER FRIENDS? PUT ON A SHOW? RULE THE WORLD?
THE CHOICE IS UP TO YOU!

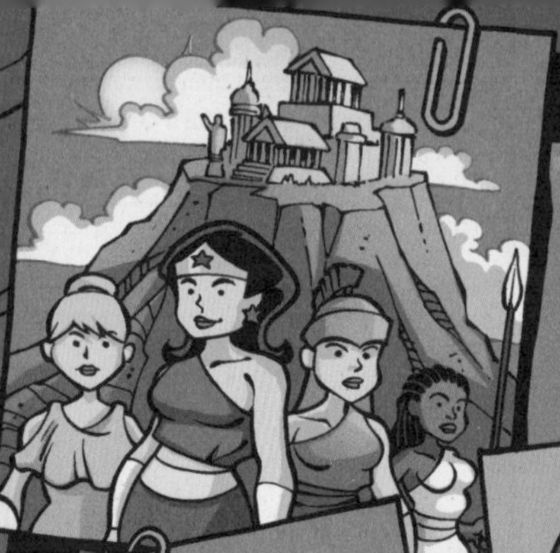

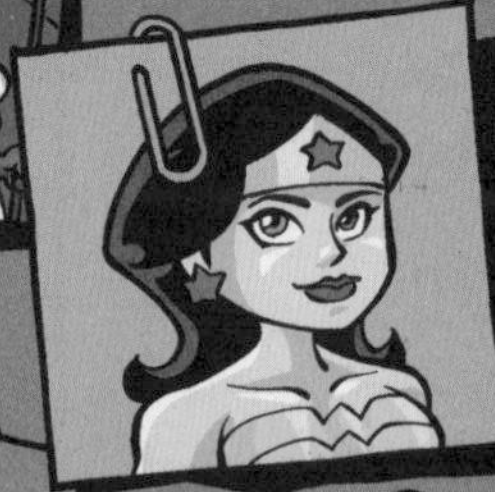

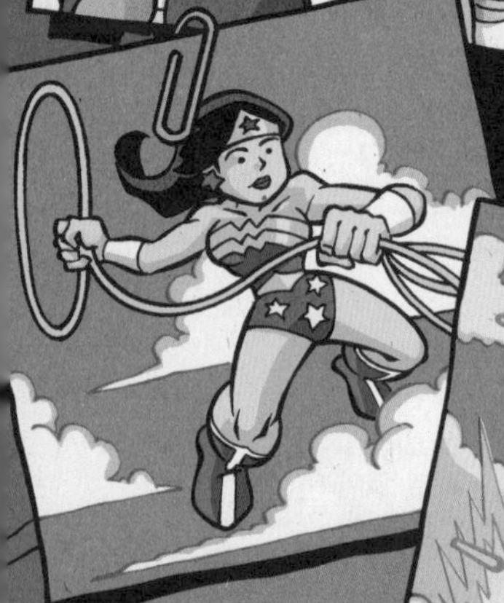

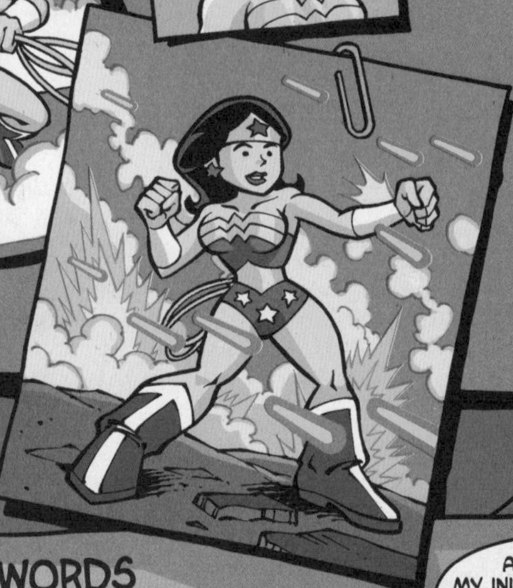

CLASSIFIED

WONDER SUPER FRIENDS FACT FILE: WONDER WOMAN

SECRET IDENTITY: PRINCESS DIANA.

POWERS: SUPER-STRONG, FASTER THAN NORMAL HUMANS, USES HER BRACELETS AS SHIELDS.

TOOLS: INVISIBLE AIRPLANE, MAGIC LASSO THAT MAKES PEOPLE TELL THE TRUTH.

ORIGIN: DIANA IS THE PRINCESS OF PARADISE ISLAND, THE HIDDEN HOME OF THE AMAZONS. WHEN DIANA WAS A BABY, THE GREEK GODS GAVE HER SPECIAL.

POWERS: THE WISDOM OF ATHENA, THE STRENGTH OF HERACLES, THE BEAUTY OF APHRODITE, AND THE SPEED OF HERMES. YEARS LATER, WHEN DIANA GREW UP, SHE LEFT HER HOME TO HELP PEOPLE ALL OVER THE WORLD AS WONDER WOMAN!

WEAKNESSES: LOSES HER POWERS IF HER BRACELETS ARE TIED TOGETHER.

WONDER WORDS

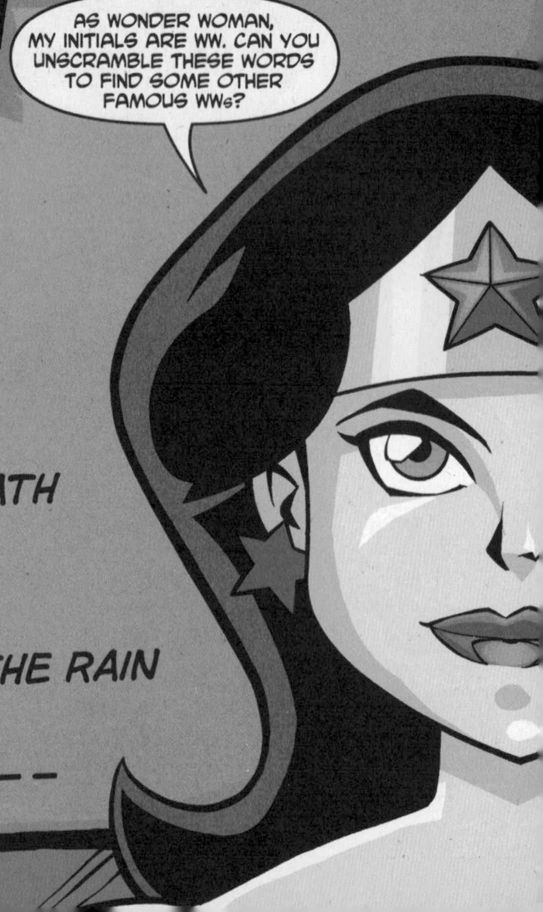
AS WONDER WOMAN, MY INITIALS ARE WW. CAN YOU UNSCRAMBLE THESE WORDS TO FIND SOME OTHER FAMOUS WWs?

AMAZON SUPER FRIEND

REDNOW NOWMA

W O N D E R W O M A N

EVIL VILLAINESS IN OZ

DIWKEC ITWCH

W _ _ _ _ _ W _ _ _ _

YOU'LL NEED THIS FOR A BATH

RMAW RETWA

W _ _ _ W _ _ _ _

THESE HELP YOUR CAR IN THE RAIN

NWISDLEIHD PREWIS

W _ _ _ _ _ _ _ _ _ W _ _ _ _ _

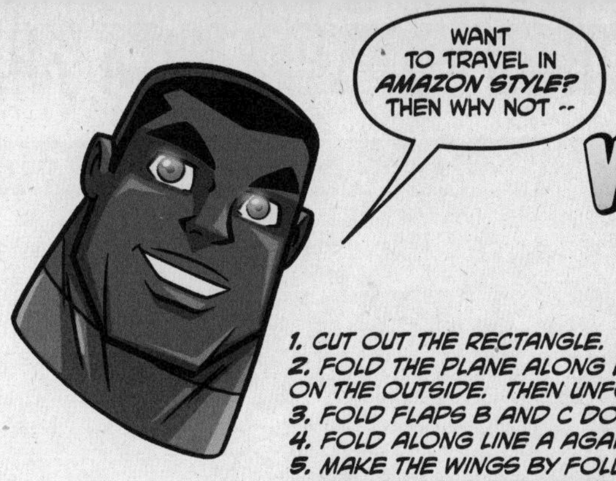
WANT TO TRAVEL IN AMAZON STYLE? THEN WHY NOT --

MAKE WONDER WOMAN'S INVISIBLE PLANE

1. CUT OUT THE RECTANGLE.
2. FOLD THE PLANE ALONG LINE A, KEEPING THE PICTURES OF WONDER WOMAN ON THE OUTSIDE. THEN UNFOLD IT AGAIN.
3. FOLD FLAPS B AND C DOWN TOWARD THE INSIDE OF THE PLANE.
4. FOLD ALONG LINE A AGAIN.
5. MAKE THE WINGS BY FOLDING THE PAPER DOWN ALONG LINES D AND E. MAKE SURE YOU FOLD THE WINGS TOWARD THE OUTSIDE OF THE PLANE.
6. TOSS IT IN THE AIR, AND LET IT FLY!

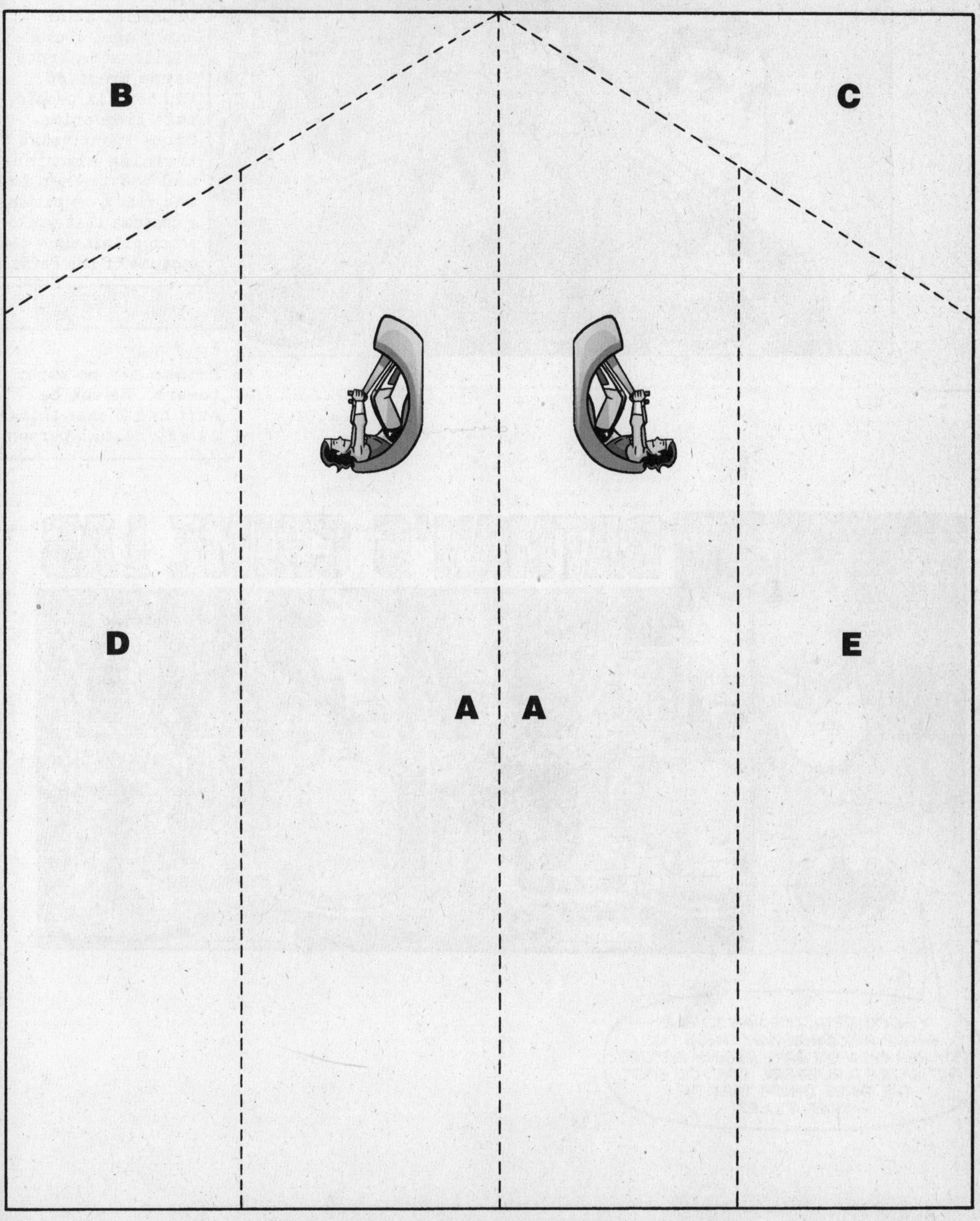
B
C
D
E
A
A

SUPER FRIENDS FACT FILE:

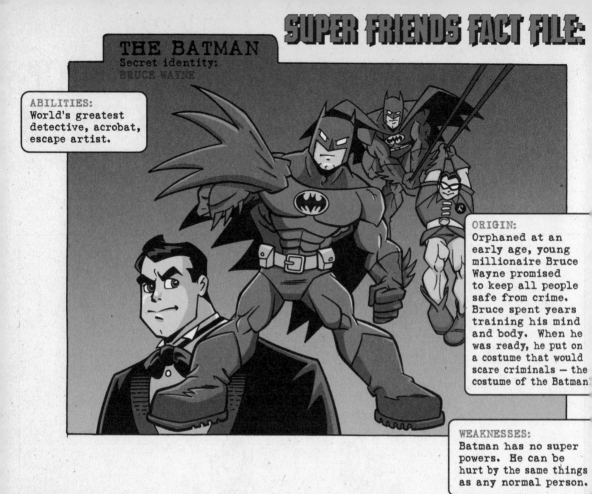

THE BATMAN

Secret identity:
BRUCE WAYNE

ABILITIES:
World's greatest detective, acrobat, escape artist.

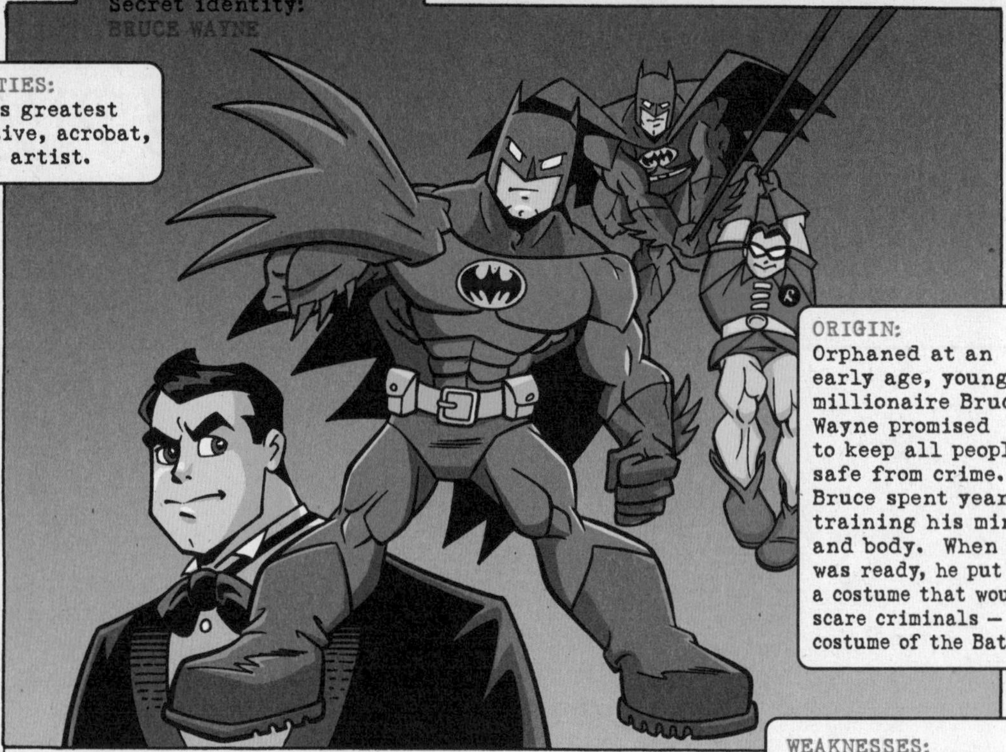

ORIGIN:
Orphaned at an early age, young millionaire Bruce Wayne promised to keep all people safe from crime. Bruce spent years training his mind and body. When he was ready, he put on a costume that would scare criminals — the costume of the Batman.

WEAKNESSES:
Batman has no super powers. He can be hurt by the same things as any normal person.

BATMAN'S CRIME LAB

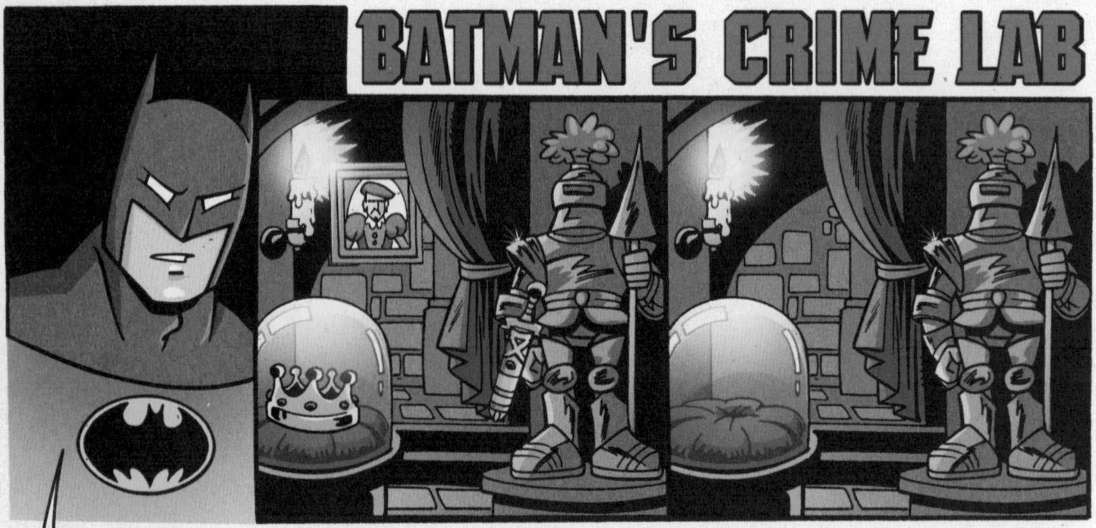
A GOOD DETECTIVE HAS TO STAY SHARP AND *OBSERVE!* THESE TWO PICTURES SHOW THE SAME MUSEUM *BEFORE* AND *AFTER* A ROBBERY. CAN *YOU* SPOT THE THREE THINGS THAT THE THIEF STOLE?

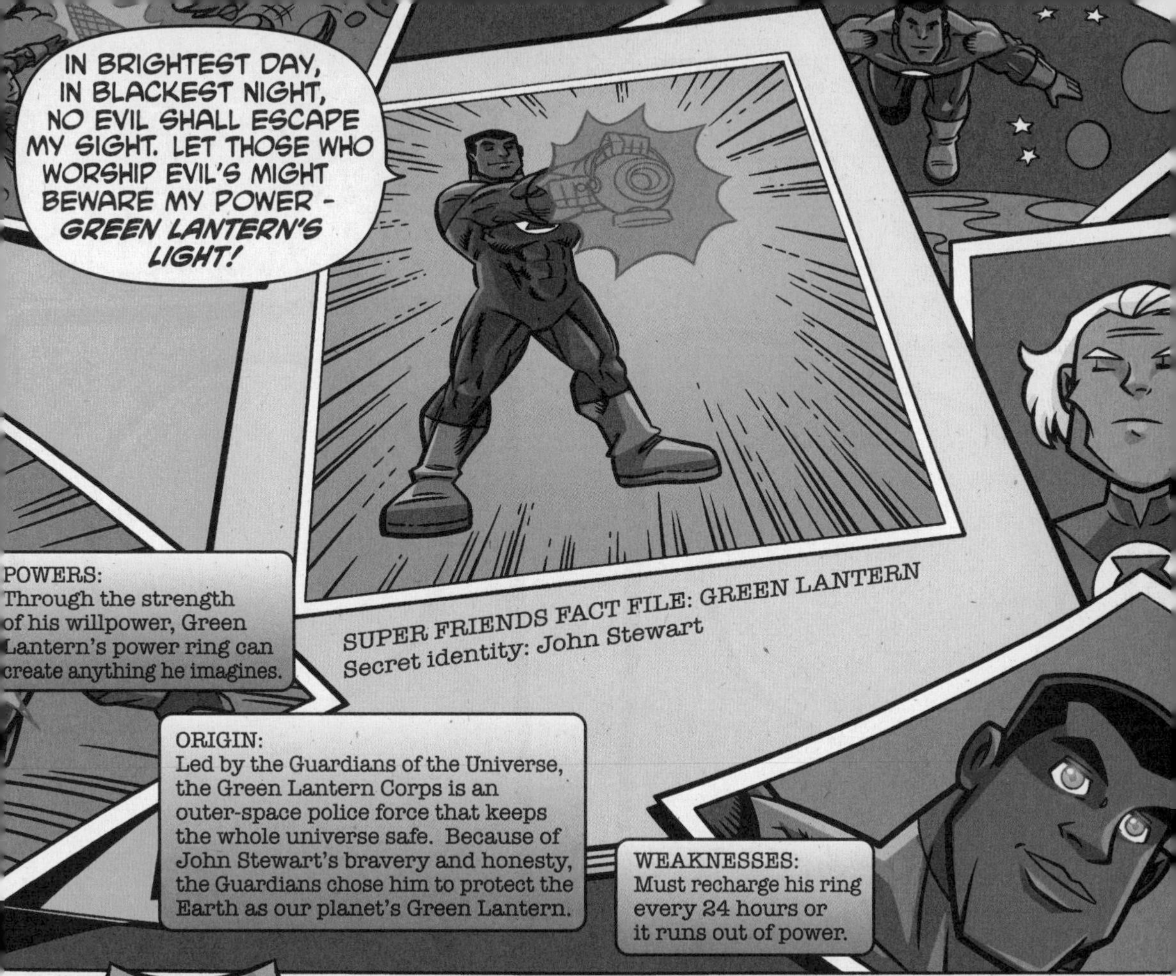
IN BRIGHTEST DAY, IN BLACKEST NIGHT, NO EVIL SHALL ESCAPE MY SIGHT. LET THOSE WHO WORSHIP EVIL'S MIGHT BEWARE MY POWER - *GREEN LANTERN'S LIGHT!*
POWERS: Through the strength of his willpower, Green Lantern's power ring can create anything he imagines.
SUPER FRIENDS FACT FILE: GREEN LANTERN
Secret identity: John Stewart
ORIGIN: Led by the Guardians of the Universe, the Green Lantern Corps is an outer-space police force that keeps the whole universe safe. Because of John Stewart's bravery and honesty, the Guardians chose him to protect the Earth as our planet's Green Lantern.
WEAKNESSES: Must recharge his ring every 24 hours or it runs out of power.

WACKY WORDPLAY

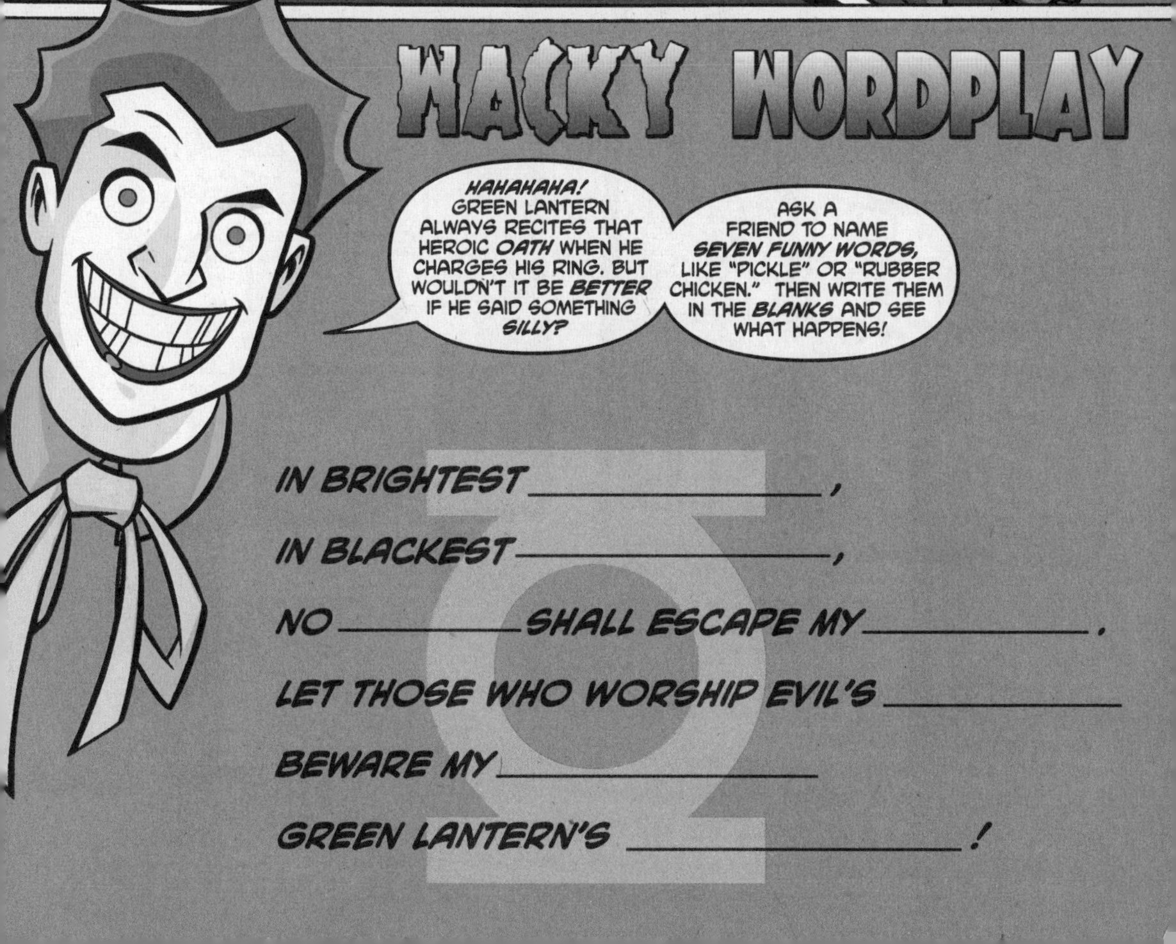
HAHAHAHA! GREEN LANTERN ALWAYS RECITES THAT HEROIC *OATH* WHEN HE CHARGES HIS RING. BUT WOULDN'T IT BE *BETTER* IF HE SAID SOMETHING *SILLY?*
ASK A FRIEND TO NAME *SEVEN FUNNY WORDS,* LIKE "PICKLE" OR "RUBBER CHICKEN." THEN WRITE THEM IN THE *BLANKS* AND SEE WHAT HAPPENS!

IN BRIGHTEST ________________,

IN BLACKEST ________________,

NO __________ SHALL ESCAPE MY ____________.

LET THOSE WHO WORSHIP EVIL'S ____________

BEWARE MY ________________

GREEN LANTERN'S ________________!

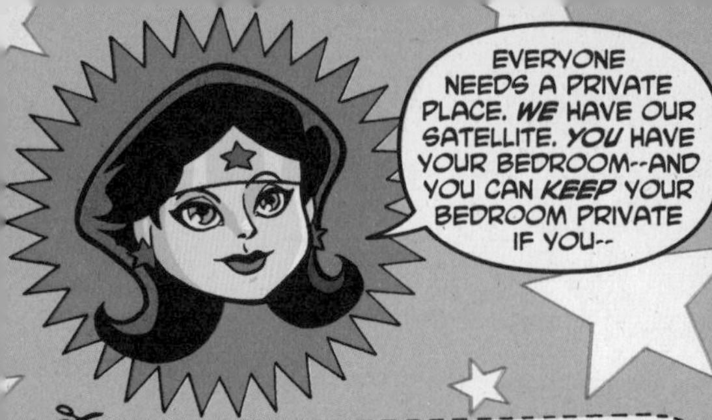
EVERYONE NEEDS A PRIVATE PLACE. *WE* HAVE OUR SATELLITE. *YOU* HAVE YOUR BEDROOM--AND YOU CAN *KEEP* YOUR BEDROOM PRIVATE IF YOU--

MAKE A SUPER FRIENDS DOOR HANGER

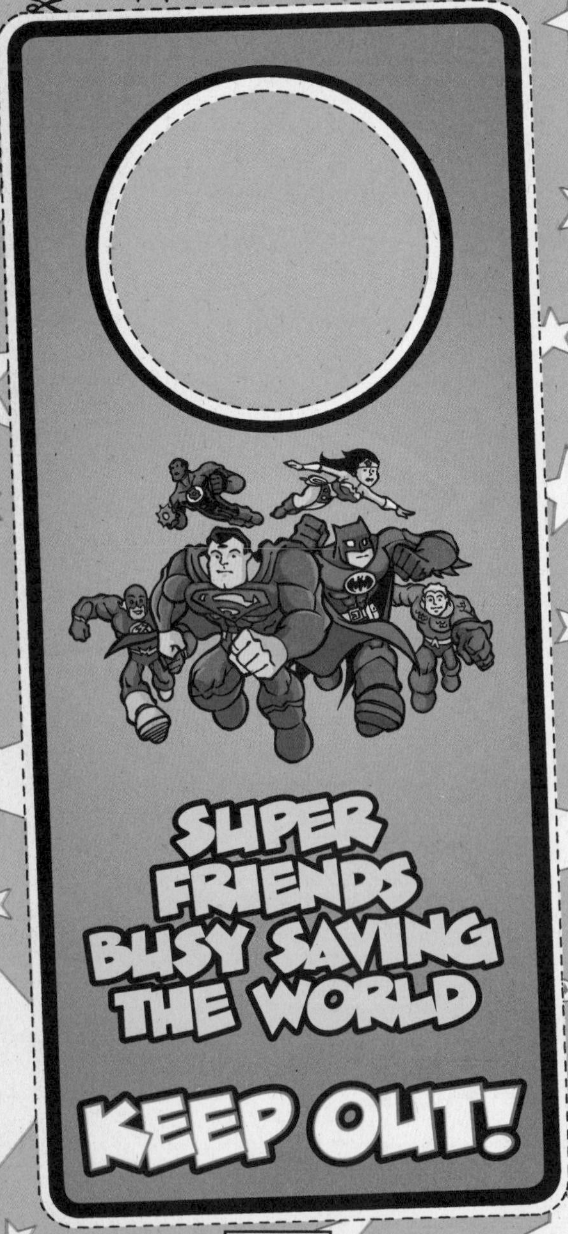
SUPER FRIENDS BUSY SAVING THE WORLD
KEEP OUT!

FRONT

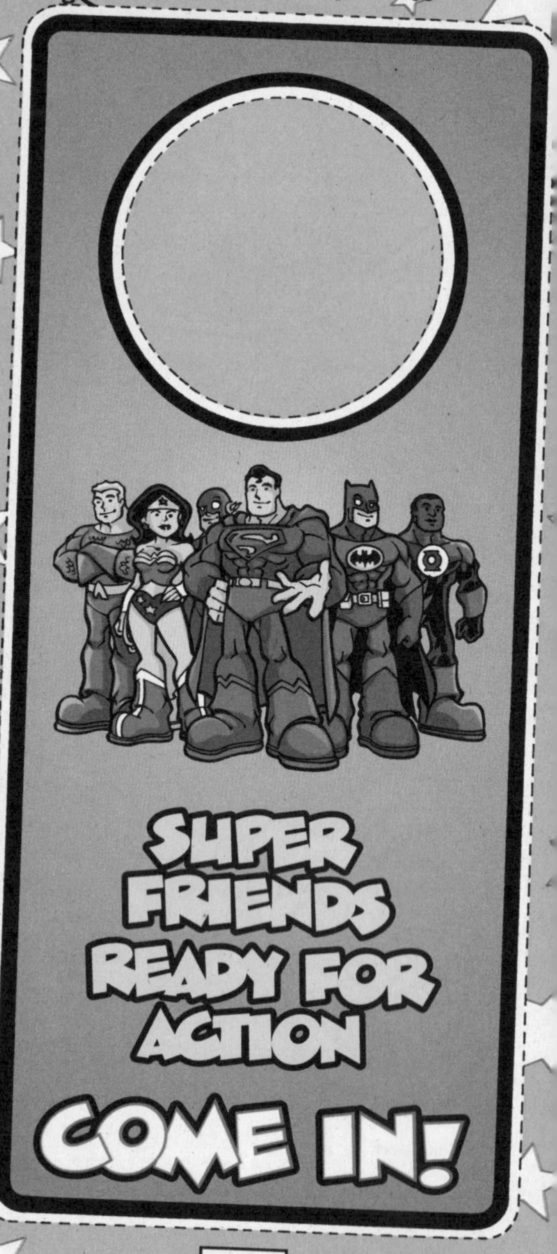
SUPER FRIENDS READY FOR ACTION
COME IN!

BACK

INSTRUCTIONS:

1. Cut out the front of the door hanger.
   Cut out the dotted circle inside the door hanger too.
2. Glue the front to a piece of cardboard. Trim the cardboard to match the door hanger.
3. Cut out the back of the door hanger. Glue it to the back of the cardboard.
4. Hang the door hanger on your door knob. Remember to turn it around when you need to!

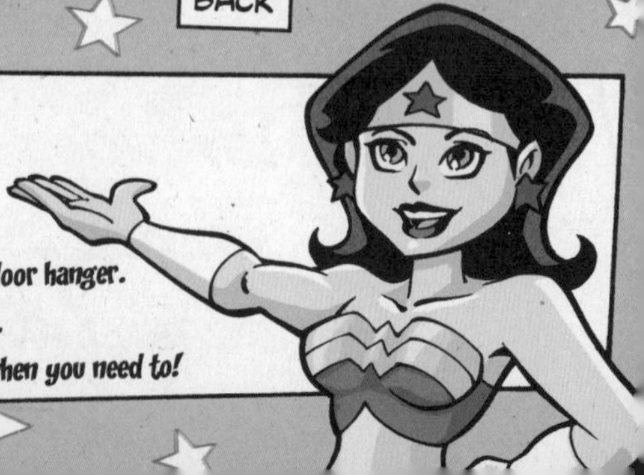

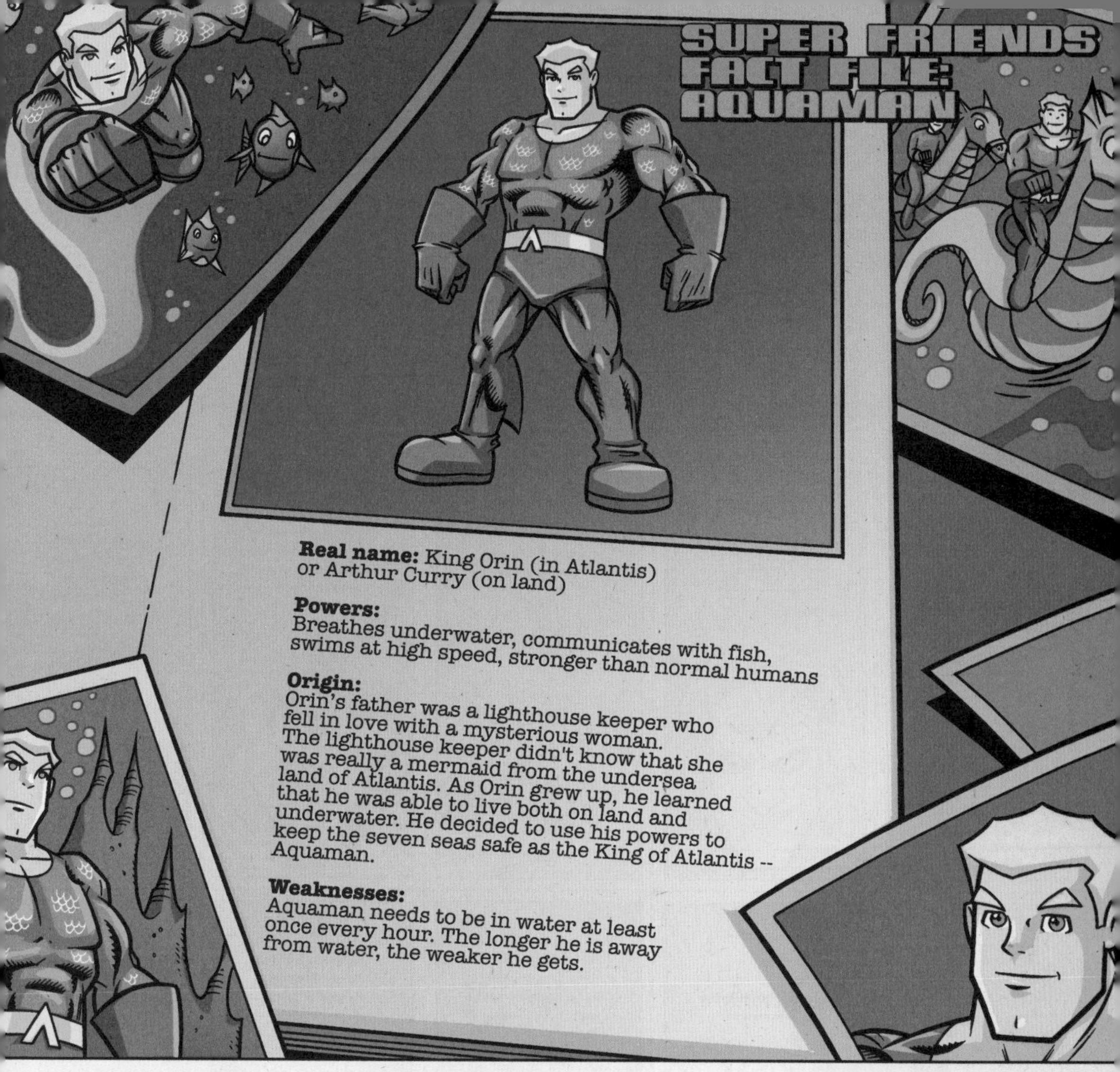
SUPER FRIENDS FACT FILE: AQUAMAN
Real name: King Orin (in Atlantis) or Arthur Curry (on land)
Powers:
Breathes underwater, communicates with fish, swims at high speed, stronger than normal humans
Origin:
Orin's father was a lighthouse keeper who fell in love with a mysterious woman. The lighthouse keeper didn't know that she was really a mermaid from the undersea land of Atlantis. As Orin grew up, he learned that he was able to live both on land and underwater. He decided to use his powers to keep the seven seas safe as the King of Atlantis -- Aquaman.
Weaknesses:
Aquaman needs to be in water at least once every hour. The longer he is away from water, the weaker he gets.

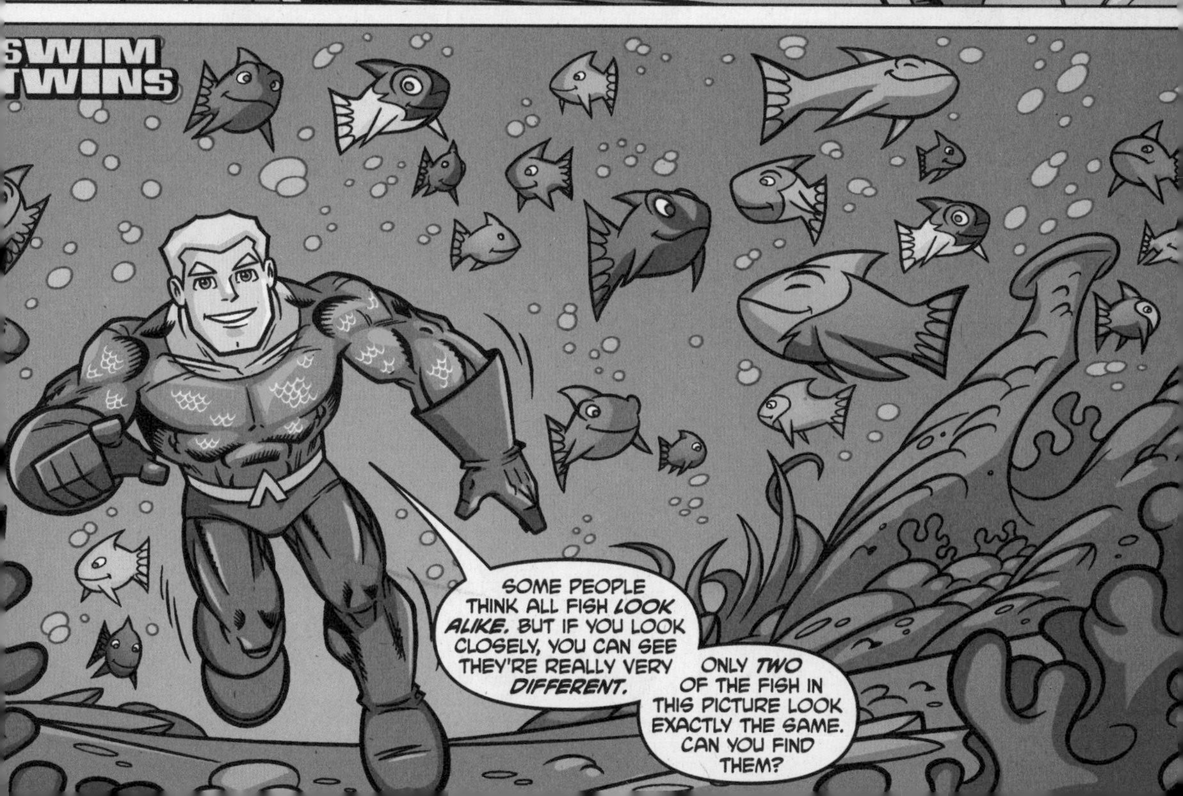
SWIM TWINS
SOME PEOPLE THINK ALL FISH *LOOK ALIKE.* BUT IF YOU LOOK CLOSELY, YOU CAN SEE THEY'RE REALLY VERY *DIFFERENT.*
ONLY *TWO* OF THE FISH IN THIS PICTURE LOOK EXACTLY THE SAME. CAN YOU FIND THEM?

DC SUPER FRIENDS™

"RACE TO THE RESCUE" GAME

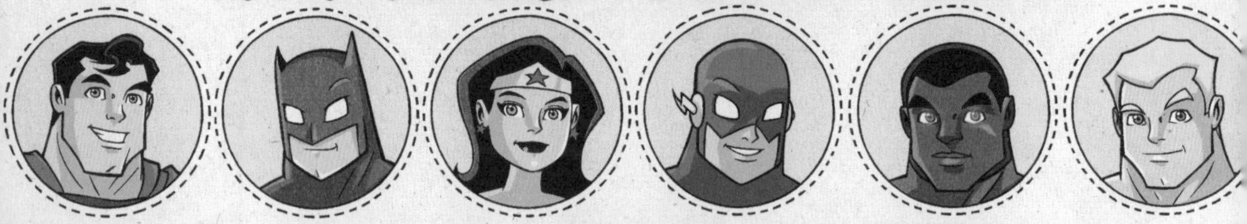

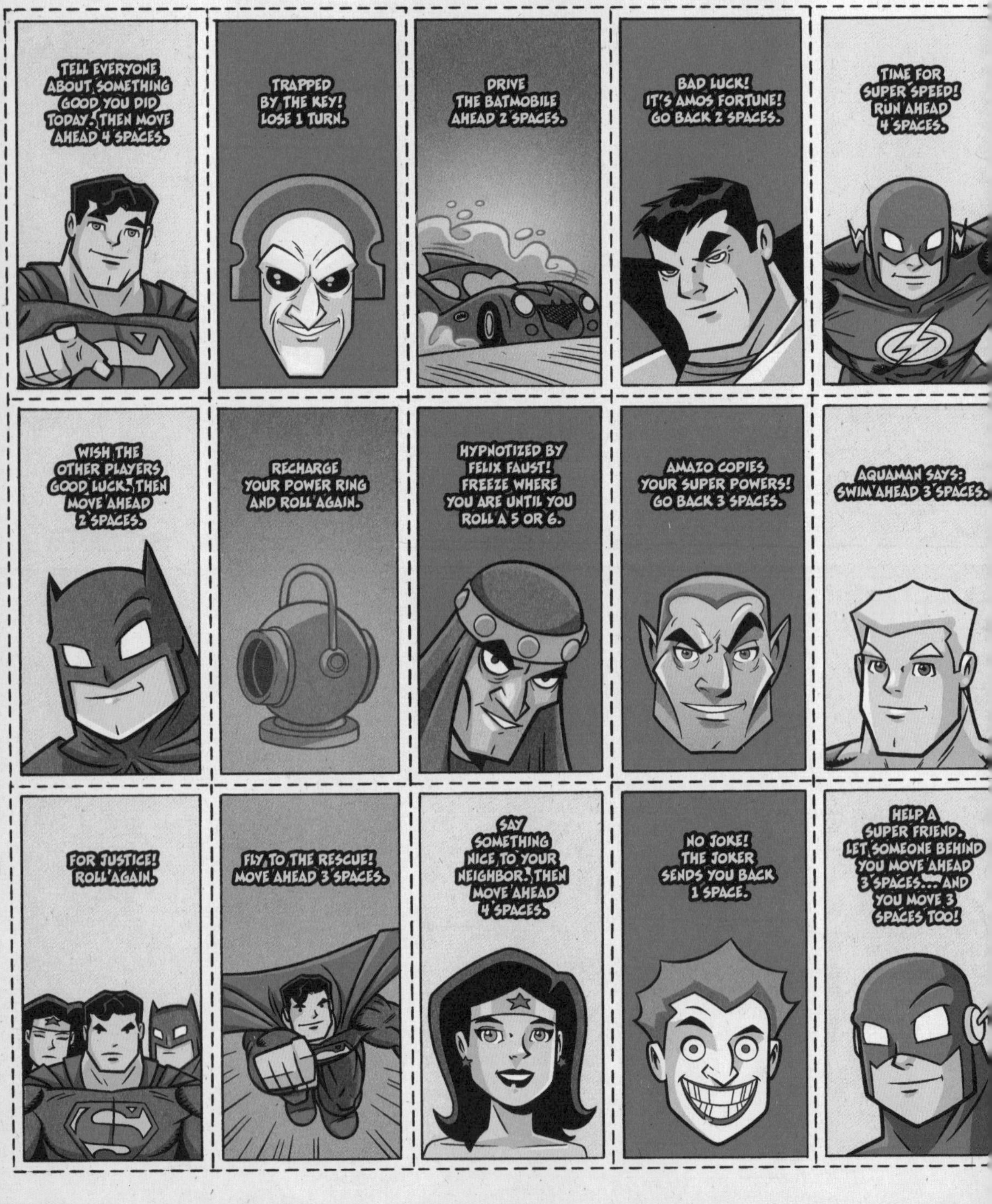

TELL EVERYONE ABOUT SOMETHING GOOD YOU DID TODAY. THEN MOVE AHEAD 4 SPACES.
TRAPPED BY THE KEY! LOSE 1 TURN.
DRIVE THE BATMOBILE AHEAD 2 SPACES.
BAD LUCK! IT'S AMOS FORTUNE! GO BACK 2 SPACES.
TIME FOR SUPER SPEED! RUN AHEAD 4 SPACES.
WISH THE OTHER PLAYERS GOOD LUCK. THEN MOVE AHEAD 2 SPACES.
RECHARGE YOUR POWER RING AND ROLL AGAIN.
HYPNOTIZED BY FELIX FAUST! FREEZE WHERE YOU ARE UNTIL YOU ROLL A 5 OR 6.
AMAZO COPIES YOUR SUPER POWERS! GO BACK 3 SPACES.
AQUAMAN SAYS: SWIM AHEAD 3 SPACES.
FOR JUSTICE! ROLL AGAIN.
FLY TO THE RESCUE! MOVE AHEAD 3 SPACES.
SAY SOMETHING NICE TO YOUR NEIGHBOR. THEN MOVE AHEAD 4 SPACES.
NO JOKE! THE JOKER SENDS YOU BACK 1 SPACE.
HELP A SUPER FRIEND. LET SOMEONE BEHIND YOU MOVE AHEAD 3 SPACES... AND YOU MOVE 3 SPACES TOO!

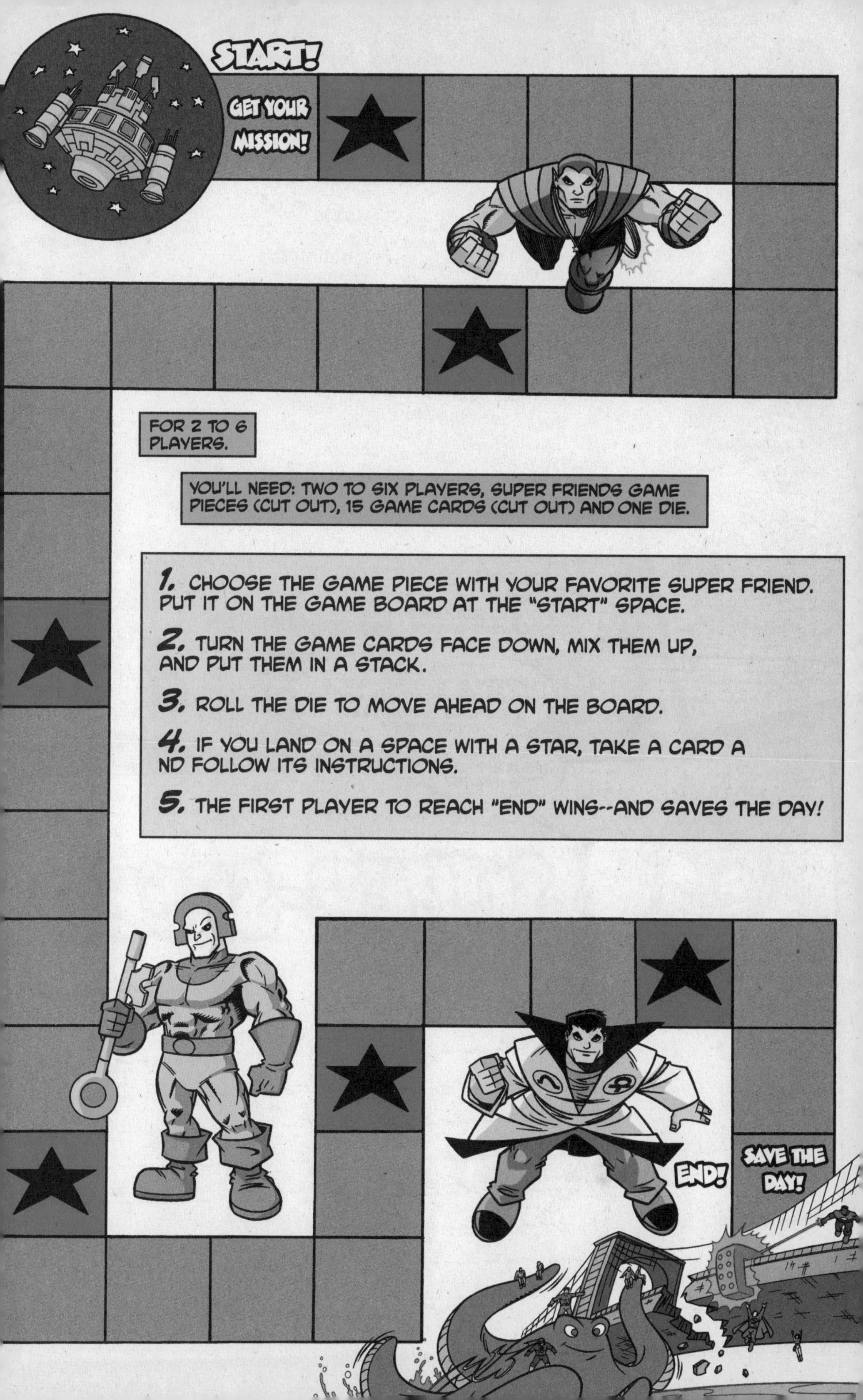
START!
GET YOUR MISSION!
END!
SAVE THE DAY!

FOR 2 TO 6 PLAYERS.

YOU'LL NEED: TWO TO SIX PLAYERS, SUPER FRIENDS GAME PIECES (CUT OUT), 15 GAME CARDS (CUT OUT) AND ONE DIE.

1. CHOOSE THE GAME PIECE WITH YOUR FAVORITE SUPER FRIEND. PUT IT ON THE GAME BOARD AT THE "START" SPACE.

2. TURN THE GAME CARDS FACE DOWN, MIX THEM UP, AND PUT THEM IN A STACK.

3. ROLL THE DIE TO MOVE AHEAD ON THE BOARD.

4. IF YOU LAND ON A SPACE WITH A STAR, TAKE A CARD A ND FOLLOW ITS INSTRUCTIONS.

5. THE FIRST PLAYER TO REACH "END" WINS--AND SAVES THE DAY!

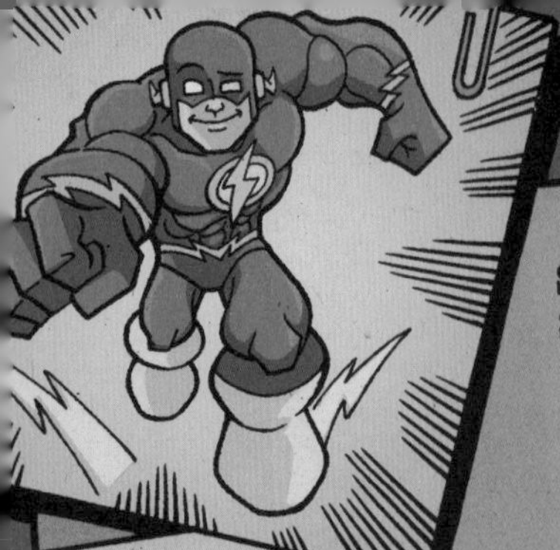

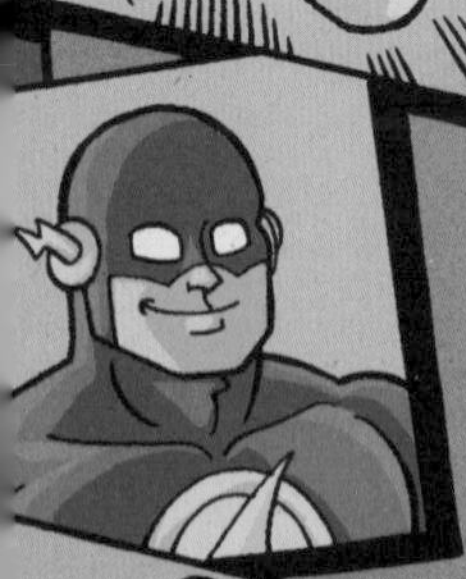

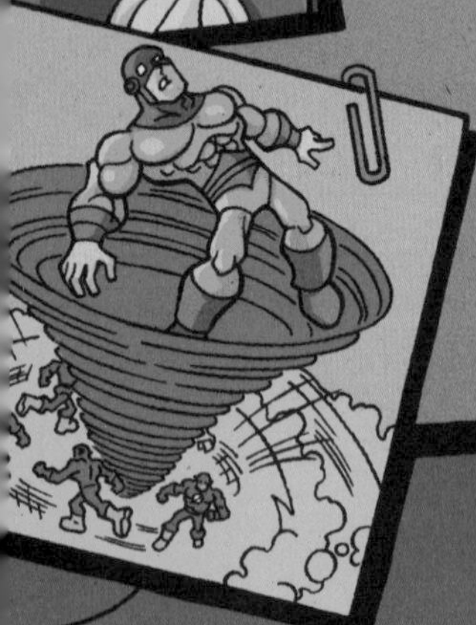

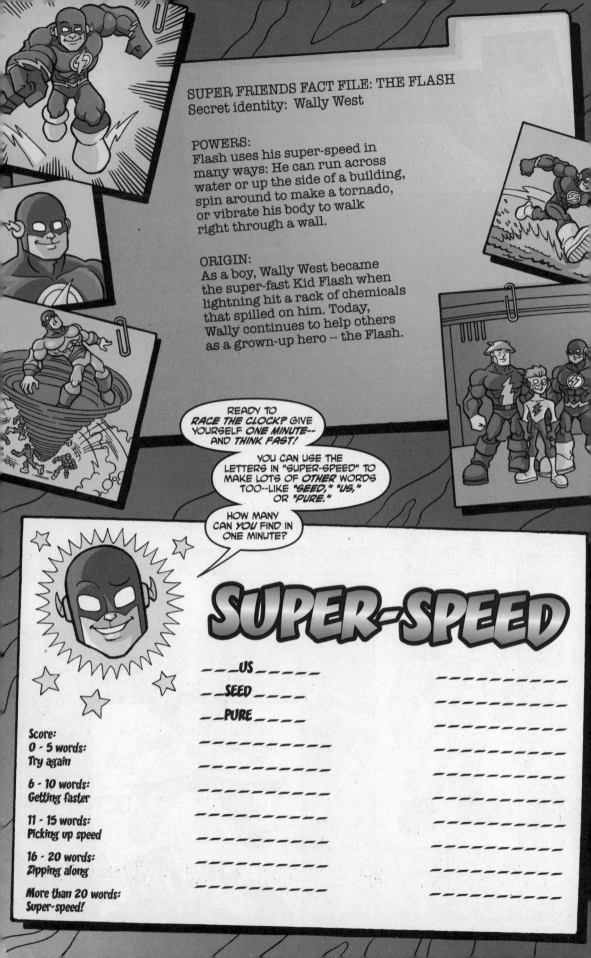

SUPER FRIENDS FACT FILE: THE FLASH
Secret identity: Wally West

POWERS:
Flash uses his super-speed in many ways: He can run across water or up the side of a building, spin around to make a tornado, or vibrate his body to walk right through a wall.

ORIGIN:
As a boy, Wally West became the super-fast Kid Flash when lightning hit a rack of chemicals that spilled on him. Today, Wally continues to help others as a grown-up hero -- the Flash.

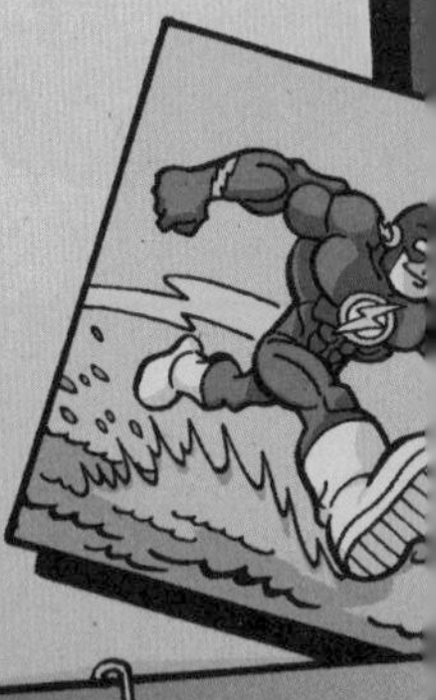

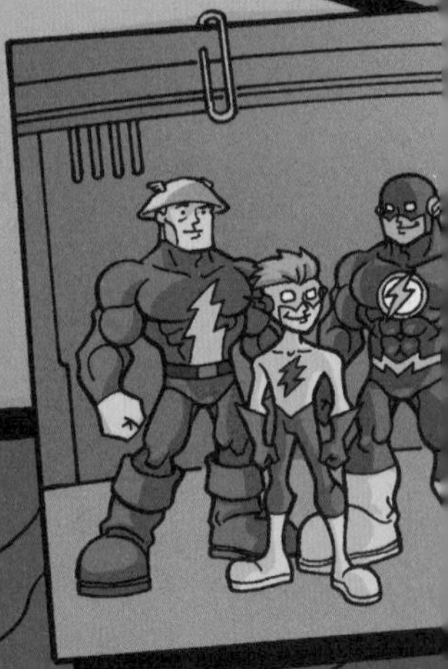

READY TO *RACE THE CLOCK?* GIVE YOURSELF *ONE MINUTE*-- AND *THINK FAST!*

YOU CAN USE THE LETTERS IN "SUPER-SPEED" TO MAKE LOTS OF *OTHER* WORDS TOO--LIKE *"SEED," "US,"* OR *"PURE."*

HOW MANY CAN *YOU* FIND IN ONE MINUTE?

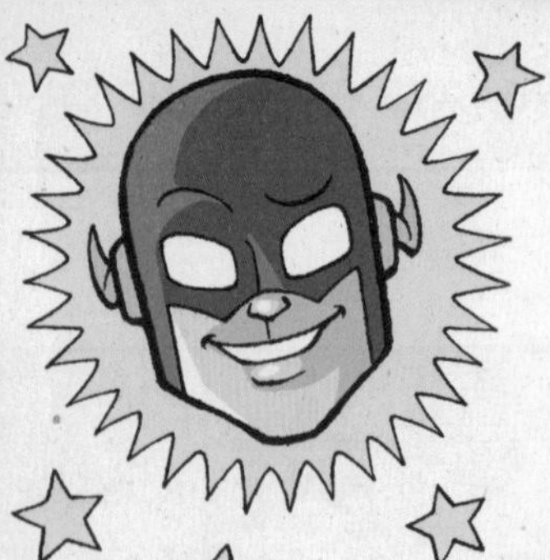

SUPER-SPEED

___US_____
__SEED____
__PURE____

Score:
0 - 5 words: Try again
6 - 10 words: Getting faster
11 - 15 words: Picking up speed
16 - 20 words: Zipping along
More than 20 words: Super-speed!